Jazz Theory

Jazz Theory: From Basic to Advanced Study, Second Edition, is a comprehensive textbook for those with no previous study in jazz, as well as those in advanced theory courses. Written with the goal to bridge theory and practice, it provides a strong theoretical foundation from music fundamentals to post-tonal theory, while integrating ear training, keyboard skills, and improvisation. It hosts "play-along" audio tracks on a Companion Website, including a workbook, ear-training exercises, and an audio compilation of the musical examples featured in the book.

Jazz Theory is organized into three parts: Basics, Intermediate, and Advanced. This approach allows for success in a one-semester curriculum or with subsequent terms. If students sense that theory can facilitate their improvisational skills or can help them develop their ears, they become more engaged in the learning process. The overall pedagogical structure accomplishes precisely that in an original, creative—and above all, musical—manner.

KEY FEATURES include 390 musical examples, ranging from original lead sheets of standard tunes, jazz instrumentals, transcriptions, and original compositions, to fully realized harmonic progressions, sample solos, and re-harmonized tunes. The completely revamped Companion Website hosts:

- 46 "Play Along Sessions" audio tracks, offering experiences close to real-time performance scenarios.

- Over 1,000 (audio and written) exercises covering ear training, rhythm, notation, analysis, improvisation, composition, functional keyboard, and others.

- Recordings of all 390 musical examples from the textbook.

- Links: *Guide to Making Transcriptions, List of Solos to Transcribe, Selected Discography, Classification of Standard Tunes*, and more.

- Lists of well-known standard tunes, including a comprehensive list of *999 Standard Tunes—Composers and Lyricists*.

NEW TO THE SECOND EDITION are instructors' tools with answer keys to written and ear-training exercises, 380 rhythmic calisthenics featuring exercises from the swing, bebop, and Latin rhythmic traditions, a new improvisation section, a set of 140 comprehensive keyboard exercises, plus an expanded ear-training section with 125 melodic, 50 rhythmic dictations, and 170 harmonic dictations, plus 240 written exercises, 25 composition assignments, and 110 singing exercises.

Dariusz Terefenko is Associate Professor of Jazz and Contemporary Media at the Eastman School of Music, University of Rochester.

Jazz Theory

From Basic to Advanced Study

Second Edition

Dariusz Terefenko

Routledge
Taylor & Francis Group

NEW YORK AND LONDON

Second edition published 2018
by Routledge
52 VAnderbilt Avenue, New York, NY 10017

and by Routledge
2 Park Square, Milton Park, Abingdon, Oxon OX14 4RN

Routledge is an imprint of the Taylor & Francis Group, an informa business

First edition published by Routledge 2014

Library of Congress Cataloging in Publication Data
Names: Terefenko, Dariusz, 1968- author.
Title: Jazz theory : beginning to advanced study / Dariusz Terefenko.
Description: Second edition. | New York ; London : Routledge, 2017.
Identifiers: LCCN 2016047510| ISBN 9781138235083 (hardback) | ISBN 9781138235106 (pbk.)
Subjects: LCSH: Jazz—Instruction and study.
Classification: LCC MT6 .T37 2017 | DDC 781.65/12—dc23
LC record available at https://lccn.loc.gov/2016047510

ISBN: 978-1-138-23508-3 (hbk)
ISBN: 978-1-138-23510-6 (pbk)
ISBN: 978-1-315-30539-4 (ebk)

Typeset in Galliard and Swiss 721
by Florence Production Ltd, Stoodleigh, Devon, UK

Visit the companion website: www.routledge.com/cw/terefenko2e

To my sister Natalia and
my brother Zenon

Contents

Figures

Tables

Preface

While teaching a theory course at the Eastman School of Music, a student came up to me after class and said: "I really enjoyed your course, but I wish that instead of countless handouts you gave us, you could write a book. It would give us something more permanent—a kind of lasting document of your teaching pedagogy that we really enjoyed." I responded that I would consider his request and began ruminating about writing a jazz theory book. I quickly realized, though, that the transition from class handouts to a well-organized textbook was not as straightforward as my eager student wanted me to believe . . .

Jazz Theory: From Basic to Advanced Study, Second Edition, is an innovative textbook designed for undergraduate and graduate jazz students, and for an ever-increasing population of classical students interested in jazz theory and improvisation. The overall pedagogy combines theory, improvisation, ear training, and keyboard skills into a comprehensive whole that enables more effective internalization and understanding of various theoretical concepts discussed in the book. Intended for 2-, 3- or 4-semester curricula in jazz theory, ear training, improvisation, harmony, keyboard skills, jazz literature, and jazz composition courses, the book can also be used as a self-study guide for professional musicians unaffiliated with an academic institution. Conveniently divided into three parts—*Basics, Intermediate, Advanced*—each major section is written with a specific demographic of students in mind: Part I for beginners, Part II for intermediate, and Part III for advanced students. While each of these sections creates a separate whole, they also form a comprehensive and cross-disciplinary narrative when taken together.

In addition to the traditional topics covered in the chapters on *Music Fundamentals, Harmonic Function, Four-Part Chords, Five-Part Chords, Modes*, and *The Blues*, the book engages the reader in an extensive discussion of *Chord–Scale Theory, Bebop*, and *Pentatonics, Hexatonics, Octatonics*. The book also offers some original thoughts on the phrase structure of standard tunes in the chapter on *Phrase Models*, and explains the principles of vertical and horizontal harmonization in the chapter on *Reharmonization Techniques*. The connection between theory and practice is an underlying motto of the book; this issue comes to the fore in the chapters on *Improvisation, Bebop Blues, The "Confirmation" Changes, The Rhythm Changes*, and *The* Tristano Style *of Improvisation*. The importance of acquiring basic keyboard skills as a necessary tool for developing comprehensive musicianship is addressed in the chapters on *Voicing Formations, Keyboard and Jazz Chorale Textures*, and *Idiomatic Jazz Progressions*. To establish more meaningful connections between different branches of theoretical discourse and jazz theory, the chapters on *Phrase Models* and *Song Forms* touch on various aspects of formal and modified Schenkerian theory, while the chapters on *Post-Tonal Jazz—Atonality, Set Classes in Jazz*, and *Twelve-Tone Techniques* make inroads into atonal and dodecaphonic music theory, offering innovative and thought-provoking ideas for the advancement of this type of interdisciplinary connections.

GOALS

Improvisational Skills

The ultimate goal of jazz theory is to improve one's improvisational skills and make one a better musician. The *Play Along Sessions* section on the Companion Website (CW) includes 46 tracks recorded by the fine musicians of the Eastman School of Music: Prof. Jeff Campbell (bass), Prof. Rich Thompson (drums), Gabe Condon (guitar), Karl Stabnau (saxophones), and myself (piano and Hammond B-3). In Chapter 10, for instance, the student is asked to play along with the prerecorded rhythm section, first in the context of the blues and modal scales and, in later chapters, in the context of complete standard songs and jazz instrumentals. Initial tracks—with the exception of the major and minor blues—place an emphasis on playing in 12 keys. Each track on modes, then, covers twelve 16- or 8-bar phrases, each in a different modal area. Similarly, the II–V–I or V–I progressions are presented in 12 keys. These progressions are meant to be practiced with the newly composed II–V–I patterns: 100 for the ii–V^7–I progression and 50 for the ii$^\emptyset$–V^7–i progression. To offer experiences closer to real time performance situations, each track is recorded at a different tempo, rhythmic feel, and with either piano, Hammond B-3 or guitar as a comping instrument.

Expanding Jazz Repertory

Aside from pedagogical concerns, a subsidiary goal of this book—one hopefully appreciated by song aficionados—is to expand the repertory of standard tunes. Chapters 20–22 discuss harmonic designs, formal models, harmonic variations, and interpretations of standard tunes. In addition to the original sheet music (with the composer's piano accompaniment, verses and lyrics) of "My Romance," "Have You Met Miss Jones?" and other tunes, these chapters include the titles of songs based on the similarity of their tonal and formal designs. By classifying standard tunes according to the harmonic structure of the A section and the type of harmonic motion in the bridge, it is my belief that students can absorb a large number of tunes with relative ease. Appendix G on the CW includes an alphabetical list of 999 titles (with their composers and lyricists), Appendix A (in the book) contains a list of 200 essential standard tunes (out of the 999) that every jazz musician should know, and Appendix I (CW) compartmentalizes standard tunes according to their harmonic and formal properties.

NEW TO THIS EDITION

- 380 Rhythmic Calisthenics featuring rhythmic exercises from the swing, bebop, and Latin rhythmic traditions.

- Comprehensive Keyboard Pedagogy with approximately 140 carefully designed keyboard exercises.

- Expanded Ear Training Section featuring 125 melodic dictations (audio files), 50 rhythmic dictations (audio files), 170 harmonic dictations (audio files), 240 written exercises, 25 composition assignments, and 110 singing exercises.

- New Improvisation Section with 500 preparatory exercises in improvisation, 200 improvisation sessions to be performed with play along tracks.

- 46 Play Along Tracks plus Scores for C, B♭, E♭ instruments and in Bass Clef.

- Scores for C, B♭, E♭ instruments and in Bass Clef for melodic patterns, improvisation drills, and others.

- Instructor's Tools with answer keys to written and ear-training exercises on the website.

- Completely revamped and enhanced Companion Website with music examples, recordings, lead sheets, exercises, list of standard tunes, and more.

HOW TO USE THE COMPANION WEBSITE (CW)

www.routledge.com/cw/terefenko2e

The Companion Website (CW) for the Second Edition of *Jazz Theory: From Basic to Advanced Study* closely follows the structure of the book and contains three large sections: *Basics*, *Intermediate* and *Advanced*, with each section partitioned into individual chapters. Each chapter, then, is further subdivided (where applicable) into smaller sections: *Play Along Sessions*, *Written Exercises*, *Ear Training*, *Rhythm*, *Improvisation*, and *Functional Keyboard*. The website for the Second Edition underwent considerable changes and sizable expansions, particularly in the areas of ear training, rhythm, improvisation, and functional keyboard. Those expansions are the result of the many valuable suggestions I received from my esteemed colleagues scattered throughout the world. For instance, the choice of specific tasks in each chapter depends on the content of the individual chapters. The main objective of Chapter 10 of the book, for instance, is to put the content of Part I to practical use. You will quickly realize that in order to be successful at playing with the rhythm section (Play Along Sessions: tracks 5–18), you need a solid command of the modes in all 12 keys (discussed in Chapter 7). Since the primary goal of these playing sessions is to familiarize the ear with the sound of the 14 diatonic/chromatic modes and to find that sound on your instrument, start by playing the most important notes from the mode (guide tones and beauty marks) and negotiate them in some kind of rhythmic fashion. Having established the connection between theoretical concepts (guide tones and beauty marks in this particular instance) and practice (the ability to effortlessly play them on your instrument), you will begin to listen to your own playing and to interact with the rhythm section. Next, start using the motifs from the book (Figure 10.10) and transpose them to 12 keys. With these motifs, focus on the techniques of motivic development (Chapter 10), select a single technique, and explore it in your playing. As you get more comfortable with handling one technique at a time, try improvising with two or more techniques.

Finally, you are ready to compose your own motifs and use them in improvisation. Tracks 5–18 (as well as other play along tracks) work just as well for advanced players as for beginners. The process described above illustrates how to work with play along tracks. This process can be summarized as follows: (1) establish a connection between theory and practice, (2) practice on your instrument, (3) begin with the material that you can handle with relative ease, (4) challenge yourself, and (5) be creative.

A measured approach to completing assignments works for the majority of keyboard drills included in the *Functional Keyboard* section. Take, for instance, Exercises 3.4.1–10. This group of exercises includes 10 four-bar progressions to be realized on the keyboard in 12 keys. The basic objective for all keyboard drills is to perform a given exercise at a steady tempo and without breaks. Start at a comfortable tempo ($\quarternote$ =40) and play the progressions from beginning to end without interruption. Using a metronome is highly recommended. Gradually increase the speed of your performance to $\quarternote$ =96. It is also imperative to follow the written instructions. In this particular case, playing the progression using three different opening chords starting on $\hat{1}$, $\hat{3}$, and $\hat{5}$, will accomplish at least two objectives: (1) familiarity with different chords shapes and (2) exploration of diverse voice-leading paths through the progression.

Performing in 12 keys is an essential skill for the contemporary musician, yet learning to play in all keys is a long and arduous process. To facilitate this process, first learn the progression in the original key. Once you master the progression in a single key and meticulously explore different positions/inversions of chords, start transposing the progression to two or three more familiar keys. Practice the progressions in two or three keys and then add more keys to your daily practice routines. You will notice that once you work diligently through five or six different transpositions, the remaining ones will not be as challenging as the earlier ones. To master the skill of playing in 12 keys, you need to be consistent and patient, commit to a daily practice regime, and allow the passing of time to see the results.

In studying jazz, it is imperative to develop an impeccable ear capable of identifying complex chord structure, melodic formations, and harmonic progressions. The CW features different kinds of ear-training activities: play-and-sing, sight singing, rhythmic/melodic/harmonic dictations, chord/mode/other scales recognition, set-class/12-tone row identification, etc. I recommend that you complete each ear-training exercise *before* proceeding to the next one, no matter how trivial that exercise might be. Without internalizing the sound of individual intervals/triads in Chapter 1 or four-part chords in Chapter 4, for instance, the ability to hear more complex five-part chords in Chapter 5 or upper-structure triads in Chapter 11 might prove too challenging. Furthermore, when individual chords or the II–V–I progressions from Part I begin to form four-bar progressions in Chapter 13 or eight-bar phrase models in Chapter 21, the ability to identify individual chords is of utmost importance to contextualize their functional role in the context of complete harmonic progressions. Since some audio tracks for ear-training drills contain multiple intervals, chords, chord progressions, or set classes, I recommend starting each audio track at a different location to avoid memorizing the sequence of events.

Recordings

In addition to different kinds of exercises, the CW also contains the recordings of all musical figures appearing in *Jazz Theory: From Basic to Advanced Study*. The *Textbook Recordings* section is organized exactly as the textbook (three parts along with individual chapters) and gives you immediate access to all audio files. By clicking on the figure, you will see the specific musical example and hear the recording. These recordings are quite useful when you are away from the keyboard (or have insufficient keyboard skills) and want to hear a particular musical example. By listening to these audio recordings you are mapping theoretical concepts (chords, modes, progressions, scales, phrase modes, set classes, etc.) with their sound and, thus, training and improving your ears.

Finally, the website contains downloadable scores for ear-training drills, extra scores (in C, B♭, E♭, and Bass Clef) for *Play Along Session* (Appendix C), an *Answer Key for Written Exercises* (Appendix A), and *Answer Key for Ear-Training Drills* (Appendix B) (with a few exercises realized in full score so you can see what I played on the recording).

Appendices/Auxiliaries

This section contains some useful material that complements the book. *Selected Discography* (Appendix F), for instance, contains the list of recordings for the standard tunes discussed in the book. For each tune, I selected representative recordings that show how the different jazz artists from different eras appropriated these tunes into their repertoire and how unique these interpretations are. This extraordinary interpretive diversity demonstrates the limitless potential of standard tunes. Listening to jazz goes hand in hand with learning how to improvise and how to find one's musical voice. Without exploring the rich canon of recorded jazz, one's quest for learning how to improvise might be deterred indefinitely. *Selected*

Discography and *List of Solos to Transcribe* in Appendix E (as well as additional footnotes in the book) provide many valuable listening resources. *Classification of Standard Tunes* in Appendix I complements the contents of Chapters 21 and 22 with 999 standard tunes classified according to the type of phrase model and the key of the bridge.

TO THE STUDENT

In Part I, the foundation of the entire pedagogical system is laid, each topic leading logically to the next. Therefore, it is imperative to study each chapter before proceeding to the next one. Use of the CW is strongly recommended; it contains numerous exercises to foster your understanding of various theoretical subjects. For optimal use of this resource read *How To Use the Companion Website*. For those already familiar with basic theoretical concepts or those who want to study more advanced topics (*Bebop, Pentatonics, Hexatonics, Octatonics, Phrase Models, Post-Tonal Jazz, Twelve-Tone Techniques*, etc.), start with a chapter that appeals to you. Each chapter, especially in Parts II and III, is a self-contained unit ready for you to explore. If you use this approach, first familiarize yourself with the terminology and various notational conventions discussed in Part I since they may be different from the one that you are already familiar with.

TO THE INSTRUCTOR

In *Jazz Theory: From Basic to Advanced Study*, I build on the existing terminology concerning chord notation and other analytical conventions. One of the main issues music theorists often grapple with is that of chord notation—a proverbial Tower of Babel in a world where notational idiosyncrasies run amok. To be fair, systems of chord notation are constantly evolving and, in spite of the best intentions, no syntactical uniformity exists that would satisfy everyone. In the Second Edition, I have adopted the notational convention recommended by the Society for Music Theory—Jazz Interest Group (SMT-jz). In June and July of 2015, the SMT-jz discussed ways to standardize jazz chord nomenclature for theory publications. The group advocated for a style guide appropriate for labeling chords in *prose text* based on the five goals: (1) familiarity, (2) clarity, (3) ease of formatting, (4) internal consistency, and (5) elegance. While the consensus was reached regarding the use of standardized/uniformed symbols in *prose text*, many have argued against the same consensus while annotating a score. Since the SMT-jz recommends that the style guide be used for *prose text* but that score annotation be more flexible, *Jazz Theory: From Basic to Advanced Study* adheres to these guidelines. For instance, C major seventh chord in *prose* is notated as CM7 and in a score as CΔ7; C major seventh sharp eleventh chord: CM7($\sharp$11) in *prose*, and CΔ7$^{(\sharp 11)}$ in a score. Given the CΔ7$^{(\sharp 11)}$ label, for instance, the chord quality is indicated with a "Δ" suffix, the essential chord tone "7" is written as a regular size Arabic number, and a chromatic extension is placed in parenthesis and written as a superscript number. The Cm$^{9(\flat 13)}$ label in a score uses a superscript for the diatonic extension "major ninth" and places the chromatic extension in parenthesis. The *prose* lead-sheet symbols employed in the book, then, follow the most recent and up-to-date effort at standardizing chord notation attempted by a large group of jazz scholars. A more loosely based system employed for score annotation reflects the author's personal preferences motivated by the role and functionality of essential chord members and extensions. Both sets of symbols, *prose* and *score*, provide a complete description of a chord's pitch structure; they are easy to interpret and show internal consistency, conformity, elegance, and clarity. In addition, *score* symbols show an inherent hierarchy that exists between essential chord tones and chordal extensions, with the former notated as regular size

Arabic numbers, and the latter notated as superscripts placed in parenthesis in the case of chromatic extensions, and written without parenthesis in the case of diatonic extensions.

Similarly marred by syntactical ambiguities in common-practice theory, the use of Roman numerals in *Jazz Theory: From Basic to Advanced Study* is reduced to four-part structures only, regardless of the actual pitch content of the chord. Roman numerals, then, represent the quality, functionality, scale-degree position, and the type of essential chord tones added to a triad. The following five basic symbols are used: X, X^7, x, $x^\emptyset$, and x^O, representing major-type chords, dominant 7th-type chords (major-minor 7th), minor-type chords, minor 7($\flat$5)/half-diminished-type chords, and diminished 7th-type chords, respectively. (Occasionally triads X^6_4 and X^6 are also used.) Though Roman numerals require some expertise to realize them in performance, they constitute excellent tools for transposing chord progressions to all 12 keys. Since Roman numerals represent essential four-part structures only, their interpretation and realization is predicated on a number of factors: melodic content, dissonance treatment, chromaticism, outer-voice counterpoint, voice leading, harmonic affects, phrase rhythm, and other considerations discussed in this book.

THEORY IS A MEANS TO AN END

As stated earlier, the ultimate goal of *Jazz Theory: From Basic to Advanced Study* is to improve one's improvisational skills and enable one to grow as a complete musician. In a sense, then, theoretical knowledge is a means to that end; for the jazz musician this is synonymous with being proficient at different styles of improvisation. To attain that goal, I discuss at length four contrasting styles of improvisation: blues, modal, bebop, and the "Tristano" school. Being the most important musical form in jazz, the blues takes precedence with extensive coverage across two chapters (Chapters 9 and 15). Modal improvisation is explained in Chapters 7, 8, and 18. The techniques of bebop improvisation are discussed in Chapter 14 and immediately put to practice in Chapters 15–17. The "Tristano" school of improvisation is codified through the prism of Lennie Tristano's solo on "Line Up," which is analyzed in Chapter 19. In addition to these four improvisational traditions, Chapters 24–26 make substantial inroads into a more experimental, yet highly organized, system of advanced harmony and improvisation. In these chapters, I attempt to create an interdisciplinary bridge between atonal/dodecaphonic music theory and jazz theory. It is my humble wish to see the ideas discussed in these chapters taking new roots and being further developed by other jazz scholars. The possibilities are truly endless and the door for new artistic directions is left wide open . . .

Dariusz Terefenko
Associate Professor of Jazz Studies
Eastman School of Music
October 2016

Acknowledgments

Witnessing a project of this magnitude take shape has left me with a sense of accomplishment and also provides a wonderful opportunity for me to thank the many people without whom this book could not have been written. First and foremost, I would like to thank Douglas Lowry (Joan and Martin Messinger Dean Emeritus of the Eastman School of Music) and Jamal J. Rossi (Dean of the Eastman School of Music) for granting me a leave of absence in the spring of 2012, during which the majority of the book was written. Dean Lowry will be greatly missed by all who had the privilege of knowing him personally. Secondly, I would like to thank my colleagues in the Jazz Department at ESM: Harold Danko, Bill Dobbins, Jeff Campbell, Clay Jenkins, Rich Thompson, Dave Rivello, and Bob Sneider, all of whom have been very supportive of the project and on whose expertise I could always count. My profoundest gratitude and heartfelt thank you go to my friend Matthew Brown for his guidance over the years and for the countless hours of stimulating conversations during which many of the concepts appearing in this book were generated. On that note, I would like to thank Robert Wason for his encouragements in pursuing the more scholarly aspects of jazz music theory.

I am indebted to many years of wonderful students at the Eastman School of Music, but perhaps particularly to: Jeff Benatar, Ben Britton, Theresa Chen, Gabe Condon, Alistair Duncan, Jonathan Fagan, Sam Farley, Brendan Lanighan, Emiliano Lasansky, Jeff McLeod, Blake Pattengale, Paulo Perfeito, Marcelo Pinto, Karl Stabnau, Alexa Tarantino, and Chris Ziemba.

I would like to thank all the amazing musicians with whom I had the privilege to record all the musical examples, play-along tracks, and ear-training drills: Jeff Campbell (bass), Rich Thompson (drums), Gabe Condon (guitar), and Karl Stabnau (saxophones). I would also like to thank the entire staff at the Technology and Media Production at the Eastman School of Music, especially Louis Chitty for his herculean job recording, editing, mixing, and producing the Play Along tracks and all the audio files available on the website.

I am indebted to the staff at Routledge, especially Constance Ditzel for showing the initial interest in my project, but also Peter Sheehy for his tireless work preparing the book for production, Laura Macy and Sophie Harding for their excellent work editing the book, and Abigail Stanley for her commendable work producing the book. I greatly appreciate their effort to find the most knowledgeable reviewers in the field of jazz theory—Keith Waters (University of Colorado at Boulder) and Chris Stover (New School)—whose many exceptional ideas and suggestions contributed greatly to the final version of this text.

Finally, I would like to thank my sister Natalia for arranging perfect conditions allowing me to work on the book, and my brother Zenon for his musical inspiration. This book is dedicated to both of them.

PART ONE

Basics

CHAPTER 1

Music Fundamentals

CHAPTER SUMMARY

Chapter 1 lays the foundation for the study of music theory. The basics of music notation are introduced as well as an understanding of intervals, their names, and the inversion of intervals. The chapter concludes with a discussion of the five triadic formations: major, minor, diminished, augmented, and suspended.

CONCEPTS AND TERMS

- Accidentals
- Bar line
- Bass clef
- Beat subdivision
- Beat value
- Chords
- Chromatic
- Clefs
- Diatonic
- Enharmonic equivalence
- Flat sign (♭)
- Grand staff
- Half step (semitones)
- Intervals:
  - Augmented
  - Compound
  - Diminished
  - Harmonic
  - Major
  - Melodic
  - Minor
  - Perfect
  - Quality
- Inversions of intervals
- Inversions of triads
- Key signatures
- Ledger lines
- Major scales
- Measures
- Meter:
  - Duple
  - Quadruple
  - Triple
- Minor scale:
  - Harmonic
  - Melodic
  - Natural
- Natural sign (♮)
- Notes
- Octave
- Octave equivalence
- Pitch
- Registers
- Relative keys
- Rhythmic duration
- Scale degrees
- Sharp sign (♯)
- Staff
- Time signatures:
  - Compound
  - Irregular
  - Simple
- Treble clef
- Triads:
  - Augmented
  - Diminished
  - Major
  - Minor
  - Suspended
- Whole steps/tones

PITCH

Pitch refers to the relative highness or lowness of musical sounds. Figure 1.1 illustrates the placement of pitches on the keyboard with the lowest notes on the left and the highest notes on the right.

FIGURE 1.1 Keyboard—Pitch Layout

To label pitches, we use the letters from the alphabet—A, B, C, D, E, F, and G—to denote the white notes and **accidentals** (sharps or flats) to denote the black notes. Each note on the keyboard has a distinct sound; notes that have the same letter name sound similar in spite of their location on the keyboard. Theorists refer to this idea as **octave equivalence**. The distance from C4 to C5 includes eight diatonic pitches (counting C4 and C5) and is therefore known as an **octave**. Integers 1 through 8 following the letter names indicate eight different **registers** or specific pitch locations characterized by their sound. With higher integers we experience higher sounding pitches, and with lower integers we experience lower sounding pitches. Labeling black notes is more complicated because they can be described in two ways. For example, the black note between C and D can be labeled either as C♯ or D♭. Since C♯ and D♭ sound the same on the piano, theorists often refer to them as being **enharmonically equivalent**.

Music is notated on a **staff** that consists of *five lines* (the first line is at the bottom of the staff) and *four spaces* (the first space is located between the first and the second line of the staff). The addition of extra lines called **ledger lines** (up to five) at the bottom or top extends the staff and allows for the notation of pitches that lie outside the boundaries of the five-line staff. A **clef** written at the beginning of the staff indicates the location of pitches, which are notated with a system of **notes**. Although there are many different clefs, only **treble** and **bass clefs** will be used in this book.[1] The grand **staff** combines two staves joined by a *brace*, with the top stave using the treble clef and the bottom stave using the bass clef. Figure 1.2 illustrates the notation of pitches from A0 to C8 on the grand staff.

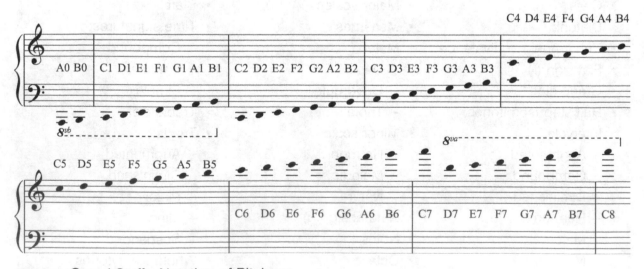

FIGURE 1.2 Grand Staff—Notation of Pitches

The octaves, C1–C2, C2–C3, etc., create a specific pattern of whole steps and half steps. A **half step** (or **semitone**) is the shortest possible distance between two keys (or notes). For instance, the distance between E4 and F4 or B4–C5 is a half step. A **whole step** (or **whole tone**) combines two half steps and represents the distance between two keys with a single key between them. For instance, the distance between C4 and D4, D4–E4, F4–G4, G4–A4, or A4–B4, is a whole step because there is a single black note between these notes.

MAJOR SCALES

The collection of notes from C4 to C5, shown in Figure 1.3, represents a specific pattern of whole steps and half steps known as a **major scale**.

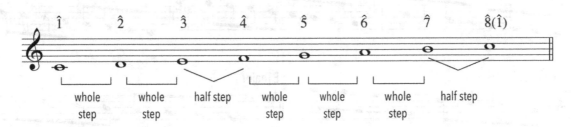

FIGURE 1.3 Major Scale

The major scale has five whole steps, beginning between **scale-degree** one (written as $\hat{1}$) and $\hat{2}$, $\hat{2}$–$\hat{3}$, $\hat{4}$–$\hat{5}$, $\hat{5}$–$\hat{6}$, and $\hat{6}$–$\hat{7}$, and two half steps between $\hat{3}$–$\hat{4}$, and $\hat{7}$–$\hat{8}(\hat{1})$. This arrangement of pitches represents one type of **diatonic scale**. The other diatonic scales also contain five whole steps and two half steps but those intervals between different scale degrees occur at a different location within the scale. For instance, the spans F4–F5 or G4–G5 filled in with white keys only (G4–A4–B4–C5–D5–E5–F5), shown in Figure 1.4, contain five whole tones and two semitones, yet their placement is different than it is in the C major scale. In order to duplicate the locations of whole tones and semitones as they occur within the C major scale, accidentals—a **sharp sign** (♯) and a **flat sign** (♭)—have to be implemented. The sharp added to F5 (in the G4–G5 octave) raises the sound of F5 by a semitone and becomes F♯5. The flat added to B4 (in the F4–F5 octave) lowers the sound of B4 by a semitone and becomes B♭4. With these added accidentals, the arrangement of whole tones and semitones occurring in the C major scale can be duplicated. These collections are labeled using their opening pitches: G major and F major, respectively.

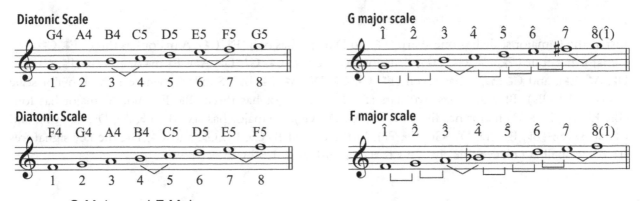

FIGURE 1.4 G Major and F Major

There are 12 possible major scales, one for each white and black note (C major, C♯/D♭ major, D major, E♭ major, E major, F major, F♯/G♭ major, G major, A♭ major, A major, B♭ major, B/C♭ major).

KEY SIGNATURES

Another method of representing major scales is to use **key signatures** written to the right of the clef. Since there are 12 distinct major scales, there will be 12 corresponding key signatures. For instance, the G major scale that we saw in Figure 1.4 has one sharp, F♯. The key signature places that sharp at the beginning of the staff immediately after the clef.

FIGURE 1.5 Key Signatures—Major Scales

Just as the G major scale has one sharp (F♯), so D major has two (F♯, C♯), A major has three (F♯, C♯, G♯), E major has four (F♯, C♯, G♯, D♯), B major has five (F♯, C♯, G♯, D♯, A♯), F♯ major has six (F♯, C♯, G♯, D♯, A♯, E♯), and C♯ major has seven (F♯, C♯, G♯, D♯, A♯, E♯, B♯). Similarly, whereas the F major scale has one flat (B♭), B♭ major has two flats (B♭, E♭), E♭ major has three (B♭, E♭, A♭), A♭ major has four (B♭, E♭, A♭, D♭), D♭ major has five (B♭, E♭, A♭, D♭, G♭), G♭ major has six (B♭, E♭, A♭, D♭, G♭, C♭), and C♭ has seven (B♭, E♭, A♭, D♭, G♭, C♭, F♭). In the case of B/C♭, F♯/G♭, and C♯/D♭, the key signatures are often spelled enharmonically. This is shown in Figure 1.5 by the arrows.

MINOR SCALES

Figure 1.6 illustrates the distribution of whole tones and semitones within the A3–A4 octave that forms a **minor scale**.

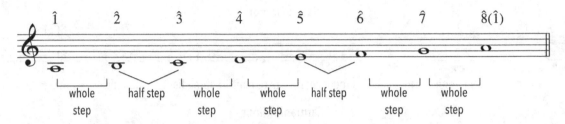

FIGURE 1.6 Minor Scale

The two semitones are located between $\hat{2}$–$\hat{3}$ and $\hat{5}$–$\hat{6}$, and the five whole tones between $\hat{1}$–$\hat{2}$, $\hat{3}$–$\hat{4}$, $\hat{4}$–$\hat{5}$, $\hat{6}$–$\hat{7}$, and $\hat{7}$–$\hat{8}$ ($\hat{1}$). Similar to C major, the A minor scale uses only the white keys of the keyboard and has no key signature. In addition to the so-called **natural** version of minor, there are two additional *shades* of minor: **harmonic** and **melodic**. The three versions of minor are illustrated in Figure 1.7 with the melodic minor shown in the ascending and descending form.

FIGURE 1.7 "Shades" of Minor

The harmonic form of minor raises $\hat{7}$ of the natural minor. The melodic form of minor raises $\hat{6}$ and $\hat{7}$ of the ascending natural minor scale. The presence of #$\hat{7}$ in the harmonic and melodic versions creates a characteristic half-step motion from #$\hat{7}$ to $\hat{8}$ ($\hat{1}$), which is analogous to the half step between $\hat{7}$–$\hat{8}$ in the major key. The use of a **natural sign** (♮) in the descending form of the melodic minor cancels out the previously attached accidentals to F4 and G4. It is important to stress that the harmonic and melodic versions of minor are not independent scalar collections; rather, they represent variants or "shades" of the minor scale. The use of key signatures always corresponds to the natural minor form and does not cover the necessary accidentals occurring in the harmonic and melodic forms. Figure 1.8 illustrates the pitch structure of C major and A minor along with the scale degree names.

As there are 12 major keys, there are also 12 minor keys, shown in Figure 1.9.

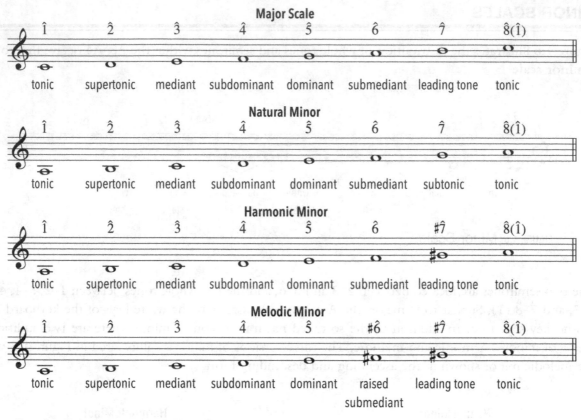

FIGURE 1.8 Scale-Degree Names

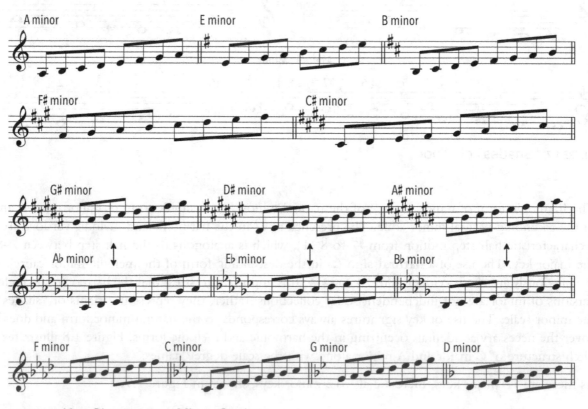

FIGURE 1.9 Key Signatures—Minor Scales

Whereas the E minor scale has one sharp (F♯), so B minor has two (F♯, C♯), F♯ minor has three (F♯, C♯, G♯), C♯ minor has four (F♯, C♯, G♯, D♯), G♯ minor has five (F♯, C♯, G♯, D♯, A♯), D♯ minor has six (F♯, C♯, G♯, D♯, A♯, E♯), and A♯ has seven (F♯, C♯, G♯, D♯, A♯, E♯, B♯). And, the D minor scale has one flat (B♭), G minor has two flats (B♭, E♭), C minor has three (B♭, E♭, A♭), F minor has four (B♭, E♭, A♭, D♭), B♭ minor has five (B♭, E♭, A♭, D♭, G♭), E♭ minor has six (B♭, E♭, A♭, D♭, G♭, C♭), and A♭ minor has seven (B♭, E♭, A♭, D♭, G♭, C♭, F♭). In the case of G♯/A♭, D♯/E♭, and A♯/B♭, the key signatures are often spelled enharmonically. This is shown in Figure 1.9 by the arrows. We refer to the pair of major and minor keys that share the same number of sharps or flats in their key signatures as **relative keys**. For example, G major and E minor both have one sharp (F♯), A♭ major and F minor have four flats (B♭, E♭, A♭, D♭).

RHYTHM

Music is notated with various rhythmic symbols that are proportionally related to one another. Figure 1.10 summarizes the basics of rhythmic notation.

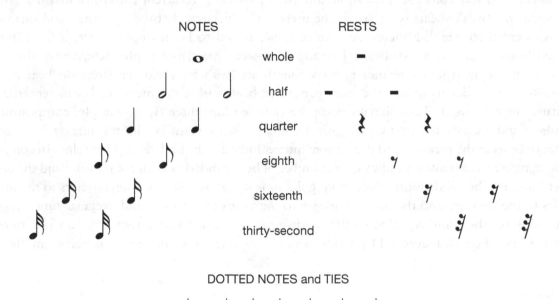

FIGURE 1.10 Basics of Rhythmic Notation

The note values and the corresponding rests are divisible by two: a *whole note* contains two *half notes*, a half note contains two *quarter notes*, etc. A *dot*, written on a space between staff lines, extends the duration of the note, rest, or dot that precedes it by half of its value. A *dotted half note* extends the duration of the half note by one *quarter note* and contains three quarter notes. A *tie* connects two or more notes at the same pitch level and creates a new duration equal to their sum. *Beams* are horizontal lines that connect multiple 8ths, 16ths, 32nds, 64ths or any combination of them. In addition to the division of note values by twos, notes can also be divided by threes creating a *triplet*, fives creating a *quintuplet*, and sevens creating a *septuplet*.

METER AND TIME SIGNATURES

Note values do not represent a fixed **rhythmic duration** until they are placed in **measures** separated with **bar lines**, and associated with a specific **beat value**. Beats are grouped in units of two, three, four (and others) and stay constant throughout a musical passage. A recurrent pattern of *accented* (strong) and *unaccented* (weak) beats is known as the **meter**. The hierarchy between accented and unaccented beats is essential to establish meter. A piece of music is said to be in **duple** meter, if the pattern of accented beats recurs every two beats (| **strong beat**–weak beat |); in **triple** meter, every three beats (| s–w–w |); and in **quadruple meter**, every four beats (with an additional stress on beat 3, as in: | s–w–s–w |). In order to specify the exact pattern of beats within the measure (i.e. meter), the **time signature** must be used. Time signatures can be classified into three types—**simple**, **compound**, and **irregular**—and are notated by two integers. In simple time signatures, the top integer indicates the number of beats in the measure and the bottom integer indicates the underlying beat value. In compound time signatures, the top integer indicates the number of **beat subdivisions** in the measure and the bottom integer indicates the subdivision value. In irregular time signatures, the top integer refers to the number of beats in the measure and the bottom integer to the beat value. Simple and irregular time signatures do not indicate the number/value of the subdivisions; compound time signatures do not show the number/value of beats. Figure 1.11 provides a summary of the aforementioned concepts and terms.

Notating Rhythm

On the score, rhythmic groupings should clearly delineate the underlying pattern of beats. In addition to representing the meter, the recurrence of these patterns also facilitates the reproduction of a song during performance. Figure 1.12 illustrates an incorrectly notated rhythm and its corrected version. The corrected version has clearly demarcated beats: this renders the rhythm easier to perform and the meter easier to perceive. More challenging rhythms may be accurately represented with the aid of different rhythmic groupings, ties, and dots.

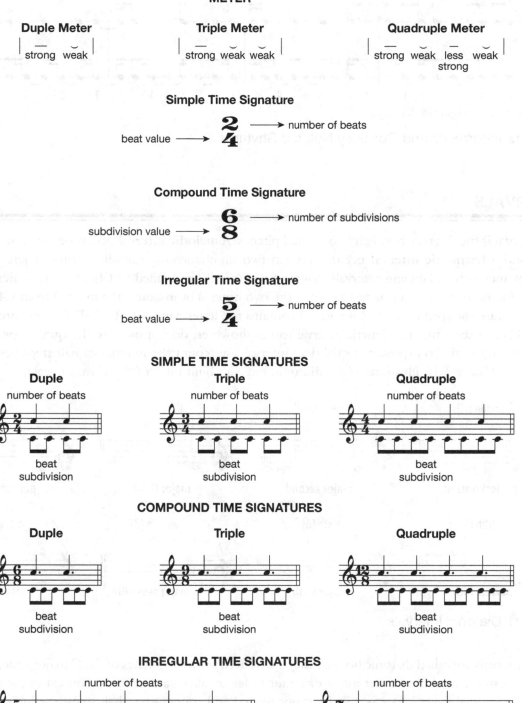

FIGURE 1.11 Meter, Time Signatures, Notating Rhythm

incorrectly notated rhythm

corrected version (visible beats)

FIGURE 1.12 Incorrectly and Correctly Notated Rhythms

INTERVALS

An **interval** is the distance between two musical pitches. A **melodic interval** occurs between two adjacent notes and a **harmonic interval** occurs between two simultaneously sounding notes. There are many different methods of labeling intervals, some of which will be detailed in Chapter 24. Generic names refer to the number of letter names between the two notes. For instance, the interval from C4 to G4 is a fifth because the span between C4 and G4 contains five letter names (C–D–E–F–G); the interval from D4 to C5 is a seventh, etc. Generic interval names, however, do not indicate the **quality** or the exact size of the interval. To express the quality of intervals, we count the number of half steps between the two notes. Figure 1.13 illustrates eight **diatonic** intervals built on $\hat{1}$ of the C major scale.

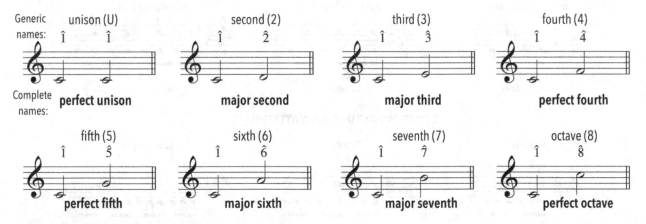

FIGURE 1.13 Diatonic Intervals

These intervals are called diatonic because they are derived from the pitches of the C major scale. Intervals derived from the pitches of other major or minor scales are also diatonic in the context of the respective keys. The interval from $\hat{1}$ to $\hat{2}$ is called a major second and contains two half steps; the interval from $\hat{1}$ to $\hat{6}$ is a major sixth and contains nine half steps. Each of these intervals can be made smaller or larger by altering one or two of their pitches by a half step. If these alterations occur in the context of C major, the resulting intervals are **chromatic** because they contain pitches that are foreign to the key of C major. Figure 1.14 shows chromatic alterations of intervals from Figure 1.13 and their full names.

To describe the quality of intervals, the following qualifiers are used: **perfect** (P), **major** (M), **minor** (m), **diminished** (D), and **augmented** (A).[2] In labeling intervals, first count the number of letter names between the two notes (including the first note) and, then, count the number of semitones between them. For instance, the interval from C#4 to A4 is a minor 6th because there are six letter names between

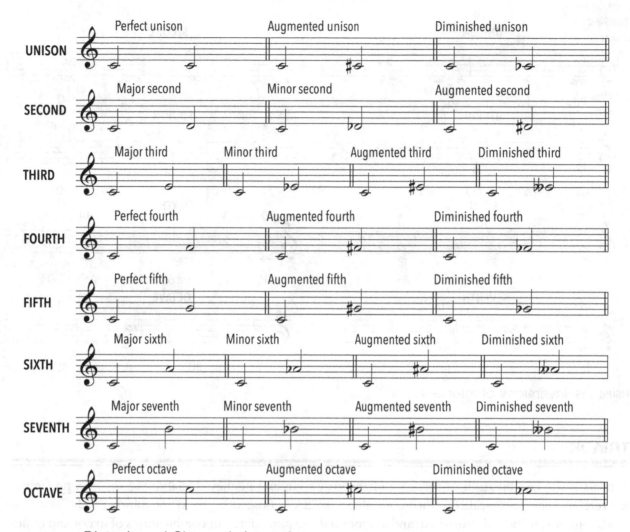

FIGURE 1.14 Diatonic and Chromatic Intervals

C♯4 and A4 (C–D–E–F–G–A) and eight half steps. But the interval from D♭4 to A4 is an augmented 5th because there are five letter names between D♭4 and A4 (D–E–F–G–A) and eight half steps. An interval that exceeds the span of an octave is known as a **compound interval**. For instance, 9ths, 11ths, and 13ths are examples of compound intervals.

INVERSION OF INTERVALS

In order to **invert** a harmonic interval, the top note is placed below the bottom note or vice versa. For instance, the interval C–G (a perfect 5th) inverts to G–C (a perfect 4th). When counting the number of semitones in both intervals, 7 and 5, respectively, their sum equals 12. This indicates the number of semitones within an octave. The same is true of other inversionally related intervals. These are illustrated in Figure 1.15. The integers above the score indicate the number of semitones.

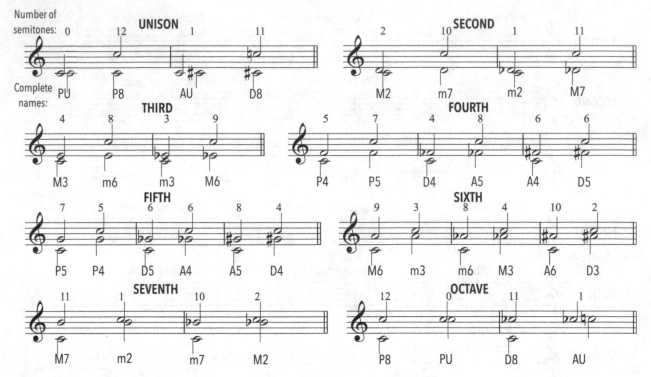

FIGURE 1.15 Inversions of Intervals

TRIADS

A **triad** is the combination of three simultaneously sounding pitches. Tonal music shows a preference for **tertian** sonorities—called **chords**, which are built of consecutive major or minor thirds. The four triads—**major, minor, diminished,** and **augmented**—explore different combinations of major and minor thirds (see Figure 1.16). Note that the tertian nature of triads is also reflected in their note spelling.

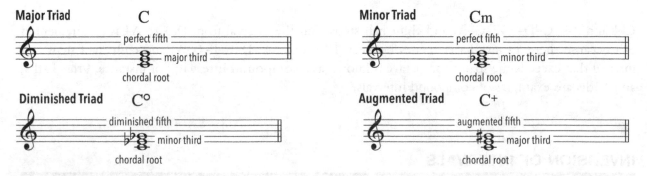

FIGURE 1.16 Basic Triads

INVERSION OF TRIADS

Figure 1.16 demonstrates complete triads in *root position*. In such cases, the *root* appears at the bottom, the *third* in the middle, and the *fifth* on top. To further explore the sound of triads, their notes can be rotated by transferring the bottom note up an octave. Since there are three different notes in the triad, the bottom note can be rotated twice before returning to the original position. These rotations are known

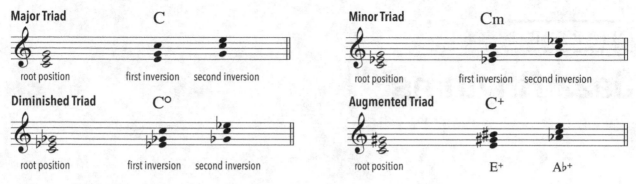

FIGURE 1.17 Basic Triads and Inversions

as **inversions**. In the case of triads, there are two inversions: *first* and *second*. Figure 1.17 illustrates four types of triads: major, minor, diminished, and augmented in root position, and first and second inversions.

The augmented triad partitions the octave into three equal parts. Each note of the augmented triad can potentially function as the root of a new augmented chord. The augmented triad is a type of **chromatic** formation because it contains a non-diatonic pitch, $\sharp\hat{5}$, which is foreign to any major or minor key. Because of its symmetrical properties, each note of the augmented triad can potentially function as the root of a new chord (Caug, Eaug, or A♭aug in Figure 1.17).

SUSPENDED TRIAD

In addition to the four triads shown in Figure 1.16, there are other possible combinations of three notes, such as the **suspended (sus4) triad** shown in Figure 1.18. It is a sonority that breaks away from the tertian organization of notes and constitutes an important formation in jazz.

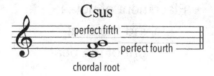

FIGURE 1.18 Suspended Triad

NOTES

1   The treble clef or violin clef is also known as the G-clef and the spiral of the lower part indicates the position of G4. The bass clef, also known as the F-clef, indicates the position of F3. In addition to these two clefs, there are various types of the C-clef of which the soprano, alto, and tenor are mostly used. The C-clefs indicate the position of the middle C: C4.

2   There are also double diminished and double augmented intervals; however, these will not be discussed in this book.

CHAPTER 2
Jazz Rhythms

CHAPTER SUMMARY

Chapter 2 identifies the main characteristics of jazz rhythm and introduces complementary rhythmic traditions from different musical cultures. Suggestions for how to practice rhythm are also provided.

CONCEPTS AND TERMS

- Bembe
- Dynamic accents
- Clave
- Cut time
- Latin music
- Metric accents
- Metronome
- Partido alto
- Phrasing:
  - Articulation
  - Dynamics
- Placement of notes:
  - Behind the beat
  - In front of the beat
- Middle of the beat
- Samba
- Strong beats
- Swing
- Swing 8th notes
- Syncopation
- Weak beats

GENERAL CHARACTERISTICS

It is not by chance that this study of jazz theory begins with the discussion of jazz rhythm. Most jazz musicians will probably agree that having a good sense of time is key to successful improvisation and to overall musicianship. Great jazz artists have always understood the importance of rhythm and time; this comes through as an individual sense of **swing** on numerous recordings. Count Basie, for instance, could play four simple quarter notes and make them swing so hard that the entire band would immediately follow his lead and play with the same energy and dedication.[1] Tito Puente—to borrow from a different, yet complementary rhythmic tradition—could create the same sensation with a few strokes on timbales or mambo bells.[2] The most effective way to learn about jazz rhythm is to *listen* and *imitate* the rhythm of great artists. Listening to music is an important part of our musical development. It allows us to focus on different aspects the musical performance, such as form, instrumentation, orchestration, rhythm, time, melodic devices, harmonic vocabulary, style, innovations, interaction, creativity, historical backgrounds, or tradition.

SYNCOPATION

Figure 2.1 illustrates the distribution of **metric accents** within a 4/4 measure.

FIGURE 2.1 Metric Accents in 4/4

Beats 1 and 3 in 4/4 time are hierarchically more important than beats 2 and 4. The former are known as **strong beats** and receive strong metric accents. Beats 2 and 4 are called **weak beats** and are hierarchically subordinate to beats 1 and 3. One of the characteristics of jazz rhythm is a shift of accents from 1 and 3 to 2 and 4. These **dynamic** (or phenomenal) **accents** create a rich and compelling dialog with the metrical accent on beat 1. By placing the dynamic accents on beats 2 and 4, jazz gets its own rhythmic identity. In addition, these accents help to create a characteristic disagreement between rhythm and meter. In jazz, rhythm seems to work against the underlying meter and that *seeming* disagreement influences the perception of time. The most immediate consequence of such a disagreement is the effect of **syncopation**; syncopation enhances the excitement of the music by distributing rhythmic figures and accents on unexpected locations within the measure. It also creates a variety of rhythmic conflicts that interact with the flow of regularly occurring metrical or phenomenal accents. Figure 2.2 illustrates a melodic line with a highly syncopated rhythmic design.

FIGURE 2.2 Syncopated Melody: "Moose the Mooche," mm. 17–24

SWING

The term *swing* has multiple meanings and associations. Sometimes it refers to a specific musical style from the 1930s called **Swing**. It may also refer to a performance practice tradition or a specific rhythmic attribute attached to the quality of 8th notes. The term **swing 8th notes** is used to indicate 8th notes that are performed unevenly with an overall rolling (swinging) time feel. Because the exact notation of swing 8th notes is neither possible nor very practical, regular 8th notes will be used with the indication *Swing* written in the top left corner of the score to denote swing 8th notes.

PRACTICING RHYTHM

Playing with a good sense of rhythm and time is not only essential to performance, it is also crucial to successful practicing. When practicing improvisation, a variety of idiomatic rhythmic figures should be used. These should be played with rhythmic integrity, convincing phrasing, and good articulation. Figure 2.3 provides a selection of one- and two-bar phrases with idiomatic jazz rhythms that can be implemented in daily practice.[3]

FIGURE 2.3 One- and Two-Bar Rhythmic Phrases

In notating 4/4 time, remember to keep beat 3 *visible*; avoid rhythmic groupings that obscure or de-emphasize beat 3. Figure 2.4 illustrates an incorrectly notated rhythm and its corrected version.

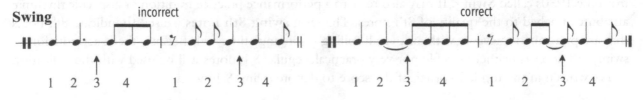

FIGURE 2.4 "Visible" Beat Three

Rhythmic integrity relates to the way swing 8th notes are performed and placed within the beat. Broadly speaking, continuous swing 8ths are played as if notated as triplet 8ths. The first two triplets tied (to become a quarter note) and the third one receives a slight dynamic accent. Figure 2.5 demonstrates this approximate notation of swing 8th notes.

FIGURE 2.5 Swing 8th Notes

Placement of Swing 8ths

Another important consideration regarding the quality of swing 8th notes relates to their placement within the beat. Swing 8ths can be placed in three different locations: **behind the beat**, in the **middle of the beat**, and **in front of the beat**. There is a huge rhetorical, conceptual, and perceptual difference between these locations. Their exact placement depends, in large part, on the overall tempo of the performance and the rhythmic tendencies of different artists. Slow and medium-slow tempi tend to use more *behind the beat* note placements, medium-up and faster tempi lend themselves for a *middle of the beat* or *in front of the beat* treatment. Certain jazz musicians show such a strong propensity towards the particular note placement, that their names have been identified with the specific performance practice technique. For instance, the great tenor saxophone player, Ben Webster, made wonderful use of the *behind the beat* playing. His many recordings convey a relaxed, laid back, and highly original time feel.[4] The guitar player active in the late 1930s, Charlie Christian, on the other hand, preferred to play in the *middle of the beat,* and his constant swing 8th notes were perfectly located in the center of the beat.[5] A jazz icon from the Post-Bop Era, the alto saxophonist Cannonball Adderley preferred his swing 8th notes slightly *in front of the beat* to energize the music with rhythmic excitement and vitality.[6]

Phrasing

The use of dynamics, legato, and especially articulation can substantially improve the overall presentation of melodic lines. Generally, the use of **dynamics** should roughly follow the contour of the melodic lines. Rising lines are typically played with a slight crescendo and descending lines with a slight diminuendo. Additionally, melodic lines should be played almost legato with barely perceptible note detachment. Carefully distributed **articulations** (dynamic accents, staccato, tenuto, marcato, etc.) are also an essential component of **phrasing**. When listening to the phrasing of the great players Wynton Kelly, Kenny Dorham, Sonny Clark, Hank Mobley, Clifford Brown, Tommy Flanagan, Lee Morgan, Sonny Rollins, Sonny Stitt, Dexter Gordon, Woody Shaw, Grant Green, Joe Henderson, Freddie Hubbard, Jackie McLean, Blue Mitchell, Barry Harris, and others, notice that their excellent use of articulation not only creates a strong sense of swing, but also defines their individual styles of improvisation.[7] The highest note within a phrase typically receives a stronger accent regardless of its position within the measure. Also, upbeats tend to be more accentuated within a phrase than downbeats. There are, however, many exceptions to these rules that will be addressed as the book unfolds.

Playing with a Metronome

As we assemble the aforementioned suggestions and put them to practical ends, the use of a **metronome** on *2* and *4* can vastly improve the quality of our swing 8th notes and solidify their placement within the measure. Playing with a rhythm section is a privilege that most jazz musicians cherish. More often than not, however, we practice alone and the metronome might be the only available recourse to check if our time and rhythm are correct. Set the metronome to 66 and make each click count as a half note on beats 2 and 4.

LATIN RHYTHMIC TRADITIONS

In addition to the swing tradition, which constitutes the backbone of contemporary jazz education, an understanding of rhythmic orientations from different musical cultures can be valuable for one's musical development. In particular, the vast array of enormously popular rhythmic grooves and dance forms from Latin America offer invaluable resources to help one cultivate his/her sense of rhythm. In a certain way, studying Swing and **Latin music** side by side allows you to better understand the complex world of rhythms, distinguish between different musical cultures, and appreciate ways in which these complementary rhythmic traditions can coexist in the form of multitudinous stylistic fusions and other cross-disciplinary blends. The term *Latin music* does not give true justice to the enormously vast and highly complex musical cultures of the different regions from Latin America. Among the myriad of rhythmic traditions, *Latin music* encapsulates the following styles: Brazilian (*samba, baião, frevo, maracatu, chorinho*), Cuban (*cha-cha-chá, mambo*), Columbian (*cumbia, currulao, porro*), Argentinean *tango*, Chilean *chacarera*, Uruguayan *candombe*, Venezuelan *joropo*, and Peruvian *zamba*, just to scratch the vast cultural plateau.[8]

Unlike Swing music, which is characterized by the distribution of phenomenal accents on beats 2 and 4 where the beat is subdivided into swing 8th notes, in Latin music the phenomenal accents generally occur on beats 1 and 3, where beat 3 receives more emphasis than beat 1. In addition, Latin music is generally played with straight 8th notes—a feature that constitutes the most fundamental stylistic difference between the two traditions. As you can see in Figure 2.6, the rhythmic patterns are notated in cut time (¢) (unlike Swing music notated in 4/4), which indicates the overall *two feel* of that music.[9] Just as Swing music can be written in 3/4, so can Latin music (particularly in *bembe* rhythms). The quality of eight notes, however, remains *swung* in a swing waltz as opposed to *straight* eights in a Latin composition.[10] The original Argentinean *tango* (as opposed to *tango nuevo*) is written in 2/4 with the 16th note beat subdivisions. That rhythmic orientation is similar to the precursor of Swing music, Ragtime, which also features a 2/4 rhythmic feel with the 16th note beat subdivisions.

Even though it is clearly beyond the scope of this book to explore the intricacies of Latin music, Figure 2.6 nonetheless provides a selection of basic rhythms and dance patterns that originated in Latin America.

Figure 2.6 contains a lot of valuable information that requires unpacking. For starters, the terms **clave**, **partido alto** and **bembe** refer to the specific structural rhythmic patterns that control the unfolding and distribution of harmony, melody, and an additional rhythmic strata in dances such as *cha-cha-chá* and *mambo* (Cuba) or *samba* and *bossa nova* (Brazil), or that are found in various Afro-Cuban polyrhythmic crossovers (*bembe*). *Samba, bossa nova, baião, choro (chorinho), cha-cha-chá, mambo, rumba, cumbia, porro, currulao, tango,* and *candombe* are the names of the specific dances from different Latin American countries. Finally, *cáscara* and *timbale* are the names of rhythmic patterns played on the specific

FIGURE 2.6 Latin American Rhythms

instruments in conjunction with an appropriate clave (either 2/3 or 3/2). As you advance your studies in jazz theory, you may return to this chapter and implement some of the rhythmic ideas introduced in Figures 2.3 and 2.6 in the manner demonstrated in Figure 2.7.

FIGURE 2.7 Bossa Nova Keyboard Realization

As emphasized in this chapter, the ability to play with a good sense of timing is key to successful improvisation in any musical style. By studying rhythmic traditions from different musical cultures you become more cognizant of the indispensable role of rhythm in music in general, and its influence on harmony, melody, form, and style in particular.

NOTES

1   Listen to "Jumpin' At the Woodside" on *First Time! The Count Meets the Duke.*
2   Listen to "Oye Cómo Va" on *El Rey* or his *Cuban Carnival.*
3   For four- and eight-bar phrases see the Companion Website (CW, henceforth).
4   Listen to "My Ideal" on *Art Tatum Ben Webster: The Album.*
5   Listen to "I Found a New Baby" on *The Genius of the Electric Guitar.*
6   Listen to "So What" on *Kind of Blue.*
7   Notable albums: Wynton Kelly (*Someday My Prince Will Come* and *Kelly at Midnight*); Kenny Dorham (*Quiet Kenny* and *Una Mas*); Sonny Clark (*Leapin' And Lopin'* and *Sonny Clark Trio*); Hank Mobley (*Soul Station* and *Workout*); Clifford Brown (*Clifford Brown And Max Roach* and At *Basin Street*); Tommy Flanagan (*Eclypso* and *Tommy Flanagan Plays The Music of Harold Arlen*); Lee Morgan (*The Sidewinder* and *Cornbread*); Sonny Rollins (*Tour De Force* and *Saxophone Colossus*); Sonny Stitt (*Sonny Stitt, Bud Powell, and J.J. Johnson* and *Constellation*); Dexter Gordon (*Go* and *The Jumpin' Blues*); Woody Shaw (*Stepping Stones* and *Imagination*); Grant Green (*Talkin' About* and *I Want to Hold Your Hand*); Joe Henderson (*Page One* and *Inner Urge*); Freddie Hubbard (*Hub Cap* and *The Artistry of Freddie Hubbard*); Jackie McLean (*McLean's Scene* and *Jacknife*); Blue Mitchell (*The Things to Do* and *Out of the Blue*); Barry Harris (*Barry Harris at the Jazz Workshop* and *Magnificent!*).
8   For representative recordings of Brazilian music listen to: Pixinguinha (*100 Anos*); Antônio Carlos Jobim (*Getz/Gilberto, Black Orpheus*); Elis Regina (*Live at Montreux*); Egberto Gismonti (*Solo*); Leny Andrade (*Ao Vivo*); Zimbo Trio (*Aqurela do Brazil*); Cuban music: Israel "Cachao" Lopez (*Cachao Descargas—The Havana Sessions*); Chano Pozo (*Manteca—The Real Birth of Cubop*); Arsenio Rodriguez (*Dundunbanza: 1946–1951*); Columbian music: Various artists (*Jende Ri Pelenge*); Argentinean music: Astor Piazzolla (*Astor Piazzolla—Essential Tango*); Uruguayan music: Hugo Fattoruso (*Trio Fattoruso*); Venezuelan music: Prisca Dávila (*Piano Jazz Venezolano*).
9   In fact, traditional Brazilian music is notated in 2/4 with the 16th note beat subdivision. Here, however, we will dispense with that tradition and use cut time and 8th note beat subdivision for the sake of readability and in keeping with the contemporary notation practice.
10   "Bluesette"—swing 8ths; "Afro-Blue"—straight 8ths, for instance.

CHAPTER 3

Harmonic Function

CHAPTER SUMMARY

Chapter 3 defines harmonic function. Its influence on the behavior of chords and harmonic progressions with triads is examined.

CONCEPTS AND TERMS

- Cadence/Cadential closure
- Cadential confirmation
- Fifth motion
- Function symbols
- Functional families
- Functional tonality:
  - Dominant
  - Predominant
  - Tonic
- Lead-sheet notation
- Leading tones
- Melodic motion:
  - Contrary
  - Oblique
  - Parallel
  - Similar
- Outer-voice counterpoint
- Pivot chords:
  - Chromatic
  - Diatonic
- Raised submediant
- Roman numerals
- Slash notation
- Structural level
- Surface level
- Tonic prolongation
- Transitional space
- Voice leading

FUNCTIONAL TONALITY

Chords and lines represent two interconnected musical forces that are capable of producing an amazing variety of linear and harmonic patterns. In tonal jazz, the behavior of these patterns is predictable, hierarchical, and systemic. In a certain sense, harmonic function can be defined as a contextual feature that can be attributed to a chord, a family of chords, harmonic progressions, or even to complete melodic phrases. These features are unique for each of the following functions: the **tonic**, the **predominant**, and the **dominant**. The interaction between these three creates a system of **functional tonality**, which undergirds the structure of tonal jazz and common-practice music.

Functional tonality is a hierarchical system wherein the predominant and the dominant are ultimately related to and controlled by the tonic. The tonic is thus at the center of this hierarchical system. The uniqueness of each harmonic function is defined by universal and well-tested characteristics of functional tonality. The tonic is synonymous with stability, rest, and the cessation of harmonic motion. The predominant generates harmonic motion by taking the music away from the tonic and leading it toward the dominant. The dominant is an antithesis of the tonic in every conceivable way: it is highly unstable, represents chords on the move, accumulates harmonic tension, and does not rest until it reaches a local or structural tonic. These very different behavioral patterns remain constant across the entirety of the tonal system in which jazz forms a distinctive musical language with its own harmonic grammar and melodic syntax. As will be demonstrated time and time again, functional tonality in jazz has different properties than that of common-practice classical music. These properties are represented by a unique set of rules dictating the unfolding of harmonic function, voice-leading conventions, and the overall behavior of chord tones and chordal extensions.

TRIADS IN MAJOR KEYS

Figure 3.1 illustrates the structure of the tonic, subdominant, and dominant triads in the key of C major.

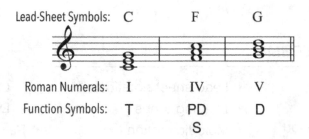

FIGURE 3.1 Tonic—Subdominant—Dominant

In all major keys, the tonic, the subdominant, and the dominant are major.

In addition to the tonic, subdominant, and dominant triads, the tonality system includes triads built on other scale degrees as well. A triad built on $\hat{2}$ is called the *supertonic*; on $\hat{3}$, the *mediant*; on $\hat{6}$, the *submediant*; and, on $\hat{7}$, the *leading tone*. Figure 3.2 illustrates triads built on each scale degree in C major.

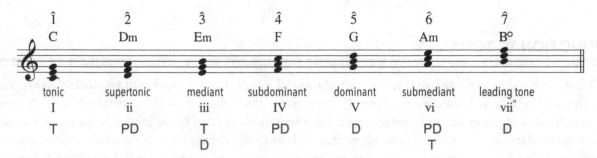

FIGURE 3.2 Triads in Major Keys

The use of a diminished triad on $\hat{7}$ expands the quality of chords occurring in a major key to three distinct types: *major*, *minor*, and *diminished*.

TRIADS IN MINOR KEYS

Figures 3.3–3.5 show the distribution of triads in the three *shades* of minor: natural, harmonic, and melodic.

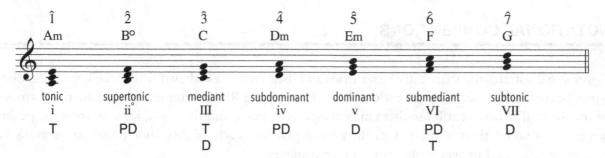

FIGURE 3.3 Triads in Natural Minor

The triads in natural minor use the same names for the scale degrees as they do in the major key, with the exception of the triad on $\hat{7}$, which is called the **subtonic**.

FIGURE 3.4 Triads in Harmonic Minor

There are two diminished triads built on $\hat{2}$ and $\sharp\hat{7}$ and one augmented triad on $\hat{3}$. The scale-degree $\sharp\hat{7}$ is called the **leading tone**.

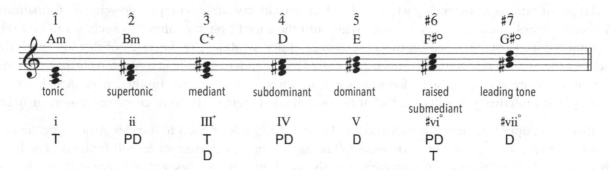

FIGURE 3.5 Triads in Melodic Minor

The scale-degree $\sharp\hat{6}$ is called the **raised submediant**. In indicating the scale degrees $\hat{6}$ and $\hat{7}$ in the melodic minor, the $\sharp\hat{6}$ and $\sharp\hat{7}$ labels are used, respectively.

The tonic, predominant, and dominant functions contain a collection of similarly functioning chords, including (but not limited to) chords built on scale degrees with which these functions are typically associated. For instance, the chords built on $\hat{4}$ and $\hat{2}$ are known as subdominant and supertonic, respectively, and they share the predominant function; the chords built on $\hat{5}$ and $\hat{7}$ share the dominant function, etc.

NOTATIONAL CONVENTIONS

Figure 3.6 illustrates the structure of four triads and their inversions labeled with three sets of notational symbols: traditional **lead-sheet notation** above the staff, and **Roman numerals** and **function symbols** below the staff. Since we will use them interchangeably throughout the book, let us make some general observations about their usefulness in theory and practice. Each of these notational conventions has unique advantages, but also some obvious shortcomings.

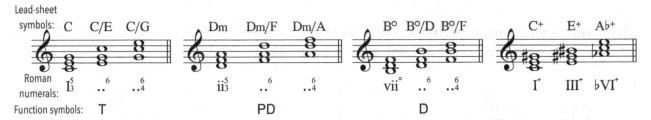

FIGURE 3.6 Notational Conventions

Lead-Sheet Notation

Lead-sheet notation, also known as popular-music notation, is by far the most widespread notational convention used by jazz musicians. It comes in a variety of forms that arise from its murky origins and subsequent vague implementations. There are many alternate notational systems in use, which for better or worse every jazz musician needs to get familiar with for purely practical, "bandstand" reasons. Here, we will only use chord symbols that are commonly found in published and respected fake books. Lead-sheet notation is very specific in showing what the chord is: it indicates the letter name, the exact number and types of extensions occurring within a chord, chordal inversions, or complex polychordal formations. A chord symbol, then, provides a quick insight into the chord's pitch content. As such, it can be easily transmitted into a voicing that captures the essence of that symbol. The downside of this labeling is the lack of contextual considerations, especially in regard to the underlying tonality. As a tonally *uninterpreted* notation, we are not quite sure, for instance, how chords relate to one another, how their behavior conveys the underlying tonality, and what the overall tonal logic of different chord successions may be.

In this book, uppercase letter names and an "M" extension will be used to indicate major-type chords. For minor-type chords an "m" extension following an uppercase letter name will be used. The lead-sheet symbols from Figure 3.6 also employ slash notation; this specifies a chord type with the lowest sounding pitch separated by a diagonal slash. An uppercase letter name to the right of the diagonal indicates the bass note. The letter name to the left of the diagonal shows a specific chord type.

Roman Numerals

Roman numerals are context-sensitive and indicate the exact position of chords with respect to the underlying tonic. This style of notation is very powerful in explaining the tonal behavior of chords, and it is mostly used in analysis. Some jazz musicians, however, have found a useful niche for this type of notation. By translating the lead-sheet notation of a standard tune to Roman numerals, jazz musicians can easily transpose and learn that tune in all 12 keys. But Roman numerals, too, have their disadvantages. Problems with this style of notation arise when a tune modulates away from the underlying tonic or frequently tonicizes new key areas. With the addition of Arabic numbers borrowed from the figured-bass tradition, Roman numerals are capable of expressing complex five-, six-, or seven-part chords. When using Roman numerals, however, complex five-, six-, or seven-part formations will be translated to their essential four-part framework. For instance, F7($\flat$13) in the key of C major will be simply notated as IV^7.

The addition of available extensions to chords is a matter of personal preference and reflects the underlying context in which specific chords occur. The practice of adding extensions or reinterpreting chords is similar to that of interpreting unfigured basses from the Baroque period. There are, however, many musical situations where more detail is desired, such as when a composer or arranger wants a specific sound or voicing. In those types of situations, a chord symbol might include more detailed information about chordal extensions, note omissions, or even a specific arrangement of notes. These chord symbols typically stand out among other, more conventionally written chords. Given the very different notation systems being used, we can start thinking more rigorously about our own notational choices.

In Figure 3.6, the tonic chord in root position is notated with an "I$_3^5$" symbol. In practice, however, a "I" will be used without the Arabic numbers because they are assumed. Also, in notating a chord in first inversion, the Roman numeral representation has already been simplified: instead of a complete "I$_3^6$" symbol, the "I$_3^6$" symbol was used. Roman numerals might also include "$\natural$," "$\sharp$," and "$\flat$." Written in front of the Roman numeral, these accidentals indicate chromatic scale degrees in relation to the underlying key. To notate major chords, uppercase Roman numerals will be implemented and to notate minor chords, lowercase Roman numerals will be used. A diminished triad will take a lowercase Roman numeral with a small raised circle, vii$^\circ$; an augmented triad will use an uppercase Roman numeral with a small plus sign, III$^+$.

Function Symbol

The function symbol notation is the least used notational system in jazz. As the name suggests, this notation specifies the harmonic function of individual chords and even complete chord progressions. It has the potential of being useful to notate specific behaviors of chords that may not—at least on the surface level—indicate that they belong to a particular functional family of chords. As such, function symbols enable the perception of harmonic progressions from a more structural perspective. Function symbols indicate neither the architecture nor the specific scale degrees of chords. This style of notation is more conceptual than it is representative of a specific surface event. The terms **surface level** and **structural level** are used to describe musical events and the degree of their importance. *Structural* events occur beneath the musical *surface* and are responsible for the overall tonal, harmonic, and melodic forces controlling the piece. Function symbols use three labels: **T** for tonic-type chords, **PD** for predominant-type chords, and **D** for dominant-type chords.

FUNCTIONAL FAMILIES

When comparing triads built on different scale degrees in Figures 3.3–3.5, notice that some of them share the same harmonic function. Some triads can even have two different functional symbols.

Major Key

A **functional family** combines chords built on different scale degrees that share the same harmonic function and voice-leading behaviors. Chords within each family are organized hierarchically according to their degree of similarity and dependency on the tonic, subdominant, and dominant triads. Figure 3.7 illustrates three families of similarly functioning chords in major.

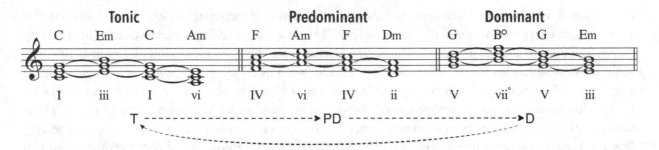

FIGURE 3.7 Functional Families in Major

Broadly speaking, functional families illustrate possible successions of chords within a tonal family and between chords of different families. The succession of T–PD–D–T, illustrated by arrows in Figure 3.7, is the most fundamental and demonstrates how chords can be combined to project a sense of tonality. This succession of harmonic functions highlights the cycle of fifths, a pattern that constitutes an essential trademark of common-practice tonality. Descending **fifth motions** are what we tend to hear as forward moving—in the sense of time or momentum—because of their drive toward tonic resolution. Any succession of chords is also dependent on its relationship to the metric and rhythmic properties of the phrase, as well as on the chord's ultimate move toward a cadence. The terms **cadence** or **cadential closure** signify an important tonal event that confirms the underlying tonic (or new key) by means of a V–I progression. Figure 3.8 demonstrates the distribution of harmonic functions within a I–vi–ii–V–I progression. Scale degrees written above the staff indicate the melodic content of the soprano voice.

FIGURE 3.8 Tonal Progression in Major

The chords I and vi are derived from the tonic family and, in certain situations, can be used as substitutes of one another. In the context of the progression from Figure 3.8, it makes sense to hear the submediant chord as a **transitional space** between I and ii or as **tonic prolongation**. Having prolonged or expanded the tonic, the vi chord moves by a fifth down to the predominant ii, which then proceeds by another fifth to the dominant on V. The progression ends with a V–I **cadential confirmation** of the tonic featuring another descending fifth motion. In this early exposition of harmonic progressions, we cannot ignore other important factors that contribute to the concept of tonality, such as metric placements and duration of chords. The vi chord occurs on beat 3 of m. 2 and lasts for 2 beats. The predominant ii occupies m. 3 and the ii–V cadential preparation of the tonic occurs in m. 4. The V–I cadential confirmation occurs over the bar lines in mm. 4–5; this progression produces forward motion and illustrates the hierarchical relationship between V and I. The tonic provides the resolution of harmonic tension and its metric placement on beat 1 in m. 5 highlights its structural and tonal significance.

Minor Key

Figure 3.9 illustrates three functional families in the minor key and demonstrates the common-tone retention between chords within each family. The predominant and dominant families combine chords from the three *shades* of minor.

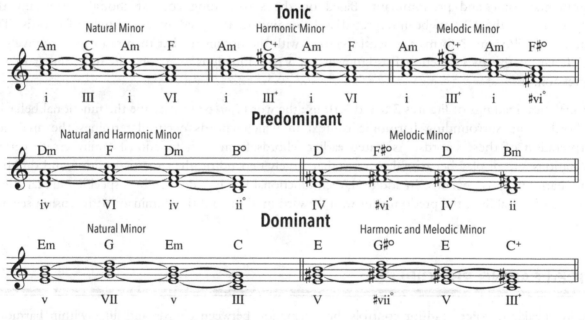

FIGURE 3.9 Functional Families in Minor

Functional families in the minor key show considerable triadic variety and are much more intricate than their major counterparts. Each family includes different types of triads, with the potential for complex functional relationships.

Figure 3.10 illustrates the succession of harmonic function in a slightly more advanced progression in 3/4.

FIGURE 3.10 Tonal Progression in Minor

The mediant chord, III⁺, occurring on beat 3, is a transitional space between i and VI. Even though the III⁺ can also function as a dominant, it functions as a tonic expansion in the context of this progression. Motion to the dominant in the second chord would have created a retrogression of harmonic function: dominant to predominant. The third chord of the progression, the submediant, also has two functional assignments: tonic and predominant. Based on the surrounding context though, especially the forthcoming iv, the VI can be interpreted as belonging to the predominant family of chords. The predominant ii° in m. 3 forms a cadential gesture with the dominant that then resolves deceptively to the VI. Given the two functional assignments of VI, it functions as a tonic in the context of this progression.

The analytical readings of Figures 3.8 and 3.10 use the word *context* to describe the functional behavior of chords. The surrounding harmonic context in which chords occur determines the analytical interpretation of these chords. As stated earlier, chords from each functional family create certain expectations and display behavioral patterns that largely depend on their metric position and duration within harmonic progressions. In addition, each functional family is defined by a specific musical affect: the tonic with stability, the predominant with forward motion, and the dominant with tension seeking resolution.

VOICE-LEADING PRINCIPLES

Broadly speaking, **voice leading** controls the interaction between chords and lines within harmonic progressions. The principles of voice leading encompass several general topics, such as the role of outer-voice counterpoint, the types of melodic motion, the retention of common tones, the treatment of dissonances, and others that will be discussed throughout the book.

At the surface level, jazz voice-leading conventions seem more relaxed than they are in common-practice music. After all, jazz musicians use forbidden parallel perfect fifths and octaves, move all the voices in the same direction, and tolerate voice crossings of different sorts. The rules of jazz voice leading are different because the syntax of jazz is largely incompatible with common-practice classical or other types of music. These differences do not mean, however, that the rules of jazz voice leading are any less strict. When jazz musicians think about dissonance treatment or highlight a linear approach to harmony as opposed to a vertical one, they rely just as much on well-defined rules of voice leading as do composers of common-practice music. The conventions of jazz voice leading depend greatly on the soprano and bass, so-called **outer-voice counterpoint**. In general, proper intervallic relationship between the outer voices guarantees a successful realization of harmonic progressions and influences the behavior of inner melodic lines. What characteristics, then, should underlie the design of outer-voice counterpoint? First, the outer-voice counterpoint should form a harmonically independent, two-voice framework. This means that the outer voices should delineate the underlying harmony without any help from inner voices. Second, the outer voices should be melodically interesting. This characteristic relates mostly to the design of the highest (or soprano) line, but in more complex progressions, it might also affect the design of the bass line. Third, outer-voice counterpoint should prioritize the use of **contrary motion**, though other types of melodic motions, such as **oblique**, **similar**, and **parallel**, are also possible.

Figure 3.11 illustrates four types of melodic motion.

FIGURE 3.11 Types of Melodic Motion

Parallel motion involves two voices moving in the same direction using the same generic interval. As far as its aesthetic value in jazz, too much parallelism might be monotonous, although in certain harmonic situations and musical styles—modal jazz in particular—this type of melodic motion is highly desirable. *Similar motion* occurs when two voices move in the same direction with different intervals between the notes. *Oblique motion* occurs when one voice ascends or descends while the other is standing still, but they are still moving homophonically. One of the most common variants of oblique motion involves pedal points; here the harmonic motion often seems to be suspended and may be reduced to a single underlying harmony, often the dominant. Although less common, oblique motion might also feature a soprano (or inner) pedal point where a stationary soprano (or inner) voice supports a melodically active bass. The most effective type of melodic motion is *contrary motion* in which two voices move in opposite direction and employ different intervals.

BASIC KEYBOARD APPLICATIONS

We will now cover some basic voice-leading principles that should prepare us for the exercises on the Companion Website (CW). Figure 3.12 illustrates an eight-bar harmonic progression with triads and triadic inversions only. Based on the progression, we will highlight some common voice-leading principles. In order to do so, let us make some analytical observations about the progression itself. In mm. 3–4, the progression modulates to the key of A minor. Boxes around Roman numerals indicate a pivot area, containing diatonic chords simultaneously functioning in the key of C major and A minor. These pivot chords provide an effective link between these two key areas. A **pivot chord** is a chord that is common to two different keys; its dual functionality allows for a smooth transition from one key to the other. More specifically, a **diatonic pivot chord** contains diatonic pitches and connects closely related keys. A **chromatic pivot chord** admits pitch alterations and connects closely, as well as distantly, related key areas.

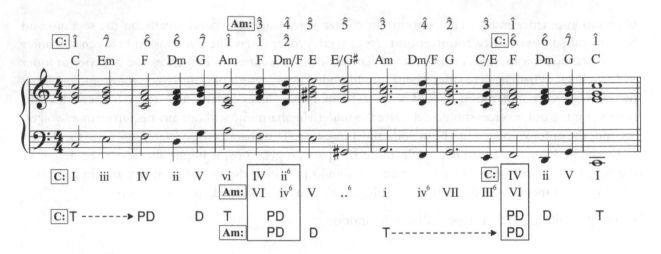

FIGURE 3.12 Keyboard Realization and Analysis

Keyboard style texture like that represented in Figure 3.12 uses three notes in the right hand (R.H.) and a single note in the left hand (L.H.). With triad formations like this, we need to consider which note in a chord to double. As a general principle, in root-position and first inversion triads we double the root (with the exception of root-position vi in the V–vi progression, see mm. 2–3 in Figure 3.12). In second inversion triads, we can double a 5th or the root. We should avoid doubling a 3rd because it is the most active tone in the triad. Finally, in connecting adjacent chords, we should strive to move via the shortest possible route and/or retain as many notes in common as possible.

When playing the outer-voice framework by itself, notice how effectively it expresses the underlying progression. In particular, the use of compound 3rds (or their inversions, compound 6ths) in the outer voices clarifies the harmonic meaning of the progression. This sound actually happens quite often and its influence on the progression is so powerful that other intervallic pairs get their harmonic definition from the relationship between the compound 3rds or 6ths. When examining the types of melodic motion between chords, notice that the outer-voice counterpoint primarily uses contrary and oblique motion. The use of contrary motion between outer voices is particularly important in progressions moving by step. The inner voices move mostly by step and employ common tones within the same voice.

In realizing progressions on the keyboard, develop a habit of starting with the outer-voice counterpoint and make sure that it features mostly contrary motion. Parallel motion between perfect intervals should be avoided, but similar motion between perfect intervals is acceptable. Strive for as many compound 3rds and 6ths as possible because these intervals clearly delineate the underlying harmony. In a triadic environment, the leading tone should be resolved up by a half step. Also, the treatment of a chordal 3rd should usually involve stepwise, upward resolution and common-tone retention, but rarely involves large leaps. Even though the progression from Figure 3.12 looks and sounds nothing like jazz, by practicing this and similar types of progressions found in the CW, the principles of voice leading are more readily internalized. This lays the foundation for more idiomatic jazz progressions in later chapters.

CHAPTER 4

Four-Part Chords

CHAPTER SUMMARY

Chapter 4 establishes the foundation of jazz harmonic syntax. Fourteen four-part chords are introduced and their functional status is examined.

CONCEPTS AND TERMS

- Chordal seventh/sixth
- Close voicings
- Dominant chords:
  - Regular
  - Suspended
- "Drop 2" voicings

- Essential chord tones
- Intermediary chords:
  - Diminished 7th
  - Diminished major 7th
  - Half-diminished 7th
  - Minor 7(♭5)

- Inversions of four-part chords
- Major chords
- Minor chords
- Open voicings
- Tritone

CHARACTERISTICS OF JAZZ HARMONY

Jazz harmonic syntax encompasses a plethora of different types of chords, from simple three-note triads to as many as eight-note structures. Within such a rich palette of possibilities, it is the four-part chord that constitutes the *fundamental formation* of jazz harmony. Just as triads were essential building blocks of common-practice music (ca. 1650–1900) so are four-part chords considered essential harmonies in jazz. Jazz harmonic syntax has evolved from common-practice music in the twentieth century in a similar manner that the latter had sprung from earlier modal theories of the 1600s and before. As such, jazz harmonic syntax is a part of a rich, constantly evolving musical language of tremendous variety. Even though we can pinpoint a lot of commonalities between jazz and common-practice music, syntactical differences between the two trump those similarities.

One essential difference between common-practice and jazz music relates to the status, role, and treatment of chordal dissonances. Unlike common-practice music, jazz allows chordal dissonances and therefore treats them in bold, new ways. The presence of four-part chords in jazz is as ubiquitous as that of triads in common-practice music. The **chordal seventh** or the **sixth** enhances the structure of chords, adds a kinetic force that energizes harmonic progressions, and permeates various levels of the musical structure. A four-part chord originates by adding one additional pitch to a triad. We refer to that note as an **essential chord tone**. To construct a four-part chord, add the following chord tones: a major 6th (6), a major 7th (M7), and a minor 7th (m7). Essential chord tones can be applied to major, minor, diminished, augmented, or suspended triads.

Figure 4.1 shows the addition of essential chord tones to the C major triad.

FIGURE 4.1 Addition of Essential Chord Tones

The addition of these three essential chord tones produces three different chords, each with a distinct intervallic structure, function, and sound. A *sixth chord*, C6, sounds very stable and is at rest. In labeling that chord, the "M" suffix in front of a "6" is omitted because C6 constitutes a commonly used label for the major triad with an added sixth. A *major seventh chord*, CM7, is a consonant entity with no particular voice leading or resolution requirements.[1] When C6 and CM7 are played in quick succession, we hear some common characteristics they share: both are major, use the same root, and are entirely *diatonic* (i.e. they only include notes from the C major scale).

Although a *dominant seventh chord*, C7, uses the same triadic foundation as C6 and CM7, it has a totally different harmonic function. The chord sounds as if it wants to move to a more stable sonority. The source of that inner tension and desire for harmonic resolution is the interval of a **tritone** between the major 3rd and the minor 7th of the dominant 7th chord.

CHORD CATEGORIES

To navigate through different chord types, the 14 four-part chords are divided into four functional categories. Even though these categories will suggest specific harmonic functions, we will discover that certain chords from different categories share the same harmonic function and that a single chord might have two different functional assignments. These functional overlaps that now might seem ambiguous will become clearer as we continue to advance in the study of jazz theory.

Major Category

Possible Harmonic Function—Tonic and Predominant

The major category includes the four chords shown in Figure 4.2. These chords, which are arranged from more stable or *diatonic* to more unstable or *chromatic*, also share the same harmonic function and are tonally stable. Different as they may sound on the surface, they can be used interchangeably in the context of various harmonic progressions. Let us examine the pitch structure of these chords more closely.

FIGURE 4.2 Major Four-Part Chords

All the chords from Figure 4.2 have at least two common tones: the root and a major 3rd. With the exception of a sixth chord, C6, all the remaining chords also include a major 7th. The 5th is an expendable note that can be chromatically altered by either lower or upper half steps. In Figure 4.2, the 5th is replaced by the ♭5th in the *major seventh flat five chord*, CM7(♭5); and, the ♯5th in the *major seventh sharp five chord*, CM7(♯5).[2] Both of these chords and their spellings preserve their tertian pedigrees. A sixth chord and a major seventh chord are diatonic because they are derived from the pitches of the diatonic scale. The *major seventh flat five* and *major seventh sharp five* chords are chromatic because they contain *pitch alterations* that are not part of the diatonic scale. A generic Roman numeral for this category is **I (X)**.

Minor Category

Possible Harmonic Function—Tonic and Predominant

Figure 4.3 shows the pitch structure of three chords from the minor category.

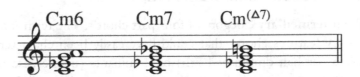

FIGURE 4.3 Minor Four-Part Chords

The *minor sixth chord*, Cm6, has a stable sound and represents a chord at rest. The *minor major seventh chord*, Cm(♯7), is more unstable. Can you identify the pitch that is responsible for that characteristic sound? The *minor seventh chord*, Cm7, is easily recognizable and one of the most commonly used chords in jazz. Its harmonic function, however, is not always apparent and largely depends on the context in which this chord occurs. For now, it suffices to say that in the context of ii–V7–I progression, a minor seventh chord built on $\hat{2}$ will always function as the predominant. In other harmonic contexts, a minor seventh chord will most likely function as a tonic chord. A generic Roman numeral for this category is **i (x)**.

Dominant 7th Category

Possible Harmonic Function—Dominant

The addition of a minor 7th to a major or suspended triad results in the creation of the two distinct dominant 7th chords: **regular** with the major 3rd and **suspended** (**sus**) with the perfect 4th.[3] Both chords are unstable and have a strong tendency to generate harmonic motion. The presence of a tritone between a major 3rd and a minor 7th of the dominant 7th chord is responsible for this harmonic and

FIGURE 4.4 Dominant Four-Part Chords

tonal instability. In the suspended dominant, a perfect 4th is the unsettling melodic agent that generates melodic motion and wants to resolve down to a major 3rd.[4] Figure 4.4 shows four chords from the dominant 7th category.

The *dominant seventh chord*, C7, clearly projects the dominant function. The *sus seventh chord*, C7sus, is most easily identifiable with modal jazz.[5] The *dominant seventh flat five chord*, C7(♭5) has a distinct intervallic structure featuring two interlocking tritones between the root and a ♭5th, and a major 3rd and a minor 7th: C4–G♭4 and E4–B♭4 in C7(♭5).[6] The *dominant seventh sharp five chord*, C7(♯5), has an augmented triad at the bottom of its structure and projects a characteristic whole-tone sound. The *dominant seventh flat five* and the *dominant seventh sharp five* contain chromatic alterations of the diatonic 5th; this makes their pitch structure even more unstable. A generic Roman numeral for this category is V^7 (X^7).

Intermediary Category

Harmonic Function—Predominant, Dominant, Tonic

Figure 4.5 illustrates the **intermediary** category of four-part chords. The term *intermediary* might seem odd; after all, this category features chords that could have easily been characterized as predominants (in the case of the m7(♭5) or half-diminished 7th) or dominants (in the case of the diminished 7th chord). The designation *intermediary* indicates that these chords have different roles in harmonic progressions.[7]

FIGURE 4.5 Intermediary Four-Part Chords

All of these chords have a diminished triad at the bottom of their structure. Chords from this category are associated with the predominant and dominant function. In more advanced harmonic situations, however, they may acquire different functional associations.

The *minor seventh flat five chord*, Cm7(♭5), or the *half-diminished seventh chord*, CØ7, has a characteristic, unresolved sound. Two different labels can be used for a chord that sounds and looks the same. For now, the former functions as the predominant in the context of iiØ–V7–i progression, and the latter participates in dominant-type situations.[8] The *diminished seventh chord*, Cdim7, constitutes a perfectly symmetrical sonority with four minor 3rds subdividing the octave into four equal parts. This important four-part formation originates from the addition of a diminished 7th to the diminished triad. This chord generally behaves as a dominant-functioning chord. The *diminished major seventh*, Cdim(♯7), acquires different harmonic functions (mostly dominant and tonic) and is probably the most dissonant formation from the collection of four-part chords.

A generic Roman numeral for the minor 7(♭5) and half-diminished 7th chords is **ii^Ø** (**x^Ø**).

The 14 four-part chords compiled in Figure 4.6 have been shown in root position with the chordal root at the bottom of their pitch structure.

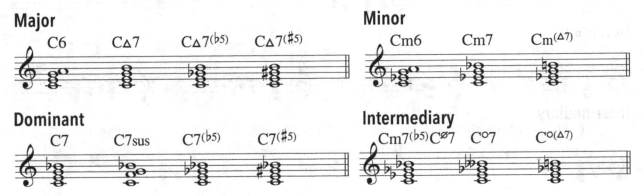

FIGURE 4.6 Fourteen Four-Part Chords

INVERSIONS OF FOUR-PART CHORDS

Broadly speaking, **inversions** illustrate different intervallic configurations of the same chord. Four-part chords can occur in four positions: *root position* (the root in the lowest voice), *1st inversion* (the 3rd in the lowest voice), *2nd inversion* (the 5th in the lowest voice), and *3rd inversion* (the essential chord tone in the lowest voice).

Figure 4.7 illustrates a root-position C6 chord with the three inversions.

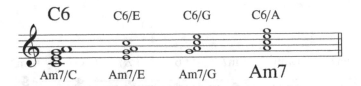

FIGURE 4.7 Inversional Equivalence of C6 and Am7

When examining each inversion, notice that the 3rd inversion of a C6 chord looks the same (i.e. is inversionally equivalent) as the root-position Am7 chord. This observation is important because it allows us to use one chord in place of the other. But this mutual relationship also means that if a sixth chord in 3rd inversion is the same as a minor seventh chord in root position, then all inversions of the sixth chord can represent some form of the minor 7th chord. Figure 4.8 illustrates the 14 four-part chords in root position and three inversions.

Major

FIGURE 4.8 Inversions of Four-Part Chords

FUNCTIONAL FAMILIES

Major Key

Figure 4.9 shows four-part chords built on each scale degree of C major. In addition to lead-sheet symbols and Roman numerals, each chord is identified with a function symbol that indicates its likely functional status in the harmonic progression.

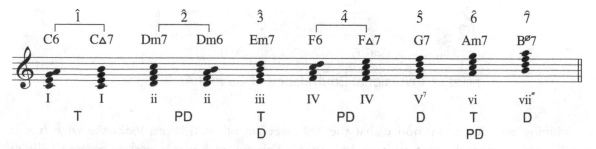

FIGURE 4.9 Four-Part Chords in Major Key

The tonic on $\hat{1}$ features two different chords: a 6th chord and a M7 chord. The supertonic ($\hat{2}$) allows two minor chords: a m7 and a m6. The mediant ($\hat{3}$) includes a m7 chord. The subdominant ($\hat{4}$) allows two major chords: a 6th and a M7. The dominant on $\hat{5}$ features a dominant 7th. The submediant ($\hat{6}$) takes a m7. And the leading tone ($\hat{7}$) features a half-diminished 7th chord. The chords built on $\hat{1}$, $\hat{3}$, and $\hat{6}$ share the tonic function, just as those built on $\hat{2}$, $\hat{4}$, $\hat{6}$ and $\hat{3}$, $\hat{5}$, $\hat{7}$ share predominant and the dominant functions respectively. Chords that share the same function will most likely share the same behavioral patterns in the context of harmonic progressions. In certain musical situations, therefore, chords of the same function can often be used interchangeably as substitutes of one another and, in more advanced situations, as chordal prolongations or expansions.

The situation gets a little more complex for chords on $\hat{3}$ and $\hat{6}$. Chords built on these scale degrees have a dual harmonic function. Depending on harmonic context, chords on $\hat{6}$ can either function as tonic or predominant. Furthermore, although chords built on $\hat{1}$ and $\hat{4}$ are major and chords on $\hat{2}$, $\hat{3}$, and $\hat{6}$ are minor, and share the same quality, they may nonetheless take a different harmonic function. What does this all mean? It means that the function of chords in jazz, as in classical music, is complex and is governed by strictly controlled laws, rules, procedures, and tonal conditions. These various principles influence voice-leading conventions, control the behavior of chords, and establish a unique musical grammar that is idiomatic for jazz. These rules also control the structure of musical compositions and allow us to make sense out of complicated harmonic progressions.

Figure 4.10 compiles three functionally related chords in major, each with the participating four-part chords.

FIGURE 4.10 Functional Families in Major Key

Minor Key

Figure 4.11 illustrates four-part chords built on each scale degree of A minor.

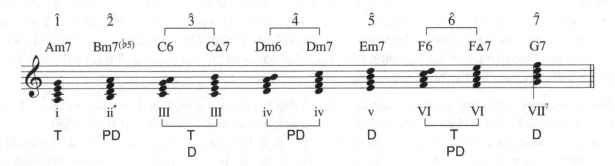

FIGURE 4.11 Four-Part Chords in Natural Minor

Once we start building chords on each scale degree of the harmonic minor as in Figure 4.12, or the melodic minor as in Figure 4.13, we are going to encounter even more chord types, intricate functional relationships, and some interesting discrepancies in chord nomenclature.

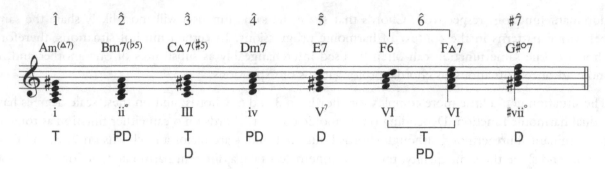

FIGURE 4.12 Four-Part Chords in Harmonic Minor

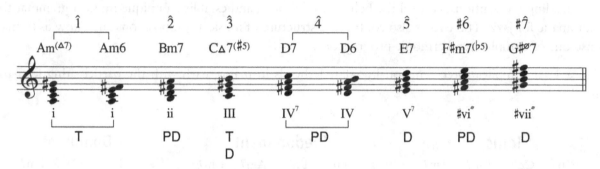

FIGURE 4.13 Four-Part Chords in Melodic Minor

Before compiling three functional families of chords in minor, let us make some general observations about the structure and quality of individual chords occurring in minor keys. The tonic note ($\hat{1}$) of the natural minor scale features a m7 chord and the tonic note of harmonic minor takes a m(♯7) chord. Scale-degree one ($\hat{1}$) of the melodic minor scale uses both a m(♯7) and a m6 chord. The supertonic ($\hat{2}$) of natural and harmonic minor uses a m7(♭5) chord, but in melodic minor it takes the form of a m7 chord. The mediant ($\hat{3}$) highlights a M7 chord in natural minor, a M7(♯5) in harmonic and melodic minor. The subdominant ($\hat{4}$) features a m7 in natural and harmonic minor, and a dominant 7th in melodic minor labeled as IV⁷. The dominant note ($\hat{5}$) uses a m7 in natural minor, and a dominant 7th in harmonic and melodic minor. The submediant on $\hat{6}$ uses a major 6th and a M7 chord in natural and harmonic minor, but the raised submediant built on ♯$\hat{6}$, takes a m7(♭5) chord. The subtonic on $\hat{7}$ of natural minor highlights a dominant 7th. The leading tone on ♯$\hat{7}$ of harmonic minor takes a diminished 7th chord, and a half-diminished 7th chord in melodic minor.

Notice that two different labels are used for a chord that has the same pitch architecture and is made up of a diminished triad and an added minor 7th: the *half-diminished 7th chord* and *the m7(♭5) chord*. In jazz, these names are often used interchangeably. The half-diminished 7th chord occurs on the leading tone of the major key and the melodic minor, and, as such, functions as a dominant or a dominant substitute that is preceded by a predominant and followed by a tonic. The m7(♭5) chord occurs on the supertonic scale degree of natural and harmonic minor and the raised submediant of melodic minor. These chords always function as predominants and carry with them the expected voice-leading and harmonic behaviors. In 99 percent of cases, the m7(♭5) chord occurs in the context of ii∅–V⁷–i progression.

Figure 4.14 compiles three functionally related chords in minor.

When examining the dominant-functioning chords in the natural minor, notice that the v⁷ chord has a minor quality typically associated with a tonic and predominant function. Its placement in this category,

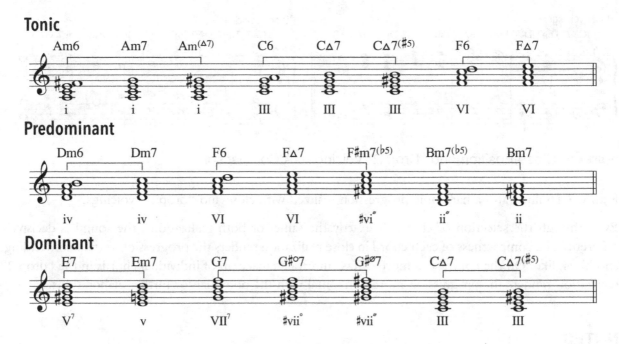

FIGURE 4.14 Functional Families in Minor Key

however, suggests that we may encounter this chord—mostly in modal tunes or minor blues tunes—functioning as a dominant.[9]

"DROP 2" VOICINGS

In jazz terminology, the term *voicing* refers to the arrangement of pitches in a chord. That arrangement can be either close or open. In a **close voicing** the arrangement of notes above the root is the most packed possible. In an **open voicing**, the arrangement of notes is intervallically more diverse. Each *root-position* four-part chord can be voiced in three different ways: (1) with a 7th (6th) as the top note, (2) with a 3rd (4th) as the top note, and (3) with a 5th as the top note. These configurations stem from the rotations of the upper three-note structure above the stationary chordal root. The most common method of generating an open voicing is to **drop** certain notes from a close-position chord down an octave. In a **"drop 2" voicing**, the *second note*, counting from the top note, is dropped down an octave. "Drop 2" refers to voicings *above the bass* in which the bass note is not counted as one of the voices being "dropped." Figure 4.15 shows three close voicings and three "drop 2" voicings for the CM7 chord.[10]

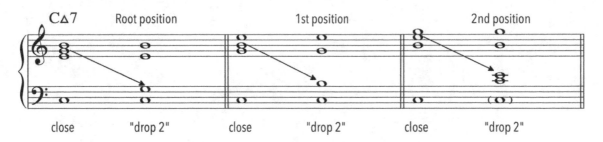

FIGURE 4.15 "Drop 2" Four-Part Voicings for CM7

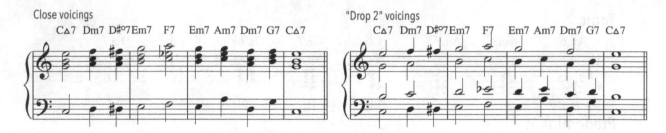

FIGURE 4.16 Close-Position and "Drop 2" Voicings—A Comparison

Figure 4.16 illustrates a harmonic progression realized with close and "drop 2" voicings.

Even though the selection of chords is exactly the same for both realizations, the sound is decisively different. The compactness of each chord in close realization renders the progression vertical, unyielding, and block like. On the contrary, a more diverse intervallic make up of individual chords in the "drop 2" realization renders the progression more horizontal with the potential for further elaborations.[11]

NOTES

1 In *italics*, I will provide complete names of chords, as jazz musicians are wont to call them. In naming chords, however, we will notice some inconsistencies and discover that certain chord symbols are spoken differently than the symbol suggests.

2 In a chord symbol, pitch alterations, diatonic and chromatic extensions are written as superscripts and placed in parenthesis. Such a notation preserves the pitch hierarchy within the chord.

3 In Chapter 5, two separate categories for the dominant 7th chord will be established: the dominant 7th category and the suspended dominant category.

4 This type of melodic motion is knows as a 4–3 suspension. In common-practice music, this type of dissonance requires a special voice-leading treatment involving three steps: preparation, suspension, and resolution. Because these three steps are related to the underlying metric and rhythmic structure, the suspension is considered rhythmic rather than melodic dissonance. In jazz, the treatment of suspended sonorities is far more relaxed when you compare it to other types of music.

5 In spite of its dominant function, the sus chord can also function as tonic in modal compositions, such as Herbie Hancock's "Maiden Voyage," Ralph Towner's "Icarus," or McCoy Tyner's "Passion Dance." The use of functional labels in the context of modal tunes, however, might be deceptive.

6 In common-practice music, C7(♭5) (enharmonically spelled as C–E–F♯–A♯) belongs to the family of augmented 6th chords, and is known as the French Sixth chord. The other two are the German Sixth chord (C–E–G–A♯) and the Italian Sixth chord (C–E–A♯).

7 The term "predominant" would have been too restrictive and would not have shown the diverse functional status of intermediary chords. Besides, "predominant" is already being used for the specific harmonic function.

8 For a more detailed explanation of the difference between the two, consult p. 49.

9 Chick Corea's "Crystal Silence," John Coltrane's "Blue Train," "Naima," or Paul Desmond's "Take Five."

10 For the complete list of four-part "drop 2" voicings consult the CW.

11 For more short harmonic progressions to practice close and "drop 2" voicings see the CW.

CHAPTER 5

Five-Part Chords

CHAPTER SUMMARY

Chapter 5 expands the repository of harmonic structures to 38 five-part chords. They are divided into five tonal categories: major, minor, dominant, suspended dominant, and intermediary.

CONCEPTS AND TERMS

- Chromatic extensions
- Diatonic extensions
- Dominant chords
- "Drop 2" voicings
- Elevenths:
  - Perfect 11th
  - Sharp 11th
- Intermediary chords
- Lower chromatic neighbor
- Major chords
- Minor chords
- Ninths:
  - Flat 9th
  - Major 9th
  - Sharp 9th
- Suspended dominant chords
- Thirteenths:
  - Flat 13th
  - Major 13th
- Upper chromatic neighbor
- Upper diatonic neighbor

CHORDAL EXTENSIONS

Chordal extensions consist of different forms of the **ninth**, the **eleventh**, and the **thirteenth**. They can be divided into two broad categories: **diatonic** and **chromatic**. Diatonic extensions enhance the structure of chords, whereas chromatic extensions modify that structure in a considerable way. The **ninth** has three distinct forms: a diatonic **major 9th**, a chromatic ♭**9th**, and a chromatic ♯**9th**. The **eleventh** has two forms: a diatonic **perfect 11th** and a chromatic ♯**11th**. The **thirteenth** has two forms: a diatonic **major 13th** and a chromatic ♭**13th**.

In jazz terminology, we frequently encounter different labels for the same harmonic extensions. Sometimes these alternate labels are acceptable, other times they are not. For instance, we can find that the ♯11th is often referred to as the ♭5th or the ♯4th, whereas the ♭13th is called the ♯5th or the ♭6th. These are all acceptable enharmonic spellings and will occasionally be implemented throughout the book. However, if we want to be more rigorous in the labeling of extensions, we must determine how a particular note or a group of notes actually functions within a chord. In Chapter 4, certain chromatic notes—the ♭5th and ♯5th in particular—were referred to as alterations of diatonic pitches. For instance, a ♭5th in the M7(♭5) chord and a ♯5th in the dominant 7(♯5) chord were called chromatic alterations and not chromatic extensions. The addition of a 9th to these four-part chords does not affect the status of these alterations. However, one would probably use the ♯11th label for an extended tertian structure with the diatonic fifth present. On the contrary, the use of the ♯11th label in the suspended dominant 7th chord is functionally and sonically incorrect because a ♯11th and a perfect 4th do not work well together. A 13th is the extension that frequently is labeled as a major or minor 6th. The note is referred to as a 13th if the 7th is present; the 6th if not. You may also wonder why there is no reference to the 9th as a 2nd. The basic reason has to do with the presence of the essential chord tone within a harmony. If a chord contains an essential chord tone, then any note added to its structure functions as an extension. The M7 chord does not include a major 2nd, but a major 9th. The dominant 7th chord does not include a ♭2nd, but a ♭9th. Therefore, chord labels, such as C7(♭2) or CM7(2,♯11) should be avoided.

ADDITION OF EXTENSIONS

Not only do we have to know how to correctly label chordal extensions, but we also have to know which extensions can be added to four-part chords and how those extensions can be used. Here are some broad generalizations.

The major chord contains two essential chord tones—a major 7th and a major 6th; two diatonic extensions—a major 9th and a major 13th; one chromatic extension—a ♯11th; and two pitch alterations—a ♭5th and a ♯5th. The minor chord admits four essential chord tones—a minor 7th, a major 6th, a major 7th and a minor 6th; three diatonic extensions—a major 9th, a perfect 11th, and a major 13th; and two chromatic extensions—a ♭13th and a ♯11th. The *minor 7(♭5) chord* (also known as the half-diminished 7th) allows one essential chord tone—a minor 7th; two diatonic extensions—a major 9th and a perfect 11th; and one chromatic extension—a ♭13th. The *diminished 7th chord* uses two essential chord tones—a diminished 7th and a major 7th; and three extensions—a major 9th, a perfect 11th, and a ♭13th. The *dominant 7th chord* contains one essential chord tone—a minor 7th; two diatonic extensions—a major 9th and a major 13th; four chromatic extensions—a ♭9th, a ♯9th, a ♯11th, and a ♭13th; and two pitch alterations—a ♭5th and a ♯5th. The *suspended dominant chord* includes one essential chord tone—a minor 7th; two diatonic extensions—a major 9th and a major 13th; three chromatic extensions—a ♭9th, a ♯9th, and a ♭13th; and two pitch alterations—a ♭5th and a ♯5th. Table 5.1 summarizes the distribution of essential chord tones, pitch alterations, and chordal extensions in M7, m7, dominant 7th (7), suspended dominant (7sus), m7(♭5), and diminished 7th (dim7) chords.

TABLE 5.1 Essential Chord Tones—Pitch Alterations—Extensions

Essential Chord Tones							
M7	**m7**		**7**	**7sus**	**m7(♭5)**	**dim7**	
diatonic	diatonic	chromatic	diatonic	diatonic	diatonic	(diatonic)	(chromatic)
6	6	♯7	♭7	♭7	♭7	♭♭7	♯7
7	♭7	♭6					

Pitch Alterations					
M7	**m7**	**7**	**7sus**	**m7(♭5)**	**dim7**
♯5		♯5	♯5		
♭5		♭5	♭5		

Extensions										
M7		**m7**		**7**		**7sus**		**m7(♭5)**		**dim7**
diatonic	chromatic	diatonic	chromatic	diatonic	chromatic	diatonic	chromatic	diatonic	chromatic	(diatonic)
9	♯11	9	♭13	9	♭9	9	♭9	9	♭13	9
13		11	♯11	13	♯9	13	♯9	11		11
		13			♯11		♭13			♭13
					♭13					

CHORD CATEGORIES

The categories for five-part chords suggest the possible harmonic function of chords in chord progressions. They are analogous to the similar categories established for four-part formations. Unlike in Chapter 4, where 14 four-part chords were built on the same starting pitch, the five-part chords are built on the specific scale degrees that suggest their likely occurrence in harmonic progressions: major on $\hat{1}$, minor chords on $\hat{2}$, dominant on $\hat{5}$, and intermediary on $\hat{2}$. By placing them in these locations, we can notice how their scale-degree position affects their pitch content. As far as the use of Roman numerals for five-part chords is concerned, we will only indicate their basic four-part structure, notating neither extensions nor alterations, just as we did with the generic Roman numerals for four-part chords. The functional behavior of five-part chords depends on the specific context in which they occur. For instance, even though minor chords appear on $\hat{2}$, which implies the predominant function, on a different scale degree they can also function as tonics. A chord from the major category might function as a tonic or a predominant depending on its role and position in the chord progression, etc. The five-part chord includes a four-part base structure and some type of a 9th. In order to keep its extension status, the 9th must be located a ninth above the root of the chord.

Major Category

Harmonic Function—Tonic and Predominant

Figure 5.1 shows six major five-part chords in close position.

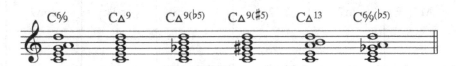

FIGURE 5.1 Major Five-Part Chords

A *sixth nine chord*, C6/9, represents the harmonic style of earlier jazz, particularly that from the Swing Era. A *major ninth chord*, CM9, is probably the most commonly utilized chord in jazz. A *major ninth flat five*, CM9(♭5), and a *major ninth sharp five*, CM9(♯5), are representatives of more contemporary jazz styles. A *major thirteenth chord*, CM13, combines two diatonic extensions (major 7th and major 13th) within its structure and a *sixth nine flat five chord*, C6/9(♭5), lowers the diatonic 5th.

Minor Category

Harmonic Function—Tonic and Predominant

Figure 5.2 shows five minor five-part chords in close position. Note that they are built on $\hat{2}$ of C major.

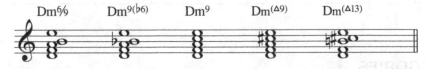

FIGURE 5.2 Minor Five-Part Chords

In the previous chapter, the minor category of four-part chords consisted of three formations: m6, m7, and m(♯7). In this category we meet a new member: *the minor ninth flat sixth chord*. The inclusion of this formation fits the present context better because of the status of ♭6th, which we have yet to discuss. The *flat sixth* added to a minor triad makes the four-part chord look and sound exactly like a major 7th chord in first inversion. In the context of five-part chords, however, the use of a ♭6th is justifiable because its addition creates an autonomous root-position five-part formation that is relatively common in more contemporary jazz styles. A *minor sixth nine chord*, Dm6/9, embodies the tonic function. A *minor ninth chord*, Dm9, is probably the most versatile chord type since it can function as a tonic or a predominant. A *minor ninth flat sixth chord*, Dm9(♭6), has a darker sound to it and is largely associated with the tonic function. Depending on its role within harmonic progressions, a *minor major ninth chord*, Dm9(♯7), can function as a tonic or a predominant. A *minor major thirteenth chord*, Dm13(♯7), prioritizes upper extensions and is primarily associated with the tonic function.

Dominant and Suspended Category

Five-part dominant 7th chords feature an impressive variety of harmonic formations. Their sonic diversity comes from the largest number of available extensions that can be added to their pitch structure. Given that diatonic and chromatic extensions can be combined with one another in a number of creative ways and that there are only two fundamental dominant 7th chords, the family of dominant chords can seem truly overwhelming. Therefore, in the investigation of five-part dominant 7ths, two distinct categories— the **dominant 7th category** and the **suspended dominant category**—are established.

Dominant 7th Category

Possible Harmonic Function—Dominant

Figure 5.3 shows 12 close-position five-part chords from the dominant 7th category built on $\hat{5}$ of C major.

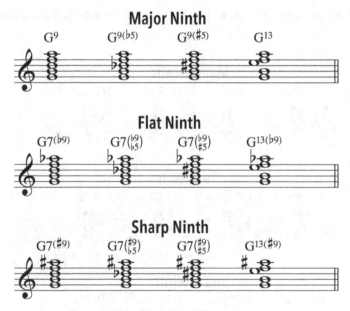

FIGURE 5.3 Dominant Five-Part Chords

Each line features a different type of the 9th added to the four-part chord. The first line contains a major 9th; the second, a ♭9th; and the third, a ♯9th. Each line features four five-part chords; they originate by replacing the 5th with a **lower chromatic neighbor**—♭5th; an **upper chromatic neighbor**—♯5th; and an **upper diatonic neighbor**—major 13th.

A *dominant ninth chord*, G9, is a diatonic formation and is derived from the notes of C major.[1] A *dominant ninth flat five*, G9(♭5), has a sound that is frequently heard on recordings from the Bebop Era. A *dominant ninth sharp five*, G9(♯5), includes an augmented triad at the bottom of its structure. A *dominant thirteenth chord*, G13, is entirely diatonic and features the characteristic minor 2nd between a major 13th and a minor 7th.[2]

A *dominant seventh flat ninth chord*, G7(♭9), contains a diminished 7th chord built on the major 3rd. A *dominant seventh flat ninth flat five chord*, G7(♭5,♭9), is highly chromatic and highlights a major triad built on the ♭5th. A *dominant seventh flat ninth sharp five chord*, G7(♯5,♭9), is commonly used as a dominant 7th in minor keys. A *dominant thirteenth flat ninth chord*, G13(♭9), includes an enharmonically spelled major triad built on the 13th.

A *dominant seventh sharp ninth chord*, G7(♯9), has a dissonant sound that is frequently used in Jazz Rock. A *dominant seventh sharp ninth flat five*, G7(♭5,♯9), contains an enharmonically equivalent minor triad built on the ♯9th. A *dominant seventh sharp ninth sharp five*, G7(♯5,♯9), is a quintessential altered chord that is frequently labeled as G7alt. A *dominant thirteenth sharp ninth*, G13(♯9), has a characteristic minor 2nd clash between a major 13th and a minor 7th that, together with the ♯9th, creates a very dissonant sonority.

Suspended Dominant Category

Possible Harmonic Function—Dominant, Predominant, Tonic

Figure 5.4 shows 12 close-position five-part chords from the suspended dominant category built on $\hat{5}$ of C major.

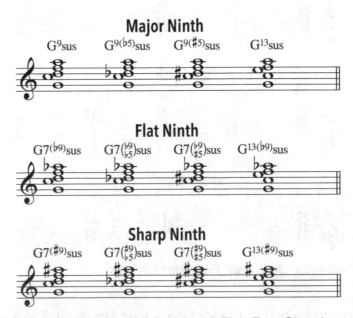

FIGURE 5.4 Suspended Dominant Five-Part Chords

The chords from Figure 5.4 can function as dominants, predominants, or even as "tonics" in certain modal tunes. The predominant status stems from the fact that they often precede a regular dominant 7th chord. That is because the suspended dominant 7th chord includes a perfect 4th which, on the one hand, initiates melodic motion that requires resolution, and on the other can be reinterpreted as the minor 7th of a local ii.

A *sus ninth chord*, G9sus, is a basic suspended formation.[3] A *sus ninth flat five chord*, G9sus(♭5), features an augmented triad built on the ♭5th. A *sus ninth flat thirteenth chord*, G9sus(♭13), has a characteristic blues flavor to it on account of an enharmonically spelled dominant 7th chord built on the 7th. A *sus thirteenth chord*, G13sus, contains a minor triad build on the 9th of the chord.

A *sus seven flat ninth chord*, G7sus(♭9), has strong voice-leading propensities that compel the 4th and the ♭9th to resolve downward by a half step. A *sus seven flat ninth flat five chord*, G7sus(♭5,♭9), features a M7 chord built on the ♭5th. A *sus seven flat ninth sharp five chord*, G7sus(♯5,♭9), contains an enharmonically respelled m7 chord built on the 7th of the chord. A *sus thirteenth flat ninth chord*, G13sus(♭9), has a m(♯7) chord built on the 7th.

A *sus seven sharp ninth chord*, G7sus(♯9), sounds like an extended minor chord and demonstrates the ambiguous nature of suspended formations. This ambiguity is something that we can capitalize on in harmonic progressions. A *sus seven sharp ninth flat five chord*, G7sus(♭5,♯9), shows strong predominant characteristics. A *sus seven sharp ninth sharp five chord*, G7sus(♯5,♯9), sounds tonally ambiguous (like all other suspended chords) and can only be tonally and functionally defined in the context of specific chord progressions. A *sus thirteenth sharp ninth chord*, G13sus(♯9), illustrates yet another tonally and functionally ambiguous suspended formation.

Intermediary Category

Possible Harmonic Function—Predominant, Dominant, Tonic

Figure 5.5 shows three intermediary chords built on $\hat{2}$ of C major.

FIGURE 5.5 Intermediary Five-Part Chords

A *minor ninth flat five chord*, Dm9(♭5), or a *half-diminished ninth chord*, Dᴼ9, has a unique characteristic sound on account of a m(♯7) chord built on the 3rd of the chord. Notice that two different labels are used for the same chord. The "m9(♭5)" suffix implies a predominant function, and the "ᴼ9" suffix suggests a dominant function. The former occurs in the context of the iiᴼ–V⁷–i progression; the latter is much rarer but can occur in the progression viiᴼ–I or, rarer still, in the progression ♯viiᴼ–i. A *diminished ninth chord*, Ddim9, has strong melodic and voice-leading tendencies. A *diminished major ninth major seventh chord*, Ddim9(♯7), has a pliable structure with interesting functional associations. Both of these chords can also function as upper structures of altered dominant 7ths.

"DROP 2" VOICINGS

The process of creating "drop 2" voicings for five-part chords is exactly the same as explained in Chapter 4. First, the chordal root remains fixed and the upper structure is rotated four times: (1) with a 9th as the top note, (2) with a 3rd (4th) as the top note, (3) with a 5th as the top note, and (4) with a 7th (6th) as the top note. These four configurations render a chord in close position. Then, the second note from the top is transferred down an octave to the left hand and, as a result, an open-position voicing is created. Figure 5.6 illustrates **"drop 2" voicings** for CM9.[4]

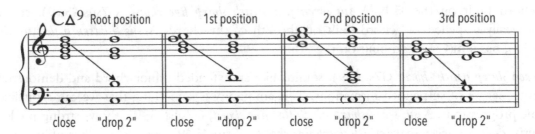

FIGURE 5.6 Positions of CM9

Figure 5.7 compares two realizations of a harmonic progression using close and "drop 2" voicings of five-part chords.

FIGURE 5.7 Close-Position and "Drop 2" Voicings—A Comparison

Both realizations sound idiomatic, which confirms the earlier premise that with the use of five-part chords you can make any jazz progression sound complete and satisfying. When you compare both realizations, however, notice that the "drop 2" harmonization is more interesting on account of the presence of intervallically diverse chordal structures. These two techniques of harmonization are important tools that contemporary jazz musicians should possess. A more detailed discussion of both textures will resurface in Chapter 12 along with other techniques of keyboard realization.

NOTES

1   The presence of a minor 7th is implied with the term *dominant ninth*.
2   In the term *dominant thirteenth*, the 13th implies a 7th, but does not require a 9th.
3   In labeling suspended chords, we do not include the 11th in the symbol. A "sus" takes care of that.
4   For the complete list of "drop 2" voicings of five-part chords consult the CW.

The II–V–I Progression

CHAPTER SUMMARY

Chapter 6 investigates the most important progression in jazz—the II–V–I—and its two tonal variants: ii–V⁷–I and ii$^{\varnothing}$–V⁷–i. A discussion of guide tones, secondary dominant 7ths, diminished 7th chords and their subsequent voice-leading transformations, further amplifies the importance of the progression.

CONCEPTS AND TERMS

- Applied dominant chords
- Chromatic ii–V⁷
- Diminished 7th chord:
  - Accented
  - Common tone
  - Neighbor
  - Passing
  - Unaccented
- Guide tones
- Harmonic elision
- Invertible counterpoint
- Melodic elision
- Secondary dominant 7th chords
- Tonicization
- ii–V⁷–I
- ii$^{\varnothing}$–V⁷–i

A BRIEF HISTORY

Nowhere are the principles of jazz harmonic syntax more evident and its grammatical rules more explicit than in the structure and behavior of the II–V–I progression. The evolution of the progression offers a fascinating journey through jazz history. The origins of the II–V–I can be traced back to fundamental V–I motion, which is the most important chord succession in common-practice music and the marker of tonality. When we compare jazz performances from different historical periods, we notice that the structure of the II–V–I progression has been in a state of constant flux. In Early Jazz, for instance, the ii–V⁷–I was not always present; the more idiomatic V⁷–I motion often implied the structural notes of the progression. Figure 6.1 illustrates mm. 1–4 of "Maple Leaf Rag" by Scott Joplin.

Even though $\hat{2}$ in the bass does not support a ii chord, the design of the bass voice seems to imply a ii–V⁷–I progression. A similar treatment of the dominant 7th, yet with an idiomatic use of chordal inversions, occurred in the Swing Era with one notable exception. The structure of V⁷–I was infused with various kinds of diminished 7th chords as demonstrated in Figure 6.2.[1]

FIGURE 6.1 "Maple Leaf Rag" by Scott Joplin, mm. 1–4

FIGURE 6.2 Diminished 7ths in V⁷–I

Harmonic expansions such as this one ultimately led to the explosion of chromaticism during the Bebop Era. By the 1940s, the ii–V⁷–I progression was fully formed and commonly implemented. In addition, intricate chromatic variants began to infiltrate the structure of harmonic progressions making improvisation more challenging. What is remarkable about Charlie Parker, Thelonious Monk, Dizzy Gillespie, and other artists from that period is that they showed endless creativity in negotiating and utilizing the major and minor versions of the II–V–I progression.[2] As the Post Bop Era rolled in, artists such as Miles Davis, Horace Silver, Lennie Tristano, and many others found new and ingenious ways to implement the progression in their music.[3] One of the most radical transformations of the progression, however, occurred in the late 1950s in the creative mind of John Coltrane.[4] His experiments with symmetrical intervallic cycles led to the development of so-called "Coltrane" substitutions.[5]

Constantly searching for a new means of personal expression while being respectful and mindful of the rich genre's traditions, jazz musicians did not advance their harmonic experiments in a creative vacuum. It seems that, in fulfilling their own artistic destiny, each generation of jazz musicians benefited from the achievements of the previous generation. This is true even today, as the merger of tonality and modality in the 1960s still resonates well with many contemporary jazz artists further transforming or disguising the structure of the II–V–I progression. The II–V–I progression, with its two tonal variants ii–V⁷–I and iiø–V⁷–i, is the fundamental harmonic block of tonal jazz, and its ubiquity in standard tunes confirms its structural importance. Yet, the sheer number of harmonic transformations that jazz musicians have been able to implement is truly remarkable and proves the progression's flexibility in adjusting to various jazz styles. This makes our study of the II–V–I progression all the more relevant.

THE ii–V⁷–I PROGRESSION

The ii–V⁷–I progression, shown in Figure 6.3, combines three harmonic functions: the predominant, the dominant, and the tonic.

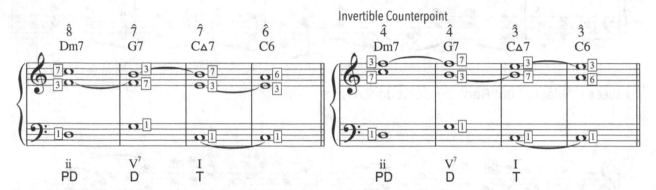

FIGURE 6.3 The ii–V⁷–I Progression—Invertible Counterpoint

Each chord of the progression is reduced to its essential members with the 3rd and 7th being known as the **guide tones**. The guide tones have two basic roles: (1) to determine the quality and functionality of chords, and (2) to dictate the voice leading and proper unfolding of chords within harmonic progressions. In this way, guide tones *guide* the improvisation and, through their careful distribution within a phrase, assure melodic continuity and harmonic clarity. Figure 6.3 includes two versions of the ii–V⁷–I progression where the second version inverts the position of guide tones of the first. The inverted version of the progression sounds a little different from the original. By exploring the potential of **invertible counterpoint** (which is inherent to two-voice and larger harmonic textures), we fundamentally redefine the way of thinking about harmony. Chords can be considered not only as vertical formations, but also as byproducts of individual lines. In a sense, we are still thinking about chords and harmonic progressions, but we are doing so from a linear rather than vertical perspective.

The guide tones in Figure 6.3 form two independently moving lines that start on the 7th and the 3rd of a predominant harmony. The voice leading of the progression depends on the kinetic force of the guide tones: the 7th of ii or V⁷ descends down to the 3rd; and the 3rd of ii or V⁷ becomes the 7th. To finish its trajectory, the major 7th of the tonic chord moves down to a more stable major 6th at the end of the progression. Besides determining the quality and function of chords, the individual tones of the guide-tone line have the potential of being reinterpreted as chord tones or as extensions of other harmonic formations.

THE ii⁰–V⁷–i PROGRESSION

The ii⁰–V⁷–i progression, shown in Figure 6.4, behaves in much the same ways as its major counterpart.[6] The presence of the m7(♭5), as a predominant, implies the choice of specific extensions in the forthcoming dominant 7th chord. In particular, the use of the ♭9th in V⁷ illustrates an ideal voice-leading scenario in which the ♭5th of ii⁰ is retained as a common tone and becomes the ♭9th of V⁷.

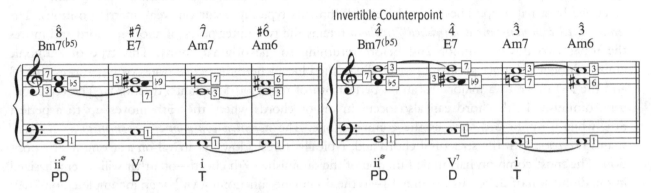

FIGURE 6.4 The ii⁰–V⁷–i Progression—Invertible Counterpoint

SECONDARY DOMINANT 7TH

One of the most common transformations of the ii–V⁷–I progression involves the use of **secondary** or **applied dominant 7th chords** (notated as **V/V** or **X⁷**). Secondary or applied dominant 7ths built on the supertonic scale degree requires a secondary leading tone on #4̂. With that addition, the secondary dominant temporarily **tonicizes** the upcoming dominant 7th on 5̂. Figure 6.5 illustrates the use of a secondary dominant within a II–V–I progression. Notice the use of five-part chords in close and "drop 2" voicings.

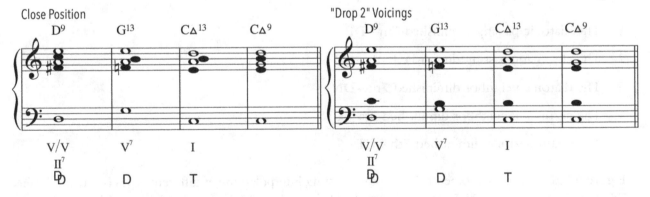

FIGURE 6.5 Close-Position and "Drop 2" Voicings—Secondary Dominant 7ths

The guide-tone line (marked with filled-in note heads) features a chromatically altered note, F♯4. The voice-leading tendency of the F♯4 up to G (leading tone motion in G) and the passing tone motion of G5 moving through F4 down to E4 are subsumed into a single descending gesture known as a **melodic elision**. The behavior of the secondary leading tone, F♯4, causes harmonic motion where no motion was before. The F♯4 replaces F4, which would have been a common tone between Dm7 and G7.

THE DIMINISHED 7TH CHORD

Although the **diminished 7th chord** and its chromatic variant, the diminished major 7th chord, belong to the intermediary family of chords, its role in harmonic progressions is quite unlike that of any other chord. There are three basic types of the diminished 7th chord: **passing**, **neighbor**, and **common tone**. The *passing diminished 7th* chord fills the space between two diatonic chords. The lower or upper chromatic *neighbor diminished 7th chord* embellishes chord tones of a structural chord from below or above by a half step. These chordal embellishments typically occur on weak metric positions. The *unaccented common-tone diminished 7th chord* retains the two outer notes of another chord and moves the inner two down a minor 2nd before returning to the original chord. This type of harmonic embellishment is highly idiomatic, especially in the blues, where the active notes or blue notes (the ♭3 and the ♭5) move to a major 3rd and a perfect 5th of major or dominant 7th chords. The common-tone diminished 7th chord can also occur in minor chords where the ♭5th moves up to a perfect 5th, while a minor 3rd stays as the common tone. The *accented common-tone diminished 7th chord* shares the root with the structural chord and, typically, foreshadows its arrival on a strong metric position. The most common harmonic function of the diminished 7th chord—one that will be emphasized in the discussion of Bebop in Chapter 14—is the dominant–functioning vii^O or an incomplete dom7(♭9) chord.

THE DIMINISHED 7TH CHORD AND THE II–V–I PROGRESSION

As an important jazz harmonic structure, the diminished 7th chord can effectively participate in the elaboration of ii–V^7–I or ii$^\varnothing$–V^7–i progressions. In order to explore the full potential of the diminished 7th chord, these progressions will be first deconstructed to their individual members. Then, specific types of the diminished 7th chord that can embellish these chords will be examined. Finally, the progressions will be assembled to their original form and embellished with different types of the diminished 7th chord. Figure 6.6 illustrates this process. Because the full names for specific diminished 7th chords are quite long, the following abbreviations will be implemented:

1. The diatonic passing diminished 7th—**DP**

2. The chromatic passing diminished 7th—**CP**

3. The diatonic neighbor diminished 7th—**DN**

4. The chromatic neighbor diminished 7th—**CN**

5. The common-tone diminished 7th—**CT**

Figure 6.7 demonstrates some of the most interesting interpolations of different types of the diminished 7th chord within the II–V–I progression realized with "drop 2" four-part voicings. Although there are far fewer choices for the use of the diminished 7th in the ii$^\varnothing$–V^7–i progression, Figure 6.7f illustrates an example that includes multiple passing diminished 7th chords. The reason that only a limited number of diminished 7th chords can participate in the ii$^\varnothing$–V^7–i progression stems from the quality and functionality of the ii$^\varnothing$ chord. Unlike its major counterpart, the m7(♭5) cannot be tonicized as a separate key area and, therefore, the diminished 7th chord cannot be used as a tonicizing formation.

Major Tonic Chords

FIGURE 6.6 Diminished 7th Chords in Context

Minor Tonic Chords

FIGURE 6.6 continued

Predominant Chords

FIGURE 6.6 continued

Dominant Chords

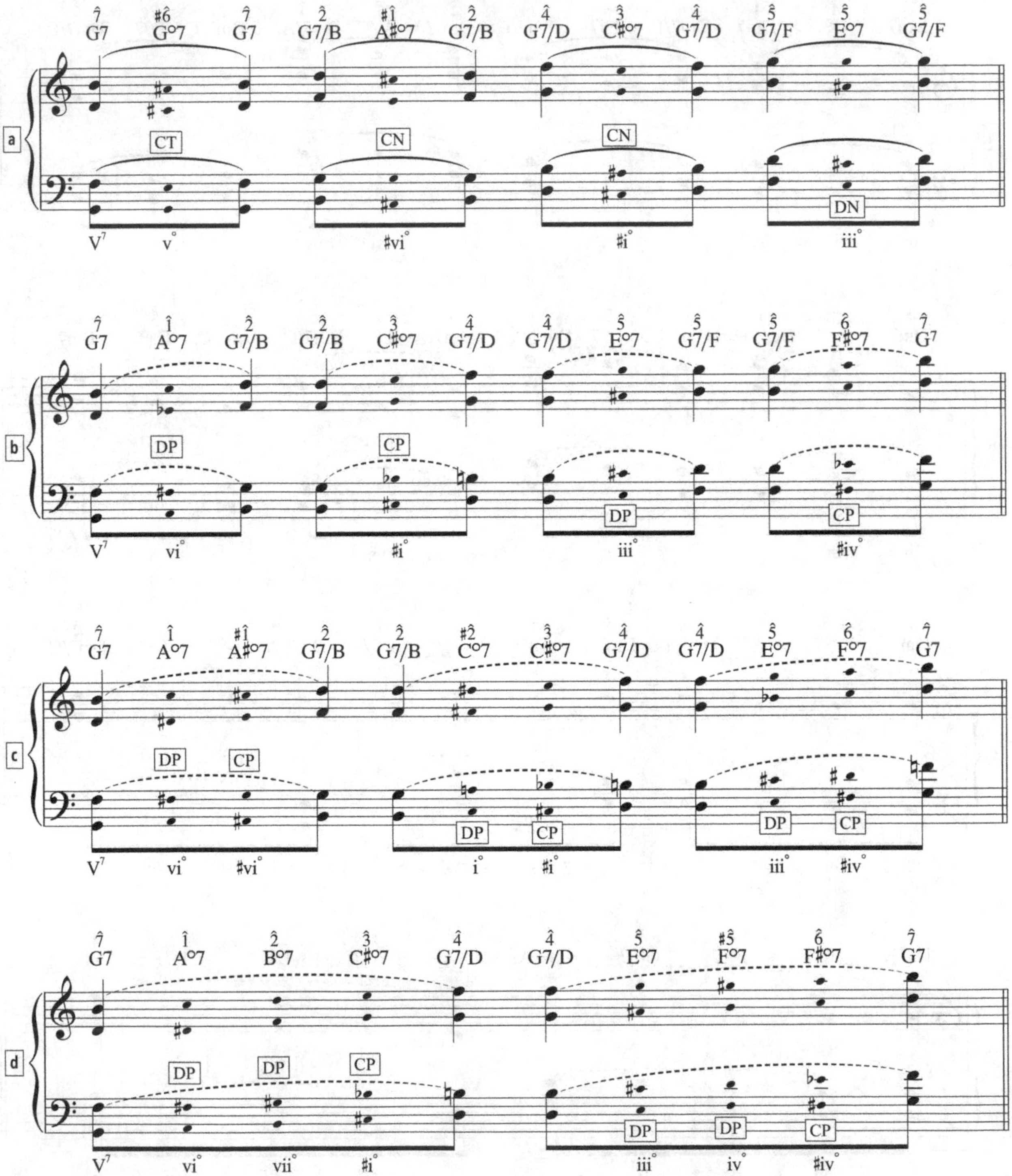

FIGURE 6.6 continued

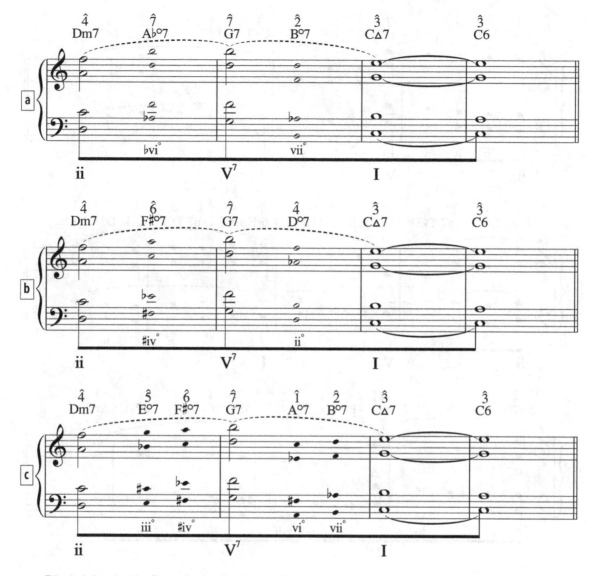

FIGURE 6.7 Diminished 7th Chords in the II–V–I Progression

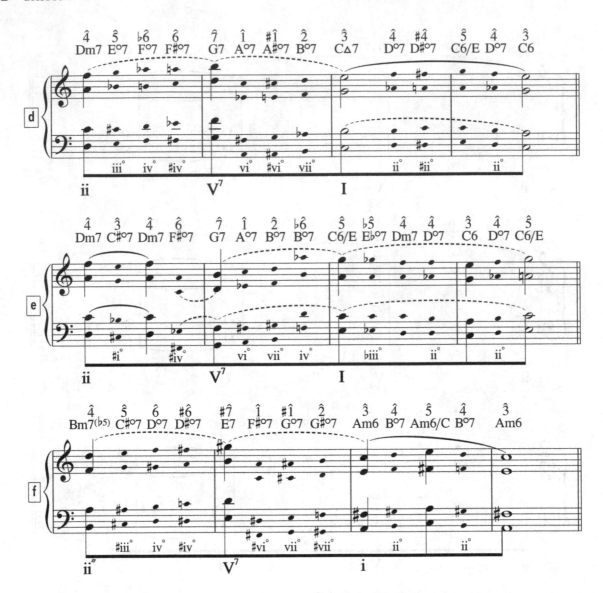

FIGURE 6.7 continued

TRANSFORMATION OF THE DIMINISHED 7TH CHORD

Figure 6.8 illustrates a voice-leading transformation of the diminished 7th chord into a **chromatic ii–V^7** using "drop 2" voicings.

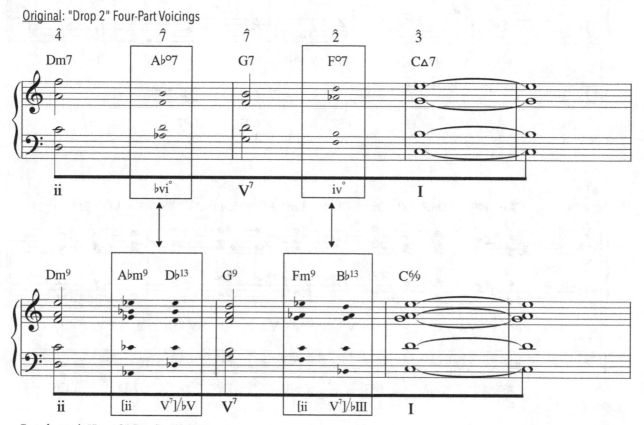

FIGURE 6.8 Harmonic Elision

A subtle contrapuntal motion (up a minor 2nd) from a ♭5th and a ♭♭7th of the diminished 7th chord to a perfect 5th and a minor 7th of the minor 7th chord generates this voice-leading transformation. A minor 7th chord, then, pairs up with its local dominant 7th to create a chromatic ii–V^7 interpolation. With the voice-leading transformation from Figure 6.8, we can further modify the structure of the diatonic ii–V^7–I from a common Swing Era progression to an idiomatic Bebop progression. The chromatic ii–V^{7}s are notated in square brackets followed by a diagonal line and a Roman numeral that indicates the subsumed resolution of the chromatic ii–V^7. This particular use of ii–V^{7}s is known as a **harmonic elision**.

The progressions in Figure 6.9 are realized with "drop 2" five-part voicings. Notice that the voice leading between chords is entirely dependent on the behavior of the guide tones. With the exception of the bass voice (which is unaffected by "drop 2"), all other voices move mostly by step.

FIGURE 6.9 Transformations of II–V–I

NOTES

1   Listen to Benny Goodman's *The Complete RCA Victor Small Group Recordings*.
2   Notable albums: Charlie Parker (*The Immortal Charlie Parker* and *Jazz At Massey Hall*); Thelonious Monk (*Genius of Modern Music, Volume I* and *The London Collection, Volumes I and II*); Dizzy Gillespie (*Groovin' High* and *School Days*).
3   Notable albums: Miles Davis (*Kind of Blue* and *At the Plugged Nickel, Volumes I and II*); Horace Silver (*Horace Silver Trio* and *The Cape Verdean Blues*); Lennie Tristano (*Intuition* and *Lennie Tristano*).
4   See, for instance, John Coltrane's *Giant Steps* and *Crescent*.
5   These idiomatic progressions are discussed in Chapter 13.
6   In order to differentiate between ii⌀ and ii, the "⌀" suffix in the m7(♭5) chord and no suffix in the minor 7th chord are used, regardless of the key signatures.

CHAPTER 7
Modes

CHAPTER SUMMARY

Chapter 7 discusses seven diatonic modes from the major scale and seven chromatic modes from the melodic minor scale.

CONCEPTS AND TERMS

- Avoid note
- Beauty mark
- Chromatic modes:
  - Altered
  - Dorian ♭2
  - Locrian ♮2
  - Lydian Augmented
  - Melodic Minor
  - Mixolydian ♯11
  - Mixolydian ♭13
- Chromaticism

- Diatonic modes:
  - Aeolian
  - Dorian
  - Ionian
  - Locrian
  - Lydian
  - Mixolydian
  - Phrygian
- Diatonic passing note
- Modal qualifiers
- Parent scale

- Pedal point
- Tetrachords:
  - Chromatic
  - Harmonic
  - Lower
  - Major
  - Minor
  - Phrygian
  - Upper
  - Whole tone

PARENT-SCALE DERIVATION OF DIATONIC MODES

In modal jazz theory, **diatonic modes** are traditionally introduced as derivatives of the **parent major scale**. What might be a bit confusing in this method is that the parent scale is also a mode, named **Ionian**. The parent-scale method is based on constructing modes on the consecutive pitches of the major scale. In Figure 7.1, **Dorian** begins on $\hat{2}$ of the C major scale and represents an ordered diatonic collection stretching from D4 to D5 (or any other octave); **Phrygian** starts on $\hat{3}$ and covers an octave from E4 to E5; **Lydian** begins on $\hat{4}$ and spans an octave from F4 to F5; **Mixolydian** starts on $\hat{5}$ and extends from

FIGURE 7.1 Parent-Scale Derivation of Diatonic Modes

G4 to G5; **Aeolian** begins on $\hat{6}$ and covers the distance from A4 to A5; and, **Locrian** starts on $\hat{7}$ and includes pitches between B4 and B5. Figure 7.1 shows the derivation of modes using the parent-scale methodology.

While parent-scale derivation is an important theoretical construct, it strips individual modes of their salient characteristics and is cumbersome in actual musical practice. Imagine, for instance, trying to quickly figure out the Phrygian mode on F♯. Using this methodology, we have to first determine which major scale contains F♯ as a major 3rd. Then, based on the fact that the D major scale indeed contains the pitch F♯ as the major 3rd, we can build the Phrygian mode using the notes from the D major scale. Cumbersome? Yes. Even more confusing than the mode derivation itself, however, is the fact that this method seems to focus on the parent scale rather than on the pitch structure of specific modes. Our methodology eliminates such two-step modal conversion and focuses on modes as individual pitch collections with their own melodic, harmonic, and structural properties. By building modes starting on the same pitch and concentrating on their sound, essential tones, and pitch hierarchy, we can better understand their pitch structure.

MODAL CHARACTERISTICS

Broadly speaking, there are two types of modes: **major** and **minor**. Major modes have a major 3rd and minor modes contain a minor 3rd. These notes are called **modal qualifiers**. This rough classification is by no means complete, but it should help to unravel the principles of modal theory. The distinction between major and minor modes enables easier aural identification. Within seven diatonic modes, three are major and four are minor. The **beauty mark** is a term that indicates the essential tone or tones indicative of the mode. The beauty mark, then, is a crucial tone to convey the sound and distinguish between different modes. **Avoid notes** are pitches within the mode that do not quite fit the structure of certain chords or melodic lines. For instance, the perfect fourth of the Ionian mode might be problematic if we try to use it over CM7 or CM9. Also, the major 3rd of the Mixolydian mode might sound dissonant if we try to use it over C7sus of C7sus(♭9) without proper preparation. Thus, the term *avoid* should alert us about potential problems that might arise while trying to use these notes in harmonic or melodic contexts. In the case of extended six- or seven-part chords (especially those that feature chromatic extensions), however, the avoid note can sometimes be admitted as one of the chord tones or unusual extensions. For instance, the fully extended tertian formation CM13(♯11) includes the perfect fifth in its structure, which in the context of CM7(♭5) and CM9(♭5), would have created a harsh dissonance against the ♭5th.

DIATONIC MODES

As mentioned in Chapter 1, the specific pattern of whole steps and half steps occurring in the major scale forms a type of diatonic collection. Other diatonic scales are formed by preserving the same number of whole and half steps yet distributing them at different locations within the scale. These types of scales are referred to as diatonic modes.

Major Modes—Ionian

Figure 7.2a provides the pitch content of the Ionian mode with each note examined according to its function within the collection. Figure 7.2b illustrates a four-bar modal phrase that projects the Ionian sound using a CM7 harmony.

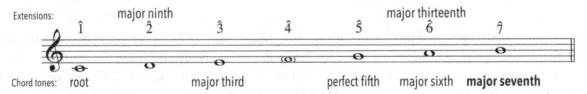

FIGURE 7.2a Ionian Mode

FIGURE 7.2b Ionian Phrase

In order to convey the sound of the **Ionian** mode, only two pitches are needed: a major 3rd as the modal qualifier and a **major 7th** as the beauty mark. The 3rd and the 7th of the mode also function as the guide tones. Scale-degree four ($\hat{4}$) of the mode is a note that should be treated with caution.[1] In Figure 7.2b it is used as a **diatonic passing note** (PN) and is located at the "and" of beat 2 or the upbeat (offbeat) in m. 2. The metric distribution of pitches within a phrase is an important factor in enabling the clear projection of a mode. In Figure 7.2b, the chord tones of CM7 are mostly located on the downbeats unless they form arpeggiation patterns, which might affect their distribution.

Major Modes—Lydian

The **Lydian** mode is a diatonic mode with a more contemporary sound. Figure 7.3a illustrates the pitch structure of Lydian and Figure 7.3b demonstrates a four-bar modal phrase with Lydian characteristics over a CM7(♭5) harmony. Henceforth, Arabic numbers are used (with appropriate accidentals) to indicate the pitch structure of modes and—in the forthcoming chapters—bebop scales, pentatonics, hexatonics, octatonics, and melodic patterns. Scale-degree labels ($\hat{1}$, $\hat{2}$, $\hat{3}$, etc.) are reserved for pitches occurring within the context of the underlying key.

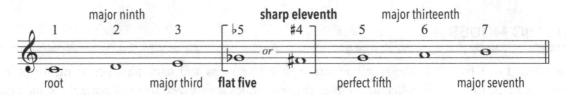

FIGURE 7.3a Lydian Mode

FIGURE 7.3b Lydian Phrase

When comparing the structure of Lydian with Ionian, the presence of ♯**11 (♯4)** as the beauty mark gives the Lydian collection its unique characteristics. Depending on its position within the chord, the beauty mark can be spelled either as a ♭5th (in chords without the perfect 5th, such as CM7(♭5)) or as a ♯11th (in chords with the perfect 5th, such as CM13(♯11)). The distribution of chord tones on metrically strong positions within a measure contributes to a clear projection of Lydian characteristics. Note that the avoid note, **5**, is excluded from the context of the phrase. The intervallic structure of the phrase prioritizes the use of fourths, one of the main building blocks in modal improvisation.

Major Modes—Mixolydian

Even though the **Mixolydian** mode belongs to the major family of modes, it has a distinct functional status and behavior that is entirely different from Ionian and Lydian modes. Figure 7.4a demonstrates the pitch structure of Mixolydian and Figure 7.4b provides a four-bar modal phrase with Mixolydian characteristics over a C7 harmony.

The presence of ♭7 as the beauty mark makes the phrase tonally unstable with a strong tendency to resolve onto a more stable chord. The status of **4** as a diatonic passing note in m. 4, deserves our attention. Since the 4th can also participate in the context of the suspended dominant and, as such, it replaces the major 3rd of the dominant 7th chord, the metric placement of that pitch within the phrase might change

FIGURE 7.4a Mixolydian Mode

FIGURE 7.4b Mixolydian Phrase

the overall chord–scale relationship from C7 to C7sus. In Figure 7.4b, the mode clearly projects the sound of the underlying C7 harmony.

Minor Modes—Aeolian

The pitch structure of the four minor modes contains ♭3, ♭6 (♮6), and ♭7 as modal qualifiers. These tones are members of the natural minor scale from which other minor modes are derived. In certain modes, however, the minor or major 6th will additionally function as the beauty mark. The natural minor scale in modal environment is known as the **Aeolian** mode. Figure 7.5a examines the pitch structure of Aeolian. Figure 7.5b illustrates a four-bar modal phrase with a characteristic Aeolian flavor over a Cm9(♭13) harmony.

FIGURE 7.5a Aeolian Mode

FIGURE 7.5b Aeolian Phrase

The beauty mark, **minor 6**, injects a darker sound to the mode that stands in stark contrast to the sound of other minor modes. The phrase in Figure 7.5b uses the Cm9(♭13) chord, which indicates an extended tertian structure. The metric distribution of chord tones and extensions shows equal metric treatment of the diatonic extensions, 9th and 11th, and the chromatic extension, ♭13th.

Minor Modes—Dorian

Figure 7.6a illustrates the pitch structure of the Dorian mode and Figure 7.6b demonstrates a four-bar modal phrase with Dorian characteristics over a Cm13 harmony.

FIGURE 7.6a Dorian Mode

FIGURE 7.6b Dorian Phrase

Even though Dorian is a minor mode, its beauty mark, **major 6**, gives the collection a characteristic *major* sound. The phrase in Figure 7.6b projects the tertian nature of the Cm13 harmony by clearly arpeggiating triads (B♭ and E♭ in mm. 1–2), four-part chords (Am7(♭5) in mm. 3 and 4, and Gm7 in m. 4), and a five-part chord (Gm9 in mm. 2–3).

Minor Modes—Phrygian

The **Phrygian** mode has a distinctive sound because of its unusual beauty mark, ♭**2**. The pitch structure of the Phrygian collection is given in Figure 7.7a. Figure 7.7b demonstrates a five-bar modal phrase with Phrygian characteristics.

FIGURE 7.7a Phrygian Mode

FIGURE 7.7b Phrygian Phrase

Even though the phrase does not have a corresponding chord and, as such, can be performed over a C pedal point, it nonetheless demonstrates strong minor qualities. A **pedal point** features a single note in the bass that controls larger sections of music. Note that the modal qualifiers and the beauty mark are featured prominently throughout the phrase.

Minor Modes—Locrian

The last diatonic minor mode deserves a special place in our discussion because of its flat out rejection from the modal family for centuries.[2] The **Locrian** mode has two beauty marks: ♭2 and ♭5. Because of its unusual pitch structure, which prevents the occurrence of a minor triad on **1**, Locrian is characterized by a highly unstable sound. It still belongs to the minor family of modes because it contains a minor 3rd. Figure 7.8a examines the pitch structure of the mode. Figure 7.8b demonstrates a four-bar modal phrase over a C pedal.

FIGURE 7.8a Locrian Mode

FIGURE 7.8b Locrian Phrase

The melodic phrase has an unsettling quality that is constantly reinforced by the tritone between **1** and ♭**5** (mm. 1, 3, and 4). The phrase in Figure 7.8b also horizontalizes four- and five-part structures. For instance, a downward arpeggiation of E♭m7 in mm. 1–2 and an upward arpeggiation of E♭m9 in mm. 3–4 create harmonic and melodic tensions with the underlying C pedal.

PARENT-SCALE DERIVATION OF CHROMATIC MODES

The **modes of melodic minor**, also known as the **chromatic modes**, are traditionally derived using the parent-scale principle. Using this method, the melodic minor collection functions as the parent scale. The pitch structure of chromatic modes is much more diverse than it is in the diatonic modes. In Figure 7.9, **Dorian** ♭**2** begins on $\hat{2}$ of C melodic minor and extends from D4 to D5; **Lydian Augmented** starts on $\hat{3}$ and spans an octave from E♭4 to E♭5; **Mixolydian** ♯**11** begins on $\hat{4}$ and covers the distance between F4 and F5; **Mixolydian** ♭**13** starts on $\hat{5}$ and spans an octave from G4 to G5; **Locrian** ♮**2** begins on ♯$\hat{6}$ (major 6th) and extends from A4 to A5; and, **Altered** begins on ♯$\hat{7}$ (major 7th) and spans from B4 to B5 of C melodic minor. Figure 7.9 illustrates the derivation of chromatic modes using the C melodic minor as a parent scale.

FIGURE 7.9 Parent-Scale Derivation of Chromatic Modes

CHROMATIC MODES

The family of chromatic modes includes three minor and four major collections—each with its unique pitch architecture, beauty marks, functional roles, and sound. Each mode will be additionally analyzed in terms of two four-note pitch segments called **tetrachords**. In this context, the **lower tetrachord** refers to the four notes derived from the scale ($\hat{1}$–$\hat{4}$); the **upper tetrachord** combines the remaining four notes ($\hat{5}$–$\hat{8}$ ($\hat{1}$)). We will encounter different combinations of the following tetrachords: **major** (2–2–1), **minor** (2–1–2), **whole tone** (2–2–2), **Phrygian** (1–2–2), **chromatic** (1–2–1) and **harmonic** (1–3–1). Arabic numbers in parenthesis refer to the number of semitones between adjacent pitches.

Minor Modes—Melodic Minor

Figure 7.10a examines the pitch structure of the **Melodic Minor** mode.[3] Figure 7.10b illustrates a four-bar modal phrase over a Cm9(#7) that captures the sound of the mode.

FIGURE 7.10a Melodic Minor

Swing
Cm(△9)

FIGURE 7.10b Melodic Minor Phrase

The structure of the mode highlights two tetrachords: lower minor and upper major that contains two beauty marks: **major 6** and **major 7**. In Figure 7.10b, the minor quality of the mode is clearly established by the presence of the minor 3rd. The mode's dissonant character is emphasized with two beauty marks located at metrically strong positions within the phrase. For instance, B5 constitutes the highest pitch within the phrase and initiates a downward arpeggiation of Baug.

Minor Modes—Dorian ♭2

The **Dorian ♭2** mode also contains two beauty marks: **major 6** and ♭2. Figure 7.11a examines the pitch structure of Dorian ♭2. Figure 7.11b demonstrates a four-bar modal phrase with Dorian ♭2 characteristics composed over a C13sus(♭9) harmony.

FIGURE 7.11a Dorian ♭2 Mode

Swing
C13(♭9)sus

FIGURE 7.11b Dorian ♭2 Phrase

The pitch structure of the mode includes two tetrachords: the lower Phrygian and the upper minor. The modal phrase in Figure 7.11b capitalizes on the two salient features of Dorian ♭2: (1) the sound of an augmented triad on ♭2 (mm. 2 and 3), and (2) the whole-tone segment stretching from ♭2 to **6** (mm. 3–4).

Minor Modes—Locrian ♮2

The **Locrian ♮2** mode contains two beauty marks: ♭5 and ♮2.[4] Figure 7.12a analyzes the pitch content of the mode and Figure 7.12b illustrates a four-bar modal phrase that utilizes salient characteristics of the mode over a Cm7(♭5) harmony.

FIGURE 7.12a Locrian ♮2 Mode

FIGURE 7.12b Locrian ♮2 Phrase

Locrian ♮2 contains two tetrachords: lower minor and upper whole tone. The melodic line in Figure 7.12b conveys the dissonant character of the mode by highlighting the beauty marks—♭5, in particular. The arpeggiation of the underlying harmony in m. 1 prioritizes chord tones (root, 3rd, ♭5th, ♭7th) and the diatonic extension (9th), which is metrically stressed on beat 3. In comparison to the phrase in Figure 7.8b, where the ♭9th occurring in the context of Locrian was metrically de-emphasized, the phrase in Figure 7.12b amplifies the status of the 9th as an extension that better fits the content of the Cm7(♭5) harmony.

Major Modes—Lydian Augmented

In addition to the three minor modes, the melodic minor scale gives rise to the four major chromatic modes, each with its own pitch structure, beauty marks, functional status, and characteristic sound. Figure 7.13a illustrates the structure of the **Lydian Augmented** mode along with an analysis of its pitch content. Figure 7.13b demonstrates the use of the mode in the context of a four-bar modal phrase over a CM7(♯5) harmony.

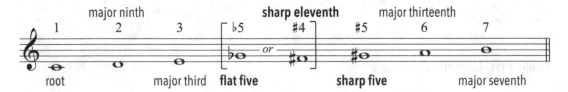

FIGURE 7.13a Lydian Augmented

FIGURE 7.13b Lydian Augmented Phrase

The pitch structure of the mode features a characteristic whole-tone segment from **1** to **#5**, which contains two beauty marks: **#11** and **#5**. The structure of Lydian Augmented also highlights two tetrachords: lower whole tone and upper chromatic. The modal phrase in Figure 7.13b has an interesting rhythmic design. The use of E and D triads in m. 3 adds another level of complexity to the line by implying a 3/8 cross rhythm.

Major Modes—Mixolydian #11

In comparison to Lydian Augmented, the **Mixolydian #11** mode (also known as **Lydian Dominant**) has a different functional status. Figure 7.14a offers an analysis of its pitch structure, and Figure 7.14b demonstrates the use of Mixolydian #11 in the context of a four-bar modal phrase over a C13(#11) harmony.

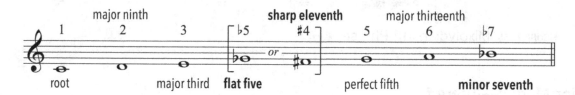

FIGURE 7.14a Mixolydian #11 Mode

FIGURE 7.14b Mixolydian #11 Phrase

The Mixolydian #11 mode has a similar pitch architecture to its diatonic counterpart, Mixolydian. The pairing of the beauty marks, ♭7 and #11, merges Lydian and Mixolydian characteristics that effectively project the sound of the dominant 7th harmony. The structure of the mode splits into two tetrachords: lower whole tone and upper minor. The phrase in Figure 7.14b projects the extended tertian nature of C13(#11) through the arpeggiation of Daug triad in m. 3 and Gm9(#7) in mm. 1–2.

Major Modes—Mixolydian ♭13

The pitch structure of **Mixolydian ♭13**, shown in Figure 7.15a, is characterized by the presence of two beauty marks: ♭7 and ♭13. Figure 7.15b shows a four-bar modal phrase written over a C9(♭13) harmony with Mixolydian ♭13 characteristics.

The additional beauty mark, ♭13, adds a minor quality to the mode. The mode splits into two tetrachords: lower major and upper Phrygian. The arpeggiation of E°7 in m. 1, A♭M7(#5) in m. 3, and C7 in m. 3 enables a projection of its extended tertian structure—C9(♭13).

FIGURE 7.15a Mixolydian ♭13 Mode

FIGURE 7.15b Mixolydian ♭13 Phrase

Major Modes—Altered

An absolute winner in the category of beauty marks is the **Altered** mode. Figure 7.16a illustrates the pitch structure of the mode and Figure 7.16b demonstrates its sound in the context of a four-bar modal phrase over a C7alt. harmony.

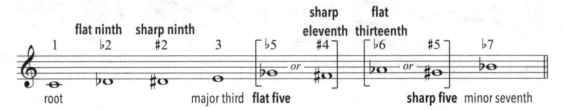

FIGURE 7.16a Altered Mode

FIGURE 7.16b Altered Phrase

The Altered mode contains four beauty marks: ♭9, #9, #11 (♭5), and ♭13 (#5). Depending on their position within a chord, the extensions, #11th and ♭13th, can also function as pitch alterations of the perfect fifth, ♭5th and #5th. The labeling of these pitches in the Altered mode indicates that they are "shades" of the diatonic fifth just as the chromatic extensions, ♭9th and #9th, are "shades" of the diatonic ninth. The mode highlights two tetrachords: lower chromatic and upper whole tone. The saturation of chromaticism in the phrase is quite overwhelming to the point that, without the root of C7alt. reminding us what the harmonic context is, it is difficult to hear this phrase in context.

Chromaticism affects all aspects of the musical fabric including harmony, melody, counterpoint, and even tonality. The use of chromaticism varies from slight surface inflections added to a single pitch to more substantial transformations of the tonal structure. Within that huge range of linear and harmonic possibilities, chromaticism is an important musical force with an inextinguishable potential. The addition of chromaticism alters the structure of harmonic formations and even redefines their functional status. Because chromaticism is such a potent force in music, it needs to be treated with caution. In short, the rule "less is more" should be at the forefront of our musical considerations. The effective use of chromaticism depends on a solid sense of time and good voice-leading skills. Chromatic notes that are foreign to the diatonic framework require correct preparation and resolution. Since the preparation and resolution of chromatic notes is inherently rhythmic, the voice-leading forces that control them have important rhythmic as well as melodic implications. The intimate relationship between chromaticism and rhythm implies that if we try to understand the former without considering its impact on meter and rhythm, our understanding will be incomplete.

In modal jazz theory, there are 14 modes: seven diatonic and seven chromatic. Modes in modal jazz typically function as independent scalar formations that are devoid of traditional tonal relationships. For instance, a complete section of a tune might feature only a single modal scale (e.g. John Coltrane's "Impressions" or McCoy Tyner's "Passion Dance").[5] In tonal jazz, however, modes exhibit similar functional behaviors comparable to those of four-, five-part, or larger structures. In Chapter 8, diatonic and chromatic modes will be combined and shown their tonal functional associations.

NOTES

1 Scale-degree four, however, is needed to give the Ionian mode identity, too. (Not major, in a tonal sense, but Ionian in a modal sense.)

2 This mode was not considered a mode in the Middle Ages and the Renaissance because of the tritone between 1 and $\flat$5 and the occurrence of the diminished triad on 1, which was unacceptable.

3 For the sake of readability, we will refer to $\sharp\hat{6}$ and $\sharp\hat{7}$ as 6 and 7.

4 This mode is also known as Locrian $\sharp$2.

5 Keith Waters in *The Studio Recordings of the Miles Davis Quintet, 1965–68* acknowledges the complexity of the term *modal jazz* and succinctly summarizes the prevailing views on the subject in six points: "(1) Modal scales for improvisation (or as a source for accompaniment); (2) Slow harmonic rhythm (single chord for 4, 8, 16, or more bars); (3) Pedal point harmonies (local bass pitch or shifting harmonies over a primary bass pitch); (4) Absence or limited use of functional harmonic progressions (such as V–I or ii–V–I) in accompaniment of improvisation; (5) Harmonies characteristic of jazz after 1959 (Suspended fourth—"sus"—chords, slash chords, harmonies named for modes: i.e., phrygian, aeolian harmonies), and (6) Prominent use of melodic and/or harmonic perfect fourths" (p. 46).

Chord–Scale Theory

CHAPTER SUMMARY

Chapter 8 establishes a relationship between the vertical and horizontal dimensions in jazz. The diatonic and chromatic modes are revisited and chord–scale relationships with four- and five-part chords, as well as the II–V–I progressions, are established.

CONCEPTS AND TERMS

- Chord–scale relationship
- Dominant category:
  - Mixolydian
  - Mixolydian ♯11
  - Mixolydian ♭13
  - Altered
- Gapped formation
- Intermediary category:
  - Dorian
  - Locrian
  - Locrian ♮2
- Major category:
  - Ionian
  - Lydian
  - Lydian Augmented
- Minor category:
  - Melodic Minor
  - Aeolian
  - Dorian
- Overtone series:
  - Fundamental note
  - Partials
- Overtones
- Quartal harmony
- Suspended dominant category:
  - Mixolydian
  - Mixolydian ♭13
  - Phrygian
  - Dorian ♭2
- Upper structures

OBJECTIVES OF CHORD–SCALE THEORY

In jazz, the relationship between chords and scales is explained using chord–scale theory. Chord–scale theory relates certain harmonies to melodies and melodies to harmonies. It also illustrates what kinds of harmonies and chord progressions can be derived from particular scales or modes. The terms *scale* and *mode* will be used interchangeably. By extension, chord–scale theory measures the harmonic identity of improvised lines and examines melodies for their harmonic clarity. Finally, chord–scale theory allows us to formulate rules of voice leading that govern the behavior of harmonic progressions and melodic lines.

In short, the relationship between scales and chords can be summarized with the following statement: *any melodic line can be represented by a chord and/or harmonic progression* and, conversely, *any chord or harmonic progression can be horizontalized as a melodic line.*

Since we will combine four- and five-part chords (as well as triads and extended tertian sonorities) that add up to some 52 harmonic formations, **chord–scale relationships** will involve many-to-one ratios. This means that certain scales can accommodate more than a single chord and certain chords can establish a chord–scale relationship with more than a single mode. The possibility that many chords can form a relationship with a single scale is of great importance to the improviser. A proper understanding of this relationship can influence our decisions in finding the most fitting harmonic match for a single scale or vice versa. Even though certain chords might not contain all the essential notes from a given mode, they can still form a convincing chord–scale relationship with that mode.

CHORD–SCALE RELATIONSHIP

A chord built entirely of thirds, so-called tertian formation, has seven notes that can be arranged in the form of a scale.[1] The notes within the scale, however, have very different melodic and harmonic behaviors. Any vertical or linear combination of notes derived from the scale has the potential to convey the sound of that scale. In order to express such a sound, the selection of pitches in a chord has to be very specific. Figure 8.1 illustrates a chord–scale relationship between CM13(♯11) and the Lydian mode.

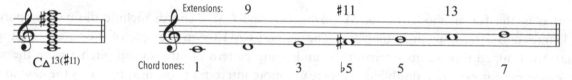

FIGURE 8.1 CM13(♯11) and Lydian Mode

There are two ways of explaining the chord–scale relationship between CM13(♯11) and Lydian. First, an extended tertian structure, CM13(♯11), can be horizontalized as the Lydian mode. Second, Lydian can be verticalized as the CM13(♯11) harmony. To project the Lydian sound, however, we do not necessarily need a complete seven-note chord; as few as three pitches, major 3rd, major 7th, and ♯11th (or ♭5th), may be used. The relationship between CM13(♯11) and Lydian means that the vertical and horizontal dimensions exhibit the same voice-leading behaviors and one can be used to represent and/or complement the other. Just as the structure of CM13(♯11) is representative of Lydian, so is the structure of other chords representative of other scales. Figure 8.2 represents the CM13(♯11) chord as a melodic phrase with characteristic modal features.

FIGURE 8.2 Lydian Phrase

In this figure, the Lydian mode has a very distinct sound. The melodic line prioritizes chord tones and the beauty mark ♯11th, avoids a perfect 5th, highlights a major triad on D, and uses successive fourths at the end of the phrase. The bottom stave projects the Lydian sound through the use of **quartal** harmonies or **quartal structures** (that is, chords built in stacked fourths). These contain the most active notes derived from the Lydian mode. The interplay between the melodic line and the underlying harmonies unifies both musical dimensions. Not only does chord–scale theory control the relationship between lines and chords, but it also suggests a particular melodic and harmonic vocabulary derived from the structure of specific chords and scales.

MAJOR CATEGORY

Possible Harmonic Function—Tonic and Predominant

In the forthcoming discussion, modes and chords are placed in the familiar functional categories. Each figure provides an analysis of the mode's pitch content in terms of chord tones and extensions along with a selection of chords and upper structures. The term *upper structure* refers to a triad or four-part chord that contains extensions or chord tones (excluding the root) of an extended harmonic formation.

The **major category** includes three scales: **Ionian**, **Lydian**, and **Lydian Augmented**. They establish a chord–scale relationship with different types of major chords. Figure 8.3 illustrates the pitch structure of these modes along with the corresponding chords.

Note that in the Ionian mode, the 6, M7, 6/9, M9, and CM13 chords include the most important chord tones and extensions from the scale. The six-part CM13 is an example of the so-called **gapped formation**. Gapped formations interrupt the underlying pattern of introducing pitches from the scale in order to prevent excessive doubling. This creates more interesting voicings, or—as is the case in this example—avoids a note that does not fit the content of a fully extended chord. Two triads, major on **5** and minor on **3**, summarize the chord–scale relationship using limited harmonic means. Scale-degree four ($\hat{4}$) is typically employed as a metrically unstressed passing or neighbor tone. In more advanced harmonic settings, however, the avoid note can also participate in the projection of a mode. For instance, harmonic structures such as C(add4) or CM7(add4) convey the sound of Ionian, but these structures require a different set of voice-leading rules and specific voicings to make them sound convincing.

In Lydian, the ♯11th is a pitch that flavors the mode in a highly recognizable manner. The chord–scale relationship in Lydian illustrates one of many spelling discrepancies that we will try to untangle. The ♯11th functions as an extension in extended tertian formations, such as in CM13(♯11). The ♯11th, then, assumes the presence of the perfect 5th. In four- and five-part chords, like CM7(♭5) and CM9(♭5), the alternate spelling ♭5th is used for the same pitch in order to preserve the tertian nature of their respective structures. A major upper-structure triad on **2** and a minor upper-structure triad on **7** convey the character of the Lydian collection using limited harmonic means.

In Lydian Augmented, the ♯5 is a pitch that injects the characteristic augmented sound into the framework of the mode or chords. The M7(♯5) and M9(♯5) chords delineate the sound of the scale. The most common triad within this mode is the one built on **3** and has a major quality. The major 13th functions as an extension in the context of a complete tertian formation, as in CM13(♯5,♯11). Otherwise it functions as a passing or neighbor tone.

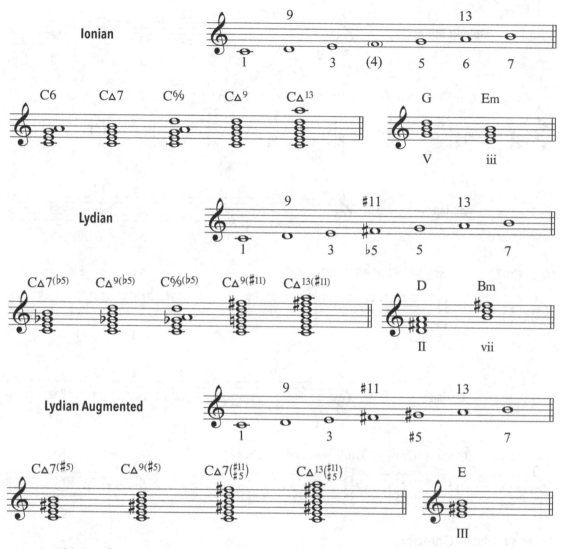

FIGURE 8.3 Major Category

MINOR CATEGORY

Possible Harmonic Function—Tonic and Predominant

The **minor category** includes three modes: **Melodic Minor**, **Aeolian**, and **Dorian**. Figure 8.4 establishes a chord–scale relationship for this category.

The first four chords, m6, m(♯7), m6/9, and m9(♯7), constitute the familiar four- and five-part formations and form a strong chord–scale relationship with Melodic Minor. The remaining ones: m11(♯7) and m13(♯7), feature extended tertian structures that incorporate six and seven notes from the scale, respectively. A major upper-structure triad on **5** captures the sound of Melodic Minor using limited triadic means.

Similarly, all the notes from the Aeolian mode can be implemented in a chord. Among the four formations from Figure 8.4, the m9(♭6) and m11(♭13) chords admit both the chord tones and the beauty mark into their structure. The first two, m7 and m9, can represent the scale too, provided that the beauty

FIGURE 8.4 Minor Category

mark occurs somewhere in the melodic line. In this particular context, the m7 and m9 chords *assume* the presence of ♭6th or ♭13th in the melodic dimension. The complementary relationship between chords and lines constitutes an important feature of chord–scale theory.

The Dorian mode is an interesting collection with equally interesting chord–scale relationships. The dual harmonic function of Dorian—tonic and predominant—slightly complicates these relationships. The Dorian mode is a symmetrical scale that features two adjacent minor tetrachords. In theory, Dorian can admit all the notes from the scale into the structure of a chord. In practice, though, the selection of notes for a melodic line or a chord is entirely predicated on the context in which the Dorian mode appears. All the chords from Figure 8.4 establish a chord–scale relationship with Dorian and can potentially function as tonic formations. Yet, only m7, m9, and m11 function exclusively as predominant chords. Therefore, the role of the beauty mark decreases in predominant-type chords and increases in tonic formations. We can also emphasize these two different functional associations of Dorian by using specific upper-structure triads. In the tonic formation, we can use a minor triad on **2**; in the predominant Dorian, a major triad on ♭7.

Dorian as Tonic and/or Predominant

Compare the sound of the two melodic phrases in Figures 8.5a and 8.5b.

FIGURE 8.5a Dorian as a Tonic

FIGURE 8.5b Dorian as a Predominant

The pitch content of these two phrases is derived exclusively from the Dorian mode. In Figure 8.5a, the line features successive fourths and prioritizes the beauty mark, **major 6**. The parallel quartal structures reinforce the melodic line and use the interval of a fourth as a basic building block. This particular pitch and harmonic architecture implies a modal style of improvisation. In Figure 8.5b, the phrase exhibits very different intervallic characteristics. The use of minor 7th completely overshadows the major 6th, which becomes de-emphasized as an unaccented passing tone at the "and" of beat 2 in m. 2. The intervallic design of the melody highlights stacked thirds; these are complemented by mostly tertian formations and/or guide tones. In this context, the use of Dorian implies a more traditional style of improvisation, which we might implement over a predominant ii in the ii–V⁷–I progression.

What can chord–scale theory tell us about the two phrases from Figure 8.5a and 8.5b? First, it tells us that the scale is a powerful entity that can exhibit either modal or tonal characteristics. Second, the intervallic design of melodic lines can potentially suggest modal or tonal environments. Third, the mode provides a structural foundation for melody and harmony. Fourth, in modal environments, upper melodic extensions function primarily as independent chord members that are not bound by the same rules of voice leading as their analogous counterparts in the tonal environment. Fifth, the pitch content of melodic lines can be effectively manipulated by exploring modal and tonal characteristics of scales.

DOMINANT CATEGORY

Possible Harmonic Function—Dominant

The **dominant category** establishes an intricate family of chord–scale relationships. The dominant category includes four scales: **Mixolydian, Mixolydian ♯11, Mixolydian ♭13,** and **Altered**. Figure 8.6 illustrates a chord–scale relationship between dominant modes and corresponding chords.

FIGURE 8.6 Dominant Category

The only pitch to be avoided is **4**. All other notes can freely participate in a chord to project the sound of these dominant-functioning collections. When examining the content of the dom7, dom9, and dom13 chords, notice that their pitch content captures the diatonic qualities of the Mixolydian mode. The sound of Mixolydian can also be expressed using two minor upper-structure triads on **5** and **6**.

The pitch structure of the Mixolydian #11 mode approximates the distribution of partials in the overtone series.[2] Figure 8.7 illustrates the **overtone series**, which distributes **partials** or **overtones** above the **fundamental note**, C1. The overtone series illustrates the sonic architecture of fundamental notes as they occur in nature. The distribution of partials above the fundamental note correlates with the location of chord tones and extensions within chords. Those closer to the fundamental (5ths, 3rds, and 7ths) form chord tones; those further removed from the fundamental (9ths, 11ths, and 13ths) constitute chordal extensions.

FIGURE 8.7 The Overtone Series

The Mixolydian ♭13 mode establishes a chord–scale relationship with the dom7(#5), dom9(#5), and dom9(♭13) chords. The mode is typically used in the context of dominant chords occurring in minor keys. Because of the potential spelling discrepancies that might arise in certain chord progressions involving a dom9(#5) chord, we will implement the syntactically correct dom9(♭13). In the key of C minor, for instance, the #5th in G9(#5) indicates D#, which does not exist. Although the G9(#5) spelling preserves the tertian nature of the chord, by referring to #5th as ♭13th we avoid making a syntactical error, which is all the more serious because it effects the minor 3rd of the tonic chord, E♭. In addition, the pitch alteration #5th becomes the chromatic extension ♭13th in the context of an extended tertian formation, such as a gapped C9(♭13) in Figure 8.6, which includes a perfect 5th as a chord tone.

Even though the dom7(♭5) and dom7(#5) chords form a relationship with the Altered mode, without the essential chromatic extensions, the Mixolydian #11 or Mixolydian ♭13 scales may actually be implied. The five-part chords that establish a chord–scale relationship with the Altered mode in Figure 8.6 have a highly chromatic pitch content and the degree of tension increases with the addition of the #9th. There are two major triads (♭5 and ♭6) and two minor triads (♭2 and ♭3) that project the sound of the Altered mode.

In the case of chromatic chords and modes (or even with certain diatonic formations and scales), the issue of providing a unified methodology for labeling extensions is extremely problematic. As we have observed, extensions can be labeled as pitch alterations and pitch alterations as extensions. Attempting to resolve these discrepancies should give us a good opportunity to think more rigorously about the choice of notation and the implications of those choices.

SUSPENDED DOMINANT CATEGORY

Possible Harmonic Function—Dominant, Predominant, Tonic

In the **suspended dominant category** there are four modes: **Mixolydian**, **Mixolydian ♭13**, **Phrygian**, and **Dorian ♭2**. They establish chord–scale relationships with different types of chord: triads, four-, five-, and six-part. The 7sus chord can function as dominant, predominant, or even as tonic in certain types of modal tunes.[3] Chord–scale theory for this category is rather complex because the 7sus chord can assume different harmonic functions. For instance, a chord–scale relationship with Phrygian and/or Dorian ♭2 might seem problematic because the major 3rd is not even present in the pitch structure of these modes. We can actually remedy this situation by reinterpreting ♭3 as #9th. And since the 7sus chord includes a perfect 4th as an essential chord tone, the absence of major 3rd from those modes is not too problematic.

Figure 8.8 illustrates chord–scale relationships for this category.

FIGURE 8.8 Suspended Dominant Category

A major triad on ♭7 and a minor triad on 2 are often used to represent the sound of the suspended Mixolydian mode. The Mixolydian ♭13 scale establishes a chord–scale relationship with two chords, 9sus(♯5) and 7sus(♭13), both of which contain a dominant 7th chord on ♭7. In the former, the ♯5th replaces the 5th; in the latter, the ♭13th implies the 5th.

Chords that establish a relationship with the Phrygian mode have an interesting selection of upper structures that can be superimposed over the root of the chord. The 7sus(♭9) chord contains a root-position half-diminished 7th chord on 5 (G–B♭–D♭–F); 7sus(♯5,♭9) includes an enharmonically spelled root-position m7 chord on ♭7, (B♭–D♭–F–G♯); 7sus(♯9) superimposes an enharmonic major triad with an added major 2nd on ♭3, (D♯–F–G–B♭); and 7sus(♯9,♭13) incorporates an enharmonically spelled major tetrachord on ♭3, (D♯–F–G–A♭). The Dorian ♭2 scale forms a chord–scale relationship with the following formations: 7sus(♭9), 13sus(♭9), 7sus(♯9), and 13sus(♯9). One of the most effective upper structures that can represent the sound of Dorian ♭2 is an augmented triad on ♭2 over the chordal root.

When comparing the chord–scale relationship between Phrygian and Dorian ♭2 in Figure 8.8, notice that the 7sus(♭9) and 7sus(♯9) chords establish a relationship with both modes. Neither of these chords, however, contains a note that is essential to the corresponding modes: the 7sus(♭9) and 7sus(♯9) chords in Phrygian do not include ♭6, while the 7sus(♭9) and 7sus(♯9) chords in Dorian ♭2 do not include **major 6th**. As was the case with other chords that *almost* captured the sound of particular modes, the missing note from the chord needs to be supplied by the melodic line or *assumed* aurally. Based on this mutual relationship, we can formulate a basic premise that underlies chord–scale theory: in order to establish the relationship between chords and scales, both musical forces—horizontal and vertical—have to complement and interact with each other in time.

INTERMEDIARY CATEGORY

Possible Harmonic Function—Predominant and Dominant

The **intermediary category** contains three modes: **Dorian, Locrian,** and **Locrian ♮2**. They establish a chord–scale relationship with m7 and m7(♭5), as well as with other extended formations. In discussing chord–scale theory for this category, we will focus on establishing a relationship between the m7 and m7(♭5) chords, and with the corresponding scales. Since these chords are frequently used in the ii–V⁷–I and ii°–V⁷–i progressions, respectively, choosing the correct scale is essential in projecting the sound of these harmonies during improvisation. Figure 8.9 illustrates a chord–scale relationship between intermediary-type modes and corresponding chords.

The Dorian mode establishes a relationship with the m7 and m9 chords in order to convey the sound of predominant ii in the ii–V⁷–I progression. In our earlier discussion of Dorian, we observed that all the notes from the scale could participate in projecting the Dorian sound. Here, the issue of the avoid note comes back and relates to the status of the beauty mark. The major 6th is excluded from the structure of predominant formations and, in the context of melodic lines, should be treated as a passing or neighbor note.

In Figure 8.9, the chromatic Locrian ♮2 is located before the diatonic Locrian. The Locrian ♮2 mode includes a major 9th, the most suitable form of the 9th that can be added to the m9(♭5) chord. We can also use upper structures: m(♮7) on ♭3, M7(♯5) on ♭5, and the augmented triad on ♭5, to convey the sound of Locrian ♮2. The m7(♭5) chord in Figure 8.9 also forms a chord–scale relationship with the diatonic Locrian mode. This scale can be used with the m7(♭5) chord, but the beauty mark ♭2 is de-emphasized

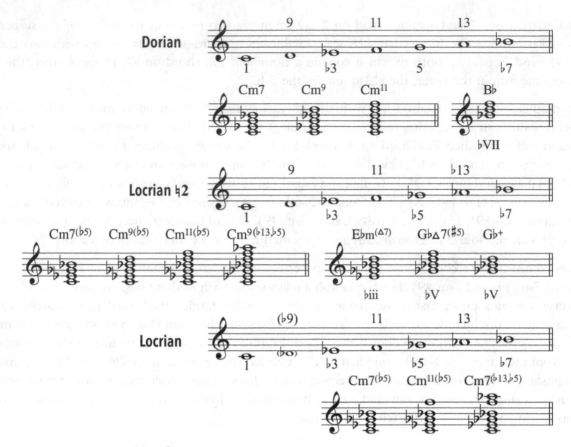

FIGURE 8.9 Intermediary Category

and treated as a passing or neighbor note.[4] The other beauty mark ♭**5** functions as a chord tone and is integral to the sound of both Locrian scales.

Chord–scale theory tells us which notes to use in melodic lines, which chords best represent the harmonic character of those lines, and which combinations of notes can participate in a chord voicing. But, the chords we use cannot always accommodate all the notes from corresponding scales. In instances when a chord does not clearly project the sound of a mode, the corresponding melodic line has to supply the missing notes from the correct scale. Depending on the context, however, even the most important notes from the mode, such as beauty marks and chord tones, might be de-emphasized and treated as passing or neighbor notes.

THE ii–V⁷–I PROGRESSION

Figure 8.10 illustrates the chord–scale relationship for the ii–V⁷–I progression in the key of C major.

Even though all the notes from Figure 8.10 are derived exclusively from the C major scale, the individual modes establish a strong metric relationship with the underlying chords. Notice that downbeats in Figure 8.10 are occupied by chord tones, while offbeats with passing notes notated with small note heads. Such a distribution of notes enables a clear projection of chords and harmonic progressions during improvisation.

In addition to the diatonic relationship shown in Figure 8.10, we can also experiment with substitute chords and their corresponding scales in order to establish more intricate chord–scale relationships, such

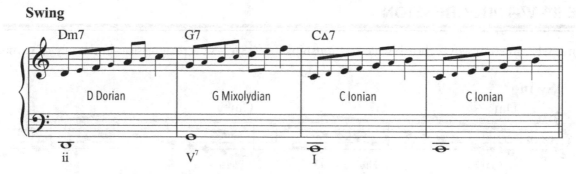

FIGURE 8.10 Chord–Scale Relationship: ii–V⁷–I

as those provided in Figure 8.11. While these relationships expand our melodic vocabulary and harmonic understanding, they also illustrate how to introduce chromatic notes. Figure 8.11 illustrates some of the most common combinations of chromatic chord–scale relationships for the ii–V⁷–I progression.

FIGURE 8.11 Chromatic Chord–Scale Relationships

In Figure 8.11a, the dominant chord in m. 2 includes the ♯11th, which establishes a chord–scale relationship with the Mixolydian ♯11 scale. The tonic in mm. 2–3 features a M7(♭5) chord, which forms a chord–scale relationship with the Lydian mode. The remaining progressions in Figure 8.11 illustrate ever more complex chord–scale relationships. In Figure 8.11d, for instance, the use of the secondary dominant 7th, V/V, in m. 1 transforms the diatonic ii–V⁷–I progression into the chromatic II⁷–V⁷–I. The use of Mixolydian ♯11 over the secondary dominant 7th is especially common in Bebop improvisation.

THE ii∅–V⁷–i PROGRESSION

Figure 8.12 illustrates two chord–scale relationships for the ii∅–V⁷–i progression in the key of C minor.

FIGURE 8.12 Chord–Scale Relationship: ii∅–V⁷–i

In Figure 8.12a, the Locrian ♮2 mode establishes a chord–scale relationship with Dm9(♭5) as it contains a major 9th that expands the m7(♭5) into the m9(♭5) formation. The choice of Mixolydian ♭13 also fits the underlying tonal context since ♭13th anticipates the arrival of minor 3rd of Cm6/9. Figure 8.12b proposes one of many chromatic chord–scale relationships that can be established for the progression. Here, the chromaticism becomes more prominent as the dominant 7th chord forms a chord–scale relationship with the Altered scale and the tonic chord with Melodic Minor.

One of the goals of chord–scale theory is to develop our practical skills. Although Figures 8.11 and 8.12 showed different chord–scale relationships, the choices in our improvisations should reflect the surrounding musical context. Even though Mixolydian ♭13 is considered a chromatic mode in the context of the progression from Figure 8.12a, it is a more fitting choice than the diatonic Mixolydian because it contains the ♭13th that better conveys the underlying tonality. The treatment of chromatic extensions is an important factor to consider while making improvisational decisions. In Figure 8.11b, for instance, the Altered mode over the dominant 7th prepares the arrival of Lydian Augmented. Since Lydian Augmented contains a dissonant ♯5th, the Altered mode one measure earlier foreshadows the occurrence of this alteration.

NOTES

1   Tertian formations complete their third span after two octaves and may contain different kinds of 3rds (minor, major, diminished, and augmented).
2   The Mixolydian ♯11 mode is also known as the "overtone" or "acoustic" scale due to its relation to the overtone series.
3   "Yes or No," "Little One," "Milestones," or "Litha," for instance.
4   In more advanced harmonic settings, however, a ♭9th can be added to the m7(♭5) chord as can be seen in Figure 23.6.

CHAPTER 9
The Blues

CHAPTER SUMMARY

Chapter 9 discusses the most important form in jazz, the blues, examines the structure of the blues scale, and provides chord–scale relationships for the basic and minor blues progressions.

CONCEPTS AND TERMS

- AA'B phrase structure
- Basic blues progression
- "Blue" notes
- Blues scale
- Call and response
- Generic blues
- Major blues scale
- Minor blues scale
- Tonicizing sonority
- 12-bar form
- Voice leading

GENERIC BLUES

The blues is an American art form. Originally, blues were primarily sung, with one of the objectives being to tell a story as vividly and expressively as possible. To tell stories, blues singers used simple repeated phrases charged with a variety of expressive devices. The ability to tell the story from one's perspective came to represent blues performance practice in particular, and jazz improvisation in general. The familiar saying that *your solo should tell a story* takes on a completely different meaning when we consider whence it came and how intricate life's stories can really be. Early blues practitioners were unconstrained by the form of the blues, as the duration of improvised lyrics often influenced the length of individual phrases. Eventually, the blues was codified as a **12-bar form** and, as such, it is by far the most common among jazz musicians.

Figure 9.1 illustrates a fundamental harmonic framework of the 12-bar blues that we will refer to as a **generic blues**.

The form of the generic blues can be partitioned into three four-bar phrases labeled as **AA'B**. Each of these four-bar phrases receives different harmonic support: the A phrase (mm. 1–4) is on the tonic, the A' (mm. 5–8) begins on the predominant and ends on the tonic, and the B phrase (mm. 9–12) begins

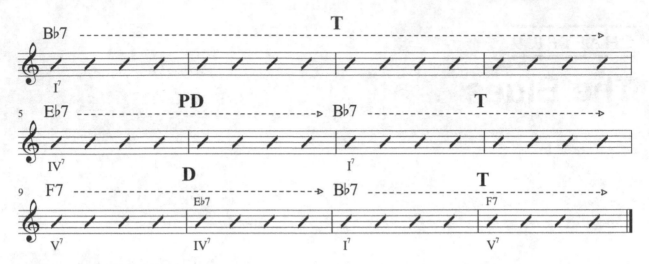

FIGURE 9.1 Generic Blues

on the dominant and ends on the tonic. Even though each phrase is analyzed with traditional functional labels, the underlying chords do not behave as specified by these labels. For instance, the tonic chord in m. 1 and the subdominant chord in m. 5 employ dominant 7th chords. In the generic blues, then, the chords on $\hat{1}$, $\hat{4}$, and $\hat{5}$ have the dominant 7th quality.

The labels A and A′ imply the same melodic content whereas the label B implies the use of new melodic material. The predominant harmonic support in mm. 5–6 of the A′ phrase, however, completely redefines the relationship between melody and harmony. The same melodic idea—which in the first A section might be heard as tonally stable—sounds unstable in the second A′ section due to the disagreement between melody and harmony. In the lyrics of early blues performances, the first two lines (A and A′) frequently introduce a problem, pose a question, or depict a specific situation. The third line (B) almost always provides a solution to those circumstances.

TELLING A STORY

Here is a sample of blues poetry from the iconic "Backwater Blues":

> *Then they rowed a little boat about five miles 'cross the pond*
> *Then they rowed a little boat about five miles 'cross the pond*
> *I packed all my clothes, throwed them in and they rowed me along.*

Figure 9.2 demonstrates a musical realization of this story.

The line in mm. 1–2 has a strong rhythmic and melodic profile. The predominant harmonic support in mm. 5–6 for the same melodic idea from mm. 1–2 redefines the relationship between melody and harmony. For instance, the A♭4s on beat 2 in m. 5 and on beat 4 in m. 6 form the interval of a perfect 4th; this creates melodic and harmonic tensions with the underlying E♭7 chord. The B phrase in mm. 9–10 resolves the accrued tension by introducing a new melodic idea. The musical answer in mm. 9–10 has a balanced melodic design that effectively complements the content of the A phrase.

FIGURE 9.2 Musical Realization of a Story

CALL AND RESPONSE

The musical depiction of the lyrics from Figure 9.2 illustrates an additional aspect of blues performance practice—the use of **call and response**. Originally practiced by a large group of people, this improvisational technique involves sharing ideas between the leader and her/his followers. Mastering the call and response technique is especially important at the beginning of our encounter with jazz improvisation. It engages us in a meaningful dialogue that includes exchanging and communicating of musical ideas. The communicative aspect of call and response is relatively straightforward in the context of verbal conversation. In a musical setting, however, when spoken words and sentences are replaced with motifs and melodic phrases, the structure of the call and response might not be as obvious. To be good communicators, we have to know how to listen, pay close attention to what the other musicians are playing, and try to be receptive to their ideas.

In certain scenarios, however, the use of the call and response technique might create less than desirable effects. For instance, when the call and response takes the form of exact and immediate repetition, it might be impressive but not necessarily in keeping with the surrounding musical context. A much more subtle way of thinking about the call and response technique involves musical interaction at the level of the entire performance in which non-adjacent sections relate to one another, and where the flow of the performance is regulated by logically introduced musical ideas. In creating a musical narrative, then, we can also respond to each other's playing, but these responses are not as obvious as simple repetitions tend to be. We can demonstrate our listening skills, for instance, by incorporating an idea that we have previously heard (i.e. a rhythmic motive from the drummer, or a melodic gesture from the guitarist) and develop it in such a way that leads to a more satisfying musical discourse. The call and response aspect of improvisation means that musicians understand each other's intentions, have an unspoken agreement, so to speak, and project them with a high level of personal expression and musical commitment.

THE BLUES SCALE

The expressiveness of the blues comes from the melodic inflections added to particular notes. When we listen to various vocal or guitar renditions of the blues, these inflections are easily recognizable; they stand out because of their emotional charge and slightly "out of tune" sound.[1] The so-called **blues scale** approximates the sound of these pitch inflections by altering $\hat{3}$, $\hat{5}$, and $\hat{7}$ of the major scale. Figure 9.3 illustrates the content of the blues scale and its derivation from the major scale.

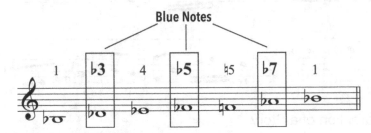

FIGURE 9.3 Blues Scale

The blues scale is a six-note collection with the **blue notes** on ♭3, ♭5, and ♭7. Although the presence of ♭7th suggests a chord–scale relationship with the dominant 7th chord, the use of the blues scale is not limited to this chord only. In the context of the blues scale, the pitches ♭3 and ♭5 constitute expressive embellishments not bound by any particular harmonic function or chord type. The blues scale, then, is as an androgynous collection that works just as well for dominant 7ths as it does for tonic and predominant chords. The unspecified functional associations of the blues scale suggest that this collection is relatively easy to implement during improvisation. Indeed, the blues scale not only allows us to add expression to our playing, but it also demonstrates our understanding of its historical importance and its role in the jazz tradition.

Major Blues Scale

Having examined the structure of the blues scale, we can now explore the tonal potential of the scale.[2] Figure 9.4 illustrates the structure of G blues scale.

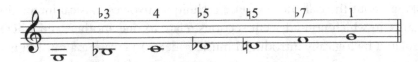

FIGURE 9.4 G Blues Scale

This scale has a minor feel to it; notice the use of ♭**3**, ♭**5** and ♭**7**. By starting the scale on B♭3 and continuing through the octave, we are able to generate a major scale that, in addition to having the *blue* 3rd, also contains the major 3rd needed for major and dominant 7th chords. A **major blues scale**, shown in Figure 9.5, starts on ♭3 of the regular blues scale, contains a perfect 5th, major 6th, major 9th, and establishes a convincing chord–scale relationship with the B♭6/9, B♭13 or other B♭-based dominant 7th chords.

In addition to more generic usage of the blues scale (where a single scale is used in the context of different chords), we can be more discerning and assign a regular blues scale to minor chords and a major blues scale to major and dominant 7th chords.

FIGURE 9.5 Major Blues Scale

BASIC BLUES PROGRESSION

In the most fundamental form, the generic blues consists of only three chords: I⁷, IV⁷, and V⁷. These harmonies control the structure of the blues, even though in some chord progressions, particularly those from the Bebop Era, they might be disguised, substituted, transformed, or omitted all together. The generic or three-chord blues, without any additional chord changes, was often employed in early jazz, particularly in Early Blues, Boogie-Woogie, and different New Orleans styles.[3] We will now examine the harmonic structure of a slightly modified blues (one that is probably the most common in jazz), and illustrate how this chord progression came about and how it relates to the generic blues. Figure 9.6 illustrates a **basic blues progression** and its relationship to the generic blues. When jazz musicians gather together to play the blues, the chances are that they will use this chord progression.

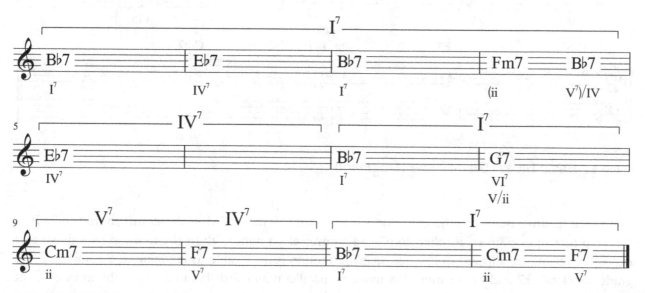

FIGURE 9.6 Basic Blues Progression

Notice that in mm. 9–12, the chord changes are different in generic and basic blues progressions. A characteristic V⁷–IV⁷ chord succession in the generic blues becomes a ii–V⁷ progression in the basic blues. Another noticeable difference between the two progressions relates to the overall unfolding of harmonic rhythm. The slow harmonic rhythm of the generic blues reflects the fixed location of the structural chords: I⁷ in mm. 1, 7, and 11; IV⁷ in mm. 5 and 10; V⁷ in m. 9. In the basic blues, the rate of harmonic rhythm is much faster, usually with one-chord-per-measure changes. Additionally, the mediant harmony VI⁷ in m. 8 introduces a chromatic chord that anticipates the arrival of a predominant ii in m. 9. This **tonicizing sonority**, V/ii, offers a momentary departure from the diatonic framework of the blues. In comparison to the generic blues, Figure 9.6 contains more tonally based progressions and, as such, lends itself for improvisation, something that we will discuss in Chapter 10.

Keyboard Realization

In addition to being fluent on our primary instruments, the ability to realize chord progressions on the piano is an essential skill that enables us to understand the harmonic structure of tunes, their voice-leading propensities, and their inherent chord–scale relationships. The most basic realization of the basic blues progression, shown in Figure 9.7, involves chordal roots in the left hand (L.H.) and guide tones in the right hand (R.H.).

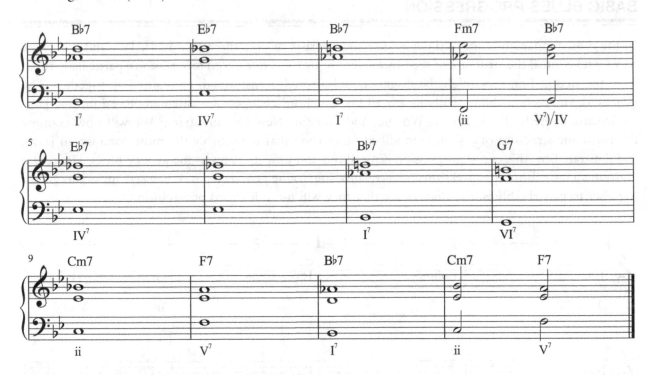

FIGURE 9.7 Basic Blues: Guide-Tone Realization

The **voice leading** between adjacent chords is very strict. A major 3rd of the dom7 chord moves by a half step to a minor 7th of another dom7 and, conversely, a minor 7th of the dom7 moves down to a major 3rd. Skips are allowed only when stepwise motion is impossible to implement. For instance, the guide tones of B♭7 and G7 in mm. 7–8 move by parallel minor 3rds because this is the most efficient way to connect these chords. Larger skips can occur in places where the guide tones are registrally too low or too high. These skips or register transfers should coincide with the overall design of phrases, distribution of cadences, and harmonic rhythm of a tune. For instance, register transfers can be made in mm. 5 and 9 because those measures mark the beginning of new phrases and are aligned with the new harmonic functions. In summary, the successful realization of harmonic progressions depends on good voice leading, which primarily relies on stepwise motion between guide tones and careful distribution of skips.

Chord–Scale Relationship

Figure 9.8 establishes a couple of chord–scale relationships for the basic blues progression in the key of B♭. Figure 9.8a uses major and minor blues scales and Figure 9.8b combines blues scales and modes.

FIGURE 9.8 Basic Blues: Blues Scales and Modes

MINOR BLUES

The progression shown in Figure 9.9 exemplifies the structure of a **minor blues**.[4]

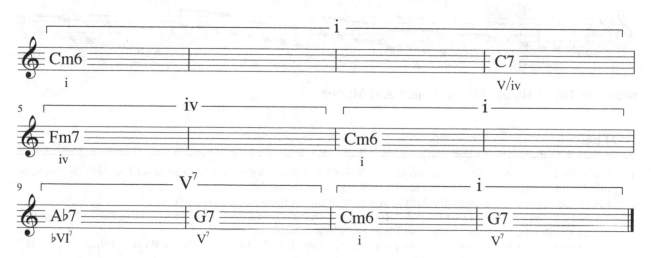

FIGURE 9.9 Minor Blues

The chord structure of the minor blues is characterized by the presence of traditional tonal progressions. For instance, the tonicization of iv in m. 4 uses a secondary dominant 7th, V/iv, and the motion to V^7 in m. 10 is prepared by the $\flat VI^7$ chord. This particular preparation of the dominant 7th, $\flat VI^7–V^7$, is one of the harmonic trademarks of the minor blues.

Chord–Scale Relationship

The two chord–scale relationships for the minor blues shown in Figure 9.10 indicate a selection of blues scales and modes that will be explored in Chapter 10.

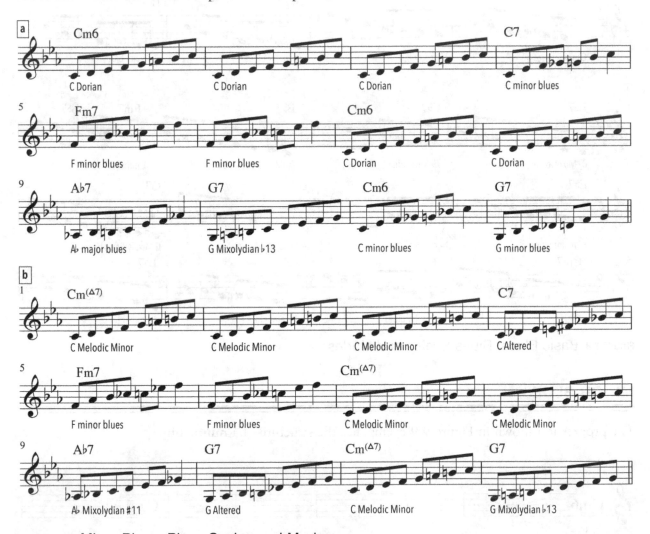

FIGURE 9.10 Minor Blues: Blues Scales and Modes

NOTES

1   Listen to the way Bessie Smith on *Essential Bessie Smith* and Billie Holiday on *Lady Sings the Blues* sing the blues, or Blind Lemon Jefferson plays the blues on *The Best of Blind Lemon Jefferson*.
2   I am indebted to Prof. Harold Danko for sharing with me his thoughts on this subject.
3   "West End Blues," "Mecca Flat Blues," "Honky Tonk Train," "Lost Your Head Blues," "Hear Me Talkin' To Ya," "Pinetop's Boogie Woogie," "Roll 'Em Pete," or "Monday Struggle."
4   Representative 12-bar minor blues compositions are: "Mr. P.C.," "Ko Ko," "Birk's Work," "Hora Decubitus," "Footprints," and "The Eye of the Hurricane."

Basic Improvisation

CHAPTER SUMMARY

Chapter 10 embarks on a study of improvisation. After initial remarks, the importance of melody in improvisation is discussed. A few basic improvisational strategies involving blues riffs, guide tones and motifs are examined, and implemented in practice.

CONCEPTS AND TERMS

- Blues riffs
- Charleston rhythm
- Compound melody
- Guide-tone improvisation
- Motivic development:
  - Inversion:
    - Real

- Tonal/modal
- Repetition:
  - Exact
  - Inexact
- Transposition:
  - Real
  - Tonal/modal

- Contraction
- Fragmentation
- Expansion
- Interpolation

GETTING STARTED

In Chapter 2, we stressed that rhythmic integrity and a good sense of time should be the focus of a performance. The quality and placement of swing 8th notes, phrasing, and articulations are essential characteristics of melodic lines. While these characteristics relate to the overall presentation of melodic lines, the content of our phrases is intimately related to the musical material with which we are working. Successful improvisation depends just as much on the ability to project the melodic line in a convincing fashion as it does on a familiarity with the melodic syntax, harmonic vocabulary, and rhythmic conventions associated with the tune being used for improvisation. In addition, the ability to listen to our own playing, articulate the form of improvisations, and make large-scale musical connections is an important skill that can improve improvisational skills.

In our initial attempts at improvisation, we might notice that instead of concentrating on *when to play*, we are spending too much time thinking about *what to play*. This is perfectly understandable; after all, improvisation is a complex musical activity. It requires complete internalization and practical understanding of theoretical concepts. In shifting our focus from *what to play* to *when to play*, the *what to play* needs to be fully internalized. This involves studying different theoretical concepts, learning different styles of improvisation, listening to music, and practicing. Improvisation is similar to learning a new language. The first step involves the acquisition of essential words and grammar rules; these are then combined in simple sentences to enable basic communication. Similarly, in jazz improvisation we first acquire a basic vocabulary of chords, scales, and motifs along some normative voice-leading rules. Once we have internalized these chords and rules, we can create idiomatic improvisations of our own.

BLUES RIFFS

We begin our study of improvisation with the blues. Improvising on the blues presents an interesting situation because the task might not seem too complicated. After all, we can negotiate different blues progressions with only a blues scale and sound quite convincing. Studying blues improvisation, however, gives us a solid foundation that we can later develop and expand. The most basic strategy in learning blues improvisation involves playing simple melodic ideas derived from the blues scale, called **blues riffs**.

FIGURE 10.1 Two-Chorus Blues Solo

In using this approach, the negotiation of chord changes is not the main concern because blues riffs fit the structure of different chords and chord progressions. There is, however, one important aspect of our playing that requires attention, namely **rhythm**. Figure 10.1 illustrates a solo on the generic blues form that employs a variety of blues riffs.

These riffs have a characteristic melodic and rhythmic profile that influences the overall flow of the solo. The design of these riffs has a unique pitch structure that prioritizes the use of the blue notes. Figure 10.2 provides a compilation of one- and two-bar blues riffs starting on different pitches of the blues scale that can be explored during improvisation. It is worth noting that these riffs are just as effective in

FIGURE 10.2 Blues Riffs

improvising on the blues as they are in improvising on other types of tunes. While improvising on blues progressions, we will use these riffs at different locations within the form so that the phrasing does not follow the regularity of four-bar phrases of the blues in a predictable way.

THE ROLE OF GUIDE TONES

In Chapter 8, it was noted that harmonies can be represented horizontally as melodic lines and that melodic lines can be represented vertically as harmonic formations. This mutual interrelationship between chords and lines implies that the same rules of voice leading that control the behavior of chords will also control the behavior of melodic lines. The keyboard realization of the blues in Chapter 9 (Figure 9.7) involved placing the guide tones in the R.H. and chordal roots in the L.H. The harmonic guide tones from Figure 9.7 can be horizontalized as a melodic line. This line can literally guide us through the chord changes while improvising, hence the term **guide-tone improvisation**. The

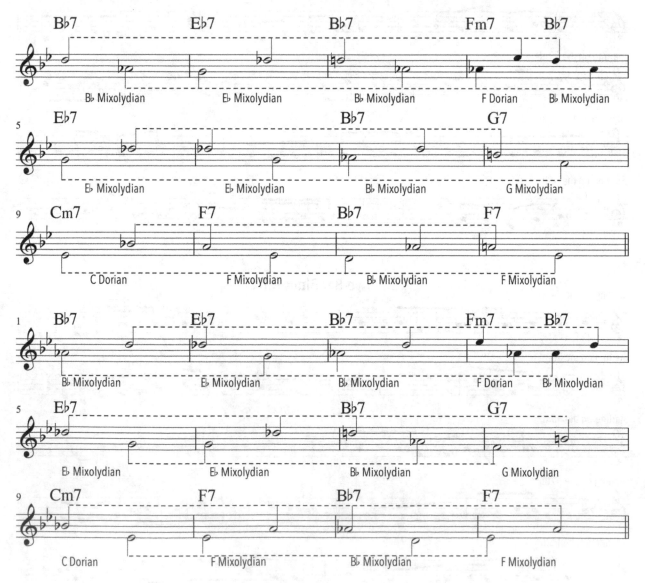

FIGURE 10.3 Guide-Tone Line: 3rds and 7ths

melodic line in Figure 10.3 consists of two half notes (or four quarter notes in m. 4) using 3rds and 7ths from the underlying harmonies. This apparently single-line melody is an example of a **compound melody**. Figure 10.3 shows the transformation of the vertical guide tones into two horizontal compound melodies beginning on the 3rd and the ♭7th, respectively, and suggests a chord–scale relationship that can be explored during improvisation. The implied contrapuntal lines are indicated with stems pointed in the same direction and attached to a dashed line.

THE CHARLESTON RHYTHM

By emphasizing a guide-tone line in our improvisation, we can clearly express the quality and function of underlying chords. To be successful at this type of improvisation, the horizontalized guide tones need to be metrically emphasized. We can begin by activating the line with the help of a two-note rhythmic gesture known as the **Charleston rhythm**.[1] This idiomatic rhythmic idea, along with the eight possible metric locations within the measure, is shown in Figure 10.4.

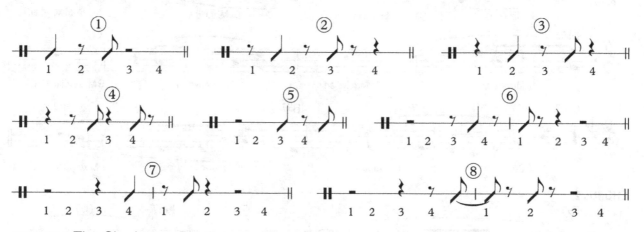

FIGURE 10.4 The Charleston Rhythm

EXPLORING GUIDE TONES

Using 3rds and 7ths

The guide-tone line establishes a chord–scale relationship with the underlying harmony that we need to preserve once we move away from improvising solely on a blues scale. Using the chord–scale relationships from Figures 10.3, 9.8, and 9.10, we will now demonstrate how the relationship between guide tones and corresponding scales might work in the context of a solo. In addition to establishing a convincing chord–scale relationship, the solo in Figure 10.5 also employs various incarnations of the Charleston rhythm.

FIGURE 10.5 Guide-Tone Improvisation

Using 3rds or 7ths

Another approach to practicing guide-tone improvisation involves embellishing only a single guide tone. Melodic activities can be organized either around the 3rd or the 7th of underlying chords. Figure 10.6 illustrates two structural lines of the blues that use the 3rds and the 7ths of corresponding chords, respectively.

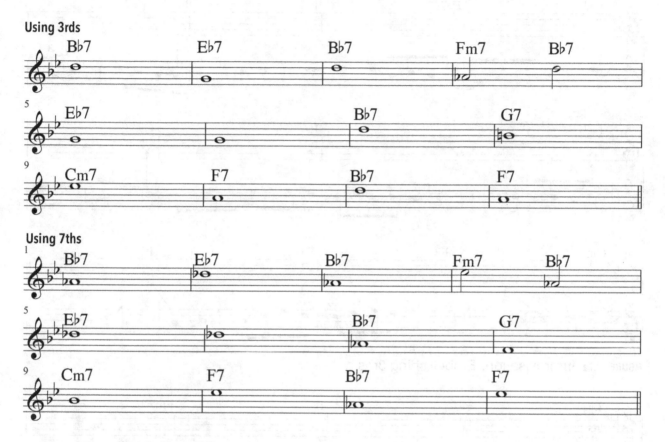

FIGURE 10.6 Two Guide-Tone Lines

With a single guide tone the structural line becomes more angular, thereby making the elaboration more challenging. Figures 10.7a and b demonstrate how to integrate individual guide tones within the context of a solo. Figure 10.7a prioritizes the 3rds and Figure 10.7b emphasizes the 7ths. Arrows indicate the metric placement of guide tones within the line.

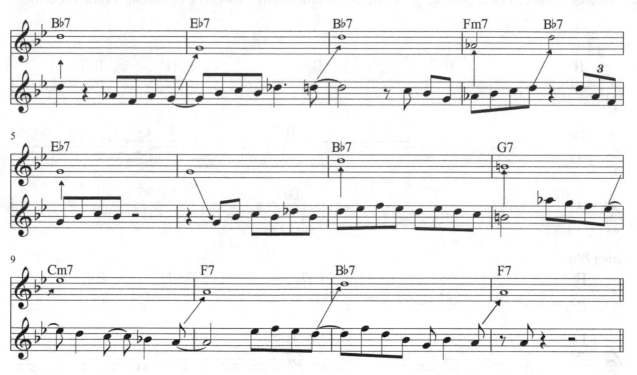

FIGURE 10.7a Improvisation: Embellishing 3rds

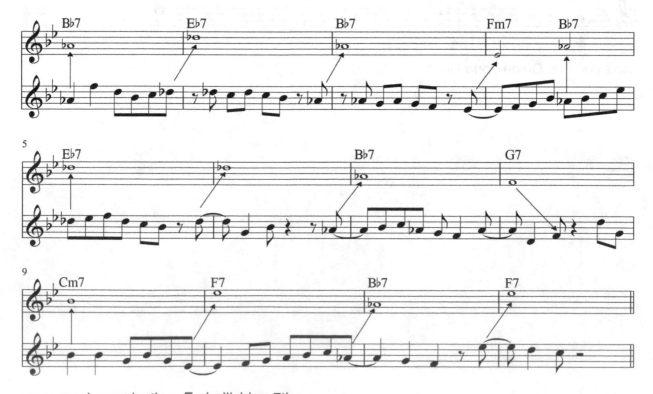

FIGURE 10.7b Improvisation: Embellishing 7ths

The 3rd and 7th lines

In preparing for improvisation, we can select a single line starting on the 3rd or the 7th and elaborate it with different melodic ideas. Such a line fulfills the rules of voice leading (the 3rd of a chord is retained

FIGURE 10.8a Improvisation: Embellishing a 3rd Line

FIGURE 10.8b Improvisation: Embellishing a 7th Line

or moves down by a half step; the 7th of a chord moves down by a half step to the 3rd of the next chord). Figure 10.8a illustrates a structural line (top staff) beginning on the 3rd and the melodic elaboration (bottom staff). Figure 10.8b shows a structural line beginning on the 7th and the subsequent elaboration. Notice the metric distribution of guide tones within these lines.

MOTIVIC DEVELOPMENT

Techniques of motivic development are innately connected with the art of composition and improvisation. Although these techniques may take many different forms, the underlying premise is to take a small melodic gesture, called a **motif**, and transform it in a logical, coherent, and musically satisfying manner. The use of motivic development provides structural coherence to improvisation. There are certain characteristics, however, that a motif should have to lend itself for musical development. These characteristics include a strong rhythmic profile, an interesting melodic shape, a clear harmonic structure, and a relatively short pitch duration. When examining motifs from jazz or classical literature (compiled in Figure 10.9), special attention should be paid to their strong rhythmic, melodic and harmonic characteristics, and above all, to their succinctness and memorability.

With their slow (or non-existent) harmonic rhythm, modal tunes are ideal vehicles for practicing improvisation and implementing different techniques of motivic development. Because the pitch content is fixed, the focus is on playing with a good sense of time and on the development of particular motifs.

FIGURE 10.9 Motifs from Literature

In the overview of techniques of motivic development, we will first demonstrate how to create a motif that successfully captures the sound of a given mode. Then the traditional techniques of motivic development will be examined, such as **repetition**, **transposition**, **expansion**, **interpolation**, **contraction**, **fragmentation**, and **inversion**. Finally, we will demonstrate how to implement these techniques in practice.

Broadly speaking, a motif should convey the sound of a specific mode, and display a strong melodic and rhythmic profile. Figure 10.10 provides a selection of motifs for diatonic and chromatic modes built on C. These will later be used for practicing motivic development with the play along tracks on the CW.

The pitch content of these motifs clearly projects the sound of corresponding modes, as each motif prioritizes the use of chord tones and beauty marks. The rhythm of each motif is representative of jazz syntax and has strong developmental potential.

FIGURE 10.10 Motifs for Practicing Improvisation

Repetition

The technique of repetition is based on either the **exact** or the **inexact** recurrence of the motif. Even though exact repetition might be redundant, occasionally it can be employed for melodic emphasis or for confirming musical ideas. Inexact repetition transforms the original motif using slight melodic and/or rhythmic modifications. These modifications typically involve pitch replacements or minor rhythmic displacements. Exact and inexact repetitions, as well as other motivic techniques, are illustrated in Figure 10.11.

Transposition

The technique of transposition transfers the original motif to a different pitch level. There are two forms of transposition: **tonal/modal** and **real**. Tonal/modal transposition preserves the underlying tonality/ modality of the motif. Thus, it allows for minor intervallic adjustments to the pitch structure of the original motif. Real transposition preserves the intervallic content of the motif when transposed to a different pitch level. The most obvious consequence of real transposition is the infusion of chromaticism and noticeable departures from the underlying tonal/modal center. With this technique, we can effectively control the ebb and flow of chromaticism and its impact on the music. To create a stark melodic contrast, for instance, we can transpose the motif by an interval that does not keep any notes in common between the original and its repetition. In order to exhibit a more controlled approach to improvisation, we can let the intervallic content of the original motif influence the level of transposition. Furthermore, to demonstrate traces of compositional thinking in our improvisation, we can control the level of transposition by implementing pitches from the original motif as roots of the transposed motifs. All of these possibilities are demonstrated in Figure 10.11.

Expansion and Interpolation

Expansions and interpolations are techniques of motivic development that add a new material to the original motif. Expansion adds a new melodic content at the end of the motif. Tangentially related to expansions, interpolations transform the original motif by inserting a new melodic material in the middle of its structure. Figure 10.11 illustrates the use of these techniques.

Contraction and Fragmentation

Contraction, which typically occurs in the context of longer gestures, shortens the length of the original motif. Subsequently, these shorter melodic cells might undergo the technique of fragmentation, which further allows for development through repetition, transposition, and/or expansion. The technique of fragmentation might be advanced through other means as well. For instance, we can partition the original motif into small melodic cells and then combine them using different motivic permutations. Figure 10.11 demonstrates the use of these techniques.

Inversion

The technique of motivic development known as inversion mirrors the intervallic content of the original motif. Just as in transposition, there are two types of inversions: **tonal/modal** and **real**. In tonal/modal inversion, the shape of the original motif is inverted in pitch space specific to the particular key or mode. Just as in tonal transposition, this technique usually does not preserve the intervallic content of the original

FIGURE 10.11 Techniques of Motivic Development

motif. Certain intervallic adjustments of the original motif are required in order to preserve the underlying tonality/modality. In real inversion, the intervallic content of the original motif is preserved and, as a result, chromatic pitches will likely occur. Using inversions in improvisation can be challenging because we have to quickly figure out intervallic inversions of the original motif and implement them in real time. In spite of these challenges, however, the use of inversion is a very powerful technique that can add more controlled variety in our playing. Figure 10.11 illustrates the use of two types of inversions, as well as other techniques of motivic development. Notice that the intervallic content of the original motif and its transformations are indicated with integers representing a number of semitones. A "+" and "–" indicate the direction of intervals: ascending and descending, respectively.

NOTE

1   The **Charleston rhythm** is derived from James P. Johnson's popular song "The Charleston" from 1923.

Intermediate

PART TWO

Voicing Formations

CHAPTER SUMMARY

Chapter 11 discusses three types of voicing paradigms: (1) upper-structure triads, (2) rootless formations, (3) incomplete, and explores their harmonic and voice-leading potentials.

CONCEPTS AND TERMS

- Dominant aggregate
- Incomplete voicings
- Polychords
- Rootless formations
- Upper-structure triads:
  - Major
  - Minor

UPPER-STRUCTURE TRIADS

The use of **upper-structure triads** involves the superimposition of major or minor triads on top of single notes, guide tones, triads, and intervallic structures. Upper-structure triads add a new set of practical and theoretical considerations. With this powerful tool, the number of ways to generate a collection of notes and harness it for compositional, improvisational, and orchestrational purposes is greatly increased. To notate these large harmonic formations, the so-called slash notation is implemented that makes complex chords relatively easy to interpret. Two types of slashes are employed: a diagonal slash that indicates an upper-structure triad written on the left side of the slash and superimposed on top of a single bass note; and a horizontal slash that indicates an upper-structure triad written on top, superimposed over a chord notated below the slash. The horizontal slash, then, denotes polychordal structures that can accommodate as many as eight distinct notes. The term **polychord** indicates two chords that sound simultaneously.

Upper-structure formations appear in different types of chords. In this chapter, they will be shown in the context of major-, minor-, and dominant 7th-type chords. While major- and minor-type chords feature some attractive voicing configurations using upper-structure triads, it is the dominant 7th that allows the largest and most diverse pairing of triads within its structure. As a result of such pairings, a remarkable family of polychordal formations with conventional and unconventional combinations of diatonic/chromatic extensions and pitch alterations occurs.

There are four **major upper-structure triads** built on **5, 2, 3,** and **7** that effectively extend the structure of any major-type chord.[1] Notice that the order in which these voicings appear in Figure 11.1 represents an inherent hierarchy that exists between them. That hierarchy refers to the degree of *dissonance* that each voicing projects and stems from the saturation of the specific extensions within each chord. In addition to four major structures, there are three **minor upper-structure triads** built on **3, 7,** and **#5** that enhance the sound of major-type chords, shown in Figure 11.1a.[2] When playing these chords in succession, notice that each chord gets gradually more intense as it accumulates more tension within its pitch content. The last polychordal structure with the minor triad on **#5** adds two highly dissonant extensions to the major chord proper: **#5** and **#9**. Whereas the former extension appears in the corresponding chromatic mode, Lydian Augmented, the latter might seem problematic on account of its close proximity to the major 3rd. As you examine the structure of that voicing more closely, however, notice that the upper chromatic extensions (**#5** and **#9**) establish a pattern of ascending thirds (starting with the root), which culminates on the **#9**. In order for that pitch to be syntactically correct and properly integrated within a voicing formation, the **#9** needs to be separated by a major 7th from the major 3rd and woven into the voicing by means of a recognizable tertian structure, such as the minor triad built on **#5**. Figure 11.1a illustrates the use of all upper-structure triads in the context of the major chord.

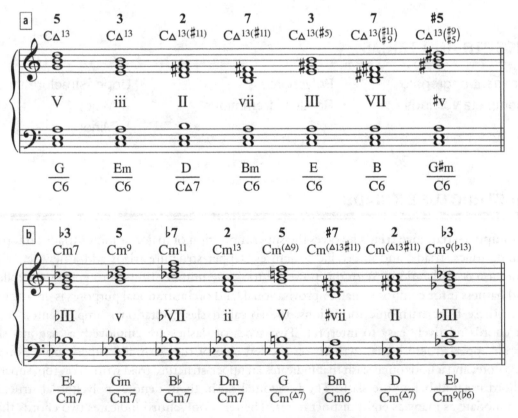

FIGURE 11.1 Upper-Structure Triads—Major and Minor Chords

In the case of minor chords shown in Figure 11.1b, there are four major upper-structure triads built on ♭3, ♭7, 5 and 2, and three minor upper-structure triads built on 5, 2, and #7. Notice that in major- and minor-type voicings, the L.H. features the root, 3rd and 6th or 7th as a harmonic foundation for the corresponding chords. The decision to use either a 6th or a 7th stems from the overall sound that the complete voicing projects. The only exception is the last minor-type chord, Cm9(♭13), which features the root, a ♭13, and a 9th in the L.H. That chord features a more contemporary sounding tonic with a characteristic major triad as the upper structure.

Broadly speaking, there are five major and five minor upper structures that can be added to the dominant 7th chord. The reason for this stems from the specific pitch combinations that these upper triads create and the voice-leading behaviors that the participating extensions and alterations project. The major upper structures are built on **2**, **♭3**, **♭5** (**♯4**), **♭6**, and **6**; they can effectively expand the dominant 7th chord with properly distributed extensions and alterations. In addition to five major upper structures, there are five minor upper structures that can also expand the structure of the dominant 7th chord. Minor triads are built on **♭2**, **♭3**, **♭5** (**♯4**), **5**, and **6**, and produce different distributions of chordal extensions and alterations. Figure 11.2 illustrates the distribution of major and minor upper-structure triads in the context of C7.

FIGURE 11.2 Upper-Structure Triads—Dominant 7th Chords

In order to implement these chords in practice, one must be able to identify them aurally. The first step in that process is to concentrate on the quality of the upper-structure triad. When the quality of the triad is identified, the recognition of the specific six-part formation depends on the ability to perceive the sound of individual extensions and pitch alterations. Extensions and alterations are characterized by a unique sound and project specific voice-leading behaviors. The ability to identify that behavior depends, in large part, on imagining the harmonic context in which a particular chord might appear. Figure 11.3 provides that context for all major and minor upper-structure triads appearing in dominant 7th chords.[3]

FIGURE 11.3 Resolution of Upper-Structure Triads

Figure 11.3 illustrates only one triadic inversion in upper parts; that choice stems from the overall sound quality of the progression as a whole. In studying these chord successions, pay close attention to the voice leading between chordal extensions and their resolutions. How would you characterize the behavior of inner voices?

Dominant Aggregate

Upper-structure formations are extremely useful in reharmonization. In order to internalize their pitch structure, they can be used to harmonize a chromatic scale without $\hat{4}$ and $\flat\hat{7}$. The ten-note scale represents all available notes that can feasibly participate in the dominant 7th chord. That collection of notes is known as the **dominant aggregate**. Simply put, in harmonizing the ten-note scale with upper-structure triads, we will explore the inversional potential of major and minor triads, exhaust all available triadic possibilities, and discover that certain pitches can support more than a single triad. Figure 11.4 demonstrates the harmonization of a dominant aggregate with the available upper-structure triads with the scale unfolding in the top voice.

FIGURE 11.4 Dominant Aggregate and Upper-Structure Triads

ROOTLESS FORMATIONS

Five-part chords are often used in an abbreviated form as **rootless formations**. As the name suggests, these types of chords leave out the root and employ the remaining notes to project the character of a chord. Without the root, a chord loses the fundamental pitch that enforces its quality, position, and function. Rootless chords tend to be harmonically and aurally more ambiguous than complete chords. Jazz musicians can capitalize on that ambiguity.

The concept of rootless formations brings up an important point about the role of the bass voice. In most performance situations the root is provided by the bass player. In chord progressions that feature rootless formations (i.e. comping) one can no longer rely on the lowest voice to articulate the changes of a tune, but should rely instead on principles of voice leading and counterpoint to supply clear indications of harmonic motion. Rootless formations are just as effective in expressing the meaning of chords and harmonic progressions as complete chords. Understandably, they are far more challenging to implement. In spite of these challenges—or because of them—they are harmonically more flexible and effective in covering all kinds of harmonic relationships.

Rootless formations can borrow chordal roots from other chords, which can redefine the harmonic/functional status of the given chord. What will soon be discovered is that most rootless chords look and sound quite familiar. In a certain sense, however, these familiar traits must be disregarded and a different root superimposed on the bottom of the chord must be imagined. Figure 11.5 provides three- and four-note rootless voicings for five-part chords along with their basic harmonic interpretations. Three-note rootless voicings further reduce the pitch content to its essential components. Some of these voicings cannot be analyzed with traditional chord symbols and get their harmonic meaning from a superimposed bass note or notes. They can, however, be analyzed as pitch-set classes (as some of them are). For the explanation of that methodology consult Chapter 24. To fully capitalize on their structural potential, explore their inversions/rotations.

FIGURE 11.5 Rootless Formations

INCOMPLETE VOICINGS

An incomplete voicing reduces the number of pitches to those that only convey the quality of a complete chord. The tonal definition of an incomplete voicing might not always be apparent. Its tonal and harmonic clarity depends on two factors: on which note or notes are going to be removed from a complete chord, and on how the intervallic content of a chord is diversified. In spite of their potentially ambiguous sound, however, incomplete voicings can be very effective as voice-leading formations, chordal substitutes, and intervallic structures. The different positions of five-part chords from Chapter 5 will be used to explore these types of formations.

To generate an incomplete voicing, follow these steps:

1. Remove a single pitch from a complete root-position five-part chord.
2. Transfer the ninth of a chord down an octave.
3. Rearrange the notes to create an open four-part voicing.

With these three steps, a large number of voicings (far too many to cover them all) are generated. Figure 11.6 demonstrates the three-step process of generating incomplete voicings.

FIGURE 11.6 Incomplete Voicing Formations

These incomplete voicings remove a 3rd, 5th, 6th, 7th, or 9th from a complete five-part chord. The choice of these notes is not entirely accidental. Granted, by not having a 3rd in the chord there is the potential risk of the lack of harmonic quality, and by not having a 7th, the functionality of a chord may be jeopardized. These incomplete voicings acquire their proper harmonic definition from a specific context in which they occur; in other words, any ambiguous sonority can be contextualized using correct voice leading and dissonance treatment. There is also an inherent logic to the removal of a 3rd and/or a 7th from a voicing. Note that the voicings lacking these pitches have a greater saturation of chromatic extensions. We can further experiment with incomplete voicing formations by removing the chordal root from a root-position five-part chord. Figure 11.7 demonstrates such a voicing for C7sus(#9,♭13) along with three harmonic progressions where that formation can be utilized.

FIGURE 11.7 Exploring Incomplete Formations

The pitch structure of this incomplete voicing hardly suggests a suspended dominant 7th chord. The notes F3, D♯4, A♭4, and B♭4 seem to be more closely related to Fm11 or a rootless B♭7sus than to C7sus(♯9,♭13). While all these harmonic readings are acceptable, in practice they need to be properly contextualized and correctly realized. In the progressions from Figure 11.7, the incomplete voicing exhibits different functional and contrapuntal behaviors. In Figure 11.7a, for instance, the Fm11 chord functions as the final tonic; in Figure 11.7b, a rootless B♭7sus functions as a suspended dominant resolving directly to the E♭M7 chord; and in Figure 11.7c, C7sus(♯9,♭13) functions as a suspended dominant resolving to C7, and subsequently, to Fm11. The same voicing can function as the tonic, dominant, or predominant, in different keys. That challenge was accomplished through careful voice-leading considerations and a proper placement of the incomplete formation within the progressions. In harmonic progressions from Figure 11.7, the rootless C7sus(♯9,♭13) sounds convincing and demonstrates that these types of chords are well suited for all kinds of harmonic and functional manipulations. Their inherent ambiguity is, in fact, their biggest asset and can be effectively explored. With such a huge potential for harmonic reinterpretation, incomplete voicings constitute great resources for advancing our own harmonic experiments and expanding our harmonic vocabulary.

NOTES

1   The relationship between the root of the major, minor, and dominant 7th chord and the root of the upper structure is explained using Arabic numbers. Major upper structures are notated with uppercase Roman numerals: II on **2**, V on **5**, ♭III on ♭**3**, etc. For instance, a B♭ major triad in the context of Gm7 is notated as ♭III, yet the same triad in the context of E7 is notated as ♭V or ♯IV.

2   Minor upper structures are notated using lowercase Roman numerals: ii on **2**, ♭ii on ♭**2**, ♭iii on ♭**3**, v on **5**, etc. For instance, an A minor triad in the context on Gm7 is notated as ii, and that same triad in the context on C7 is notated as vi.

3   For a complete list of V⁷–I (i) progressions with properly resolved upper structures, visit the CW.

Keyboard and Jazz Chorale Textures

CHAPTER SUMMARY

Chapter 12 introduces six basic models of realizing harmonic progressions on the keyboard. These models establish the foundation for more advanced methods of keyboard realization referred to as *jazz chorale five-voice* and *jazz chorale four-voice* texture.

CONCEPTS AND TERMS

- Ghost notes
- Jazz chorale style
- Keyboard style
- Model I
- Model II
- Model III
- Model IV
- Model V
- Model VI
- Walking bass line
- Walk down
- Walk up

MODELS OF KEYBOARD STYLE TEXTURE

The ability to realize harmonic progressions on the keyboard is an essential skill for the contemporary jazz musician, regardless of her/his primary instrument. The forthcoming models of keyboard playing will help to accomplish this objective. Models I through VI feature techniques of keyboard playing that are fully functional (models II, IV, and VI) and preparatory (models I, III, and V). Mastery of these models is required to advance one's skills and progress to more complex techniques of keyboard realization known as **jazz chorale styles**. Just as models I through VI get progressively more intricate, so do the two jazz chorale styles: (1) in five voices and (2) in four voices. The fundamental difference between the six models of keyboard playing and the two jazz chorale styles is the overall distribution of voices between hands. In **keyboard style**, the left hand provides the harmonic support using: (1) roots only in 1:1 ratio, (2) roots, thirds, or fifths in 2:1 ratio (two feel), and (3) walking bass line (with idiomatic melodic embellishments). Although each model introduces a specific bass pattern, it is highly recommended to practice all models with alternate left hand patterns. These models (particularly models II, IV, and VI) can be used as effective textures for accompaniment. The overall perception of harmony in *keyboard style* textures is more vertical rather than linear.

In jazz chorale textures, the distribution of voices between hands is more equitable; in five-voice jazz chorale, the left hand (L.H.) controls two voices and the right hand (R.H.) three voices; in four-voice jazz chorale, both hands control two voices. Not only do jazz chorale textures prioritize individual voices and focus on linear characteristics of harmonic progressions, but they also pave new paths for the discovery of less conventional harmonic substitutions. Needless to say, both keyboard style and jazz chorale textures are very practical, and their mastery will enable you to develop a more cultivated insight into the wonderful world of jazz harmony.

Model I

- Guide-tone lines in the R.H.

- Roots of chords in the L.H. in 1:1 ratio with the R.H.

Figure 12.1 demonstrates **Model I** using a basic blues progression in F. In your practice, invert the content of the R.H.

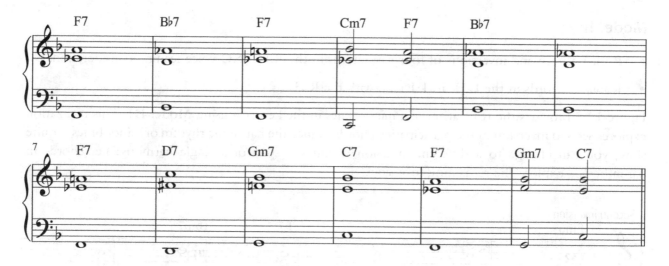

FIGURE 12.1 Keyboard Realization: Model I

Model II

- Rhythmicized guide tones in the R.H.

- Roots, 3rds, or 5ths (and diatonic/chromatic passing notes) in the L.H. in 2:1 ratio with the R.H.

Figure 12.2 illustrates the use of **Model II** in the context of a basic blues progression in C. The R.H. distributes the Charleston rhythm at different locations within the measure. A faster harmonic rhythm in the L.H. creates what jazz musicians call the *two feel*, which is an attractive way of energizing the harmonic content of a progression. In the case of two chords per measure, the L.H. alternates between roots and 3rds (5ths) or roots and 5ths (3rds). In the case of a single harmony occupying the space of two measures (mm. 5–6), the L.H. anticipates the arrival of the next harmony in a linear fashion by employing the diatonic B♭2 and the chromatic B♮2 passing notes. These two notes make the arrival of the root of C7 more forceful and inevitable. The arrival of A7 in m. 8 is prepared with a diatonic passing note, B♭2. In your practice, explore the potential of invertible counterpoint in the R.H. and come up with a different L.H. content.

FIGURE 12.2 Keyboard Realization: Model II

Model III

- Root-position and inversions of four-part chords in the R.H. (NO voice-leading considerations).

- Roots of chords in the L.H. in 1:1 ratio with the R.H.

Figure 12.3 provides the realization of a minor blues in the key of F using **Model III**. This realization explores second inversion of the participating chords. (Since the harmonic rhythm of minor blues is quite slow, you can change to a different inversion within the span of a single harmony: i.e. chords in parenthesis.) Explore the remaining inversions.

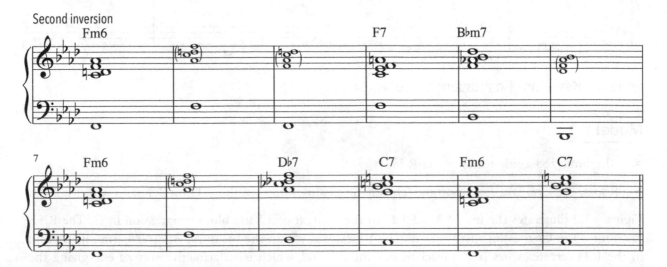

FIGURE 12.3 Keyboard Realization: Model III

Model IV

- Root-position and inversions of four-part chords in the R.H. realized with good voice leading.

- Roots, 3rds, or 5ths in the L.H. in either 1:1 or 2:1 ratio with the R.H.

In order to realize harmonic progressions using **Model IV**, you need to resolve the 3rds and 7ths of corresponding chords properly and remember about the rules of good voice leading between chords (i.e. common-tone retention, stepwise motion, and contrary outer-voice counterpoint). The realization of a minor blues begins on the first inversion of Fm6, which in turn affects the subsequent voice leading of the entire progression. In your practice, explore the remaining inversions of chords.

FIGURE 12.4 Keyboard Realization: Model IV

Model V

- Rootless five-part chords in the R.H. (NO voice-leading considerations).

- Roots, 3rds, or 5ths of chords in the L.H. in 2:1 ratio with the R.H.

Broadly speaking, rootless formations omit the root of the chord from their structure. With rootless five-part chords, the upper four-part structure is placed in the R.H. and the root in the L.H. Some of the R.H. shapes look, sound, and feel familiar, since they have already been encountered as four-part chords in the context of **Model III** and **Model IV**. Similar to **Model III**, we will first acquaint ourselves with four rotations of the rootless formation. Figure 12.5 shows the use of **Model V** in the context of the A section of Jerome Kern's "All the Things You Are." This realization investigates only the third position of the participating chords.[1]

FIGURE 12.5 Keyboard Realization: Model V

Model VI

- Rootless five-part chords in the R.H. realized with good voice leading.

- Roots of chords in the L.H. in 1:1 ratio with the R.H.

- Walking bass line in the L.H. with rhythmicized rootless formations in the R.H.

Figure 12.6 illustrates a realization of "All the Things You Are" using **Model VI**. Figure 12.6a demonstrates a more basic realization of the progression and Figure 12.6b highlights a full-fledged rendition of the progression with the walking bass in the L.H. In both realizations, the motion between chords is governed by the principles of good voice leading.

FIGURE 12.6 Keyboard Realization: Model VI

A good walking bass line clearly delineates the underlying chords with stepwise motion and chordal arpeggiation. The use of chordal arpeggiation is an effective technique and it clearly captures the tonal essence of the underlying harmonies. If overused, however, this technique tends to be predictable and bereft of melodic interest. A better way of generating convincing walking bass lines mixes the use of stepwise motion with arpeggiation in a balanced way. The design of the bass line in mm. 1–2 features an arpeggiation of Fm9 immediately followed by a stepwise **walk up** in m. 2. The melodic ascend from Bb2 to Eb3 in m. 2 employs a chromatic passing note on beat 4 offset by a diatonic descend, **walk down**, from Eb3 to Ab2 in m. 3. As a rule of thumb, when connecting chords related by 5ths, the melodic ascend requires a chromatic passing note on beat 4 and the melodic descend travels that distance diatonically. In the case of two chords per measure, as in m. 6, a straightforward arpeggiation pattern alternating the root/5th and root/3rd pairs should suffice. The use of **ghost note** embellishments constitutes yet another idiomatic feature of an effective bass line. Ghost note embellishments in Figure 12.6b employ an array of melodic intervals (3rd in m. 4; 4th in m. 8; 5ths in mm. 2 and 5; and 8ves in mm. 3, 4, 6, and 7) and triplet figures (m. 7). In conclusion, a convincing walking bass balances the use of arpeggiation with stepwise motion, changes the melodic contour with the arrival of new chords, introduces chromaticism in the context of passing notes, uses ghost note and triplet note embellishments, and clearly delineates the underlying harmonic progression.

JAZZ CHORALE—FIVE-VOICE TEXTURE

The aforementioned models of keyboard realization offer a solid foundation for more advanced methods of realizing chord progressions on the keyboard known as **chorale style**. In the traditional *chorale style* four-voice texture (i.e. J.S. Bach's renditions of chorale melodies or Abbé Vogler's "improved" modal harmonizations of chorales), both hands control two voices: the R.H. the soprano and the alto voices, and the L.H. the tenor and the bass voices.[2] The reason for the equal voice distribution is both practical and conceptual. With two voices per hand, it is much easier to handle the content of each voice in a complementary fashion especially when supplying additional melodic diminutions. By focusing on linear properties of participating voices, the resulting harmony becomes a byproduct of contrapuntal interactions between lines and *not* a collection of vertically unfolding block-like structures.

In this section, the focus is on the two variants of jazz chorale texture: (1) in five voices, with 2+3 voice distribution, and (2) in four voices, with 2+2 voice distribution. Since both variants employ different four-part, five-part, and larger harmonic structures, some formations need to be reduced to their five- or four-part counterparts, respectively. The control and projection of larger structures in four voices is more challenging as it involves necessary pitch omissions. In five-part jazz chorale texture the issue of pitch omission also exists, but to a much lesser degree than it does in four-voice texture. As far as voicings of chords in jazz chorale texture are concerned, we will rely on the familiar "drop 2" technique introduced in Chapter 4 with slight modifications.

The most common way of handling "drop 2" chords places two voices in the L.H. and three voices in the R.H. In the case of five-part chords, the upper four-part structure can be rotated four times. There are four unique "drop 2" voicing arrangements for any complete five-part chord.[3] Figure 12.7 summarizes these techniques using the C9(b5) chord as a model.

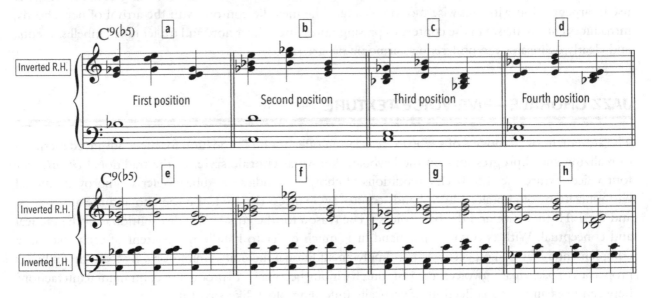

FIGURE 12.7 Positions of C9(♭5)

In order to be prepared for every eventuality that comes our way while realizing chord progressions, we can think more carefully about the structure of five-part chords in terms of invertible counterpoint. Since the R.H. contains three-note voicings, its content can be inverted three times; the L.H. content can be inverted twice. Figure 12.8 illustrates this principle using C9(♭5).

FIGURE 12.8 Voicing Explorations of C9(♭5)

In Figures 12.8a–12.8d, the content of the R.H. features three inverted structures superimposed over a fixed L.H. content. As far as the structure of individual chords is concerned, make sure that the distance between the top note in the L.H. and the lowest note in the R.H. does not exceed an octave. Figures 12.8e–12.8h exploit the potential of the inverted L.H. pitch content. The inverted L.H. renders certain chords without the root; this transformation might redefine the tonal status of some chords (Figures 12.8f and 12.8h) and leave them unusable in certain harmonic situations, particularly if the root functions as a harmonic provider.[4] On the other hand, the tonal status of rootless chords can be determined based on the context in which they occur, and their tonal status can be confirmed based on the voice leading, counterpoint, and metric position.

Figure 12.9 realizes a II–V–I progression using jazz chorale texture in five voices.

Figure 12.9 includes four realizations of the progression. Each realization begins with a different "drop 2" five-part voicing, which, in turn, influences the unfolding of the progression and the underlying voice leading. If the first chord, Dm9, is in the *first position*, as in Figure 12.9a, then the following chord, G9sus, is in the *third position*. The third chord of the progression, G7(♭9,♭13), retains its structure from

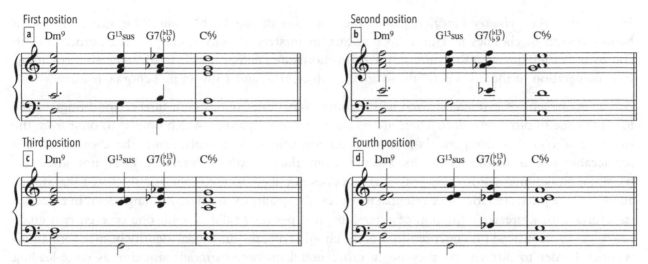

FIGURE 12.9 The II–V–I Progression—Jazz Chorale Texture in Five Voices

the predominant preparation, G13sus, and moves down a fifth to the *first position* of C6/9. In chords moving by descending 5ths (the most common chord succession in tonal jazz), the specific predictions and generalizations can be made regarding the behavior of chords: if the opening chord is in *first*, *second*, *third*, or *fourth* position then the subsequent chord is in *third*, *fourth*, *first*, or *second* position, respectively. Keeping in mind these general observations helps to navigate through any jazz progression with a correct and predetermined voice leading.

Figure 12.10 explores the potential of the inverted R.H. content.

FIGURE 12.10 Jazz Chorale Texture in Five Voices—Invertible Counterpoint

The opening chord, Dm9, is in the *second position*, which features an attractive intervallic structure with a characteristic major 9th in the L.H. There are three unique renditions of this progression based on the inverted R.H. content. Even though the pitch content stays exactly the same, the sound of each progression is considerably different on account of the unique pitch organization of each voicing.

JAZZ CHORALE—FOUR-VOICE TEXTURE

The jazz chorale four-voice texture follows in the footsteps of the time-honored harmonizations of chorale melodies by J.S. Bach. As such, the jazz chorale texture features equal distribution of voices between the hands. The most crucial difference between chorale harmonizations by Bach and our attempt at imitation is the greatly expanded harmonic palette that we have at our disposal. Whereas Bach's harmonies consist primarily of triads and 7th chords, jazz harmonies feature extended structures where the

7th chord is the *primary* sonority, just as the triad was during Bach's time. One glance at Bach's harmonization of chorales in Figure 23.1 reveals his mastery of voice leading, and treatment of 7th chords and other dissonant formations. Just as 7th chords are carefully handled with a stepwise/common-tone preparation of the dissonant 7th, so are the 9ths, 11ths, and 13ths in jazz chorale texture.

A rich assortment of extended harmonic structures complicates things even further and brings to the fore the issue of pitch omission. There are no clear-cut rules regarding which note(s) to omit from the structure of complete five-part, six-part, or larger formations. As a general rule, the chordal 5th is a replaceable chord member and its absence from the chord's architecture does not affect its harmonic/functional status. This generalization does not apply to the chromatic shades of the 5th: ♭5 and ♯5. These pitch alterations are essential to express the quality of chords containing them. In extended structures with a greater saturation of extensions, it is perfectly valid to omit one or even two guide tones and focus instead on upper tensions of the chord. True, the functional identity of such formations is much harder to discern, yet they might prove useful in some harmonic situation as voice-leading formations. In some instances, the incomplete chord may also appear without the root, which further conceals its intended tonal meaning. Tonal and functional ambiguities are innately entwined with the structure of incomplete chords and these ambiguities lead to the exploration of their inexhaustible harmonic potentials.

Figure 12.11 illustrates a II–V–I progression realized in jazz chorale four-voice texture.

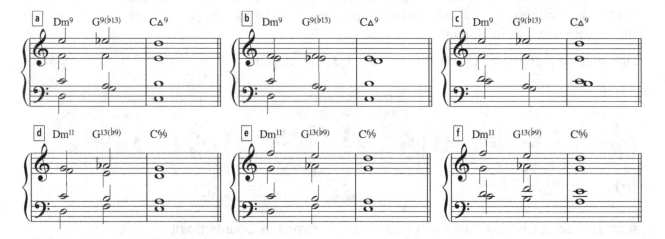

FIGURE 12.11 The II–V–I Progression—Jazz Chorale Texture in Four Voices

Figures 12.11a–c include four-part reductions of chords with the root in the bass coupled with the use of invertible counterpoint in both hands; Figures 12.11d–f add some rootless chords to the mix. Notice that Dm9 (Figures 12.11a–c) omits the chordal 5th; G9(♭13) substitutes the 3rd with the 9th; and CM9 dispenses with the 5th. In Figures 12.11d–f, Dm11 omits the 5th and the 9th; G13(♭9) is a rootless formation with the guide tones in the L.H., and C6/9 is yet another rootless formation. The use of invertible counterpoint is reserved for the specific structures that lend themselves for such contrapuntal manipulations. For instance, the R.H. content can be freely inverted, as demonstrated in Figures 12.11b and 12.11e, without jeopardizing the identity of participating chords. The use of inverted L.H. proceeds more judiciously and applies only to the chords that remain tonally and functionally intact. For instance, in Figure 12.11c the L.H. of Dm9 is inverted and, as a result, that inverted sonority is heard as a clear predominant formation. If you try to invert the original major 2nd in the L.H. (G9(♭13) in Figure 12.11a or 12.11c), the new structure would not have been too convincing because: (1) a much greater intervallic distance between the bass and the tenor voice would have influenced the status of the lowest pitch as the chordal root (which it is not), and (2) the overall perception of functionality/tonality of the progression would have been impacted as a result. Figures 12.11d–f feature rootless formations. Here, the issue of pitch omission is fairly straightforward because in rootless structures the chordal root is simply omitted. These types of formations are perfectly invertible. As stated earlier, the guide tones in the L.H. are ideal candidates for invertible counterpoint; when inverted, they change neither the functional status of chords nor their quality.

NOTES

1   In your practice, explore the remaining positions of the participating chords.
2   J.S. Bach's *371 Harmonized Chorales and 69 Chorale Melodies with Figured Bass* and Abbé Vogler's *Choral-System*.
3   As a reminder, the "drop 2" technique does not affect the chordal root; the second pitch from the top is dropped down an octave and placed above the chordal root.
4   The inverted L.H. works best with rootless chords, particularly those that feature guide tones and/or pairs of extensions.

Idiomatic Jazz Progressions

CHAPTER SUMMARY

Chapter 13 investigates two- and four-bar jazz progressions. It also focuses on aural identification and keyboard realization of non-modulatory and modulatory phrases with various ii–V^7 or ii$^\emptyset$–V^7 interpolations.

CONCEPTS AND TERMS

- *Coltrane* substitutions
- Dominant saturation
- Harmonic contrafact
- Harmonic ellipsis
- Harmonic progressions:
  - *Countdown*
  - *Giant Steps*

- – *Lady Bird*
- Major-third cycles
- Modulation
- Symmetrical intervallic cycles
- Tag endings
- Tonic prolongation

- Tritone invariance
- Tritone substitutions
- Turnarounds
- Turnbacks
- ii–V^7 diminutions

TRITONE SUBSTITUTIONS

The ii–V^7–I progression constitutes the perfect vehicle to introduce one of the most important features of jazz harmony: the **tritone substitution**, notated as **TR/X**. The tritone substitution has its theoretical origins in the equal or symmetrical division of the octave. This substitution is associated with the dominant 7th chord and capitalizes on inversional **invariance** of the tritone inherent to the dominant 7th formation. The interval of a tritone between the 3rd and the 7th is invariant (i.e. remains unchanged) when the root of a dominant 7th is replaced by the root of another dominant 7th chord tritone away. By virtue of sharing the same tritone, which contains the most essential notes from the chord, the two dominant 7th chords also share the same functional status. The symbol **TR/X** indicates a tritone substitute formation in relation to some dominant 7th chord. For instance, a TR/V in the key of C major stands for the Db7 chord, because Db7 is the tritone substitution of G7; a TR/VI in the same key indicates

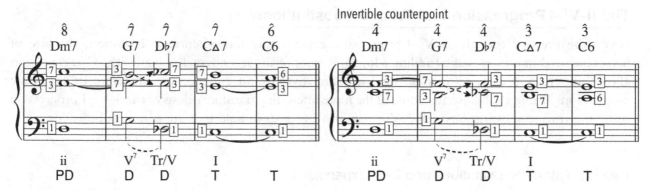

FIGURE 13.1 Tritone Substitution

E♭7 as the tritone substitution of A7. In both cases the chordal roots of the diatonic and chromatic 7th chords are a tritone apart. Figure 13.1 explains inversional invariance of the tritone using a ii–V⁷–I progression in C major.

The tritone F4–B4 is invariant when the root of D♭7 replaces the root of G7. With that root replacement, the 3rd and the 7th swap their chord tone status: the 3rd of V⁷ becomes the enharmonic 7th of TR/V, and the 7th of V⁷ becomes the 3rd of TR/V. As functionally equivalent dominant 7ths, V⁷ and TR/V are ideal substitutes of one another. If any dominant 7th chord is replaced by its tritone substitution then the chord tones, extensions, and alterations swap their melodic status as well. Table 13.1 illustrates that relationship.

TABLE 13.1 The Status of Chord Tones, Alterations, and Extensions

Dominant 7th—X⁷	Tritone Substitution—TR/X
root	flat five—♭5 or sharp eleventh—♯11th
third—3rd	flat seventh—♭7th
fifth—5th	flat ninth—♭9th
flat seventh—♭7th	third—3rd
major ninth—9th	flat thirteenth—♭13th
flat ninth—♭9th	fifth—5th
sharp ninth—♯9th	major thirteenth—13th
flat five—♭5 or sharp eleventh—♯11th	root
major thirteenth—13th	sharp ninth—♯9th
sharp five—♯5 or flat thirteenth—♭13th	major ninth—9th

The ii–V⁷–I Progression and Tritone Substitutions

Given the premise that the ii–V⁷–I progression expands the fundamental V–I motion, the rate of harmonic rhythm is increased by adding a local ii in front of any secondary dominant 7th. That expansion allows for creative ways to manipulate harmonic rhythm and enhance the structure of harmonic progressions. Table 13.2 illustrates some of the more interesting transformations of the ii–V⁷–I progression using the tritone substitutions and ii–V⁷ expansions. Chords in bold indicate tritone substitutions.

TABLE 13.2 Tritone Substitutions and ii–V⁷ Expansions

Dm7	G7	CM7	C6
Dm7	G7 **D♭7**	CM7	C6
D7	G7	CM7	C6
A♭7	G7	CM7	C6
A♭7	**D♭7**	CM7	C6
A♭7	A♭m7 **D♭7**	CM7	C6
E♭m7 **A♭7**	Dm7 G7	CM7	C6
D7 **A♭7**	G7	CM7	C6
D7 **A♭7**	G7 **D♭7**	CM7	C6
E♭m7 **A♭7**	A♭m7 **D♭7**	CM7	C6
Dm7 E♭m7 **A♭7**	G7 A♭m7 **D♭7**	CM7	C6
Dm7 **A♭7**	E♭m7 **A♭7** Dm7 **D♭7**	CM7	C6
D7 E♭m7 **A♭7**	A♭m7 **D♭7** D7 **D♭7**	CM7	C6
D7 E♭m7 **A♭7**	D7 **A♭7** G7 **D♭7**	CM7	C6

TURNAROUNDS

In addition to the ii–V⁷–I and ii⁰–V⁷–i progressions, there are other harmonic progressions that often occur in standard tunes. Probably the most recognizable progression is a **turnaround**, also known as a **turnback**. The turnaround is a two- or four-bar progression, usually with a faster harmonic rhythm that typically occurs at the end of 8- or 16-bar phrases. One of the formal functions of the turnaround is to effectively prepare the arrival of the *top of the chorus* by ushering in a familiar chord progression.[1] Just as the ii–V⁷–I progression can be transformed with different harmonic substitutions, so too can turnarounds.

The I–vi–ii–V⁷ Progression

Figure 13.2 shows a diatonic I–vi–ii–V⁷ progression realized using **Model IV** of keyboard style playing.

FIGURE 13.2 The I–vi–ii–V⁷ Turnaround

This progression extends the diatonic ii–V⁷–I by another fifth-related chord built on $\hat{6}$. The submediant chord in the major key has a dual harmonic function: tonic and predominant. In the context of this progression, the vi chord functions as a **tonic prolongation** or tonic expansion. To *prolong* a chord means to use an auxiliary chord (or chords) that shares the same harmonic function with the chord being prolonged.

Harmonic Transformations

Jazz musicians often use different harmonic substitutions to modify the content of diatonic progressions. The most common harmonic modifications of the I–vi–ii–V⁷ progression involve the use of secondary dominant chords (V/X), and tritone substitutions (TR/X). Figure 13.3 demonstrates these substitutions using **Model VI** of harmonic realization.

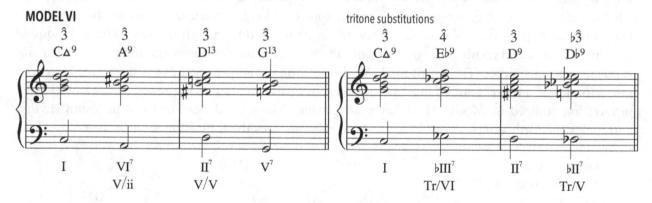

FIGURE 13.3 Tritone Substitutions in the I–vi–ii–V⁷ Progression

The secondary dominant 7ths A9 and D13 are analyzed with two different Roman numeral labels: (1) VI⁷ and V/ii, and (2) II⁷ and V/V, that can be used interchangeably. The tritone substitutions, E♭9 and D♭9, also use two Roman numerals: (1) ♭III⁷ and TR/VI, and (2) ♭II⁷ and TR/V, respectively.

TAG ENDINGS

Tag endings are somewhat related to turnarounds in their basic harmonic structure, but play different roles in tunes and complete performances. A tag ending occurs at the very end of a tune, repeats a chord sequence (which in the course of subsequent repetitions becomes harmonically transformed), and has an indeterminate duration. Only the final repetition of the tag ending progression is harmonically closed with a clear confirmation of the tonic. Its basic role in the performance is to provide a satisfactory, coda-like ending with a final improvisational flair. As Miles Davis demonstrated on his many recordings, tag endings may take a life of their own—especially with Herbie Hancock, Ron Carter, and Tony Williams in the rhythm section—and frequently exceeded the length of his solos.[2]

Tag endings and turnarounds often share similar chord progressions: the only difference between the I–vi–ii–V[7] and the iii–vi–ii–V[7] is that the former begins on the tonic and the latter on the mediant chord. These two chords, I and iii, are said to be functionally equivalent and are frequently used as substitutes of one another. Figure 13.4 illustrates a iii–vi–ii–V[7] tag ending progression realized with **Model II** of keyboard playing. Each measure displaces the Charleston rhythm by a half beat.

FIGURE 13.4 Tag Endings

Each of these chords can be further substituted by a secondary dominant 7th and, subsequently, by a TR/X. Since a tag ending progression is usually four bars long, we can demonstrate the use of two harmonic techniques that will double the rate of harmonic rhythm in each measure. The technique of **dominant saturation** combines two dominant 7th chords, diatonic or chromatic and its TR/X (or vice versa) next to each other. The use of the **ii–V[7] diminution** technique expands any dominant 7th chord into a local ii–V[7] progression. Figure 13.5 demonstrates these techniques in the context of a iii–vi–ii–V[7] progression realized in **Model II** of keyboard playing. The second note of the Charleston rhythm anticipates the forthcoming chord by a half beat; this enhances the forward motion of the progression.

FIGURE 13.5 Harmonic Expansions

THE CYCLE OF DOMINANT 7ths PROGRESSION

Probably the most famous occurrence of the cycle of dominant 7ths progression is in the bridge of "I Got Rhythm," by George and Ira Gershwin. In the discussion of secondary dominants the term *the dominant of the dominant* was used to indicate the relationship between the secondary dominant, V/V, and the structural dominant 7th, V^7. Since the cycle of dominant 7ths progression uses three secondary dominants prior to the structural dominant 7th, that progression can be called by a very long and impractical name: *the dominant of the dominant of the dominant of the dominant 7th.* Or a more practical way to name it is to use Roman numerals: V/vi–V/ii–V/V–V^7 or III^7–VI^7–II^7–V^7.

Figure 13.6 illustrates two cycles of dominant 7ths progression in the key of C major: *diatonic* realized in **Model IV** of keyboard playing, and chromatic with tritone substitutions in m. 2 and m. 4 using **Model VI.**[3]

FIGURE 13.6 The Cycle of Dominant 7ths Progression

THE *LADY BIRD* PROGRESSION

The terms *turnaround* and *tag ending* are generic labels that do not indicate a particular chord sequence; rather, they suggest the specific formal function of these progressions. In jazz, there is a certain subset of harmonic progressions whose names suggest specific chord successions. When jazz musicians use the term the **Lady Bird** progression, for instance, it connotes a particular chromatic turnaround from Tadd Dameron's tune of the same title recorded in 1947. Figure 13.7 illustrates the chord structure of that progression using **Model VI** of keyboard playing. Notice that each progression features slightly different walking bass patterns and the rhythmic content in the R.H.

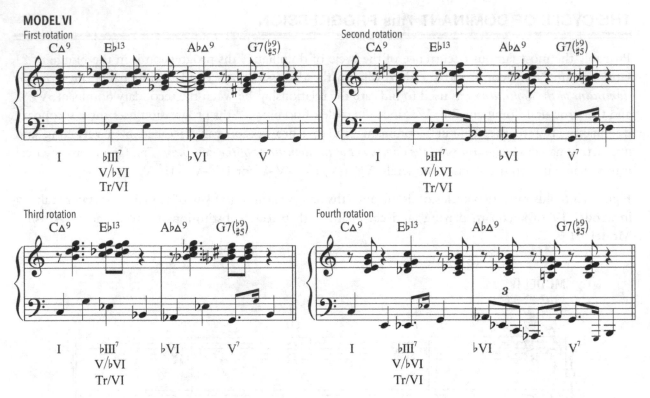

FIGURE 13.7 The "Lady Bird" Progression

As indicated with Roman numerals, the E♭7 chord can be explained as a tritone substitution of A7 or as a tonicization of the ♭VI key area. The ♭VI key area establishes a major third-relation with the underlying tonic. Dameron's iconic progression foreshadows even more daring harmonic experiments with the complete major-third cycles that came to fruition in John Coltrane's composition "Giant Steps."

COLTRANE SUBSTITUTIONS

John Coltrane's recording of *Giant Steps* in 1959 epitomized his three-year period of harmonic explorations, most notably with **symmetrical intervallic cycles**.[4] His composition "Countdown," which is a **harmonic contrafact** on Miles Davis's "Tune Up," illustrates the use of *Coltrane* substitutions. Characterized by fast harmonic rhythm, this substitution projects a **major-third cycle** in which each local major 7th chord is tonicized with the corresponding dominant 7th. In the context of the Dm7–G7–CM7 progression shown in Figure 13.8, the first member of the major-third cycle, ♭VI, is accessed through its dominant 7th that follows the structural predominant, ii. The next member of the major-third cycle, III, is also preceded by its dominant, V/III, before the progression completes its trajectory with the structural dominant 7th resolving to the tonic. The progression in Figure 13.8 is realized with the jazz chorale five-part texture using two voices in the L.H. and three voices in the R.H.

The *Giant Steps* **progression** is closely related to the *Countdown* **progression** with one exception: it forms a complete major-third cycle, thus dividing the octave into equidistant major 3rds. Figure 13.9 illustrates the harmonic structure of the *Giant Steps* progression in the key of C major using **Model VI** of keyboard playing.

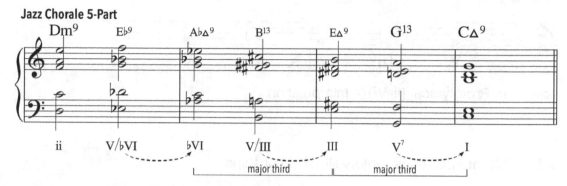

FIGURE 13.8 The "Countdown" Progression

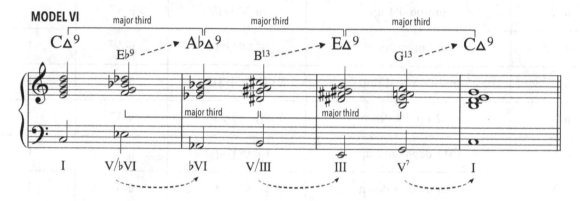

FIGURE 13.9 The "Giant Steps" Progression

AURAL IDENTIFICATION OF FOUR-BAR PROGRESSIONS

The [ii–V⁷]/X Interpolation

The focus now shifts to identifying and realizing four-bar phrases with diatonic or chromatic [ii–V⁷]/X interpolations. A [ii–V⁷]/X indicates an incomplete ii–V⁷ of one of 11 possible local tonics to which the progression could potentially resolve. This type of chord interpolation represents a **harmonic ellipsis**. The harmonic ellipsis, which in this case includes an incomplete II–V progression, is notated in square brackets with a Roman numeral indicating the *non-existent* resolution. In other words, square brackets indicate the use of incomplete II–V progressions and the Roman numeral shows the resolution had the progression been carried to its conclusion. In the generic prototype shown in Figure 13.10, a [ii–V⁷]/X is inserted between two structural ii–V⁷s.

In learning to identify these progressions aurally, two approaches are employed: (1) focus on the intervallic distance between individual chords, and (2) focus on the intervallic distance between diatonic and interpolated ii–V⁷s. Table 13.3 lists all possible [ii–V⁷]/X and specifies the intervallic relationship between the structural ii–V⁷ and a [ii–V⁷]/X interpolation: the first interval indicates the distance between V⁷ and [ii] and the second interval between the ii and a [ii]. The phrases in Table 13.3 are organized from the easiest to the most difficult to identify aurally.

Figure 13.11 realizes these progressions using various models of keyboard playing introduced in Chapter 12. Play these (and the forthcoming) progressions at your own comfortable speed with a metronome (set on "2 and 4" to ♩=58) then gradually increase the tempo. Invert the opening sonority in order to familiarize yourself with less familiar chordal shapes.

FIGURE 13.10 Prototypical [ii–V⁷]/X Interpolation

TABLE 13.3 [ii–V⁷]/X Interpolations—Intervallic Relationships

Diatonic	Intervallic relationships	Interpolations	Diatonic	Tonic
ii–V⁷	unison–P4 up	[ii–V⁷]/**IV**	ii–V⁷	I
ii–V7	m2 up–tritone	[ii–V⁷]/♯**IV**	ii–V⁷	I
ii–V⁷	m2 down–M3 up	[ii–V⁷]/**III**	ii–V⁷	I
ii–V⁷	M2 up–P4 down	[ii–V⁷]/**V**	ii–V⁷	I
ii–V⁷	M2 down–m3 up	[ii–V⁷]/♭**III**	ii–V⁷	I
ii–V⁷	m3 up–M3 down	[ii–V⁷]/♭**VI**	ii–V⁷	I
ii–V⁷	m3 down–M2 up	[ii–V⁷]/**II**	ii–V⁷	I
ii–V⁷	M3 down–m2 up	[ii–V⁷]/♭**II**	ii–V⁷	I
ii–V⁷	M3 up–m3 down	[ii–V⁷]/**VI**	ii–V⁷	I
ii–V⁷	P5 down–M2 down	[ii–V⁷]/♭**VII**	ii–V⁷	I
ii–V⁷	tritone–m2 down	[ii–V⁷]/**VII**	ii–V⁷	I

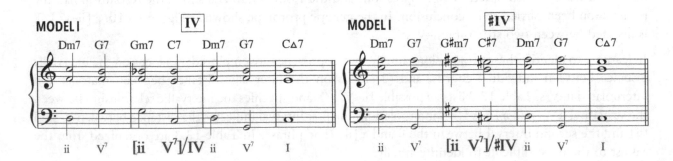

FIGURE 13.11 Model Realizations

FIGURE 13.11 continued

FIGURE 13.11 continued

Four-Bar Modulations

Figure 13.12 illustrates the distribution of chords within a modulatory four-bar phrase. An "X" indicates the new tonic.

FIGURE 13.12 Four-Bar Modulations

The permanent shift to a new tonal area is referred to as a **modulation**. There are specific conditions for a modulation to take place. To begin with, a clearly established tonic is necessary from which to modulate. Next, the original tonic must be destabilized and proceed towards a predominant key area. A motion away from the tonic, however, is not considered a modulation and neither is a chromatic [ii–V^7]/X interpolation. In order for a modulation to have occurred, the new key must be prolonged and confirmed by a cadence. In jazz harmony, that cadential confirmation typically uses some sort of a ii–V^7–I progression. The four-bar generic model from Figure 13.12 summarizes these events. For instance, mm. 1–2 illustrate the initial tonic and its subsequent prolongation and confirmation; mm. 3–4 summarize possible activities in a new key area and its final confirmation.

Table 13.4 compiles 11 four-bar modulatory phrases divided into two broad categories: closely related keys and remotely related keys. They are organized hierarchically according to their degree of remoteness from the initial tonic. The ability to hear modulations will help to identify these types of tonal shifts in standard tunes, particularly between individual sections of the tune.

Figure 13.13 realizes these progressions using various models of keyboard playing from Chapter 12.

Figure 13.14 provides three generic prototypes for modulations from major to minor, minor to major, and minor to minor keys.

Table 13.5 illustrates possible modulatory paths that you will practice on the CW.

TABLE 13.4 Prototypical Four-Bar Modulations

Closely Related Keys			
I	ii–V^7	(ii–V^7)/**IV**	**IV**
I	ii–V^7	(ii–V^7)/**V**	**V**
I	ii–V^7	(ii–V^7)/**II**	**II**
I	ii–V^7	(ii–V^7)/**♭VII**	**♭VII**
I	ii–V^7	(ii–V^7)/**VI**	**VI**
I	ii–V^7	(ii–V^7)/**♭III**	**♭III**
Remotely Related Keys			
I	ii–V^7	(ii–V^7)/**III**	**III**
I	ii–V^7	(ii–V^7)/**♭VI**	**♭VI**
I	ii–V^7	(ii–V^7)/**VII**	**VII**
I	ii–V^7	(ii–V^7)/**♭II**	**♭II**
I	ii–V^7	(ii–V^7)/**♯IV**	**♯IV**

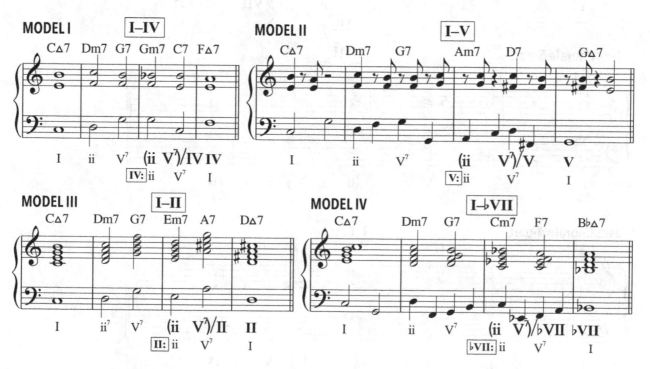

FIGURE 13.13 Model Realizations

FIGURE 13.13 continued

FIGURE 13.14 Generic Prototypes for Four-Bar Modulations

TABLE 13.5 Possible Modulatory Paths

Major to Minor Keys			
I	ii–V^7	(ii$^\emptyset$–V^7)/**ii**	**ii**
I	ii–V^7	(ii$^\emptyset$–V^7)/**vi**	**vi**
I	ii–V^7	(ii$^\emptyset$–V^7)/**iii**	**iii**
I	ii–V^7	(ii$^\emptyset$–V^7)/**iv**	**iv**
Minor to Major Keys			
i	ii$^\emptyset$–V^7	(ii^7–V^7)/**III**	**III**
i	ii$^\emptyset$–V^7	(ii^7–V^7)/**VI**	**VI**
i	ii$^\emptyset$–V^7	(ii^7–V^7)/**VII**	**VII**
i	ii$^\emptyset$–V^7	(ii^7–V^7)/**V**	**V**
i	ii$^\emptyset$–V^7	(ii^7–V^7)/**♭II**	**♭II**
Minor to Minor Keys			
i	ii$^\emptyset$–V^7	(ii$^\emptyset$–V^7)/**iv**	**iv**
i	ii$^\emptyset$–V^7	(ii$^\emptyset$–V^7)/**v**	**v**
i	ii$^\emptyset$–V^7	(ii$^\emptyset$–V^7)/**ii**	**ii**
i	ii$^\emptyset$–V^7	(ii$^\emptyset$–V^7)/**vii**	**vii**
i	ii$^\emptyset$–V^7	(ii$^\emptyset$–V^7)/**iii**	**iii**

The [ii⌀–V⁷]/x Interpolation

Figure 13.15 illustrates the rhythmic structure of a four-bar phrase in the minor key with a chromatic [ii⌀–V⁷]/x interpolation.

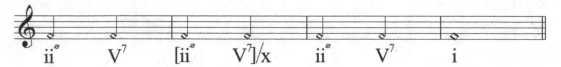

FIGURE 13.15 Prototypical [ii⌀–V⁷]/x Interpolation

Table 13.6 lists all possible [ii⌀–V⁷]/x interpolations and specifies the intervallic relationship between the V⁷ in m. 1 and [ii⌀] in m. 2, and the structural ii⌀–V⁷ and a [ii⌀–V⁷]/x, respectively. These four-bar progressions are organized from the easiest to the most difficult to identify aurally.

TABLE 13.6 [ii⌀–V⁷]/x Interpolation

Diatonic	Intervallic relationships	Interpolations	Diatonic	Tonic
ii⌀–V⁷	unison–P5 down	[ii⌀–V⁷]/**iv**	ii⌀–V⁷	i
ii⌀–V⁷	m2 up–tritone	[ii⌀–V⁷]/**♯iv**	ii⌀–V⁷	i
ii⌀–V⁷	m2 down–M3 up	[ii⌀–V⁷]/**♯iii**	ii⌀–V⁷	i
ii⌀–V⁷	M2 up–P4 down	[ii⌀–V⁷]/**v**	ii⌀–V⁷	i
ii⌀–V⁷	M2 down–m3 up	[ii⌀–V⁷]/**iii**	ii⌀–V⁷	i
ii⌀–V⁷	m3 up–M3 down	[ii⌀–V⁷]/**vi**	ii⌀–V⁷	i
ii⌀–V⁷	m3 down–M2 up	[ii⌀–V⁷]/**ii**	ii⌀–V⁷	i
ii⌀–V⁷	M3 down–m2 up	[ii⌀–V⁷]/**♭ii**	ii⌀–V⁷	i
ii⌀–V⁷	M3 up–m3 down	[ii⌀–V⁷]/**♯vi**	ii⌀–V⁷	i
ii⌀–V⁷	P5 down–M2 down	[ii⌀–V⁷]/**vii**	ii⌀–V⁷	i
ii⌀–V⁷	tritone–m2 down	[ii⌀–V⁷]/**♯vii**	ii⌀–V⁷	i

Two II–V Interpolations

Figure 13.16 provides a generic four-bar phrase with two different interpolations in mm. 2 and 3: the one in m. 2 is a harmonic ellipsis and the other confirms a new tonic.

Table 13.7 shows possible progressions utilizing these interpolations that you will encounter on the CW.

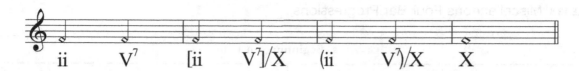

FIGURE 13.16 Four-Bar Modulations with Two Interpolations

TABLE 13.7 Two II–V Interpolations

Less Challenging			
Diatonic	First Interpolation	Second Interpolation	New Tonic
ii–V^7	[ii–V^7]/**IV**	(ii–V^7)/**VII**	**VII**
ii–V^7	[ii–V^7]/**VII**	(ii–V^7)/♭**VII**	♭**VII**
ii–V^7	[ii–V^7]/♭**V**	(ii–V^7)/**VI**	**VI**
ii–V^7	[ii–V^7]/**III**	(ii–V^7)/♭**VI**	♭**VI**
ii–V^7	[ii–V^7]/♭**VII**	(ii–V^7)/**V**	**V**
ii–V^7	[ii–V^7]/♭**III**	(ii–V^7)/♭**V**	♭**V**
ii–V^7	[ii–V^7]/**V**	(ii–V^7)/**IV**	**IV**
ii–V^7	[ii–V^7]/♯**IV**	(ii–V^7)/**III**	**III**
ii–V^7	[ii–V^7]/**IV**	(ii–V^7)/♭**III**	♭**III**
ii–V^7	[ii–V^7]/**III**	(ii–V^7)/**II**	**II**
ii–V^7	[ii–V^7]/**II**	(ii–V^7)/♭**II**	♭**II**
More Challenging			
Diatonic	First Interpolation	Second Interpolation	New Tonic
ii–V^7	[ii–V^7]/**III**	(ii–V^7)/**VII**	**VII**
ii–V^7	[ii–V^7]/**II**	(ii–V^7)/♭**VII**	♭**VII**
ii–V^7	[ii–V^7]/♭**VI**	(ii–V^7)/**VI**	**VI**
ii–V^7	[ii–V^7]/**IV**	(ii–V^7)/♭**VI**	♭**VI**
ii–V^7	[ii–V^7]/♭**III**	(ii–V^7)/**V**	**V**
ii–V^7	[ii–V^7]/**VI**	(ii–V^7)/♭**V**	♭**V**
ii–V^7	[ii–V^7]/**VI**	(ii–V^7)/**IV**	**IV**
ii–V^7	[ii–V^7]/♭**VII**	(ii–V^7)/**III**	**III**
ii–V^7	[ii–V^7]/**VII**	(ii–V^7)/♭**III**	♭**III**
ii–V^7	[ii–V^7]/♯**IV**	(ii–V^7)/**II**	**II**
ii–V^7	[ii–V^7]/**V**	(ii–V^7)/♭**II**	♭**II**

TABLE 13.8 Miscellaneous Four-Bar Progressions

a. Beginning on I			
I vi	ii V⁷	iii vi	ii V⁷
I ♯i°	ii ♯ii°	ii ♭VI⁷	(ii–V⁷)/IV
I	(ii–V⁷)/IV	IV	ii V⁷
I	[ii∅–V⁷]/vi	(ii–V⁷)/IV	IV
I IV	iii ♭VII⁷	vi II⁷	ii TR/V
I	IV ♯iv°	I VI⁷	II⁷ V⁷
I ♭V⁷	IV⁷ ♭VII⁷	I VI⁷	II⁷ TR/V
I	♯iv° iv	iii VI⁷	ii ♭VII⁷
I	[ii∅–V⁷]/iii	[ii–V⁷]/♭III	ii V⁷
I	(ii∅–V⁷)/ii	ii	(ii∅–V⁷)/vi
I	[ii–V⁷]/♭II	ii V⁷	I
I	[ii–V⁷]/♭VII	[ii–V⁷]/♭VI	ii V⁷
I	(ii–V⁷)/♭VI	♭VI	ii V⁷

b. Beginning on ii			
ii V7	I vi	[ii–V7]/♭III	ii TR/V
ii V⁷	vi II⁷	iii ♭iii°	ii V⁷
ii V⁷	[ii–V⁷]/♭III	[ii–V⁷]/♭V	(ii–V⁷)/VI
ii V⁷	[ii–V⁷]/II	vi II⁷	ii TR/V
ii∅ V⁷	I	[ii–V⁷]/III	ii V⁷
ii∅ V⁷	I ♭V7	IV⁷ ♭VII⁷	I
(ii∅–V⁷)/iv	iv	ii V⁷	I

c. Beginning on IV			
IV	[ii–V⁷]/♭III	I	ii TR/V
IV	ii V⁷	I vi	(ii∅–V⁷)/vi
IV	iii vi	ii V⁷	TR/V
IV	♯iv°	I	I
IV	[ii∅–V⁷]/iii	(ii∅–V⁷)/ii	ii TR/V
IV	(ii∅–V⁷)/vi	vi II⁷	ii V⁷

TABLE 13.8 continued

d. Beginning on vi			
vi	ii	V^7	I
vi	II^7	ii	TR/V
vi	ii V^7	I	$(ii^\emptyset-V^7)/ii$
vi	$[ii^\emptyset-V^7]/vi$	$(ii^\emptyset-V^7)/iii$	iii
vi	$[ii^\emptyset-V^7]/vi$	$[ii-V^7]/IV$	ii V^7

Miscellaneous Four-Bar Progressions

Having discussed different combinations of the ii–V^7–I and ii$^\emptyset$–V^7–i progressions, we can now explore four-bar progressions that might be found in standard tunes. Table 13.8a–d illustrates common four-bar phrases that begin on I, ii, IV, and vi.

Table 13.8a compiles 13 four-bar phrases that begin on the tonic chord: some of these phrases are harmonically open and end with the structural ii–V^7 progression; others feature substitute dominants, such as TR/V or $\flat VII^7$; still others end with a tonicization of two closely related keys—IV and vi.[5] Table 13.8b illustrates seven four-bar phrases that start with the ii–V^7 or ii$^\emptyset$–V^7 progressions.[6] Table 13.8c shows six four-bar phrases that begin on the subdominant chord.[7] The IV opening makes them challenging to identify and easily confused with phrases that start on I. Table 13.8d demonstrates five four-bar phrases that begin on the submediant chord.[8]

NOTES

1   The term *top of the chorus* refers to the beginning of the form.
2   Listen to Miles Davis's solo on "All of You" from *My Funny Valentine* (1964).
3   For the use of different inversions and rotations in the context of dominant 7th progressions consult the CW.
4   This album marked a zenith of his harmonic experiments largely influenced by Nicholas Slonimsky's *Thesaurus of Scales and Melodic Patterns.*
5   Representative tunes are: "Long Ago and Far Away," "Memories of You," "I'm Old Fashioned."
6   Representative tunes are: "I Hadn't Anyone Till You," "For Heaven's Sake," "I've Got You Under My Skin."
7   Representative tunes are: "A Ship Without a Sail," "I Can't Believe That You're in Love With Me," "September Song."
8   Representative tunes are: "Cry Me a River," "In a Sentimental Mood," "Blue Skies."

Bebop Improvisation

CHAPTER SUMMARY

Chapter 14 discusses the main characteristics of the bebop style and proposes a pedagogy of bebop improvisation.

CONCEPTS AND TERMS

- Altered dominant bebop scales:
  - Altered
  - Dominant #11
  - Dominant ♭13
  - Dominant ♭9/#11/♭13
- Bebop scales:
  - Dominant

- Intermediary
- Major
- Minor:
  - Dorian bebop
  - Minor ♭7 bebop
  - Minor #7 bebop
- Chromatic alterations
- Chromatic passing note

- Direct cadential gesture
- Double neighbor figures
- Indirect cadential gesture
- Intermediary/dominant bebop complex
- Triplets

BEBOP SCALES

The Bebop revolution in the late 1930s was probably one of the most important musical events in the history of jazz. Bebop brought about the advent of modern jazz and, with it, jazz pedagogy. Bebop syntax is considerably different from more traditional types of jazz, such as Early Jazz, Ragtime, New Orleans styles, Kansas City style, Chicago style, and Swing, not only in its approach to improvisation, but also in its treatment of form, harmony, melody, and rhythm. Broadly speaking, solos became longer, musical forms more codified, harmonies more chromatic, melodies more angular, and rhythmic patterns more intricate. This chapter discusses the pitch structure of four **bebop scales: major, minor, dominant,** and **intermediary.**[1] Each of these is further analyzed in terms of their possible functional associations. These associations enable us to choose a correct bebop scale for a specific chord and/or harmonic progression. The functional behavior of bebop scales is similar to the behavior of modes. The most obvious difference between bebop scales and modes relates to the number of pitches in these collections.

Unlike seven-note modes, bebop scales are composed of eight distinct pitches. The addition of an extra note to a seven-note scale has vast melodic and harmonic implications, particularly in the domain of chromaticism.

Major Bebop Scale

Possible Harmonic Function—Tonic and Predominant

Figure 14.1 shows the pitch content of the **major bebop scale**.

FIGURE 14.1 Major Bebop Scale

The use of a **chromatic passing note** between **5** and **6** transforms the Ionian mode into the major bebop scale.[2] This chromatic addition allocates all the chord tones on strong beats and passing notes on weak beats in relation to the underlying 4/4 meter. The metric distribution of pitches shown in Figure 14.1 conveys the harmonic and functional forces that are inherent to the structure of the scale. In the major bebop scale, beats 1, 2, 3, and 4 delineate the 6th chord and the offbeats spell out the diminished 7th chord. Figure 14.2 illustrates this scenario. Since bebop scales are associated with different tonal behaviors, harmonic functions, and locations in relation to the underlying key, Arabic numbers (without carets, written in bold) are used to represent their pitch content.

FIGURE 14.2 Major 6th and Diminished 7th Chords

What is the significance of this particular distribution of pitches within the major bebop scale? Figure 14.2 demonstrates that the major bebop scale combines two different tonal forces: the tonic represented by the 6th chord and the dominant represented by the diminished 7th chord. The diminished 7th chord is frequently employed as an incomplete dom7(♭9) as it contains a major 3rd, 5th, 7th, and ♭9th of the dom7(♭9) whose root is a major 3rd down from the root of the corresponding diminished 7th chord. The diminished 7th chord built on 7 from Figure 14.2 represents the rootless G7(♭9).

Figure 14.3 illustrates the distribution of C6 and its inversions on the chord tones of C major bebop and Ddim7 with its inversions on the passing notes of the scale.

FIGURE 14.3 Distribution of Major 6th and Diminished 7th Chords

The use of a single chromatic pitch like the one the bebop scale offers allows us to fully explore the metric, melodic, and harmonic potential of that note. It also enables us to control the behavior of two opposing tonal forces, tonic and dominant, and explore their potential during improvisation. This type of control refers to the placement of chord tones and passing notes within the measure. When chord tones are displaced from downbeats to offbeats, for instance, their metric position is de-emphasized at the expense of passing notes, which now receive metric stress. With this subtle metric shift, the content of the lines might become more unstable, without needing to add extra chromatic notes.

Minor Bebop Scales

Possible Harmonic Function—Tonic and Predominant

There are three unique **minor bebop scales** with a similar pitch structure to the major bebop scale. Minor bebop scales employ a passing note between **5** and **#6**, and **♭7** and **8**. The upper tetrachords of these scales are derived from the Melodic Minor and Dorian modes respectively. The former includes **#7**, which enables the projection of a diminished 7th chord, and the latter contains **♭7**, which injects a subtle modal flavor to the sound of this scale. The pitch structure of these collections is shown in Figure 14.4.

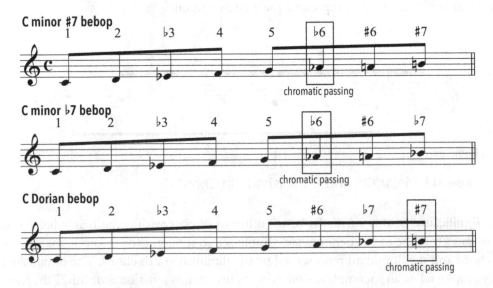

FIGURE 14.4 Minor Bebop Scales

As far as the distribution of chord tones and passing notes is concerned, in **minor #7 bebop** the strong beats form a minor 6th chord and the offbeats create a diminished 7th chord. In **minor ♭7 bebop**, the strong beats also produce a minor 6th chord, but the offbeats generate a dominant 7th chord built on

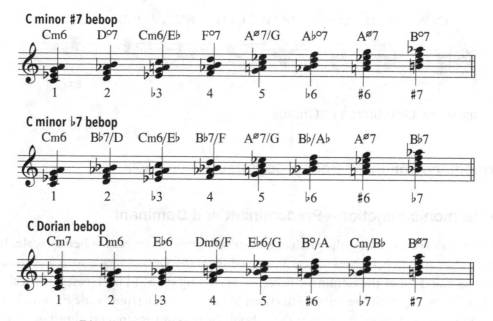

FIGURE 14.5 Distribution of Chords

♭7. In **Dorian bebop**, the strong beats create a minor 7th chord and the offbeats project a minor 6th chord. Figure 14.5 illustrates the distribution of chords on each scale degree of minor #7 bebop, minor ♭7 bebop, and Dorian bebop.

Dominant Bebop Scale

Possible Harmonic Function—Dominant

The **dominant bebop scale** is derived from the Mixolydian mode and uses a chromatic passing note between ♭7 and **8** (**1**).[3] The spelling of #7 indicates that ♭7 from the dominant bebop scale is raised. Figure 14.6 illustrates the structure of the scale.

FIGURE 14.6 Dominant Bebop Scale

The addition of the chromatic note enables the formation of a half-diminished 7th chord on #7. The presence of a passing half-diminished 7th further intensifies the dominant character of the scale and implies that #7 can be used in the context of dominant 7th chords in more advanced melodic and harmonic settings. Figure 14.7 demonstrates the distribution of chords on each scale degree of the dominant bebop scale.

FIGURE 14.7 Distribution of Chords

The Intermediary/Dominant Bebop Complex

Possible Harmonic Function—Predominant and Dominant

There are two ways of rationalizing the pitch organization of the **intermediary bebop scale**. Its structure can be examined as an independent collection derived from the Dorian mode with a chromatic passing note between ♭3 and **4**, or as the dominant bebop scale starting on **5**. In both cases, the scale establishes a chord–scale relationship with the minor 7th chord built on the supertonic scale degree. Both methods yield the same pitches and reveal important facts about the pitch structure and chord–scale relationships embedded in this scale. The former method of scale derivation suggests that intermediary bebop is an independent collection that establishes a relationship with the predominant minor 7th chord. The latter method explains ways in which the scale is also inherently tied to dominant bebop.

Because the intermediary bebop scale has the same pitch content as dominant bebop, the scale mediates between the two tonal functions, predominant and dominant. This succession of tonal functions most often occurs in the context of ii–V^7; this makes the progression an ideal vehicle for the implementation of the **intermediary/dominant bebop complex**. The only difference between intermediary and dominant bebop scales is the different metric distribution of chord tones and passing notes in relation to the corresponding harmonies. Figure 14.8 illustrates this scenario.

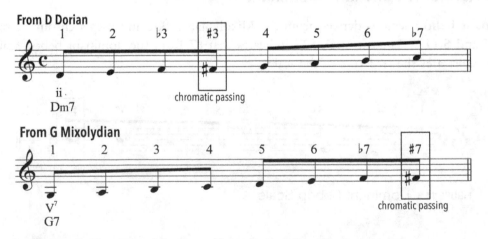

FIGURE 14.8 Derivation of Intermediary Bebop Scale

When the pitch structure of G dominant bebop is compared with D intermediary bebop, their content is exactly the same. The root and the 3rd of Dm7 occur on beats 1 and 2. The chromatic passing note F♯4 falls on the offbeat because of its melodic and harmonic instability. This metric placement impacts the distribution of notes on beats 3 and 4. It seems that the placement of a 4th and a 6th on beats 3 and 4 stymies the logical distribution of chord tones over Dm7. When we consider, however, that these notes—reinterpreted as the root and the 3rd of G7—foreshadow the dominant 7th harmony by two beats, we can conclude that the use of the intermediary/dominant 7th bebop complex has the potential for manipulating harmonic rhythm and approaching improvisation more from a linear as well as a harmonic perspective.

PRACTICING BEBOP IMPROVISATION

We will now begin to practice bebop improvisation using several different routines organized into the following categories: (1) the metric placement of pitches, (2) the addition of extra chromatic notes, (3) the alterations of dominant bebop scales, (4) the exploration of the diminished 7th chord, and (5) the use of triplets.

Metric Placement—Scalar and Arpeggiation Patterns

Figures 14.9a–d illustrate basic routines for internalizing the structure of major and minor bebop scales and for practicing the correct metric placement of pitches from these scales. Since each routine shown below demonstrates a specific scalar or arpeggiation pattern in the context of a single scale, in your practice try exploring different scales with each routine.

ROUTINE 1: Start the scale on a chord tone (downbeat) as shown in Figure 14.9a. Play the scale up and down for two octaves.

FIGURE 14.9a Routine 1: Scalar Patterns

ROUTINE 2: Start the scale on a passing tone (upbeat) of the scale as shown in Figure 14.9b. Play the scale up and down for two octaves.

FIGURE 14.9b Routine 2: Scalar Patterns

ROUTINE 3: Arpeggiate chords built on each scale degree of the bebop scale using different patterns shown in Figure 14.9c.

FIGURE 14.9c Routine 3: Arpeggiation Patterns

ROUTINE 4: Combine scalar segments with arpeggiation patterns as shown in Figure 14.9d.

FIGURE 14.9d Routine 4: Scalar and Arpeggiation Patterns

Practice these (and all the remaining) routines with a metronome on two and four starting at a medium-slow tempo. Set the metronome to ♩=60 and make each click count as a half note. Gradually increase the tempo to medium-up at ♩=96.

Addition of Extra Chromatic Notes

The **addition of extra chromatic notes** can further intensify the content of bebop lines. Just as the metric placement of single chromatic passing notes (**5–6** in major, **5–♯6** in minor, **♭7–8** in dominant, and **3–4** in intermediary) is strictly controlled, so is the addition of extra chromatic notes. Figures 14.10a and 14.10b illustrate two routines for practicing the addition of extra chromatic notes. These two routines can be fully realized in the context of major and dominant bebop scales. The minor and intermediary bebop scales can only accommodate one extra chromatic passing note between **2** and **1**. The minor 3rd in their pitch structure prevents us from implementing two chromatic passing notes.

ROUTINE 1: Start the bebop scale on the downbeat of **2** (ascending/descending) and **1** (descending). Add a single upper/lower chromatic passing note (depending on the direction of the line) (Figure 14.10a).

ROUTINE 2: Start on the downbeat of **3**, **5**, and **6** of major and dominant bebop, then add two chromatic passing notes between **3–2** and **2–1** (Figure 14.10b).

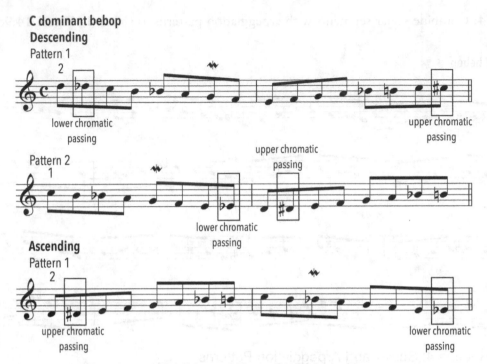

FIGURE 14.10a Routine 1: Addition of Extra Chromatic Note

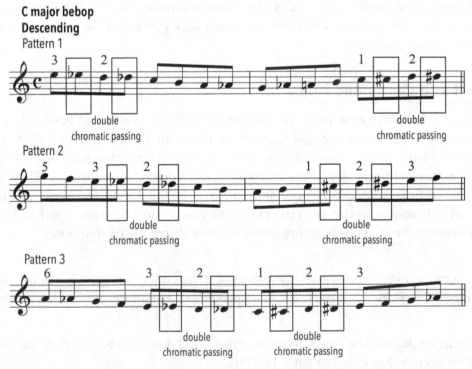

FIGURE 14.10b Routine 2: Addition of Extra Chromatic Notes

Altered Bebop Scales

Since the dominant function is associated with harmonic tension, the pitch structure of the dominant bebop scale can be modified by applying additional **chromatic alterations**. In theory, dominant bebop can be enhanced with available chromatic extensions. In practice, however, these alterations should reflect the overall musical context, particularly as it relates to the underlying tonality. Figure 14.11 shows four **altered dominant bebop scales**.

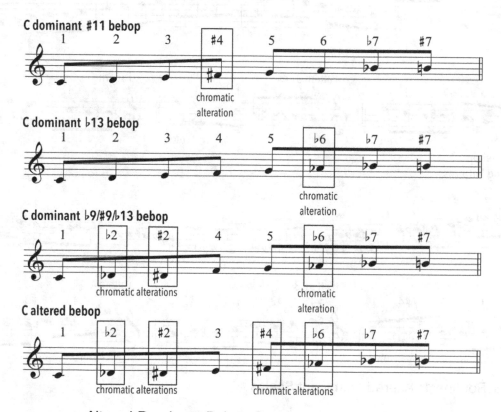

FIGURE 14.11 Altered Dominant Bebop Scales

Because of the presence of ♭13th in dominant ♭13, dominant ♭9/♯9/♭13, and altered bebop scales, these scales work best in the context of dominant 7th chords occurring in minor keys. Notice that in the dominant ♭9/♯9/♭13 scale, **3** is omitted from the structure of the scale and substituted with **♯2**, which functions as an accented dissonance. This substitution preserves the metric placement of **5** and **♭7** on the downbeats 3 and 4, respectively. In the altered bebop scale, the chord tone **3** is relegated to the status of the passing note occurring between **♯2** and **♯4**. The placement of chromatic extensions on the downbeats further accentuates the dissonant status of the scale. Figures 14.12a–c suggest routines for practicing these scales.

ROUTINE 1: Start the scale on a chord tone (downbeat) as shown in Figure 14.12a. Play the scale up and down for two octaves.

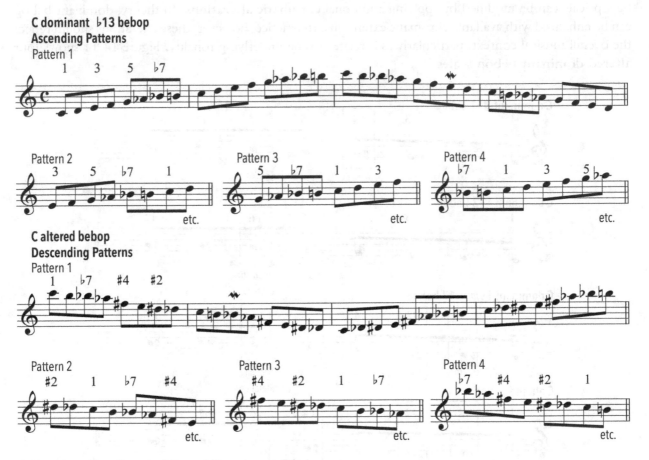

FIGURE 14.12a Routine 1: Altered Dominant Scales

ROUTINE 2: Start the scale on a passing tone (upbeat) as shown in Figure 14.12b. Play the scale up and down for two octaves.

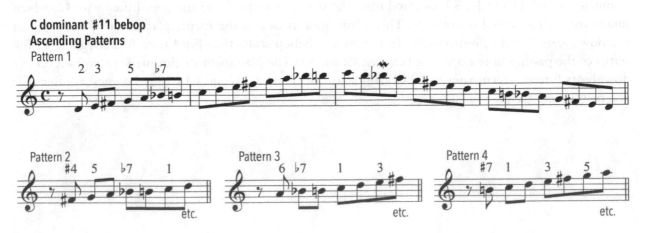

FIGURE 14.12b Routine 2: Altered Dominant Scales

C dominant ♭9/#9/♭13 bebop
Descending Patterns
Pattern 1

FIGURE 14.12b continued

ROUTINE 3: Use the specific arpeggiation pattern with each altered scale, as shown in Figure 14.12c.

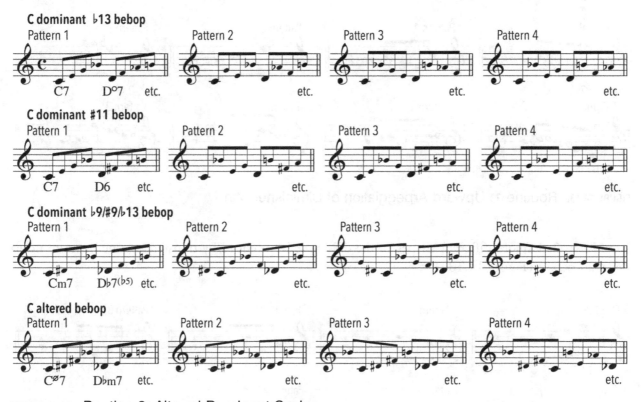

FIGURE 14.12c Routine 3: Altered Dominant Scales

The Diminished 7th Chord

The diminished 7th chord is an essential building block of bebop improvisation. As a rootless dom7(♭9), the diminished 7th chord is very effective at projecting the tonality of chord progressions with dominant 7th formations. As a chromatic passing sonority occurring on the offbeats of selected bebop scales, the diminished 7th chord can be quite effective at adding chromatic tension to melodic lines, at manipulating the harmonic rhythm of underlying chord progressions, and at providing voice-leading connections between stable formations. All of these applications are ultimately related to the metric placement of the diminished 7th chord. Figures 14.13a–f demonstrate six different routines for practicing the diminished 7th chord.

ROUTINE 1: Explore different shapes of the diminished 7th chord by transferring one or more notes *up* an octave (Figure 14.13a).[4]

FIGURE 14.13a Routine 1: Upward Arpeggiation of Diminished 7th

ROUTINE 2: Explore different shapes of the diminished 7th chord by transferring one or more notes *down* an octave (Figure 14.13b).

FIGURE 14.13b Routine 2: Downward Arpeggiation of Diminished 7th

ROUTINE 3: In the context of a V^7–I progression, resolve the diminished 7th chord using the **direct cadential gesture**. A direct cadential gesture establishes a strong chord–scale relationship with the underlying harmony (Figure 14.13c).

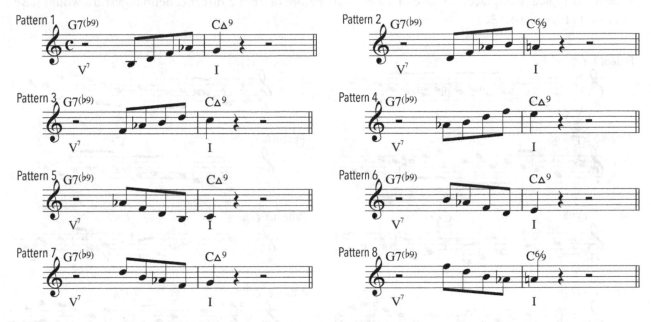

FIGURE 14.13c Routine 3: Direct Cadential Gestures for V^7–I

ROUTINE 4: In the context of a V^7–i progression, resolve the diminished 7th chord using direct cadential gesture (Figure 14.13d).

FIGURE 14.13d Routine 4: Direct Cadential Gestures for V^7–i

ROUTINE 5: In the context of a V⁷–I progression, resolve the diminished 7th chord using the **indirect cadential gesture**. An indirect cadential gesture can take many different forms, but it mainly relates to the relationship with the underlying harmony and its overall metric placement. This type of melodic cadence is typically displaced by one or more beats before or after a direct cadential gesture would have occurred (Figure 14.13e).

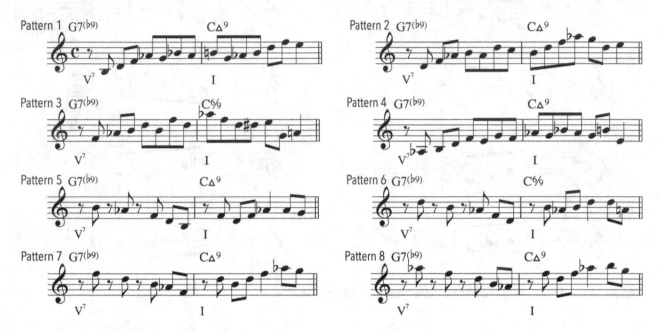

FIGURE 14.13e Routine 5: Indirect Cadential Gestures for V⁷–I

ROUTINE 6: In the context of a V⁷–i progression, resolve the diminished 7th chord using indirect cadential gesture (Figure 14.13f).

FIGURE 14.13f Routine 6: Indirect Cadential Gestures for V⁷–i

Triplets

The use of **triplets** adds extra energy and forward motion to melodic lines. Triplets work very well in the context of chordal arpeggiation with single or **double neighbor figures** preparing the triplet as shown in Figures 14.14a–d.

ROUTINE 1: Add the following triplet arpeggiation patterns with the lower chromatic/diatonic neighbor into the structure of bebop scales (Figure 14.14a).

FIGURE 14.14a Routine 1: Triplet Arpeggiation with a Lower Neighbor

As a rule of thumb, each scale degree should be approached with a lower neighbor a half step below the target note. Such a melodic approach results in either diatonic or chromatic neighbors.

ROUTINE 2: Add the following triplet arpeggiation patterns with the upper diatonic neighbor into the structure of the bebop scales (Figure 14.14b).

FIGURE 14.14b Routine 2: Triplet Arpeggiation with an Upper Neighbor

Diatonic upper neighbors are derived from the corresponding scale and are located a half and/or whole step above the first note of the triplet figure.

ROUTINE 3: Add the following triplet arpeggiation patterns with a double neighbor figure into the structure of the bebop scales (Figure 14.14c).

FIGURE 14.14c Routine 3: Triplet Arpeggiation with a Double Neighbor

ROUTINE 4: Add the following arpeggiation patterns with double neighbor figure into the structure of the bebop scales (Figure 14.14d).

FIGURE 14.14d Routine 4: Arpeggiation with a Triplet Double Neighbor

The extended double neighbor figure utilizes two lower neighbors, diatonic and chromatic. To prevent excessive chromaticism, a lower diatonic neighbor initiates the pattern and a lower chromatic neighbor occurs prior to its target note, with the exception of half steps that naturally occur in the scale (i.e. **3**, **5**, and **7** of major bebop; **2**, **5**, and **#7** of minor **#7**; **3**, **6**, and **b7** of dominant; and **3**, **5**, and **b7** of dominant **b13**).

The ii–V⁷–I Progression

Figure 14.15 establishes a chord–scale relationship for the ii–V⁷–I progression using bebop scales.

FIGURE 14.15 Bebop Scales for ii–V⁷–I

Each scale features a descending sixth span from the root to the third of the underlying chord. The first two chords of the progression use the same scale—hence the intermediary/bebop complex label—albeit starting on a different note of the corresponding chords.

Negotiating the Minor Seven Flat Five Chord

Before illustrating the chord–scale relationship for a ii⁰–V⁷–i progression using bebop scales, let us discuss how to negotiate the m7(♭5) chord with bebop scales. The chord–scale relationship between the predominant ii⁰ and bebop scales is more intricate that it is for the predominant ii. Figure 14.16 demonstrates this relationship.

FIGURE 14.16 Chord–Scale Relationship for the Minor 7(♭5) Chord

In order to understand this relationship, the m7(♭5) chord should be examined as if it were a four-part upper structure of the corresponding dominant 9th chord. In Figure 14.16, Dm7(♭5) constitutes the upper structure of B♭9. Bebop scales that fit the content of m7(♭5), then, are derived from the dominant bebop scales that work for a dominant 9th chord, whose root is a major 3rd down from the root of the m7(♭5) chord. The two scales in Figure 14.16—**intermediary ♭2** and **intermediary ♮2**—begin on the root of m7(♭5) and share the pitch content with the dominant and dominant ♯11 bebop scales. In addition to working well with the m7(♭5) chord, these two intermediary bebop scales also capture the melodic characteristics of Locrian and Locrian ♮2 modes—both of which are associated with the predominant ii⁰.

The ii⁰–V⁷–i Progression

Figure 14.17 illustrates three chord–scale relationships for the ii⁰–V⁷–i progression using different bebop scales.

FIGURE 14.17 Bebop Scales for ii⁰–V⁷–i

In comparison to the ii–V⁷–I progression, the chord–scale relationship for the ii⁰–V⁷–i progression is more intricate: unlike in the former, where the first two chords are negotiated with the same dominant bebop scale starting on the roots of respective chords, in the latter each chord can potentially establish a relationship with two different scales. Thus the ii⁰ chord establishes relationships with intermediary ♭2 and intermediary ♮2; the V⁷ chord with dominant ♭13, dominant ♭9/♯9/♭13 and altered bebop scales; and the i chord with minor ♯7th, minor ♭7th, and Dorian bebop.

NOTES

1 In the current discussion, the term **bebop scales** is used loosely to depict particular eight-note constructs with one or more chromatic passing notes at different locations in their structure. The *one* scale that traditionally goes by this name is the dominant bebop scale (with a passing note between ♭7 and 1); there are Jerry Coker's additional *three* bebop scales and Mark Levine's *four* bebop scales, all of which present different scalar constructs. A common misconception about bebop scales is that they originated during the Bebop Era, when, in fact, they were quite common in the repertory of rags, marches, and other popular genres of the late 19th and early 20th centuries. For a clear manifestation of the dominant bebop scale in Early Jazz, listen to the transition material after the trio of Lew Pollack's ragtime composition "That's a Plenty" (1914). The pitch succession, F5–E♮5–E♭5–D–C–B♭–A–G–F, clearly delineates what we now call the *bebop scale*.

2 The spelling of the chromatic passing note as ♭6 (A♭ in C major bebop) is in keeping with the correct spelling of the diminished 7th chord (B⁰7) that forms the essential chord–scale relationship with this scale.

3 This is what most texts refer to as *the* bebop scale.

4 The great piano player Barry Harris is credited with having codified this technique.

CHAPTER 15

Bebop Blues

CHAPTER SUMMARY

Chapter 15 analyzes three blues progressions from the Bebop Era and proposes additional approaches to blues improvisation.

CONCEPTS AND TERMS

- Blues progressions:
  - "Billie's Bounce"
  - Bird
  - "The Dance of the Infidels"
- Entry windows
- Structural line

THREE HARMONIC VARIANTS

During the Bebop period, the blues underwent significant harmonic, melodic, and rhythmic developments. The harmony became more chromatic and saturated with all kinds of chord substitutions. The rate at which chords changed, i.e. *harmonic rhythm*, increased exponentially and became one of the trademarks of bebop harmony. What is interesting about bebop harmony is that some of the chromatic extensions can be traced back to the old-fashioned blues. For instance, a ♯11th (♭5th) or ♯9th over the dominant 7th chord represent the notes of the blues scale: ♭5 and ♭3, respectively. The melody in the bebop blues ceased to be purely vocal in character (as had been the case earlier) and became more virtuosic with an influx of idiomatic chromaticism. The rhythmic organization of the bebop blues experienced some considerable developments particularly in the use of intricate syncopations, metric displacements, cross rhythms, double-time figures, and others. Gone were the static rhythmic gestures from earlier blues tunes and in their place, complex rhythmic ideas began infiltrating the rhythmic organization of bebop compositions.

Along with the transformation of harmony, melody and rhythm, the Bebop blues also saw some remarkable changes concerning the ways jazz musicians approached improvisation. Instead of focusing on mere chord arpeggiations, occasional chromaticism and *blue notes* embellishments, bebop musicians emphasized a more horizontal approach to soloing, which resulted in the plasticity of harmonic rhythm and the infusion of idiomatic chromaticism. The use of different bebop scales (as those discussed in Chapter 14) not only guaranteed a correct dissonance treatment, but it also helped to negotiate chord progression more linearly without being confined to the rigidity of vertical harmonies.

Although the harmonic surface of certain blues tunes from the Bebop Era might not resemble the harmonic paradigm of the basic blues discussed in Chapter 9, the background harmonic structure always preserves the essential chords of the blues no matter how complex that surface might be. A quick glance at the harmonic properties of the three blues variants discussed in this chapter reveals how completely different their chord progressions are. Measures 1–4, for instance, feature three sets of changes that prolong the governing tonic in imaginable ways. What is interesting about these surface substitutions is that they inevitably and logically lead to the structural harmony in m. 5. To show how diverse mm. 1–4 of the blues can be and how they relate to the governing tonic, Figure 15.1 tallies some of the more interesting harmonic paths through that section.

FIGURE 15.1 Harmonic Paths—Mm. 1–4

Variant 1—The *Billie's Bounce* Progression

Figure 15.2 illustrates an F blues with harmonic substitutions typical of the Bebop Era. This **blues progression** is based on "Billie's Bounce" by Charlie Parker.

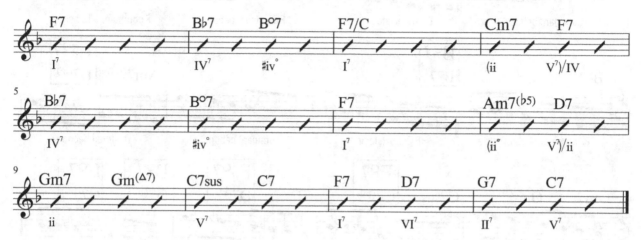

FIGURE 15.2 "Billie's Bounce"—Chord Changes

There are a few significant differences between "Billie's Bounce" and the basic blues progression. The presence of #iv° in m. 2 and a (ii∅–V⁷)/ii progression in m. 8 offers new improvisational possibilities. The diminished 7th passing chord in m. 2 leads to F7/C in m. 3. The structural V⁷ in mm. 9–10 is prolonged with four chords: Gm7–Gm(#7)–C7sus–C7. As a consequence, the occurrence of V⁷ is postponed until m. 10. The preparation of ii in m. 8 uses a (ii∅–V⁷)/ii progression. The two harmonic events from mm. 2 and 8 are unique to the structure of this particular blues progression.

In addition to the passing status of the diminished 7th chord in m. 2, this important chord can occur in other harmonic situations, albeit with different functional capacities. Since the diminished 7th chord functions as an upper structure of the dom7(♭9), any dominant 7th chord can potentially utilize this sound. Figure 15.3 establishes a chord–scale relationship for "Billie's Bounce" and indicates places where the diminished 7th chord can be implemented. The use of a single octatonic scale in m. 2 demonstrates an economical approach to improvisation wherein a single scale establishes a chord–scale relationship with two different harmonic formations.[1]

Figure 15.4 provides a realization of "Billie's Bounce" using **Model VI** of keyboard playing. The content of the R.H. is rhythmicized with the Charleston rhythm placed at different metric locations. When this rhythmic gesture appears on beat 3 (or later in the measure) then the second part of the figure anticipates the forthcoming harmony.

The realization in Figure 15.4 includes two sets of chord progressions: (1) original, which indicates only four-part chords, and (2) complete, which shows pitch expansions of the original progression. Since **Model VI** of keyboard realization uses rootless formations in the R.H., the analysis of these chords *assumes* the presence of the root *whether or not* that root actually appears in the L.H.

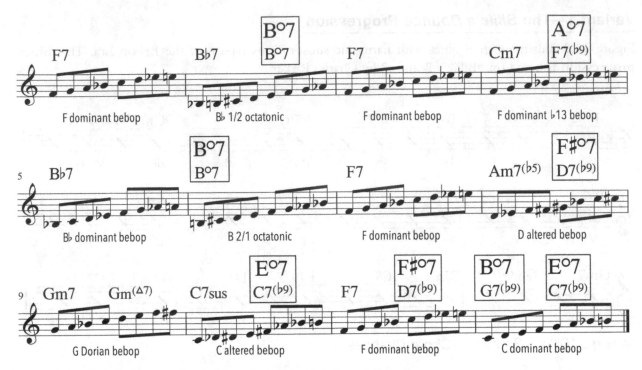

FIGURE 15.3 "Billie's Bounce"—A Chord–Scale Relationship

FIGURE 15.4 "Billie's Bounce"—Model VI Realization

Variant 2—The *Bird Blues* Progression

Figure 15.5 illustrates the harmonic structure of the **Bird** blues in E♭.[2]

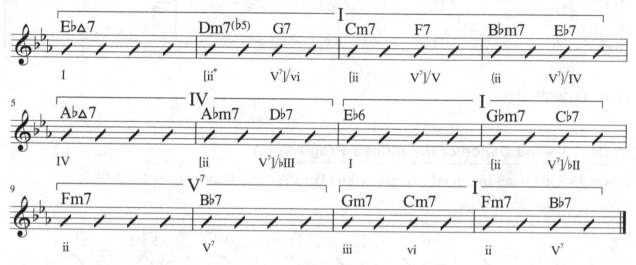

FIGURE 15.5 "Bird Blues"—Chord Changes

In this progression, the structural chords in mm. 1 and 5 still occur on the tonic and subdominant scale degrees, respectively, yet instead of dominant 7ths they feature major 7th chords. The motion from I to IV in mm. 1–4 is packed with idiomatic harmonic activity. The parallel motion between the guide tones of E♭M7 and Dm7(♭5) activates the circle of 5ths progression. The second phrase (mm. 5–8) features two chromatic ii–V7s in mm. 6 and 8. The former, [ii–V7]/♭III, is a back-door dominant 7th preparation of the major tonic in m. 7. The chromatic [ii–V7]/♭II in m. 8 anticipates the arrival of the structural ii–V7 in mm. 9–10 by a half step. The third four-bar phrase of Bird blues in mm. 9–12 has a chord structure similar to the basic blues progression. Figure 15.6 provides a realization of the progression using jazz chorale five-part texture. The turnaround in mm. 11–12 features substitute harmonic changes.

FIGURE 15.6 "Bird Blues"—Jazz Chorale Texture in Five Voices

FIGURE 15.6 continued

Variant 3—The *Dance of the Infidels* Progression

Figure 15.7 illustrates the chord changes for Bud Powell's "**The Dance of the Infidels**" in C.[3]

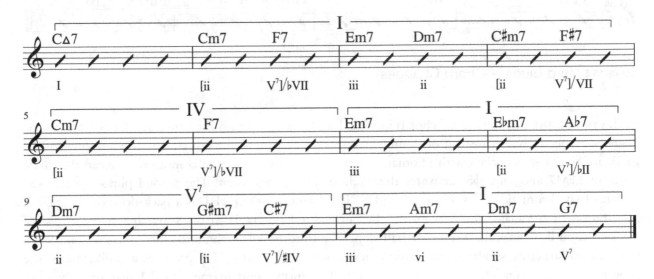

FIGURE 15.7 "The Dance of the Infidels"—Chord Changes

The opening phrase in mm. 1–4 includes two chromatic ii–V^7s. The [ii–V^7]/$\flat$VII progression in m. 2 functions as a tonic expansion and the [ii–V^7]/VII in m. 4 functions as a ii–V^7 tritone expansion of C7. Note that in m. 3, the voice-leading preparation of [ii–V^7]/VII uses two parallel minor 7th chords: iii and ii. The occurrence of the structural subdominant in m. 5 is delayed until m. 6 by its corresponding predominant. This predominant expansion forms a minor 2nd relationship with the preceding [ii–V^7]/VII. One of the most effective chord substitutions of this blues progression occurs in mm. 9–10. The structural dominant 7th, which should have occurred in m. 10, is replaced by a [ii–V^7]/$\sharp$IV progression. The nature of this substitution is analogous to the [ii–V^7]/VII progression from m. 4. In both cases, the ii–V^7 tritone expansions prepare and/or disguise the occurrence of structural harmonies. Figure 15.8 provides a realization of "The Dance of the Infidels" using **Model VI** of keyboard playing. Measures 11–12 feature alternate changes for the turnaround.

FIGURE 15.8 "The Dance of the Infidels"—Model VI Realization

IMPROVISATION

We will now discuss two approaches to improvisation using Variants 2 and 3 of the blues. The first approach is based on arpeggiations of rootless five-part chords over the **structural line**. The second approach is based on finding the most efficient way of connecting closely or distantly related chords. Arpeggiation of rootless formations using the notes of a structural background line is an effective improvisational strategy demonstrating one's understanding of chord structures and voice leading. Such a background line uses whole and half notes (depending on the rate of harmonic rhythm) that are derived from the underlying harmony and move primarily by step. The individual notes function as *roots* of the corresponding rootless five-part formations that are subsequently arpeggiated. Figure 15.9 demonstrates two structural lines derived from the Bird blues embellished with chord arpeggiations.

The use of common-tone (or stepwise) connections is based on finding a pitch called an **entry window**. This pitch allows for a smooth connection between closely or distantly related chords or key areas. If we know, for instance, that the 7th of ii also functions as the 3rd of ♭VI⁷, then this particular note can be used as an entry window to connect these two chords. If we also know that it is possible to connect ii and ♭VI⁷ by moving the 9th of ii by a half step (in either direction) to land on the 5th or 13th of ♭VI⁷, then doing so will guarantee good voice leading between these distant harmonies. Figure 15.10 illustrates available entry windows in "The Dance of the Infidels" and the bottom staff integrates these pitches in the context of melodic lines.

FIGURE 15.9 "Bird Blues"—Arpeggiation of a Structural Line

FIGURE 15.10 "The Dance of the Infidels"—Entry Windows

NOTES

1   For a discussion of octatonic scales, see Chapter 18.
2   This progression (originally in F) is based on Charlie Parker's "Blues For Alice."
3   The original composition is in the key of F major.

The "Confirmation" Changes

CHAPTER SUMMARY

Chapter 16 provides an analysis of Charlie Parker's "Confirmation" as a representative composition from the Bebop Era. A transcription of the solo by the pianist Hank Jones is analyzed and two chord–scale relationships for the tune are provided.

CONCEPTS AND TERMS

- Arpeggiation
- Cadential melodic gestures
- Chromaticism
- Diminished 7th chords
- Metric displacement
- 32-bar AABA form

"CONFIRMATION"—AN ANALYSIS

Figure 16.1 shows the lead sheet of "Confirmation" by Charlie Parker.[1]

Form and Harmony

"Confirmation" features a **32-bar AABA** formal design with slight melodic variations in each A section. The chord progression in the A section employs a chain of local II–Vs preparing the arrival of the structural IV in mm. 5, 13, and 29. This characteristic chord sequence bridging two harmonic pillars, I and IV, is one of the most interesting harmonic expansions associated with the blues and other tunes as well.[2] As is the case with most compositions from the Bebop period, the harmonic rhythm of "Confirmation" is fast and intricate. For instance, mm. 1–4 feature an idiomatic progression with a sequence of dominant 7ths that begins on $\hat{3}$ in m. 2, descends by whole steps to $\hat{1}$ in m. 4, and resolves to the subdominant in m. 5. Each dominant 7th in mm. 2–4 is subsequently expanded with the ii$^\emptyset$–V or ii–V^7 progressions, thereby doubling the rate of harmonic rhythm. In m. 2, then, A7 becomes Em7(♭5)–A7; in m. 3, G7 turns into Dm7–G7; and, in m. 4, F7 expands into Cm7–F7.

FIGURE 16.1 "Confirmation"—Lead Sheet

Comparing the second half of each A section shows that the first A is harmonically open and ends on a ii–V⁷ in m. 8, while the second and the final A sections feature closed harmonic cadences on I in m. 16 and m. 32, respectively. The bridge in mm. 17–24 has a symmetrical phrase structure and slower harmonic rhythm, which redirects the harmony from I to IV in m. 19 and then to ♭VI in m. 23. These key areas are tonicized with local ii–V⁷ progressions. The choice of these tonal areas corroborates an interesting fact about the overall tonality of bebop tunes with respect to jazz traditions. The subdominant key area has always had strong blues connotations and the flat submediant was one of the few chromatic regions that ragtime or early jazz tunes allowed in their harmonic structure.[3]

Melody and Rhythm

The melody of "Confirmation" has an interesting structural design. The background line $\hat{3}$–$\hat{2}$–$\hat{1}$ in mm. 1–4, for instance, controls the unfolding of the melodic surface. The beginning of each measure highlights the structural tones at prominent metric positions. Scale-degree two in m. 2—which in the context of the underlying chords functions as the 3rd and the 7th, respectively—resolves to the 3rd of Dm7 in m. 3, completing the $\hat{3}$–$\hat{2}$–$\hat{1}$ span. In mm. 17–19, the pitch succession $\hat{5}$–♭$\hat{5}$–$\hat{4}$–$\hat{3}$–$\hat{2}$ (local 8–♯7–♭7–6–5)—although occurring over the ii–V⁷–I in B♭—is an idiomatic line that also controls the content of the melodic diminutions. Figure 16.2 illustrates these two melodic spans.

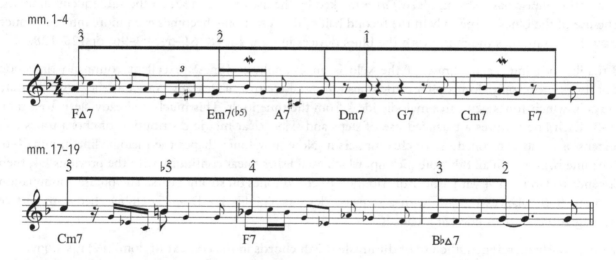

FIGURE 16.2 "Confirmation"—Structural Spans

The melody also features some interesting blues inflections. With the arrival of the structural harmony in m. 5, for instance, the melody highlights a pitch succession that utilizes two blue notes: ♭$\hat{5}$ and ♭$\hat{3}$. In mm. 9–10, ♭$\hat{3}$ and ♭$\hat{7}$ continue to embellish the melody with ♭$\hat{7}$ in m. 10 implicating a ♭5th of the A7 harmony. In m. 22, the same blue notes, ♭$\hat{3}$ and ♭$\hat{7}$, become harmonically redefined in the context of V/♭VI.

As stated in Chapter 15, one of the characteristic sonorities in the Bebop Era was the diminished 7th chord. This chord typically functions as a rootless dom7(♭9). In m. 8, the pitch D♭5, which constitutes the ♭9th of C7, is featured prominently on beat 1; in m. 24, D♭4 occurs in the context of a phrase that anticipates the return of the final A section. In both cases, the resolution of these notes follows the rules of good voice leading.

The rhythm of "Confirmation" is likewise typical of the Bebop Era. The melody features syncopations, upbeats, 8th-note anticipations of the forthcoming harmony, and effective cadential gestures. The rhythmic design of the melody is particularly effective at the end of each phrase. In mm. 2–3, for instance, a short two-note gesture occurring at the "and" of 4 and 1 concludes the presentation of the opening phrase. In m. 7, another two-note figure on beat 2, utilizing a major 13th and a major 9th of G7, effectively terminates the preceding phrase. In m. 15, a four-note figure on beats 3 and 4 delineates the underlying harmony and, at the same time, anticipates the forthcoming harmony.

AN ANALYSIS OF THE TRANSCRIPTION

Hank Jones's solo on "Confirmation," shown in Figure 16.3, is from the album *Bebop Redux* recorded in 1977. In this solo, Jones shows how two jazz traditions—blues and bebop—can be integrated in a musically convincing manner. He also demonstrates a stunning command of the bebop language manifested in a linear approach to improvisation.

As indicated in the analysis of the tune, the A section of "Confirmation" contains elements of the blues, such as single blue-note inflections and characteristic blues harmonies. Jones capitalizes on the blues potential of the tune in a number of creative ways. At the end of chorus 1 in mm. 29–32, for instance, the entire phrase has a strong *bluesy flavor* marked by the use of $\flat\hat{3}$ and $\flat\hat{7}$. In the subsequent choruses, the use of the blues—especially in the second half of the A section—becomes even more intense. Notice how Jones saturates the music with the blues devices in mm. 45–48, 61–64, 93–96, or 125–128.

Broadly speaking, each phrase of the solo is an example of Jones's excellent command of bebop vocabulary; not only do his phrases demonstrate total control of the language, but they also illustrate ways in which Jones generates melodic ideas from the tune itself. This much is already clear from mm. 1–8. Each line features a balanced use of steps and skips, clear metric distribution of chord tones and extensions, and controlled use of **chromaticism**. Note how Jones shapes the melodic line in mm. 4–6. The line begins with an 8th-note pick up, which establishes linear continuity with the previous E4, then ascends to G5 in m. 4 with a clear distribution of chord tones on strong beats. The phrase continuation in mm. 5–6 balances the line with a stepwise descent, G5–F5–E5–D5–C5, embellished with surface arpeggiations of the underlying chords.

As previously mentioned, the use of **diminished 7th chords** in the context of dom7($\flat$9) is synonymous with bebop syntax and Jones often highlights this chord in his solo. His treatment of the sonority is very creative and includes **arpeggiation** (mm. 10 and 34), **incomplete diminished 7th** (mm. 24 and 98), and **metric displacement** (mm. 26–27 and 40).

The solo is unified through the use of similar melodic devices at the same locations within the form. For instance, in mm. 4, 12, and 28 of the form, Jones frequently employs a dom7($\sharp$5) chord (mm. 4, 12, 36, 92, 100, and 108). The melodic ideas seem to foreshadow the arrival of the main tonic, rather than to articulate the underlying harmony, and occur in mm. 7, 71, and 103. More importantly, the beginning of each chorus emphasizes $\hat{5}$, which occurs in various guises in the original tune (mm. 1, 17, and 25). At the beginning of each chorus, Jones comes back to $\hat{5}$ and slightly modifies its status from the previous chorus: in m. 1, $\hat{5}$ is prepared with a two-note pick up derived from the tonic bebop scale; in m. 33, $\hat{5}$ initiates a diatonic scalar ascent; in m. 65, $\hat{5}$ introduces a chromatic scalar ascent; and, in m. 97, $\hat{5}$ begins an idiomatic line with varied contour.

FIGURE 16.3 "Confirmation"—Improvised Solo by Hank Jones (transcribed by Dariusz Terefenko)

CHORUS 2

FIGURE 16.3 continued

CHORUS 3

FIGURE 16.3 continued

CHORUS 4

FIGURE 16.3 continued

Among many features of the solo, Jones's treatment of chromaticism is masterly. In the discussion of bebop scales in Chapter 14, I emphasized that the addition of a single chromatic note to a seven-note scale creates an ideal metric scenario in which chord tones are distributed on strong beats and non-chord tones on weak beats. Some interesting examples of the use of controlled chromaticism occur in: (1) m. 4, where Gb5 functions as an unaccented passing note; (2) m. 20, where C#5 serves as an accented passing note; (3) m. 42, where D#5 initiates the phrase; (4) m. 99, where Eb5 ends the phrase; (5) m. 87, where D major is a chromatic upper-structure triad over DbM7; and, (6) m. 59, where C#m7 functions as a chromatic upper-structure four-part chord over G7.

Jones also uses an impressive assortment of **cadential melodic gestures**. These patterns usually accomplish two objectives: (1) they provide a logical phrase conclusion and (2) they foreshadow the arrival of the next phrase. In m. 23, for instance, a two-note succession Eb4–Ab3 ends the two-bar phrase. This simple gesture is very effective because it: (1) clearly delineates the underlying harmony, provides voice-leading resolution of the chromatic notes E4–A3 from m. 22, (2) anticipates the beginning of the next phrase that starts an octave higher on Ab4, and (3) recurs in the middle of the phrase (m. 24) at a different pitch level, G4–C4.

CHORD–SCALE RELATIONSHIP: MODES

Figure 16.4 provides a chord–scale relationship for "Confirmation" using modes only.

Although the rate of harmonic rhythm is relatively fast (with the ubiquitous II–V progressions), each measure contains only a single mode. In establishing chord–scale relationships for other chords, we need to determine their function, analyze their quality, and choose an appropriate mode that fits the underlying context. For instance, each tonic chord occurring in the tune establishes a chord–scale relationship with the Ionian mode only. Although Lydian and Lydian Augmented could potentially have been used as substitute scales, they would have been too chromatic in the context of this tune and clearly outside the stylistic conventions of the bebop style. The underlying motion from I–IV is rooted in the blues tradition and the selection of modes for the subdominant in m. 5 is in keeping with that tradition. Even though the subdominant on IV features a dominant 7th chord, in the context of this progression it functions as a predominant.

There are two ways of establishing chord–scale relationships for ii–V⁷ or ii⁰–V⁷ progressions: (1) select a mode that works for V⁷ or (2) select a mode that works for ii or (ii⁰). As shown in Figure 16.4, mm. 2–4 feature a descending sequence of incomplete II–Vs connecting the tonic on I with the predominant on IV. Each II–V progression establishes a chord–scale relationship with the corresponding dominant 7th. Notice that in m. 2, the use of Mixolydian b13 fits the underlying context much better than the diatonic Mixolydian mode. The tonic note F4 functions as the b13th of Mixolydian b13 and is retained as a common tone in mm. 1–2. The second A section (mm. 9–16) demonstrates a different approach to chord–scale theory. The selection of modes for the II–V progression in Figure 16.4 is based on the quality of the predominant chord. Thus in m. 10, Em7(b5)–A7 uses E Locrian, while in m. 11, Dm7–G7 establishes a chord–scale relationship with D Dorian, etc.

The bridge of "Confirmation" (mm. 17–24) features two four–bar phrases with ii–V⁷ tonicizations of the IV and bVI key areas. The chord–scale relationship for the bridge in Figure 16.4 includes a different selection of modes: Dorian, Mixolydian, and Ionian for Cm7–F7–BbM7, and Dorian, Altered, and Lydian for Ebm7–Ab7–DbM7. Tonal and contextual considerations are particularly evident with the choice of

FIGURE 16.4 Chord–Scale Relationship: Modes

Altered mode in m. 22, which accommodates notes from the tonic key and prepares the arrival of FM7 in m. 25. The last A section (mm. 25–32) features a much bolder selection of modes. The choices of A Altered in m. 26 and F Locrian in m. 28 are particularly poignant. The former injects chromatic notes into the structure of dominant 7th chord. The choice of F Locrian over Cm7–F7 in m. 28 might seem out of place because neither chord (at least not in the present form) establishes a convincing relationship with this mode. But, the F Locrian mode forms a chord–scale relationship with F7sus(♭9,♯9), which is an effective harmonic substitution for Cm7–F7.

While the selection of modes in Figure 16.4 is overcrowded with different options, an improvisation may focus on only a few modes. In fact, each A section contains a selection of modes that could be implemented in the course of an entire solo. In establishing a successful chord–scale relationship for the tune, be mindful of three important considerations: (1) modal hierarchy, (2) chromatic treatment, and (3) voice leading. Chromatic modes, for instance, contain notes that typically need preparation. This preparation usually takes place anywhere from one beat to one measure before the chromatic notes occur. The succession of modes in mm. 5–6—B♭ Mixolydian and D Mixolydian ♭13—illustrates such a case. The latter mode contains the chromatic ♭13th that was introduced as ♭7th of B♭7 in m. 5.

CHORD–SCALE RELATIONSHIP: BEBOP SCALES

Figure 16.5 provides a chord–scale relationship for "Confirmation" using bebop scales only.

The selection of bebop scales is analogous to the use of modes from Figure 16.4. In m. 2, for instance, Em7(♭5)–A7 uses A Mixolydian ♭13, which accommodates $\hat{1}$ in its pitch structure, as does A dominant bebop ♭13, making them much better choices than their diatonic counterparts.

Demonstrating slightly different and more advanced organization of bebop scales, the last A section alternates between ascending and descending scalar patterns. In addition, the last note of each measure forms a stepwise connection with the first note of the next, thereby ensuring effective voice leading between different scales. Thus the last note of m. 26, C♯4, resolves up to D4, which begins the G dominant bebop scale on **5**. Similarly, the use of B♭3 in m. 31 is a consequence of the C4 in m. 30 resolving down to the ♭7th of C7.

NOTES

1   For representative recordings, consult Appendix F on the CW.
2   Parker's "Blues For Alice" has the same harmonic substitutions in mm. 1–4. Standard tunes, such as "Come Rain or Come Shine" and "There Will Never Be Another You," also feature this characteristic progression.
3   See, for instance, "Tin Roof Blues," "Copenhagen" or "Maple Leaf Rag."

FIGURE 16.5 Chord–Scale Relationship: Bebop Scales

The Rhythm Changes

CHAPTER SUMMARY

Chapter 17 provides an analysis of Charlie Parker's "Moose the Mooche." This chapter also suggests a pedagogy of rhythm changes improvisation.

CONCEPTS AND TERMS

- Appoggiatura
- Contrafact
- Eight-bar blues
- Hypermetric organization
- Pitch enclosure
- Rhythm changes

"I GOT RHYTHM" CONTRAFACTS

With the exception of the blues, the **rhythm changes** progression is probably the most important chord progression in jazz. The term rhythm changes refers to a 32-bar AABA form based on the harmonic structure of "I Got Rhythm" by George and Ira Gershwin. The song appeared in the Aarons and Freedley production *Girl Crazy* (1930) and originally featured a 34-bar AABA form with a two-bar extension in the last A section. The two-bar extension was eventually cut and the chord changes of the last A section replicated those from the second A. A newly composed line based on the rhythm changes progression is known as a **contrafact**. The enormous popularity of rhythm changes has been well documented by an ever-increasing number of composed contrafacts and recordings.[1]

"MOOSE THE MOOCHE"—AN ANALYSIS

Charlie Parker wrote a number of contrafacts on rhythm changes among which "Moose the Mooche" shown in Figure 17.1 is one of the most well known.[2]

FIGURE 17.1 "Moose the Mooche"—Lead Sheet

Form and Harmony

"Moose the Mooche" features a 32-bar AABA form.[3] The first A section is harmonically open and ends on a ii–V^7 in m. 8. The second A features a full-cadential closure on I in m. 16. The bridge traverses through a cycle of dominant 7ths progression and interrupts the form on V^7 in m. 24. The final A section is harmonically closed but, in order to allow for the circularity of the chorus improvisation, it features a I–VI^7–ii–V^7 turnaround progression (or any acceptable substitute variant).

The tonic is prolonged in mm. 1–4 and then morphed into a V/IV in m. 5. The tonic prolongation takes the form of an idiomatic I–vi–ii–V^7 progression, which lends itself to a variety of harmonic substitutions. The subdominant controls mm. 5–6 and is capable of many surface realizations. Next, mm. 7–8 proceed to the dominant, which can also be idiomatically expanded, transformed, and/or confirmed. The A section of rhythm changes is also known as an **eight-bar blues** because it contains the harmonic paradigm of the blues: tonic in m. 1, subdominant in m. 6, and dominant in m. 8.[4] This foreshortened blues preserves the structural weight of the fundamental chords, as the tonic controls the longest span (mm. 1–4), the subdominant occupies the shorter span (mm. 6–7), and the dominant (m. 8) becomes subject to various harmonic modifications.[5]

Melody and Rhythm

The melody of "Moose the Mooche" confirms the premise that contrafacts are far more dexterous than the tunes from which they borrow their chord progressions. The melodic rhythm of "Moose the Mooche" is typical of bebop syntax. In m. 1, the Charleston rhythm is highlighted with an octave leap from F4 to F5. This rhythmic gesture appears in various guises throughout the tune. Other rhythmic figures, such as 8th-note triplets in mm. 2 and 8, and 16th-note triplet turn figures in mm. 14, 31, and 32, are idiomatic decorations that enhance the melodic surface.

The presence of chromaticism is integral to the structure of bebop melodies. Some of the chromatic additions, such as the metrically accented C♯5s in mm. 2, 6, 26, and 30, make subtle references to the blues. Other chromatic notes emphasize structurally important harmonies. For instance, a carefully prepared A♭4 occupies beat 1 in mm. 5 and 29, and constitutes the ♭7th of the underlying V/IV harmony. The preparation of A♭4 in mm. 4 and 28 features an upward stepwise ascent: F4–G4. The end of m. 12 illustrates another idiomatic preparation of this pitch. Here, the A♭4 anticipates V/IV by a half beat and occurs at the "and" of 4 in m. 12. The downward tritone leap from D5–A♭4 further intensifies its status and injects yet another blues characteristic into the framework of the melody. Other chromatic notes, such as unaccented passing and **pitch enclosures**, have primarily ornamental functions. The chromatic passing note G♭4 in mm. 5 and 29 moves between $\hat{6}$ and $\hat{5}$. A chromatic pitch enclosure occurs in m. 18 where the melodic cell E4–C4–C♯4–D4 encircles the root of D7. The C♯5s in mm. 2, 6, 26, and 30 constitute melodic **appoggiaturas** because they are accented and approached by a leap.

The rhythmic structure of the melody is interesting hypermetrically: in mm. 1–4, the hypermetric downbeat occurs in mm. 1 and 3 and emphasizes $\hat{5}$ as the melodic anchor. The continuation of the phrase features a less regular **hypermetric organization** with metrical downbeats occurring in mm. 5, 6, and 7. This hypermetric organization corroborates yet another characteristic of contrafacts, namely that they have a fairly irregular and purposefully unpredictable phrase structure. The irregular hypermetric organization of the A section is balanced by a symmetrical unfolding of hypermetric two-bar phrases in the bridge.

HARMONIC REWORKINGS OF RHYTHM CHANGES

The A section of rhythm changes can be realized with different harmonic progressions. Some of the most interesting realizations are shown in Figure 17.2. With each progression, the level of harmonic complexity increases.

When comparing mm. 1–2 with mm. 3–4, which essentially feature similar tonic expansions, B♭M7/D, D7(♭9), Dm7, B♭7, DM7, B♭M7/F, or D7 at the beginning of m. 3 can all be used to replace the original tonic chord B♭M7. In comparing the substitute options for the submediant in m. 1 or the supertonic in m. 2, there is also a variety of available choices. Figure 17.2e–i demonstrates more advanced transformations of the original progression. In Figure 17.2e, the submediant in m. 1 (Gm7) and the supertonic in m. 4 (Cm7) are replaced with the dominant tritone substitutions (D♭7(♭5) and G♭7, respectively). Figure 17.2g experiments with the *Coltrane* substitutions. In Figure 17.2h, a dominant pedal point supports the chord progression in upper parts. In Figure 17.2i, an extended cycle of dominant 7ths beginning on ♭6̂ substitutes for the original progression.

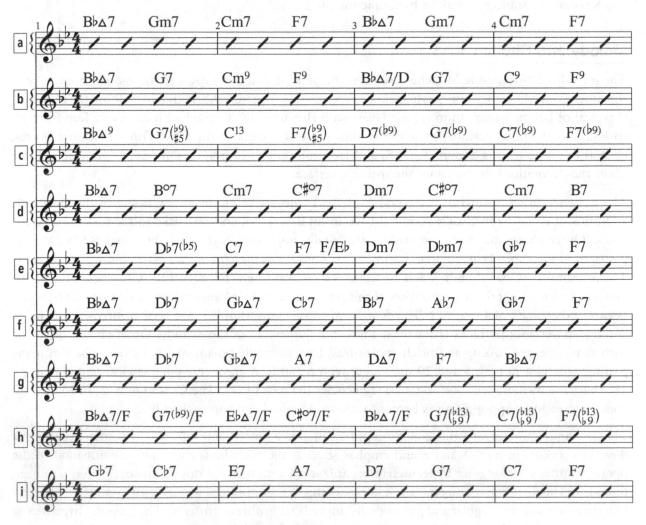

FIGURE 17.2 Alternate Progressions for the A Section

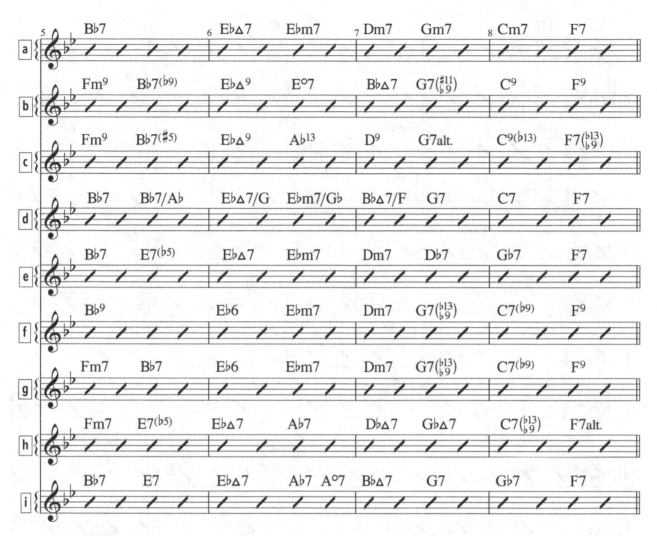

FIGURE 17.2 continued

The bridge of rhythm changes can be realized in many different ways as shown in Figure 17.3.

All the harmonic options in Figure 17.3 rely on the use of dominant 7th tritone substitutions, ii–V⁷ diminutions, and/or [ii–V⁷]/X interpolations. The use of a dominant 7th tritone substitution in its clearest manifestation is shown in Figure 17.3b. Chords in mm. 18, 20, 22, and 24 function as tritone substitutions of the preceding dominant 7ths. The use of ii–V⁷ diminutions results in the faster harmonic rhythm, as each dominant 7th of the bridge can be potentially expanded with a predominant ii. In Figure 17.3c, the ii–V⁷s occurring in mm. 18, 20, 22, and 24 expand the underlying dominant 7th chords. The combination of ii–V⁷ diminutions with [ii–V⁷]/X interpolations can produce more intricate harmonic progressions as demonstrated in Figure 17.3d and 17.3e. The most obvious consequence of such combinations is even faster harmonic rhythm with two chords per measure. For instance, in Figure 17.3d, the [ii–V⁷]/X interpolations in mm. 18, 20, 22, and 24 establish a logical voice-leading connection with the upcoming ii–V⁷ progression. In addition, the ii–V⁷s in mm. 17–18, 19–20, 21–22, and 23–24 are a half step away from each other, which further assures good voice leading. The neighboring ii–V⁷s are also on display in Figure 17.3e. But unlike Figure 17.3d, the [ii–V⁷]/X progressions in mm. 18, 20, 22, and 24 from Figure 17.3e function as lower chromatic neighbors in relation to the diatonic ii–V⁷ progressions.

FIGURE 17.3 Alternate Progressions for the B Section

RHYTHM CHANGES IMPROVISATION

The A Section: A Single-Scale Approach

The chord structure of the A sections of rhythm changes can be reduced to the fundamental framework shown in Figure 17.4.

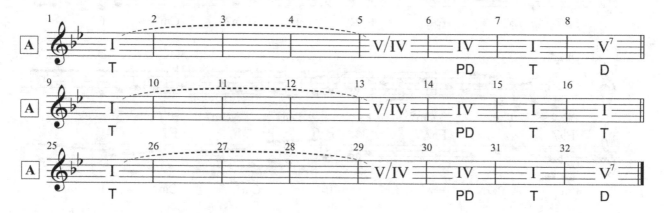

FIGURE 17.4 Fundamental Harmonic Frameworks

While mm. 1–4 of any A section feature a tonic prolongation, mm. 5–8 are more complicated even at the background level. For instance, the predominant in mm. 6, 14, and 30 can take the form of major 7th or dominant 7th chords. Also, the tonally closed second A section features two bars of I in mm. 15–16 instead of a half cadence in mm. 8 and 32. Figure 17.5 establishes a chord–scale relationship between structural chords and bebop scales.

FIGURE 17.5 A Basic Chord–Scale Relationship for the A Section

With a single major bebop scale controlling mm. 1–4, we can concentrate on improvising melodic lines that are entirely derived from the B♭ major bebop scale without being too preoccupied with the surface chord changes. In fact, when improvising against a more complex harmonic accompaniment, the melodic lines—albeit with a single chromatic passing note and the diminished 7th chord—will balance the chromatic accompaniment with controlled melodic tensions. Since mm. 5, 13, and 29 tonicize the subdominant harmony, this harmonic event needs to be well planned, prepared, and executed. Take the clue from the original melody and see how Parker introduced ♭$\hat{7}$ in those measures. In short, ♭$\hat{7}$ is an essential pitch that is necessary to make a convincing transition from the tonic to the predominant key

FIGURE 17.6 Phrases for the A Section

area. Figure 17.6a–c demonstrates how to negotiate the A section of rhythm changes using the chord–scale relationship from Figure 17.5.

The A Section: A Two-Scale Approach

The next step in rhythm changes improvisation involves adding a dominant 7th bebop scale in mm. 2 and 4. As a result, we must now negotiate two chromatic notes, $\flat\hat{6}$ from major bebop and $\sharp\hat{4}$ from dominant bebop. These additions will considerably chromaticize the content of melodic lines. Except for m. 6, mm. 5–8 remain the same as in Figure 17.4; the subdominant is expanded with a passing diminished 7th on $\sharp\hat{4}$. Figure 17.7 provides a chord–scale relationship for the A section of rhythm changes.

Figure 17.8a–c demonstrates a melodic realization of the chord–scale relationship from Figure 17.7.

FIGURE 17.7 An Alternate Chord–Scale Relationship for the A Section

FIGURE 17.8 Phrases for the A Section

FIGURE 17.9 The A Section—Arpeggiation Patterns

The A Section: Chord Arpeggiations

Having introduced two scalar choices for mm. 1–4, we can now focus on improvising over more harmonically advanced A sections with various arpeggiations of four- and five-part chords. These options are shown in Figure 17.9 with different harmonic settings for the A section.

The use of arpeggiation capitalizes on good voice leading between adjacent chords. When examining the content of lines in Figure 17.9b–e, notice that the low (or high) notes that begin arpeggiation patterns create a stepwise line spanning the entire A section. Such a line uses common tones and/or features stepwise motion between adjacent chords.

The B Section: A Single-Scale Approach

With only dominant 7th chords, the bridge of rhythm changes has a relatively uniform chord–scale relationship. Figure 17.10 establishes a basic chord–scale relationship for the B section. The use of D dominant bebop ♭13 at the beginning of the bridge is in keeping with the overall tonality of rhythm changes.

FIGURE 17.10 A Basic Chord–Scale Relationship for the B Section

Figure 17.11a–c provides a melodic realization of the chord–scale relationship from Figure 17.10.[6]

FIGURE 17.11 Phrases for the B Section

FIGURE 17.11 continued

NOTES

1   Some of the most well-known contrafacts on rhythm changes include: Lester Young's "Lester Leaps In," Sonny Stitt's "Eternal Triangle" (modified bridge) and "Sonny Side Up," Thelonious Monk's "Rhythm-A-Ning," Benny Harris's "Crazeology," Dizzy Gillespie's "Ow" and "Shaw 'Nuff" (with Parker), Fats Navarro's "Eb–Pob," Sonny Rollins's "Oleo," John Lewis's "Delauney's Dilemma," George Coleman's "Lo-Joe," Bill Evans's "Five," Miles Davis's "The Theme" and "The Serpent's Tooth" (modified bridge), Harold Danko's "Not In the Mood," Bill Dobbins's "TJRC," Brian Dickinson's "Splash," Jan Jarczyk's "Fifteen Years," Clay Jenkins's "Habitat," and Jeff Campbell's "Exit 41."

2   Other contrafacts on rhythm changes by Parker include: "Ah-leu-cha," "Anthropology," "Dexterity," "Kim," "Constellation," "An Oscar For Treadwell," "Celerity," "Chasin' The Bird," "Passport," "Red Cross," and "Steeplechase."

3   For representative recordings, consult Appendix F on the CW.

4   The term *eight-bar* blues was pointed to me by Prof. Harold Danko, who played in the Thad Jones/Mel Lewis Orchestra from 1976 until 1978; he remembers Thad Jones using this term in reference to the A section of rhythm changes and "Don't Get Sassy."

5   Eight-bar blues progressions often use the progression I–III–IV–I. Matthew Brown mentions this in his paper: "'Little Wing': A Study in Music Cognition," in *Understanding Rock*, ed. John Covach and Graeme Boone (Oxford: Oxford University Press, 1997), 155–169 [161]. A good example is J. J. Cale's "After Mignight."

6   For the example of a great solo on rhythm changes as performed by Hank Jones visit the CW.

Pentatonics, Hexatonics, Octatonics

CHAPTER SUMMARY

Chapter 18 embarks on a study of pentatonic, hexatonic, and octatonic scales. These collections are classified according to their possible chord–scale relationships and explored from different vertical and horizontal perspectives.

CONCEPTS AND TERMS

- Cardinality
- Double-diminished 7th chord
- Gapped formation
- Hexatonic voicings
- Hexatonics:
  - Altered
  - Regular
- Mixolydian ♭9
- Modes of Limited Transposition (MOLT)
- Mode II

- Mode IV
- Mode VI
- Octatonic scales:
  - Half-whole (**1/2**) octatonic I, II, III
  - Whole-half (**2/1**) octatonic I, II, III
- Palindrome
- Pentatonic system
- Pentatonic voicings
- Pentatonics:
  - Altered

- – Chromatic
- – Diatonic
- – Dominant
- – Major
- – Minor
- – Suspended
- Pitch aggregate
- Quartal voicings
- Scalar transposition
- Stacked fourth
- Transposition through the scale

METHODOLOGY

A thorough understanding of chord–scale theory allows us to prioritize certain notes and de-emphasize others. Hierarchically important notes occurring in the context of harmonic progressions and melodic lines (beauty marks, chord tones, alterations, and extensions) should receive melodic, harmonic, and rhythmic stress. Avoid notes, meanwhile, require careful metric and voice-leading considerations, because their uncontrolled presence might affect the clarity of chord progressions and melodic lines. In the structure of seven-note modes, there is a distinct hierarchy among pitches: the use of **4** in Ionian or **5** in Lydian, for instance, might have an undesirable effect on the content of corresponding chords or lines. The exclusion of these notes from Ionian and Lydian (and other notes from other modes as well) creates intervallically diverse six-note hexatonic scales (i.e. scales of cardinality of six).

The removal of two notes from seven-note modes produces even more intervallically diverse five-note pentatonic scales (i.e. scales of cardinality of five). The intervallic variety of pentatonic and hexatonic scales is very attractive to the improviser. In seven-note modes, scalar transpositions of a melodic pattern tend to sound predictable after a few repetitions. In pentatonic or hexatonic collections, however, the same pattern often sounds less predictable because the intervallic content of these scales is much more diverse. The reduction of pitch content to only five or six *essential* tones highlights the most crucial notes from the mode and imbues them with the capacity to make chords or melodic lines sound convincing. The development of pentatonic and hexatonic systems is analogous to the methodology of mode classification discussed in Chapter 7 and chord–scale theory in Chapter 8. **Pentatonics** and **hexatonics** are placed in functional categories and analyzed for their melodic and harmonic potential.

Unlike pentatonic and hexatonic collections whose pitch content is derived from the specific seven-note modes, the **octatonic scale** is an example of the symmetrical scale. Also known as the **Mode of Limited Transposition** (MOLT, henceforth), the octatonic scale (or **Mode II** using Oliver Messiaen's nomenclature) has only three unique pitch transpositions on account of its symmetrical structure. This characteristic renders the scale extremely useful in all kinds of harmonic and melodic environments.[1] In addition to the familiar octatonic scale (Mode II), there are two additional octatonic scales with a different, yet perfectly symmetrical pitch content. Largely overlooked by jazz musicians, Mode IV and Mode VI in Messiaen's Modes of Limited Transposition offer interesting pitch contents for generating unorthodox harmonic formations and melodic lines.

PENTATONICS

In jazz, pentatonics represent a rich assortment of scales with a vast potential for improvisation. They come in a variety of flavors, from the simple blues inflections added to diatonic pentatonics popularized by Lester Young in the 1930s to the chromatically altered five-note segments common in contemporary jazz styles.[2]

Basic Pentatonics

There are three basic pentatonics: major, minor, and dominant.[3] **Major pentatonic**, shown in Figure 18.1, is derived from the Ionian mode excluding **4** and **7**.

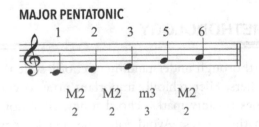

FIGURE 18.1 Major Pentatonic

The absence of semitones from its structure affects the scale's tonal character and removes the traces of harmonic tension from the collection. The sound of this scale conveys an aura of tonal neutrality, which makes major pentatonic, and other pentatonics as well, ideal choices for modal improvisation and modal harmony.

Minor pentatonic is derived from the Aeolian mode by excluding the tritone between **2** and ♭**6**. Figure 18.2 illustrates the derivation of a minor pentatonic.

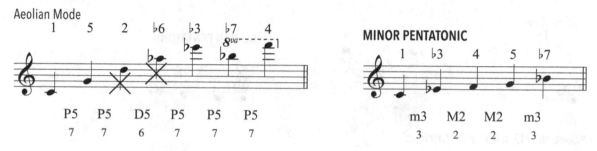

FIGURE 18.2 Minor Pentatonic

The content of a minor pentatonic prioritizes the intervals of major 2nds and minor 3rds, just as in the major counterpart. Similar to major pentatonic, the absence of the tritone and the leading tone contributes to the scale's independent tonal status.

Figure 18.3 illustrates two types of dominant pentatonic scales: dominant and suspended. Both can be derived from the Mixolydian mode and, as such, establish a convincing chord–scale relationship with the dominant 7th and suspended dominant chords, respectively.

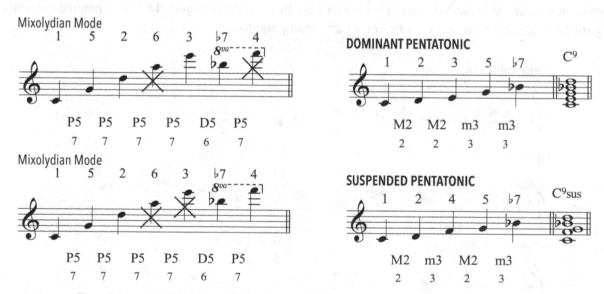

FIGURE 18.3 Dominant and Suspended Pentatonics

The pitch content of **dominant pentatonic** includes the tritone between **3** and ♭**7** that is inherent to the structure of the scale. The omission of **6** prevents the occurrence of a minor 2nd. This is in keeping with the overall character of other pentatonic collections. The intervallic content of **suspended pentatonic** prioritizes major 2nds and minor 3rds and the inclusion of **4** enables a chord–scale relationship with corresponding suspended formations.

Diatonic Pentatonics

In Chapter 7, diatonic and chromatic modes were generated using rotations of two parent scales: the major to construct diatonic modes and the melodic minor to create chromatic modes. **Diatonic pentatonics** can be derived in a similar manner. For the derivation of diatonic pentatonics, **Dorian pentatonic** is employed as the parent scale. The reason for this selection stems from its symmetrical pitch organization.[4] Figure 18.4 illustrates the pitch structure of the Dorian pentatonic.

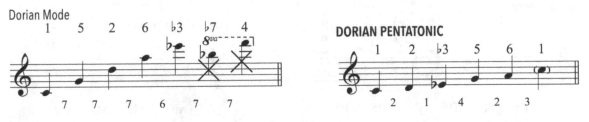

FIGURE 18.4 Dorian Pentatonic

Unlike other pentatonics discussed thus far, the Dorian pentatonic has a much more diverse intervallic content and includes four distinct intervals: two major 2nds, a minor 2nd, a major 3rd, and a minor 3rd (when you wrap the scale around the octave). Although reduced to only five notes, the pitch content of the scale embodies the essential Dorian characteristics: it has minor qualities and includes the beauty mark, major 6th.

By rotating the pitch structure of Dorian pentatonic, five distinct pentatonics are created: *Phrygian*, *Lydian*, *Mixolydian*, *Aeolian*, and *Locrian*. These scales are referred to as **diatonic pentatonics**. The Ionian pentatonic is excluded since it was previously introduced in Figure 18.1 as a major pentatonic. Figure 18.5 illustrates these five rotations of a Dorian pentatonic.

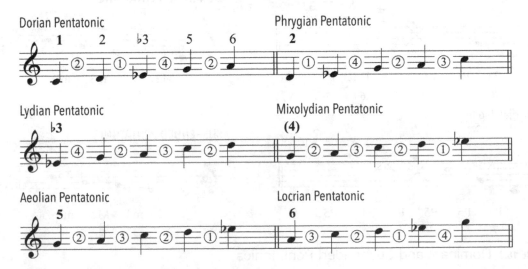

FIGURE 18.5 Rotations of Dorian Pentatonic

The Phrygian pentatonic starts on **2**, the Lydian pentatonic begins on **3**, the Mixolydian pentatonic starts on the *non-existent* **4**, the Aeolian pentatonic originates from **5**, and the Locrian pentatonic begins on **6**. When transposing these pentatonics to the same starting pitch, all but Mixolydian begin on the same note. The Mixolydian does not, since its pitch content is built on the *non-existent* root of the scale **4**. When comparing the structure of Mixolydian and Aeolian from Figure 18.5, notice that they have the same pitch content. The difference between the two, however, becomes apparent when comparing their transpositions. Figure 18.6 shows six pentatonics transposed to C4.

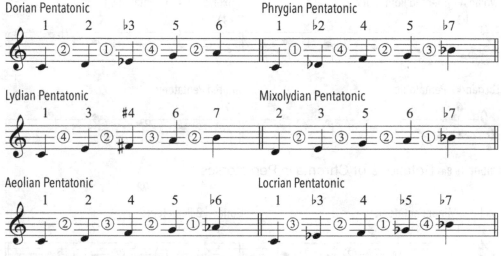

FIGURE 18.6 Pentatonics Transposed to C4

Based on what is already known about the modal theory, observe that the diatonic pentatonics have the same salient features as the corresponding seven-note modes. The Phrygian pentatonic contains the beauty mark ♭**2**, the Lydian pentatonic includes ♯**11**, and the Mixolydian pentatonic contains all the essential notes from the dominant 7th formation. The Aeolian pentatonic features the beauty mark ♭**6**, and the Locrian pentatonic highlights the characteristic ♭**5**.

Chromatic Pentatonics

Figure 18.7 shows the pitch content of the Melodic Minor pentatonic, which can serve as the parent scale for the generation of **chromatic pentatonics**.

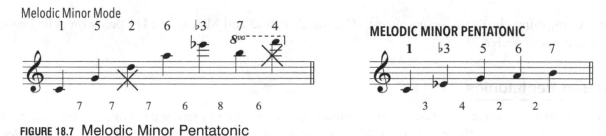

FIGURE 18.7 Melodic Minor Pentatonic

Figure 18.8a illustrates the rotations of the chromatic pentatonics and Figure 18.8b transposes them to C4.

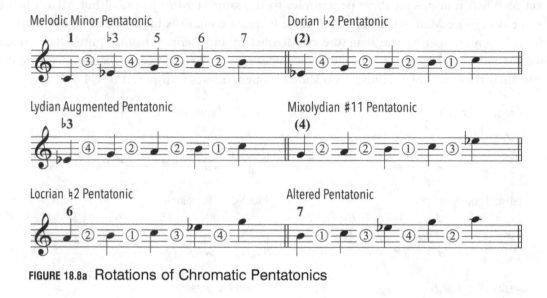

FIGURE 18.8a Rotations of Chromatic Pentatonics

FIGURE 18.8b Chromatic Pentatonics Transposed to C4

After transposing chromatic pentatonics to C4, the Dorian ♭2 and Mixolydian ♯11 pentatonics begin on ♭2 and 2 respectively.[5]

Altered Pentatonics

The structure of diatonic and chromatic pentatonics can be modified by minor pitch displacements and/or chromatic alterations. These pitch modifications result in the creation of the **altered pentatonics**; these scales share essential qualities with the regular pentatonic scales that they purport to modify. Figure 18.9 compiles altered pentatonics and shows their relationships with the diatonic and chromatic pentatonics.

BASIC PENTATONICS

DIATONIC PENTATONICS

Altered Pentatonics

Altered Pentatonics

FIGURE 18.9 Altered Pentatonics

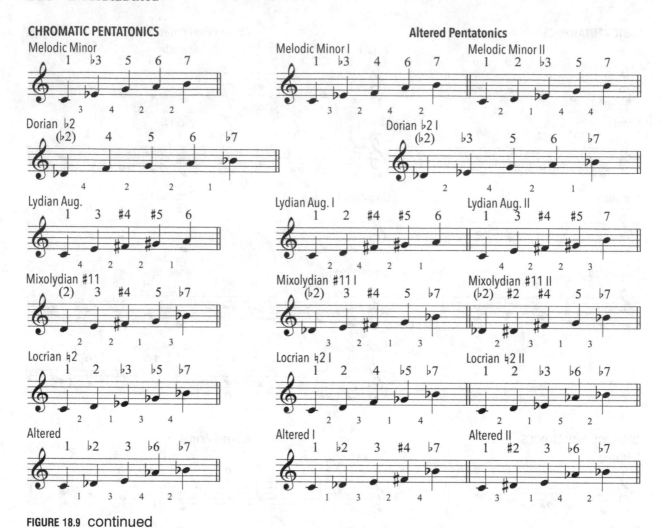

FIGURE 18.9 continued

With the exception of the Mixolydian pentatonic, altered versions of diatonic pentatonics include different combinations of pitches derived from the corresponding modes. **Mixolydian I** and **Mixolydian II** include chromatic alterations of **2**; these result in the inclusion of ♭9 in the former, and ♭9 and ♯9 in the latter.[6]

THE PENTATONIC SYSTEM

Broadly speaking, there are three types of pentatonic scales: **diatonic**, **chromatic**, and **altered**. The diatonic and chromatic pentatonics can be derived from the Dorian and Melodic Minor pentatonics, respectively. Altered pentatonics result from minor pitch displacements and/or alterations of diatonic and chromatic pentatonics. Even though pentatonics are primarily associated with modal improvisation and modal harmony, it is possible to invoke traditional functional relationships to make them useful in tonal improvisation and harmony. The **pentatonic system** attempts to illustrate the tonal potential of different pentatonic collections. To facilitate this discussion, the diatonic, chromatic, and altered pentatonics are compartmentalized into the familiar functional categories.

Major Category

Possible Harmonic Function—Tonic and Predominant

Figure 18.10 illustrates a collection of major pentatonics and establishes chord–scale relationships with selected chords.

FIGURE 18.10 Chord–Scale Relationship: Major Category

Minor Category

Possible Harmonic Function—Tonic and Predominant

Figure 18.11 compiles minor pentatonics and provides chord–scale relationships with selected chords.

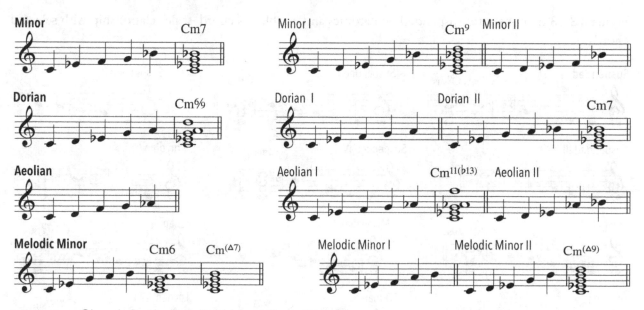

FIGURE 18.11 Chord–Scale Relationship: Minor Category

Dominant Category

Possible Harmonic Function—Dominant

Figure 18.12 shows dominant pentatonics and establishes chord–scale relationships with selected chords.

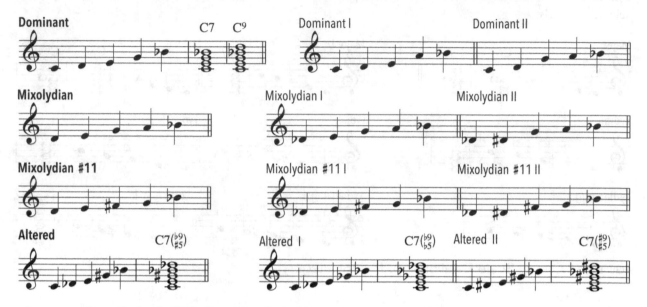

FIGURE 18.12 Chord–Scale Relationship: Dominant Category

Suspended Dominant Category

Possible Harmonic Function—Dominant and Predominant

Figure 18.13 demonstrates suspended pentatonics and establishes chord–scale relationship with selected chords.

FIGURE 18.13 Chord–Scale Relationship: Suspended Dominant Category

Intermediary Category

Possible Harmonic Function—Predominant and Dominant

Figure 18.14 features intermediary pentatonic collections and establishes chord–scale relationships for this category.

FIGURE 18.14 Chord–Scale Relationship: Intermediary Category

Harmonic Potential

Pentatonic collections are very useful for the generation of **quartal voicings**. Although voicings introduced in this section primarily have modal characteristics, they are just as effective in various tonal contexts. Figure 18.15 demonstrates five quartal voicings that can be derived from the Dorian pentatonic. In this and the forthcoming figures, boxed chords indicate the projection of a complete pentatonic collection.

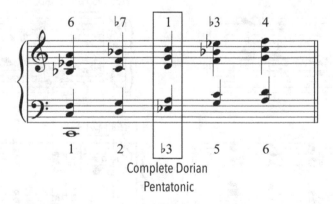

FIGURE 18.15 Dorian Family of Voicings

The structure of the voicings in Figure 18.15 features the notes from the Dorian mode arranged as **stacked fourths**.[7] Even though occasional thirds or other intervals might appear in quartal voicings, they tend to balance the overall structure of the sonority. As long as the interval of a fourth is prioritized (especially at the bottom of the chord), voicings should display typical modal characteristics.

The methodology for generating **pentatonic voicings** can be summed up as follows:

1. Create a quartal voicing that includes all or the majority of the pitches from the pentatonic collection.

2. The pitches from the pentatonic scale function as the *roots* of the subsequent chords derived from this pentatonic.

3. Transfer the opening voicing up to the *next* pitch from the *pentatonic scale* unfolding in the *bass*. Think of transferring all the voices (excluding the bass voice) up to the next available pitch derived from the corresponding *seven-note mode*. In generating Phrygian pentatonic voicings, for instance, use a Phrygian pentatonic to create five unique transpositions of the opening sonority and the Phrygian mode to supply the pitch content.

4. While the lowest note of each voicing projects the specific pentatonic scale, the inner voices are derived from the corresponding mode.

5. These voicings represent a useful collection of sonically related voicings that can be used interchangeably in a variety of tonal or modal contexts.

Figure 18.16 illustrates the families of pentatonic voicings for selected basic, diatonic, chromatic, and altered pentatonic collections.

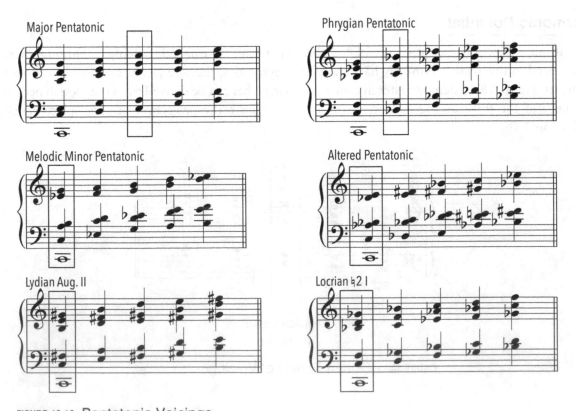

FIGURE 18.16 Pentatonic Voicings

Melodic Potential

Even though the methodology described above focuses on voicings, the idea that chords can be horizontalized as lines and vice versa allows us to explore the melodic potential of pentatonics. Figure 18.17 shows how it is possible to extract three-note melodic cells from a specific pentatonic and then how to use those cells to create a pentatonic line.

Dorian Pentatonic

Lydian Aug. Pentatonic

Phrygian II Pentatonic

Suspended IV Pentatonic

FIGURE 18.17 Pentatonic Lines

These pitch transfers preserve the overall shape of the original cell, but not always the intervallic contour of the cell. The diverse intervallic structure of pentatonics is very useful in rendering different pitch transfers of the original motive less symmetrical and devoid of intervallic predictability.

HEXATONICS

The **hexatonic** scale is a six-note collection that conveys characteristics similar to the seven-note modes. Just like pentatonics, hexatonic scales have interesting intervallic properties and provide essential notes for melodic lines and harmonic formations. First, the hexatonic collections are compartmentalized into familiar functional categories. Then, the individual scales are derived from the aggregates of pitches that contain all available notes from the particular category. Since the **pitch aggregate** for the major category, for instance, combines eight distinct notes, there are a lot of options for generating different major hexatonics. Given the enormous range of possibilities, it is best to pick a scale whose pitch content best expresses a specific modal or tonal context.

The derivation of hexatonics from the aggregate puts the understanding of pitch hierarchy to the test. The pitch structure of hexatonic collections prioritizes only those notes that are essential to projecting the exact harmonic function and/or intended chord–scale relationship. Each category below includes two types of hexatonic collections: regular and altered. **Regular hexatonics** share common characteristics with the corresponding modes. For instance, Mixolydian ♯11 hexatonic has similar properties to the seven-note Mixolydian ♯11 mode, etc. **Altered hexatonics** are derived from the specific pitch aggregate and their structure includes minor variations from regular hexatonics. In labeling altered hexatonics, use the name of the category with Roman numerals specifying different variations (i.e. Major Altered I, Dominant Altered II, etc.).

Major Category

Possible Harmonic Function—Tonic and Predominant

Figure 18.18 illustrates the pitch aggregate for the major category: three regular hexatonic collections and three altered hexatonics.[8] The only notes that cannot be used in the aggregate are: ♭2, ♭3, and ♭7. All other notes can be freely combined as six-note segments to create altered hexatonics. Notice that the Major Altered II and III combine the characteristics of three regular hexatonics (**5** from Ionian, **♯4** from Lydian, and **♯5** from Lydian Augmented).

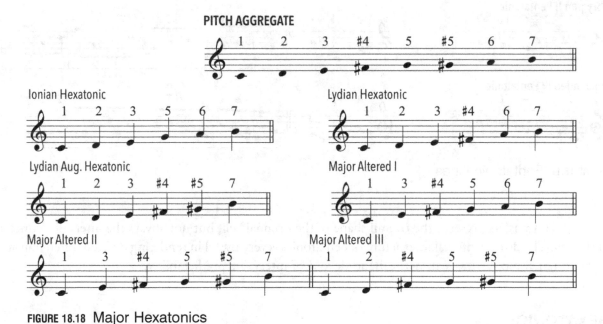

FIGURE 18.18 Major Hexatonics

Minor Category

Possible Harmonic Function—Tonic and Predominant

Figure 18.19 provides the pitch aggregate for the minor category: three regular hexatonic collections and three altered hexatonics. The inclusion of ♯4 in the aggregate raises several issues. Until now, the ♯4 (♭5th) has participated only in the context of major or dominant chords. In a more advanced harmonic syntax, however, the addition of ♯4 (functioning as a ♯11th) expands the structure of minor formations. Since the extended tertian structure derived from C Melodic Minor, for instance, features two overlapping four-part formations, Cm(♯7) and B∅7, the upper formation can be substituted with the Bm7 chord. This substitution preserves the tertian nature of the extended formation and infuses the seven-part chord with the Lydian characteristics: C–E♭–G–B–D–F♯–A.

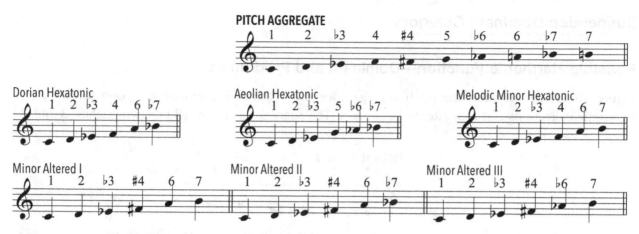

FIGURE 18.19 Minor Hexatonics

Dominant Category

Possible Harmonic Function—Dominant

Figure 18.20 shows the pitch aggregate for the dominant category: four regular hexatonic collections and four altered hexatonics. The only pitches excluded from the aggregate are **4** and **7**. Notice the presence of Mixolydian ♭9, which was not encountered in the discussion of modal theory. Since this scale includes a single chromatic alteration ♭9—just as do the two other chromatic modes, Mixolydian #11 and Mixolydian ♭13—this collection is labeled as **Mixolydian ♭9**.

FIGURE 18.20 Dominant Hexatonics

Suspended Dominant Category

Possible Harmonic Function—Dominant and Predominant

Figure 18.21 demonstrates the pitch aggregate for the suspended dominant category: three regular hexatonic collections and four altered hexatonics. The aggregate contains all but two pitches, **3** and **7**.

FIGURE 18.21 Suspended Hexatonics

Intermediary Category

Possible Harmonic Function—Predominant and Dominant

Figure 18.22 shows the pitch aggregate for the intermediary category: four regular hexatonic collections and four altered hexatonics.

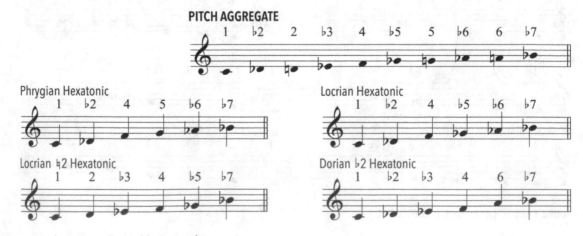

FIGURE 18.22 Intermediary Hexatonics

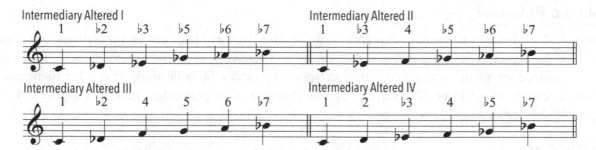

FIGURE 18.22 continued

Harmonic Potential

Just as with pentatonics, the hexatonic collections provide useful pitch resources for creating interesting voicings of different cardinality. The procedures for generating voicings of various sizes are similar to those discussed earlier in this chapter and utilize transfers of the initial voicing through the hexatonic scale. The resulting six voicings represent the sound of the specific hexatonic and constitute potential substitutes for one another in different harmonic scenarios. **Hexatonic voicings** can be generated using the following procedures:

1. Establish the initial close-position voicing that captures the sound of the hexatonic scale.

2. Transfer the close-position voicing up to the next pitch from the hexatonic scale. Use notes from the corresponding hexatonic scale only.

3. Rearrange the pitches of the initial close-position voicing to create different open-position voicings.

4. Transfer the open-position voicing through the hexatonic scale.

Figure 18.23 demonstrates these procedures using four- and five-part voicings derived from Lydian hexatonic.

FIGURE 18.23 Hexatonic Voicings

Melodic Potential

Based on the fundamental premise that chords can be linearized and lines can be verticalized, hexatonic scales can be explored by using different melodic cells. These cells are derived from the scale's content and transferred to all the notes from the corresponding hexatonic collection. The subsequent pitch transfers feature more intervallic variety, as was the case with pentatonic scales in Figure 18.17. Figure 18.24 demonstrates this process.

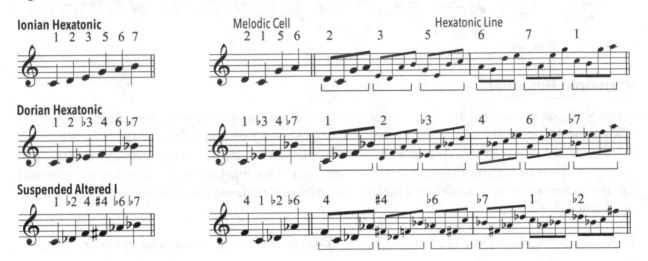

FIGURE 18.24 Melodic Potential

THE 1/2 OCTATONIC SCALE—MODE II OF LIMITED TRANSPOSITION

In Chapter 14, we saw how bebop scales expand the number of pitches from seven to eight. Theorists often refer to this expansion as a change in the **cardinality** of the scale. The term *octatonic* denotes a scale whose cardinality is eight, i.e. the scale consists of eight distinct pitches. The **octatonic scale** covered in this chapter comes in two forms that alternate between half– and whole–tones. Those intervals are normally represented by the Arabic numbers 1 and 2 respectively.

The terms *half whole* and *whole half* refer to the order in which those two intervals recur within these scales. The term half–whole (or 1/2) designates octatonic scales that begin with two notes a half step apart, whereas the term whole–half (or 2/1) designates octatonic scales that begin with two notes a whole step apart. Each version has very different functional behaviors and establish important chord-scale relationships, though the symmetrical properties of both scales allow for some interesting functional overlaps and a multiplicity of harmonic associations.

The **1/2** octatonic scale is primarily associated with the dominant function. It establishes impressive chord–scale relationships with a variety of dominant 7th formations. The **1/2** octatonic scale is a symmetrical collection that repeats the **1/2** intervallic pattern every other note. The scale partitions the octave into two tritones or four minor 3rds. It also includes two overlapping minor 3rd cycles a half step apart. In C **1/2** octatonic, these cycles feature the following pitch segments: C–E♭–F♯–A and D♭–E–G–B♭. The symmetrical properties of the scale have profound harmonic and melodic implications. They mean that *any* voicing, chord progression, scalar segment, or melodic cell when transposed up or down a minor 3rd will retain the original shape and functional status. A single **1/2** octatonic will therefore establish the chord–scale relationship with as many as four distinct harmonic formations a minor 3rd apart. The **1/2** octatonic scale has **three unique transpositions** shown in Figure 18.25. These scalar transpositions are referred to as **1/2 octatonic I**, **1/2 octatonic II**, and **1/2 octatonic III**.

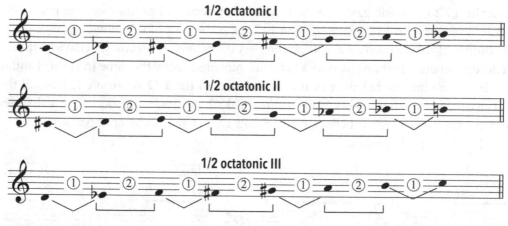

FIGURE 18.25 **1/2** Octatonic I, II, III

Before exploring the harmonic potential of the scale, let us examine the pitch structure of **1/2** octatonic I in terms of chord tones, pitch alterations, and chordal extensions. Figure 18.26 provides a pitch analysis of **1/2** octatonic I built on C4.

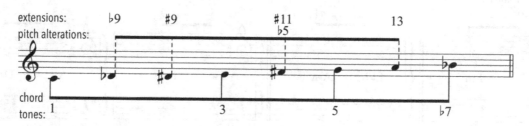

FIGURE 18.26 **1/2** Octatonic I—Pitch Analysis

The scale includes all the chord tones of the C7 harmony: the root, major 3rd, perfect 5th, and minor 7th. It also contains three chromatic extensions ♭9th, ♯9th and ♯11th, one diatonic extension, major 13th, and one pitch alteration, ♭5th. As such, the **1/2** octatonic establishes a convincing chord–scale relationship with C7(♭5) and C13(♭9,♯9,♯11). In addition, the **1/2** octatonic I scale is a perfect match for the C7(♭9) chord that, until now, has been paired with neither a scale nor a mode. Since the pitch content of any **1/2** octatonic is invariant under minor 3rd transposition, the dominant 7th chords a minor 3rd apart establish chord–scale relationships with the same **1/2** octatonic scale. Therefore, any **1/2** octatonic can be used in conjunction with four distinct dominant 7ths. This ratio of chords to scale relationships is a distinctive feature of the octatonic collection and allows for a highly economical use of the scale. Figure 18.27 examines the pitch structure of **1/2** octatonic I in the context of four dominant 7ths minor 3rd apart.

A7	♯9	3	♯11/♭5	5	13	7	1	♭9	A7
F♯7	♯11/♭5	5	13	♭7	1	♭9	♯9	3	F♯7
E♭7	13	♭7	1	♭9	♯9	3	♯11/♭5	5	E♭7
C7	1	♭9	♯9	3	♯11/♭5	5	13	♭7	C7

FIGURE 18.27 **1/2** Octatonic I and Four Minor 3rd-Related Dominant 7ths

Each note of the **1/2** octatonic has a unique chordal membership. For instance, the pitch C5 functions as #9th in A7, #11th/♭5th in F#7, major 13th in E♭7, or as the root of C7. What does it mean? It means that in the context of these chords, C5 will exhibit very different voice-leading behaviors that are unique to the specific dominant 7th chord. A note's behavior remains exactly the same in vertical and horizontal dimensions. In examining the behavior of the second note of the **1/2** octatonic I, D♭4, all the possible harmonic scenarios in which all other notes from the **1/2** octatonic can occur are exhausted. Figure 18.28 illustrates the voice-leading behavior of C5 and D♭5 (C#5) in the context of C7, E♭7, F#7, and A7 using V⁷–I or V⁷–i progressions.

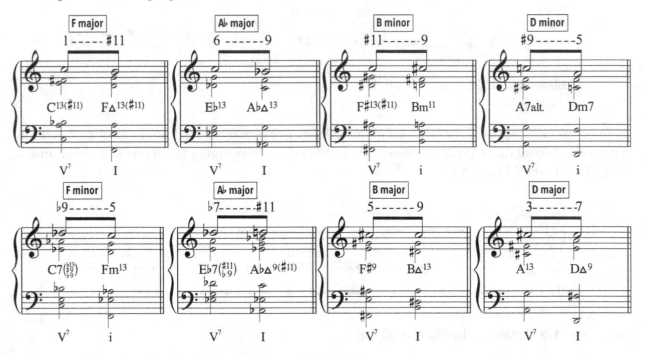

FIGURE 18.28 Voice-Leading Behavior of C5 and D♭5 (C#5)

Harmonic Potential

In exploring the harmonic potential of **1/2** octatonic, let us examine what happens to a chord in **transposition through the scale**. Transposition through the scale takes the initial formation and moves it linearly to the nearest available formation derived entirely from the pitches of the scale. For instance, a major triad in root position built on **1** becomes a minor triad in 2nd inversion on ♭**2**; a half-diminished chord on **1** becomes a dim(#7) chord on ♭**2**, etc. The two initial chords, shown in Figure 18.29, create

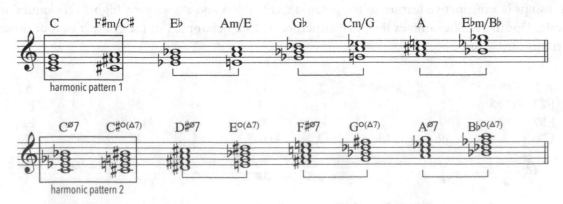

FIGURE 18.29 Harmonic Transpositions Through the **1/2** Octatonic I Scale

a harmonic pattern that repeats every other note. In transposition through the scale, then, the initial sonority can be thought of as comprised of three or four (depending on the chord's cardinality) melodic lines traversing through the scale in a stepwise fashion.

Melodic Potential

Let us now examine what happens to a motivic cell in transposition through the scale. Just as the structure of harmonic formations built on **1** and **♭2** is different from one another, so is the intervallic design of motivic cells occurring on these pitches. If the original motivic cell built on **1** of **1/2** octatonic features a specific intervallic design, in transposition to **♭2**, the order of pitches is preserved yet the intervals between the notes change. A melodic pattern combines two recurrences of the original motive on **1** and **♭2** that is subsequently repeated every other note. Figure 18.30 illustrates a few motivic cells transposed through the **1/2** octatonic. The circled numbers between adjacent pitches indicate the semitone count.

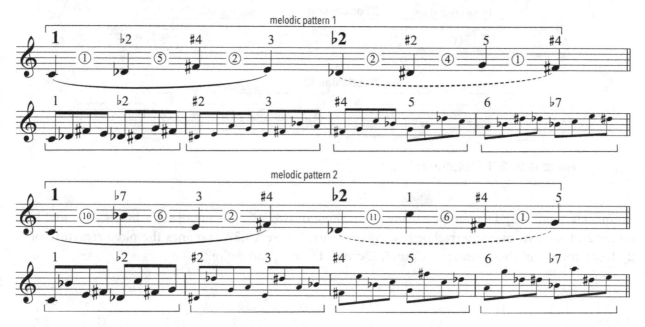

FIGURE 18.30 Melodic Transpositions Through the **1/2** Octatonic I Scale

What we now know about the structure and behavior of the **1/2** octatonic scale is summarized below:

1. The pitches—**1**, **♭3**, **♯4**, and **6**—can potentially function as either roots, ♯9ths, ♯11ths (♭5ths), or major 13ths of four dominant 7th chords built on **1**, **♭3**, **♯4**, and **6**.

2. The pitches—**♭2**, **3**, **5**, and **♭7**—can potentially function as either major 3rds, perfect 5ths, minor 7ths, or ♭9ths of four dominant 7th chords built on **1**, **♭3**, **♯4**, and **6**.

3. Any harmonic formation or melodic pattern built on **1** retains its original form when transposed up or down a minor 3rd.

4. Any harmonic formation or melodic pattern built on **♭2** retains its original form when transposed up or down a minor 3rd.

5. Any harmonic/melodic pattern combines two occurrences of the initial chord/cell built on **1** and **♭2** and repeats every other note.

THE 2/1 OCTATONIC SCALE—MODE II OF LIMITED TRANSPOSITION

Since the **2/1 octatonic** constitutes the inversion of the **1/2** octatonic, the principles regarding symmetry and transpositional invariance are exactly the same for both scales. The fundamental difference between the two relates to their very different functional associations. The **2/1** octatonic functions largely as a predominant and establishes a basic chord–scale relationship with the diminished 7th chord. The scale has three unique transpositions: **2/1 octatonic I**, **2/1 octatonic II**, and **2/1 octatonic III**. Figure 18.31 illustrates the pitch structure of these scales.

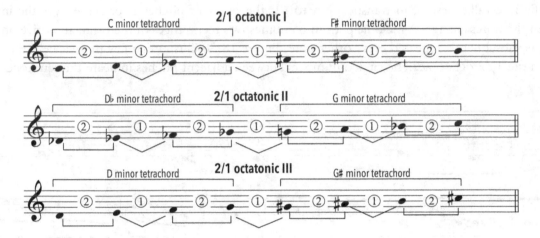

FIGURE 18.31 **2/1 Octatonic I, II, III**

To quickly build a **2/1** octatonic on any pitch, think of two adjacent minor tetrachords separated by a minor 2nd, or two minor tetrachords a tritone apart. Figure 18.32 examines the pitch structure of C **2/1** octatonic I in the context of Cdim7, E♭dim7, F♯dim7, and Adim7.

A°7	♭3	11	♭5	♭13	♭♭7	#7	1	9	A°7
F♯°7	♭5	♭13	♭♭7	#7	1	9	♭3	11	F♯°7
E♭°7	♭♭7	#7	1	9	♭3	11	♭5	♭13	E♭°7
C°7	1	9	♭3	11	♭5	♭13	♭♭7	#7	C°7

FIGURE 18.32 **2/1 Octatonic I and Four Minor 3rd-Related Diminished 7ths**

Similar to the relationship between the **1/2** octatonic and the dominant 7th chord, the **2/1** octatonic contains only chord tones and extensions of the diminished 7th chord. By arranging all the notes from the **2/1** octatonic as shown in Figure 18.33, the **double-diminished 7th chord** is created that contains two gapped diminished 7th formations. A **gapped formation** uses an interval, which lies outside of the underlying cyclic pattern, to link two symmetrical chords: a major 2nd in this case.

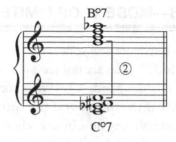

FIGURE 18.33 Double-Diminished 7th Chord

Once we realize that **2/1** octatonic II has the same pitch content as **1/2** octatonic I, then it becomes clear that a single octatonic scale can establish a relationship with dominant 7th and diminished 7th chords. Since the diminished 7th chord often functions as a rootless dom7(♭9), it can use the same scale in different harmonic situations.

OTHER OCTATONIC SCALES—MODE IV OF LIMITED TRANSPOSITION

Mode IV of Limited Transposition is a symmetrical scale with the **1/1/3/1** intervallic pattern repeated at the tritone. Since the symmetrical segment of the scale is much longer than the **2/1** patterns in Mode II, Mode IV has six unique transpositions and, as such, is less symmetrical than Mode II. The pitch content repeats itself at the tritone. The structure of the scale is shown in Figure 18.34.

Mode IV

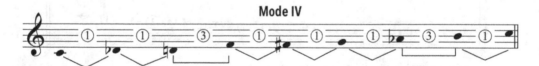

FIGURE 18.34 Mode IV of Limited Transposition

Even though Mode IV is neither associated with particular harmonic function nor establishes a convincing chord–scale relationship with traditional chords, it can nonetheless furnish some fresh harmonic and melodic ideas to experiment with while reharmonizing tunes or composing your own material. Figure 18.35 demonstrates how to explore the harmonic potential of the scale by taking the initial formation and transposing it through the scale in the manner shown in Figure 18.29.

FIGURE 18.35 Harmonic Transpositions Through Mode IV

OTHER OCTATONIC SCALES—MODE VI OF LIMITED TRANSPOSITION

Mode VI of Limited Transposition is a symmetrical scale with the **2/2/1/1** intervallic pattern repeated at the tritone. Similar to Mode IV, Mode VI has six unique pitch transpositions. Among seven MOLT, three are octatonic: Mode II, Mode IV, and Mode VI. When comparing Mode II with Mode VI, the former conjoins two *minor* tetrachords at the tritone and the latter combines two *major* tetrachords at the tritone. Similar to Mode IV, Mode VI has no obvious chord–scale relationships except for some distant traces of tonic and dominant function. The pitch structure of Mode VI is given in Figure 18.36.

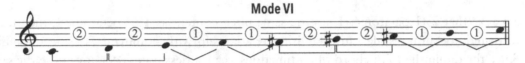

FIGURE 18.36 Mode VI of Limited Transposition

Figure 18.37 illustrates how to explore the harmonic potential of Mode VI by transposing the initial sonority through the scale.

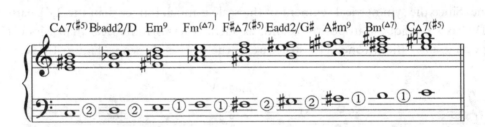

FIGURE 18.37 Harmonic Transpositions Through Mode VI

As limited as their usage is in mainstream jazz, Modes IV and VI are great scalar resources to experiment with while improvising, harmonizing and composing in a more modern jazz idiom. Just as Oliver Messiaen created a whole new harmonic and melodic universe using MOLT, so jazz musicians can also adopt them for their own artistic needs.

NOTES

1   The term **Modes of Limited Transposition** (MOLT) was introduced by Oliver Messiaen in his *The Technique of My Musical Language*. Mode I is based on the recurring major 2nd intervallic pattern (notated as 2) and is commonly known as the whole-tone scale; Mode II is the octatonic scale discussed here and features the recurring 2/1 intervallic pattern; Mode III features the 2/1/1 pattern; Mode IV, the 1/1/3/1; Mode V, the 1/4/1; Mode VI, the 2/2/1/1; and Mode VII the 1/1/1/2/1 pattern. The indication "2/2/1/1" refers to the number of semitones between adjacent pitches of the scale: "1"—one semitone, "2"—two semitones, "3"—three semitones, etc. For Messiaen's explanation of modes see the English translation (1956) pp. 58–62.

2   See, for instance, Lester Young's *The Kansas City Sessions* and *The Complete Aladdin Recordings*.

3   The major, minor, and "suspended" pentatonics are rotations of one another.

4   From ca. 800 until the 1600s, Dorian was considered the first mode in the eight-mode (or 12-mode) system. Significantly, Dorian is also a **palindrome**: it has the same intervallic structure upwards and downwards.

5   Since the Mixolydian ♭13 pentatonic does not contain ♭7 in its structure, it is omitted from the list of available chromatic pentatonics.

6 The use of Roman numbers "I," "II," etc. indicates the pitch variations of the basic, diatonic, or chromatic pentatonics.
7 These types of voicings are also known as the *So What* voicings because they resemble similar chords performed by Bill Evans on the iconic *Kind of Blue* recording from 1959.
8 Since hexatonic collections and modes share the same chord–scale relationships, the forthcoming figures do not include chords.

CHAPTER 19

The *Tristano Style* of Improvisation

CHAPTER SUMMARY

Chapter 19 provides an analysis of Lennie Tristano's "Line Up." Based on this analysis, specific characteristics of his style of improvisation are discussed and codified.

CONCEPTS AND TERMS

- Compound/polyphonic melody
- Escape tones
- Melodic interpolation
- Motivic parallelism
- Neighbor figures
- Passing notes
- Playing outside
- Rhythmic displacement
- Sidestepping
- Slurs
- Structural approach
- Tristano school

INTRODUCTION

"Line Up" is an overdubbed solo performed by Lennie Tristano with a pre-recorded rhythm section.[1] The solo is a superb demonstration of an important style of improvisation, which is characterized, above all, by a highly innovative approach to rhythm and meter. The remarkable feature of the **Tristano school**, whose illustrious alumni include Lee Konitz, Warne Marsh, Billy Bauer, and others, is that it lends itself for improvisation as much as it does for composition. In fact, contrafacts such as "Lennie's Pennies" and "317 East 32nd Street" composed by Tristano, "Subconscious-Lee" and "Kary's Trance" written by Konitz, or "Marshmallow" and "See Me Now, If You Could" composed by Marsh, sound like improvisations worked out in advance.

"Line Up" exemplifies the essence of the Tristano style and, as such, constitutes a great pedagogical tool for summarizing various characteristics of jazz musical syntax discussed in this book. It also demonstrates how specific theoretical concepts work in practice. You will be surprised at the amount of information encoded in this solo and how much you can learn by cracking Tristano's musical code. In the forthcoming analysis, the discussion focuses on the aspects of his playing that have practical applications and eventually leads to a broader codification of his style of improvisation.

ANALYTICAL ANNOTATIONS

Figure 19.2 shows a partially annotated transcription of Lennie Tristano's "Line Up." To facilitate comprehension, various analytical markings and symbols are used, and these are summarized in Figure 19.1. **Neighbor figures** prepare chord tones or structural tones by step from below and/or above. In the transcription, **UN** indicates upper neighbor, **LN** lower neighbor, and **DN** double neighbor (which some jazz musicians also call pitch enclosure). Double-neighbor figures typically involve three- or four-note groupings, but in the case of longer gestures, they are designated **EDN** (extended double neighbor). The chord tone decorated with a neighbor figure is analyzed with an Arabic number written in parenthesis to show its chord membership. Somewhat related to neighbor figures is the **escape note, EN**, which leaves a chord tone with a step and resolves to another chord tone by a skip in the opposite direction. In addition to neighbor and escape notes, Tristano employs a variety of **passing notes, PN**. Those derived from bebop scales are designated **BPN** (bebop passing note). In the score, passing and escape notes are placed in parenthesis and analyzed accordingly. Occasionally, **D** (diatonic) and **C** (chromatic) are written in front of **LN, DN, PN**, etc.: for instance, **CUN** stands for chromatic upper neighbor, **DDN** for diatonic double neighbor, etc. In the case of accented figures, **A** written in front of the symbol is used: **ALN** indicates accented lower neighbor; **ACPN**, accented chromatic passing note, etc.

Neighbor figures often occur in the midst of a phrase making them difficult to isolate from the surrounding notes; they are therefore marked by **slurs** in the score. *Dashed slurs* show various scalar passages, such as modes, bebop scales, pentatonics, chromatic segments, melodic patterns, and characteristic gestures. *Dotted slurs* indicate prolongation of notes across larger sections of music and a stepwise voice-leading connection between (with possible octave transfers) adjacent phrases. *Brackets* below the score are reserved for chord arpeggiations and harmonic substitutions, which are analyzed with additional chord symbols, scale degrees, and Arabic numbers. Chords written below the brackets represent harmonic departures from the underlying progressions. These departures are essential to Tristano's style and include: *superimposition of chromatic structures* (three-, four-, or five-part), *harmonic sequences*, and *chromatic sidestepping*. Chromatic **sidesteppings** are indicated with vertical arrows pointing to the direction of a departure from the structural harmony. For the purpose of readability, these departures are analyzed with enharmonic chord symbols, which do not coincide with the structurally appropriate spellings.

Scale degrees specify important tones in the tonic key and underscore *structural melodic spans* or *motifs* occurring at the background level. For instance, a $\hat{6}–\flat\hat{6}–\hat{5}$ stands for the melodic span F–F♭–E♭ in the key of A♭ major. There is frequently a lot of melodic activity at the surface level between structural tones; therefore, these tones are marked with longer stems connected to a *horizontal beam*. *Dashed stems* indicate non-structural notes, such as local chord tones or melodic patterns connected to a horizontal beam. *Arabic numbers* are utilized for specific pitch successions occurring over local harmonies. For instance, a C:1–2–3–5 illustrates a C–D–E–G melodic pattern.

Abbreviations

UN/DUN	upper neighbor/diatonic upper neighbor
LN/CLN	lower neighbor/chromatic lower neighbor
DN/DDN/CDN	double neighbor/diatonic double neighbor/chromatic double neighbor
ELN/DEDN/CEDN	extended lower neighbor/diatonic extended double neighbor/chromatic extended double neighbor
EN	escape note
PN/CPN/BPN	passing note/chromatic passing note/bebop passing note
ALN/AUN/ACPN/ACDN	accented lower neighbor/accented upper neighbor/accented chromatic passing note/accented chromatic double neighbor
INT	melodic interpolations

Symbols

	groups different neighbor figures
	shows modes, bebop scales, pentatonics, chromatic scales, melodic patterns, and interpolations
	note prolongations and stepwise voice-leading connections (with octave transfers) between adjacent phrases
	indicates chord arpeggiations and harmonic substitutions
	connects structural tones to a horizontal beam
	connects notes of lesser structural significance to a horizontal beam
	shows chromatic sidestepping in relation to the structural harmony
	combines structural spans and motives
( )	represents passing and escape notes in the score

Integers

$\hat{1}$, $\hat{2}$, $\hat{3}$, $\hat{4}$, etc.	structural tones
1–2–3–5; 1, 2, 3, etc.	chord members over local harmonies
(3), (5), etc.	local chord tones decorated with neighbor-tone figures

FIGURE 19.1 Analytical Symbols and Annotations

FIGURE 19.2 "Line Up"—Lennie Tristano (transcribed by Dariusz Terefenko)

CHORUS 2

FIGURE 19.2 continued

FIGURE 19.2 continued

CHORUS 4

FIGURE 19.2 continued

FIGURE 19.2 continued

CHORUS 6

FIGURE 19.2 continued

CHORUS 7

FIGURE 19.2 continued

AN ANALYSIS OF THE TRANSCRIPTION

When listening to the recording of "Line Up," notice the inherent complexity of Tristano's lines, their incessant drive, and their swinging quality. As had been the case with numerous instrumental contrafacts from the bebop period (and as was definitely the prevalent compositional strategy of his school) Tristano borrowed the chord progression from the repertory of standard tunes. In this case he chose "All of Me" by Gerald Marks and Seymour Simons. An interesting fact about "Line Up" is the absence of a clearly defined thematic statement at the outset of the piece. With each passing chorus, the music seems to build up a forward momentum giving listeners numerous jolts by shifting to chromatic key areas or engaging in complex rhythmic displacements. With the exception of a few places (mm. 97–104 and 149), the solo employs a single-line texture, which makes it ideal for studying and performing by different instrumentalists. But what is truly remarkable about "Line Up" is that, in spite of the listener's initial reaction to its complex nature, Tristano uses relatively simple melodic ideas that he effectively synchronizes with different structural patterns. He employs a variety of rhythmic devices that give the solo an innovative character and fully capitalizes on the relationship between melody and meter. The interplay between melody and meter occurring at various levels of the musical fabric is the driving force behind this solo, which demonstrates Tristano's heightened awareness of musical discourse.

Rhythmic Displacement

The idea of **rhythmic displacement** is central to the Tristano style and is announced in the very first phrase of his seven-chorus *tour de force* solo. The line begins in m. 9 with an iambic rhythmic motive, which is immediately answered in m. 10 by an anapestic figure.[2] The placement of the anapestic figure on beat 4, coupled with an accent on the first note, makes the entire phrase sound metrically ambiguous, almost as if the beat got turned around. By displacing the second half of the phrase by a beat, Tristano cleverly overrides the predictable phrase symmetry and, with relatively simple melodic means, begins his solo in a highly original manner. Play the opening phrase with a metronome and pay close attention to the way the accents and note placements influence the overall perception of the underlying meter. To compare how the phrase might have sounded if Tristano had retained the expected phrase symmetry without rhythmic displacement, start the second phrase on beat 1 in m. 11.

Tristano explores the concept of rhythmic displacement using different improvisational strategies, such as phrase displacement, metric displacement, manipulation of phrase accents, and melodic interpolations. *Phrase displacement* occurs when the phrase is shifted by a beat (or more) and creates a dissonance with the underlying harmonic and metric framework. Probably the most effective use of this technique occurs in m. 77 where the line begins on beat 2 with a downward arpeggiation of the E major upper-structure triad over the structural B♭7 and is further emphasized with a strong accent on the first quarter note, E♮4. The *manipulation of phrase accents* shifts regular metrical accents, thereby creating metric ambiguity. This technique occurs when the phrase temporarily renders beats 2 and 4 as beats 1 and 3. The phrase in mm. 159–160 illustrates these features. Notice how beat 4 in m. 159 influences the perception of beat 2 in the next measure.

Metric displacement implies the use of cross rhythm to create a characteristic rhythmic jolt and accumulation of tension within the phrase. The phrase in mm. 81–83 displays these characteristics. The distribution of accents and phrase groupings in mm. 81–83 creates an interesting superimposition of 3/4, 3/8, 2/4, and 4/4 respectively. Notice how the use of 3/8 influences the metric location of sub-phrases in 2/4 and 4/4 in mm. 82–83, and how the perception of the meter in the ensuing measures is constantly being challenged.

Melodic Interpolation

Melodic interpolation is a relatively straightforward improvisational technique based on the addition and repetition of a few notes in the midst of a phrase that results in subsequent rhythmic displacement. The two-note melodic interpolations in m. 57 and mm. 116–117 demonstrate the use of this technique.

The simplicity of Tristano's melodic ideas is truly remarkable. These ideas vary from simple *triadic arpeggiations* (mm. 97–99), *diatonic scalar patterns* (mm. 13–15), and *pentatonic scales* with chromatic passing notes (mm. 65–67). Hand in hand with these simple devices goes the manner in which Tristano terminates his melodic lines. The repository of his melodic cadential gestures is quite impressive and includes various *intervallic skips* (mm. 95, 124, 156, 224), *stepwise descents* (mm. 147–148, 167), and *neighbor figures* (mm. 63, 177, 184).

Playing Outside

Along with rhythmic displacement, **playing outside** of the underlying tonality is another hallmark feature of Tristano's style of improvisation and results in his highly original approach to chromaticism. In "Line Up," the use of chromaticism is pervasive, yet the manner in which Tristano controls it deserves attention. Just like his use of rhythmic displacements, Tristano's use of chromaticism is elegant and logical. When his lines temporarily leave the underlying tonal area and venture into a chromatic space, they retain strong melodic and harmonic identities and remain *inside* of the *outside* key areas. Figure 19.3 compares two phrases from mm. 25–28 and 63–68.

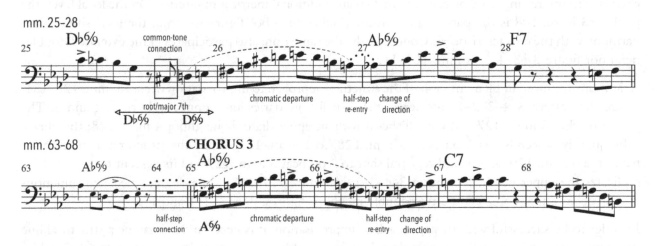

FIGURE 19.3 Playing "Outside"

Notice how similar these chromatic departures are. In the former, Tristano employs C♯3 (enharmonic D♭3) to access the chromatic neighboring area up a minor 2nd from the structural harmony D♭6/9. As a common tone between the two key areas, D♭3 functions as the root of D♭6/9 and the major 7th of DM7, and as such constitutes the ideal choice (entry window) for connecting these key areas. During mm. 65–66, the chromatic upper neighbor harmony A6/9 embellishes the A♭6/9 harmony, capitalizing on a common tone reinterpretation and an intricate double-neighbor preparation. Although the top of chorus 3 begins with a chromatic neighbor harmony without prior preparation, the opening note E♮3 is a half step away from the previous note in m. 63 and thus establishes a smooth voice-leading continuation between adjacent phrases. In m. 65, what seems to be excessive chromaticism on beats 3 and 4 turns out to be an intricate pivot area where the two keys, A and A♭, converge and interact.

This pivot area hovers around $\hat{3}$. On the one hand, the segment C4–D♭4–D♮4–C4 in m. 65 functions as a double-neighbor figure foreshadowing the occurrence of C♯4 on beat 1 in m. 66; on the other, it reminds us that the line is still in the key of A♭ major. Notice the overall melodic flow and phrase contour of these two measures. Beats 1 and 2 of m. 65 initiate a pentatonic segment in A major; beats 3 and 4 introduce a double-neighbor pivot area. Beats 1 and 2 of m. 66 return to the same pentatonic segment as m. 65 in the opposite direction, and continue onward, via a half-step re-entry, to a resolution in m. 67 with a double-neighbor figure encircling $\hat{3}$.

Structural Approach

Some of Tristano's phrases, such as in mm. 13–15, 33–36, 105–112, 125–131 and others, have an intricate architecture and demonstrate what can be described as a **structural approach** to improvisation. These spans provide structural frameworks for surface melodic elaborations, thereby giving the solo remarkable coherence. When you consider that these spans can, and often do, contradict the predictable phrase symmetry and, in more advanced situations, can even disguise the formal boundaries, the benefits of using this approach in practice is evident. What transpires in mm. 13–15 is a basic illustration of a structural approach to improvisation. The $\hat{8}$–$\hat{7}$–$\hat{6}$–$\hat{5}$ melodic pattern controls the surface melodic elaborations, which basically consist of simple upper diatonic neighbors and a single escape note. A similar approach occurs in the context of a compound melody in mm. 33–36. Here, the span $\hat{8}$–$\hat{7}$–$\hat{6}$ begins in the lower voice and is subsequently answered by the melodic pattern 8–♯7–♭7 from C7. At the same time, the upper voice of this seemingly polyphonic texture emphasizes the 5th of the corresponding chords with interesting note placements that create additional metric ambiguities. On the local level, the pitch C♭3 in m. 108 is the part of a chromatic double-neighbor figure flavoring the local submediant harmony with the characteristic ♭5. Concurrently, the same note also participates in the extended double-neighbor figure $\hat{3}$–♭$\hat{3}$–$\hat{4}$–$\hat{3}$ in mm. 105–112.

A far more advanced implementation of the structural approach to improvisation occurs in mm. 125–131, where the pattern $\hat{3}$–$\hat{4}$–$\hat{3}$–$\hat{2}$–$\hat{1}$ cuts across the formal boundaries and connects choruses 4 and 5. The phrase reaches $\hat{3}$ in m. 127 and embellishes it with an upper diatonic neighbor $\hat{4}$ in m. 128; the phrase subsequently descends, via $\hat{2}$ on beat 4 in m. 128, to $\hat{1}$ in m. 129. While the structural span seems to have ended in m. 129, an upward registral shift to $\hat{2}$ on beat 3 in m. 129 and its descent to $\hat{7}$ in m. 131, replicates the upper neighbor motion $\hat{3}$–$\hat{4}$–$\hat{3}$–$\hat{2}$ from mm. 127–128. Scale-degree one, then, functions as a pivot note that connects the two double-neighbor figures: $\hat{3}$–$\hat{4}$–$\hat{3}$–$\hat{2}$–$\hat{1}$ and $\hat{1}$–$\hat{2}$–$\hat{1}$–$\hat{7}$.

In order to be successful with this approach to improvisation, it is necessary to imagine a structural line that moves *mostly* by step in larger note values and establishes a convincing chord–scale relationship. The creation of structural lines depends on the ability to *hear* and to *isolate* them from the underlying chord progressions, and, subsequently, to embellish them with different melodic ideas.

Advanced Techniques

Tristano employs more advanced techniques of improvisation, particularly in later choruses. These techniques include unprepared chromaticism, harmonic interpolations, manipulation of harmonic rhythm, superimposition of chromatic progressions, motivic parallelism, and compound melody. *Unprepared chromaticism* occurs in m. 185, where Tristano begins his line up a minor 2nd from the structural harmony D♭6/9. Although he does not prepare this passage immediately, Tristano anticipates it in the previous choruses. *Harmonic interpolation* expands the underlying chord structure with substitute chords or new chord progressions. In "Line Up" these interpolations are relatively easy to spot because Tristano clearly delineates them with straightforward arpeggiation or other easily recognizable melodic patterns. The most stunning use of this technique occurs during mm. 201–206, where the succession, | Dm(♯7)–C♯m(♯7) | C6/9 | F♯m(♯7) | Fm6–D♯°7 | D°7 | BM7 | expands the underlying C7–Fm7–B♭7 progression.

Tristano's *manipulation of harmonic rhythm* is borne out of his horizontal approach to improvisation and comes in two guises: *harmonic displacement* and *harmonic omissions*. The former is based on the placement of regularly occurring chords on metric locations different than expected. The latter omits certain structural chords altogether, giving priority to the independent nature of melodic lines. Some of Tristano's lines are unconstrained by the predictable symmetry of chord progressions and display a fair amount of linear independence. In disregarding certain structural harmonies, Tristano demonstrates how lines influence the harmonic outcome and not the other way around. In m. 37, for example, the melodic line continues in the harmonic space of C7 begun in m. 35 and only gradually merges with the underlying harmony F7. The *superimposition of chromatic progressions* in place of structural chords is an effective technique that can be implemented to introduce controlled chromaticism into your own playing. It requires the use of simple melodic devices, such as in mm. 215–216, where the G♭7–C♭M7 and F7–B♭m7 progressions are clearly superimposed over the structural B♭m7 harmony.

Motivic parallelism is a technique that affects the musical surface and background. The use of motivic parallelism at the background level is quite common in composition, but when it happens in the context of improvised music it proves the advanced artistry of the improviser. On a more local level, an $\hat{8}$–$\hat{7}$ pattern in m. 138 is immediately answered by a $\hat{4}$–$\hat{3}$ pattern in the same measure. Scale-degree three on beat 4 of m. 139 initiates an enlarged version of a half-step motive utilizing the blue 3rd on beat 4 of m. 140. These illustrate how salient intervallic gestures—in this case, a minor 2nd down—influence the unfolding of the melodic phrase. In mm. 189–190, Tristano introduces a background span, $\hat{8}$–♭$\hat{7}$–$\hat{6}$–$\hat{5}$–$\hat{4}$–$\hat{3}$, and immediately repeats it in an incomplete form and with subtle metric displacements in mm. 191–192.

Motivic parallelism also indicates surface devices that reappear throughout the solo—one's favorite melodic devices, so to speak. For instance, the four-note figure with two ascending half steps followed by a larger intervallic skip in m. 45, mm. 142–143, and m. 207 (slightly varied), or the 1–2–3–5 melodic patterns in mm. 27, 30, 69, 123, 163, 217, etc., show Tristano's penchant for these types of surface devices. Yet, in comparison to the more structural use of motivic parallelism, they seem like simple recurrences of familiar and well-internalized melodic patterns.

The use of **compound** or **polyphonic melody** adds yet another level of complexity to his solo and demonstrates Tristano's contrapuntal approach to improvisation. This technique implies the use of two-voice texture in the context of a single-line melody. Figure 19.4 illustrates a voice-leading reduction of mm. 157–161.

FIGURE 19.4 Compound Melody

The upper voice forms a $\hat{3}$–$\hat{2}$–$\hat{1}$ melodic span that cuts across the formal boundaries. Scale-degree two in m. 158 becomes temporarily suspended and the melodic activity is transferred to the lower voice with a diatonic scalar descent. In mm. 159–160, the lower voice forms a $\hat{3}$–$\hat{4}$–$\sharp\hat{4}$–$\hat{5}$ melodic pattern embellished with unfolding thirds, which also contributes to the polyphonic nature of the phrase. At the top of chorus 6, $\hat{2}$ is restored and resolves down to $\hat{1}$ on beat 2. The cadential gesture A♭3–E♭3 on beat 2 of m. 161 unifies the two melodic strands. One of the conditions for the use of the compound melody is a clear registral separation between the implied voices.

The treatment of chromaticism and voice leading are intimately related to one another and are essential elements of Tristano's cultivated approach to improvisation. Notice how he introduces chromatic segments into his lines in mm. 16 and 41. In m. 16, Tristano arpeggiates D♭M9 as an upper structure of E♭7, which contains three diatonic extensions: 9th, 11th, and 13th. On the way down, he supplies chromatic versions of the two extensions, ♭13th and ♭9th, and resolves the perfect 11th down to a major 3rd. These linear connections occur in the same register. When the line enters the chromatic region in m. 41, Tristano uses an octave displacement preparation as the diatonic B♭2 from m. 40 foreshadows B3 at the outset of the chromatic departure in m. 41. Even though there is an upward octave leap in this preparation, it is perfectly justifiable from a voice-leading perspective.

Tristano's lines are notoriously long; observe the one running uninterruptedly in mm. 81–91. Within this melodic stretch, Tristano creates a nicely balanced line that features the measured use of stepwise motion, arpeggiation, and chromaticism. In addition to all this, Tristano's playing swings hard—a trait that anyone should admire and imitate.

THE *TRISTANO STYLE* OF IMPROVISATION

Based on the analysis of "Line Up," the essential features of *Tristano's style* of improvisation are summarized using the following rubrics:

Rhythmic Syntax

- Phrase displacement
- Metric displacement
- Manipulation of phrase accents
- Agogic accents
- Juxtaposition of different time signatures

Melodic Syntax

- Melodic devices:
  - Lower/upper neighbors
  - Double neighbors
  - Extended double neighbors
  - Escape notes

- Passing notes
- Bebop passing notes

- Upper structures:
  - Triads
  - Four-part chords

- Arpeggiation

- Diatonic scalar patterns

- Modes

- Pentatonic scales

- Bebop scales

- Chromatic segments

- Cadential gestures:
  - Intervallic skips
  - Stepwise descents
  - Neighbor figures

- Chromaticism

Harmonic Syntax

- Tritone substitutions

- Modification of the quality of chords

- Harmonic interpolations

- Manipulation of harmonic rhythm:
  - Harmonic shifts
  - Harmonic omissions

- Superimposition of sequential progressions

Voice Leading

- Common-tone retentions

- Common-tone connections

- Stepwise connection between adjacent phrases

- Preparation of chromatic extensions

- Melodic resolutions

- Registral shifts

Phrasing

- Length

- Flow

- Shape

- Contour

- Dynamics

- Articulation

- Balance

Advanced Techniques

- Structural approach to improvisation

- Unprepared chromaticism

- Harmonic interpolations

- Manipulation of harmonic rhythm

- Superimposition of chromatic progressions

- Motivic parallelism

- Compound melody

NOTES

1 "Line Up" was recorded in 1955 and released on the album *Lennie Tristano* on Atlantic Records. *Lennie Tristano* and the sequel *The New Tristano* from 1962 remain two of his most well-known projects.
2 The terms *iambic* and *anapestic* represent two types of Greek poetic metric units associated with the length and groupings of syllables. An *iambic* rhythmic figure consists of short (unaccented)–long (accented) notes; an *anapest* consists of short–short–long notes.

Advanced

PART THREE

Analyzing Jazz Lead Sheets

CHAPTER SUMMARY

Chapter 20 provides an analysis of two standard tunes: "My Romance" and "All the Things You Are." The analysis of "My Romance" focuses on a structural reading of the tune. The analysis of "All the Things You Are" concentrates on the ubiquity of the II–V–I progression.

CONCEPTS AND TERMS

- Back-door dominant 7th
- Fake book
- Lead sheets

- Two-level analysis:
  - First level
  - Second level

- II–V–I:
  - Incomplete
  - Structural
  - Tonicizing

WHAT DOES A LEAD SHEET TELL US?

In order to become a successful jazz musician, one has to learn how to read, interpret, and modify **lead sheets**. Improvising from a lead sheet is a unique performance skill that jazz musicians cultivate on a daily basis and perfect over a long period of time. Comparable to other shorthand notations from classical music, such as figured bass, tablature, partimento, or others, lead-sheet notation contains just enough essential information to create a complete performance.

A typical jazz lead sheet includes a single-line melody, chord symbols, and lyrics. Lead sheets can be a part of larger compilations of songs known as **fake books**. They can also exist as individual song folios; these types of lead sheets are probably the most accurate and valuable. Musicians can create their own fake books to play with other musicians and to agree on harmonic changes. Jazz lead sheets from reputable publishers contain relatively few mistakes. This is helpful since in the not-so-distant past illegal fake books contained many mistakes. Reputable publishers sometimes incorporate dubious editorial decisions and present a certain historical performance as somehow iconic of that song's performance practice. Although the accuracy of fake books has certainly improved, the best method of learning and retaining tunes is to find the original recording and transcribe the melody and chord changes from the record.

Songs that constitute the core of jazz repertory were once widely popular. They were continually heard on the radio and often topped the charts. Artists who performed them were treated like celebrities and had cult-like followings. Jazz musicians have appropriated these tunes into their repertoire for obvious reasons: they are great songs written by composers who, above all, valued and understood the importance of a good melody. Their popularity among jazz musicians is probably the best testimony that great music never loses its appeal. The original chord progressions of standard tunes might include the harmonic vocabulary typical of the popular idiom during the Golden Age of the American Popular Song, ca. 1900–1960.[1] Just as in decades past, when jazz musicians offered personal interpretations of these tunes, it is important to learn how to interpret lead sheets in a manner that convincingly expresses the nature, affect, and *feel* of the song.

TWO-LEVEL ANALYSIS

A method of analysis known as **two-level analysis** enables us to differentiate between chords that are structurally important and those that are not. In this method, the **second level** is more general. It stands back from surface-level details to examine larger harmonic gestures and functions. It also determines the large-scale key distribution and the harmonic character of individual phrases. Such examination forces one to look at the tune from a more global perspective. The **first level** of analysis goes back to a chord-by-chord, measure-by-measure unfolding of harmonic changes. In conjunction with the initial observations, it helps to determine how chords interact with one another, how progressions project harmonic function, and how chords behave on a local level. This analytical method establishes a hierarchical relationship between chords, illustrates the functional relationships at the phrase level, and explains how the tonality of a tune works. It merges global and local perspectives into a unified analytical synthesis.

"MY ROMANCE"

This analytical demonstration discusses the difference between chords that are structurally important and those that are not. Figure 20.1 illustrates a lead sheet of "My Romance" by Richard Rodgers and Lorenz Hart.[2]

The A section of "My Romance" is divided into two four-bar phrases. The first phrase begins on the tonic and features a strong cadential confirmation of the tonic in m. 4 that establishes the key of the song. Remember that to establish a key it is necessary to have a statement of the tonic, a motion away from the tonic, and some kind of cadential gesture to confirm the tonic. In standard tunes, that cadential gesture almost exclusively takes the form of the ii–V^7–I progression. Figure 20.2 provides a two-level analysis of mm. 1–16. Measures 1–4 of "My Romance" exhibit these characteristics, as indicated by Roman numerals in Figure 20.2. The second phrase in mm. 5–8 begins on the submediant and leads back to the tonic.

Even though the harmonic rhythm is relatively fast, with two chords per measure, not all the chords have the same structural and functional weight. For instance, mm. 1–2 expand the underlying tonic with a I–IV–iii–vi progression, whereas mm. 5–6 expand the submediant with a local i–V^7–i progression before tonicizing the predominant ii with a V/ii on beat 3 in m. 6. The second level of analysis, however, reveals a simpler and more fundamental tonal architecture for the A section: mm. 1–4 establish the tonic with a I–ii–V^7 tonic expansion; mm. 5–6 feature tonal motion to the submediant followed by a ii–V^7

FIGURE 20.1 "My Romance"—Lead Sheet

confirmation of the tonic in mm. 7–8. These harmonies occur on metrically strong positions and, by and large, reflect the symmetrical nature of eight-bar phrases.

The B section features a harmonic departure away from the tonic. In particular, mm. 9–13 are controlled by a IV–I progression with local blues inflections highlighting the ♭VII⁷ harmony. The ♭VII⁷ chord in mm. 9 and 11 is also known as a **back-door dominant 7th** because it subsumes its natural voice-leading tendencies and deceptively resolves up a whole step to the tonic chord. The music departs even further away from the main key in the second four-bar phrase of the B section. To make tonal sense out of that progression, let's start in m. 16 and move backwards. The B section is harmonically open and ends on the dominant in m. 16. That dominant 7th is reached through a sequence of fifth-related chords that begins on F#m7(♭5) in m. 13. Each measure, with the exception of m. 15, contains some kind of a ii–V⁷ progression. The second level of analysis indicates a more fundamental harmonic architecture of the B section: mm. 9–12 elaborate a diatonic IV–I progression; mm. 13–16 then expand the underlying tonality with chromatic motion to the mediant and a subsequent return, via a cycle of fifths progression, to the dominant.

FIGURE 20.2 Two-Level Analysis—"My Romance," mm. 1–16

By looking at the overall tonal architecture of a tune, it is possible to learn and memorize the essential harmonies in the first half of the tune. In fact, if a seasoned jazz musician were to explain the harmonic progression of mm. 1–16 to a novice, he would probably say something like this:

> The first A section has two four-bar phrases: the first in I, the second in vi, which returns back to I. The B section features a IV–I progression with a back-door $\flat$VII^7 in the first four-bar phrase, and a cycle of fifths with local ii–V^{7}s starting on $\sharp\hat{4}$, in the second four-bar phrase that closes on the dominant 7th.

Notice that this succinct explanation omits a lot of harmonic details and focuses instead on a big tonal picture. The harmonic details absent from that description are either theoretically assumed or aurally picked up during the performance.

"ALL THE THINGS YOU ARE"

This analysis focuses on only one aspect of the tune, namely the presence and function of the ii–V^7–I progression. Figure 20.3 shows a lead sheet of "All the Things You Are" by Jerome Kern and Oscar Hammerstein II. With a beautiful melody, gorgeous lyrics, interesting harmonic progressions, and an extended 36-bar AABA' form, "All the Things You Are" has become an ultimate favorite among jazz musicians.[3]

What is particularly striking about "All the Things You Are"—and about the majority of standard tunes as well—is the sheer number of ii–V^7–I progressions permeating its harmonic structure.[4] In standard tunes, the two basic types of the ii–V^7–I progression are commonly implemented: **structural** and **tonicizing**. The **structural ii–V^7–I** may or may not always be present at the outset of a tune, but will definitely occur at the end of it in order to confirm the underlying tonality. In "All the Things You Are," mm. 33–36 feature a clear statement of the structural ii–V^7–I. The same progression also occurs in mm. 2–4, but in this context, it provides a harmonic support for the melody and is a part of the larger harmonic span. The structural weight of both progressions is very different and depends on their placement within the tune (see Figure 20.4).

The **tonicizing ii–V^7–I** progression functions as a local cadential preparation and/or confirmation of secondary key areas. In mm. 6–8, a local (ii–V^7)/III tonicizes the mediant key, III. Why the mediant key? Because the tune appears to be in the key of A$\flat$ major and any harmonic departure from the main tonic is labeled accordingly. This tonicizing progression also occurs within a phrase and, as such, plays a purely supportive role. Remember that the tonicizing ii–V^7 is placed in parenthesis, followed by the diagonal slash and a Roman numeral that indicates a tonicized key area, hence the (ii–V^7)/III label in m. 6. At the end of the second A section, there is another local ii–V^7 progression tonicizing the leading-tone key, VII.

When comparing the two tonicizing ii–V^7–I progressions from mm. 10–12 and 21–23, notice that they occur in different locations and therefore have very different structural roles. Which one is more important? The one from mm. 21–23 because it closes the B section of the song with yet another tonicization of a chromatic key area: the flat submediant, $\flat$VI. The (ii–V^7)/V in mm. 10–12, meanwhile, is located within a phrase and barely passes through the dominant key area. Even though it tonicizes a secondary tonal area, that tonicization is not confirmed as the phrase continues and closes in a different key, namely G major. This type of tonicization has a prolongational aspect to it. Finally, in m. 30, there

FIGURE 20.3 "All the Things You Are"—Lead Sheet

FIGURE 20.4 Roman Numeral Analysis—"All the Things You Are"

is another type of a ii–V^7 progression, yet without the resolution. This progression is notated in square brackets (representing a harmonic ellipsis) with a Roman numeral indicating its *non-existing* resolution to ♭III. This is referred to as an **incomplete ii–V^7** progression. Figure 20.4 illustrates the location of different ii–V^{7}s occurring in the tune.

NOTES

1   The original harmonic progressions are found in the original song folios, which might include a verse and piano accompaniment.
2   For representative recordings, consult Appendix F on the CW.
3   For representative recordings, consult Appendix F on the CW.
4   Even though most musicians would agree that "All the Things You Are" is in A♭, this and other "problematic" tunes can be considered from many tonal angles. A parallel narrative might suggest an emerging tonality of A♭ that begins with an F minor "shadow" tonality (to borrow a metaphor from Frank Samarotto's essay: "Strange Dimensions: Regularity and Irregularity of Deep Levels of Rhythmic Reductions").

Phrase Models

CHAPTER SUMMARY

Chapter 21 introduces 13 phrase models that illustrate the essential harmonic, contrapuntal, and structural properties of the different eight-bar phrases commonly found in standard tunes.

CONCEPTS AND TERMS

- Cadential confirmation:
  - Complete
  - Harmonically closed
  - Harmonically open
  - Incomplete
- Modulatory
- Chromatic phrase models
- Diatonic phrase models:
  - Off-tonic
  - On-tonic
- Harmonic departure
- Incomplete phrase model
- Jazz rule of the octave
- Phrase identifiers
- Phrase models

PHRASE PROTOTYPES

The phrase structure of standard tunes is fairly predictable.[1] It consists of a finite number of mostly eight-bar phrases that are easily classified according to their melodic, harmonic, and contrapuntal properties.[2] Melodic properties, for instance, are characteristic successions of melodic tones common to particular families of standard tunes. The same can be said about harmonic and contrapuntal features. The supporting harmonies are constrained by certain principles of chord formation and by various rules of counterpoint and harmonic function. These relationships are demonstrated using the concept of **phrase models**. Although phrase models are classified according to the differences in the melodic structure and supporting harmonies, it is important to stress that these properties are mutually intertwined. The behavior of the melody is shaped by its supporting harmonies, just as the sense of harmonic progression is dictated by the behavior of melodic patterns.[3] This intimate relationship means that if we attempt to understand the phrase structure of standard tunes in exclusively melodic terms or from a purely harmonic perspective that understanding will be incomplete.

In the discussion of II–V–I in Chapter 6, a distinction between different rhetorical types and the functional role of the progression was made. Aside from their melodic, harmonic, and contrapuntal characteristics, phrase models can be described in terms of their rhetorical layout. Typically, a phrase model has three main parts: phrase identifier, harmonic departure, and cadential confirmation. A **phrase identifier** is a short harmonic progression with two, three, or four chords that appears at the beginning of a phrase and gives the entire phrase its harmonic identity. Given the pliability of jazz harmony—especially its huge transformative potential—phrase identifiers occur in various substitute forms without actually changing the status of the phrase model. Since each phrase model has a different phrase identifier, it is considered the most recognizable feature of the model.

Harmonic departures typically occur in the middle of a phrase and feature different diatonic or chromatic interpolations as well as tonicization of closely or distantly related key areas. Given the plethora of available harmonic options, this section of a phrase model is the most ambiguous and challenging to codify. In the context of the prototypical phrase model, then, the exact location and type of harmonic departures is ultimately related to the design of the melody and the type of underlying chord progressions.

In contrast to the inherent ambiguity of harmonic departures, the harmonic implications of the **cadential confirmations** are fairly straightforward. The cadential confirmation is a progression—typically a **complete/incomplete** II–V or its common harmonic variants—that concludes a phrase model. Depending on the rate of harmonic rhythm, cadential confirmations typically occur in m. 8 or mm. 7–8 of an eight-bar phrase. Figure 21.1 shows a generic phrase model with three structural components: phrase identifier, harmonic departure, and cadential confirmation.

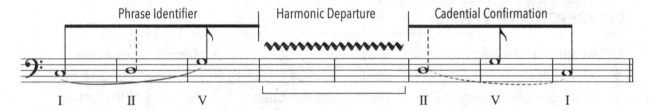

FIGURE 21.1 Generic Phrase Model

The hierarchy among chords is indicated with different note stems and flags connected to the beam. Slurs group chords comprising the phrase identifier. Dashed slurs illustrate cadential confirmations. Brackets indicate the space occupied by harmonic departures. The two empty measures in Figure 21.1 are reserved for a harmonic departure that is unique to the structure of a particular tune. The beam connects chords belonging to the phrase identifier and cadential confirmation features a complete cadential closure.

Normally, all three components of the phrase model are present but, under special conditions, a phrase model can be truncated. The B section of a tune with a complex harmonic setting may, for instance, utilize only parts of the phrase model without cadential closure or harmonic departure. This type is referred to as an **incomplete phrase model**.

Phrase models provide background harmonic frameworks for the tonality of standard tunes. These models draw on traditional tonal features, such as root movement by fifths, monotonality, stepwise motion of the supporting counterpoint, and the T–PD–D–T chord succession. Let's briefly revisit these features and examine the ways in which they explain the tonality of standard tunes. A root movement by fifths is the overarching characteristic of tonal music. With a single tonic at the center of tonality, all other chords are dependent on the tonic. Chord progressions, especially those with the structural visibility (i.e. ii–V^7–I), follow the traditional root movement by 5ths, the most fundamental harmonic motion defining tonality and tonal relationships.[4] This motion exemplifies the succession of harmonic functions from the instability of the dominant to the stability of the tonic or—at the background level—controls the proper distribution of the secondary key areas. Even though other root movements may (and frequently do) occur, they are hierarchically dependent on fifth motion and can even be derived from it. Since the tonal system places a single tonic at the center of all melodic, harmonic, and contrapuntal activity, the concept of monotonality is central to tonality. Even though certain tunes, such as "I Hear a Rhapsody," "Just Friends," "Dream Dancing," and many others, might begin in apparently different keys, they ultimately lead to the home key. This is decisively confirmed by a cadence featuring a root movement by fifths.

Counterpoint is a driving force that propels different harmonic progressions to their destinations. In the context of standard tunes, the term *counterpoint* is applied to signify the behavior of guide tones within chord progressions and to indicate the overall characteristics of voice leading. Since the behavior of counterpoint is predictable yet quite flexible, it is a powerful agent influencing the interaction of melodic lines and chord progressions. Figure 21.2 illustrates the harmonic flexibility of a counterpoint using a $\hat{1}$–$\hat{7}$–$\hat{1}$ melodic pattern. These distinct harmonic realizations employ root movement by fifths, use a stepwise motion in inner voices, and demonstrate the transformative power of counterpoint. The rules of counterpoint in both harmonizations are exactly the same; the respective outcomes, however, could not be more different.

FIGURE 21.2 Harmonic Flexibility of Counterpoint

Figure 21.2a illustrates the harmonic realization of a $\hat{1}$–$\hat{7}$–$\hat{1}$ melodic pattern using a diatonic I–ii–V[7]–I progression. Figure 21.2b demonstrates a more intricate realization of the same melodic pattern. After the initial support from the tonic chord, $\hat{1}$ in Figure 21.2b is reinterpreted as a ♭5th of the F♯m7(♭5) chord, which launches the sequence of fifth-related progressions before converging on the final tonic chord. The harmonic space between the two tonic chords in Figure 21.2b is heavily elaborated with different diatonic and chromatic formations. One of the most striking features of Figure 21.2b is that it preserves the same basic rules of tonal voice leading and harmony as Figure 21.2a. The intervening chords do not violate any traditional rules of tonal voice leading and harmony; they do not, for example, create parallel perfect 8ves and 5ths with adjacent chords—not that parallel perfect 8ves and 5ths are unwelcomed in jazz syntax—nor do they violate the rules of functional syntax. Since the harmonic realization of the $\hat{1}$–$\hat{7}$–$\hat{1}$ pattern in Figure 21.2a satisfies the traditional rules of tonal voice leading and harmony, and the processes of transformation preserve those rules, the resulting progression shown in Figure 21.2b constitutes a correct tonal progression.

JAZZ RULE OF THE OCTAVE

During the Baroque Era, the *Rule of the Octave* was a practical tool that enabled musicians to gain harmonic flexibility at the keyboard.[5] The rule prescribed how to harmonize a major or minor scale unfolding in the bass using idiomatic chord successions.[6] A similar rule can be developed for jazz. Instead of placing the scale in the bass, the major scale is placed in the soprano voice. The **jazz rule of the octave** explains how to harmonize a descending major scale with idiomatic jazz progressions. By examining different harmonic outcomes, the relationship of melodies to chords and chords to melodies becomes clear. The jazz rule of the octave also helps us to realize the harmonic potential of different melodic segments and examines their behavior in the context of underlying chord progressions. Figures 21.3a–21.3d illustrate four distinct harmonizations of the descending major scale.

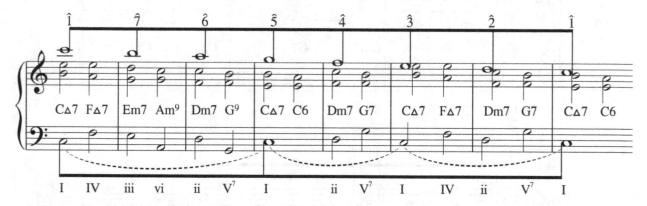

FIGURE 21.3a Jazz Rule of the Octave: Variant 1

Figure 21.3a features a diatonic realization of the scale. The tonic note is prolonged throughout the harmonization (dashed slurs) and only momentarily is left to create a harmonic contrast. As expected, the final harmonic gesture is in the form of a ii–V^7–I progression.

Figure 21.3b illustrates a much bolder harmonization of the scale employing a root movement by fifths. Scale degrees $\hat{1}$ and $\hat{4}$ become reinterpreted as a ♭5th and ♭9th of (ii$^\emptyset$–V^7)/iii and (ii$^\emptyset$–V^7)/vi, respectively. It is worth noting that the initial tonic is absent from this harmonization. Known as an **off-tonic** progression, this and other off-tonic progressions are hallmarks of **Phrase Models 2, 3, 5,** and **13**.[7]

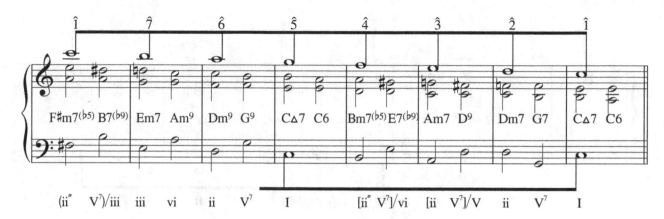

FIGURE 21.3b Jazz Rule of the Octave: Variant 2

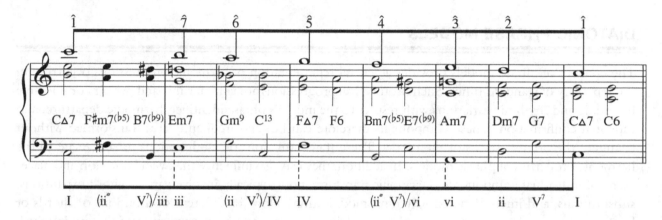

FIGURE 21.3c Jazz Rule of the Octave: Variant 3

Figure 21.3c illustrates how to infuse the scale with various tonicizations of closely related key areas. The notes of the descending scale become reinterpreted as different chord tones and extensions of supporting harmonies. For instance, the tonicization of IV capitalizes on reinterpreting $\hat{6}$ as a major 9th of Gm7 and a major 13th of C13 before resolving to FM9 with $\hat{5}$ in the soprano. Special attention should be paid to the behavior of the inner voices as they continue to move by step and clearly delineate the structure of underlying chords.

Unlike other harmonizations in the preceding figures, Figure 21.3d begins in the submediant key with a clear cadential confirmation of the submediant using the $(\text{ii}^{\varnothing}-V^7)/\text{vi}$ progression. This particular off-tonic progression is especially common in the repertory of standard tunes. Before converging on the tonic, however, this harmonization also features tonicizations of IV and ♭III, and an elided motion to V with a II^7 as harmonic support for $\hat{3}$. Even though this realization prioritizes the predominant collection of chords (as the confirmation of vi and tonicization of IV indicate) and modal mixture harmonies, these local key areas are ultimately related to the governing tonic. These eventually synchronize the melodic and harmonic forces at the end of the progression. In keeping with the notational practice employed in this book: parentheses are used to indicate the secondary ii–V^7s that resolve to their tonicized key areas; and square brackets to indicate secondary ii–V^7s (harmonic elisions) that do not. For instance, the progression $(\text{ii}-V^7)/\text{IV}$ in the key of C major indicates Gm7–C7–FM7; the progression $[\text{ii}-V^7]/\text{IV}$ stands for Gm7–C7 followed by some other chord.

FIGURE 21.3d Jazz Rule of the Octave: Variant 4

DIATONIC PHRASE MODELS

The concept of phrase models provides a general representation of harmonic progressions occurring in the repertory of standard tunes. Such prototypical progressions are fairly flexible and permit considerable harmonic and rhythmic variations with respect to the model's phrase identifier, harmonic departure, and cadential confirmation. These components therefore can be (and frequently are) transformed without changing the original status of the model. These transformations or modifications usually relate to the harmonic properties of phrase models. In addition, they can also influence the overall duration and placement of individual components. Harmonic transformations typically involve various chord expansions, substitutions, and interpolations. Rhythmic modifications allow for different distributions of chords or harmonic progressions in relation to the underlying rhythmic and metric structure of the model. Such a degree of harmonic and rhythmic freedom allows for the classification of similar phrases within the rubric of a single phrase model.

Each **diatonic phrase model** is derived from a fundamental $\hat{1}$–$\hat{7}$–$\hat{1}$ melodic pattern and appears in two distinct forms: (1) as a harmonic progression with essential chords analyzed only with Roman numerals, and (2) as a contrapuntal framework with guide-tone lines navigating through the supporting harmonies of the model. The use of analytical symbols is in keeping with a notational practice commonly used by music theorists: dashed slurs indicate the prolongation of essential tones or harmonies, beams show phrase groupings, open note heads illustrate tones of greater structural significance than black note heads (these are further distinguished with either extended stems and/or flags), and scale degrees analyze notes of the tonic key. The discussion of each phrase model ends with a fully realized model using jazz chorale five- or four-voice texture and a partial list of standard tunes that share the harmonic characteristics of a particular phrase model. For additional standard tunes and harmonic transformations of individual phrase models, visit the CW.

Phrase Model 1

The overview of phrase models begins with the basic eight-bar progression. The use of a I–II–V progression as the phrase identifier is balanced with the use of a complete or incomplete II–V as the cadential confirmation. Notice that in Figure 21.4 (and in all the remaining figures showing the properties of phrase models) the structural chords of the model are notated with uppercase Roman numerals. The phrase identifier (I–II–V) and the cadential confirmation (II–V) of **Phrase Model 1** combine two tonal variants of the progressions: I–ii–V^7 or i–ii$^\emptyset$–V^7 and ii–V^7 or ii$^\emptyset$–V^7 respectively. The middle part of **Phrase Model 1** is reserved for the harmonic departure. This features a simple prolongation of the tonic or temporary tonicizations of closely or distantly related key areas. As stated earlier, these modifications do not alter the overall character of the model. **Phrase Model 1** in Figure 21.4 features a relatively slow harmonic rhythm with one chord per measure. Frequently, however, the rate of harmonic rhythm is much faster, usually with two chords per measure.

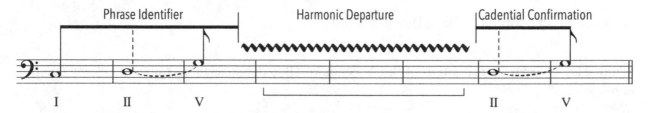

FIGURE 21.4 Phrase Model 1

Figure 21.5 illustrates a contrapuntal framework of **Phrase Model 1** and its derivation from a diatonic $\hat{1}$–$\hat{7}$–$\hat{1}$ melodic pattern. Notice that in Figure 21.5 (and in all the remaining figures showing contrapuntal properties of phrase models) the chords are analyzed with complete Roman numerals. One of the advantages of such a representation (without bar lines and with essential harmonies only) is that it clearly shows the hierarchy between chords and contrapuntal forces generating the model. The exact distribution of chords and the type of harmonic departure are ultimately related to the characteristics of a specific standard tune.

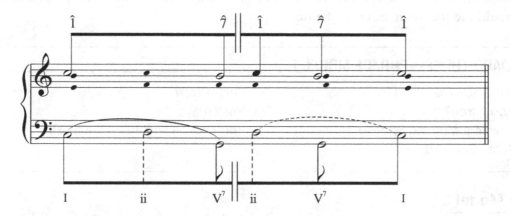

FIGURE 21.5 Phrase Model 1: Contrapuntal Framework

The most salient feature of **Phrase Model 1** is an **on-tonic** phrase identifier, which clearly projects the tonality of the tune. As a form-building entity, the cadential confirmation comes in two different types, **complete** and **incomplete**, and can be further classified as **harmonically open, modulatory,** or **harmonically closed**. A harmonically open pattern typically ends the first A section of the AABA-type or the B section of the ABAC-type tunes. A modulatory cadential closure uses a ii–V^7 progression that prepares the arrival of a new key area in the B section of the AABA-type or the B or C sections of the ABAC-type tunes. A harmonically closed cadential confirmation utilizes a ii–V^7–I progression at the end of the tune. **Phrase Model 1** can also accommodate a minor version of the phrase identifier (i.e. ii$^\emptyset$–V^7–i) as in "You and the Night and the Music" or "Softly, As in a Morning Sunrise." But the contrapuntal framework of the model remains unchanged.

FIGURE 21.6 Phrase Model 1: "Bye Bye Blackbird"

Figure 21.6 illustrates a realization of the A section of "Bye Bye Blackbird" using jazz chorale texture in five voices.[8]

The list of songs that concludes the presentation of each phrase model contains a selection of familiar standard tunes that share the harmonic characteristics of a particular model. For a more thorough list of tunes sharing the same phrase model, visit the CW. By studying these tunes, you can begin to notice the familiar traits and common characteristics between them. You can also observe how different harmonic transformations depart from the original phrase model and how they are generated. This and the other lists on the CW are by no means exhaustive, but are an attempt to show the wealth of harmonic progressions in standard tunes sharing similar properties. One of the challenging aspects of this classification, however, is the proliferation of different versions of standard tunes in many fake books of questionable provenance. While such sources naturally present problems, they also present an opportunity to take a fresh look at the repertory of standard tunes from the viewpoint of a practicing musician who has to frequently *improve* the existing lead sheet or sift through the surface chord progressions in order to understand the harmonic essence of a tune.

STANDARD TUNES—PHRASE MODEL 1

Bye Bye Blackbird	This Is New
How About You?	Yesterdays
Softly, As in a Morning Sunrise	You and the Night and the Music
The More I See You	

Phrase Model 2

The main characteristic of **Phrase Model 2** is an **off-tonic** phrase identifier II–V, which can occur in the form of ii–V^7 or ii$^\emptyset$–V^7 progressions. Figures 21.7a–21.7c provide a basic harmonic layout of the model with an incomplete cadential confirmation, show a contrapuntal framework derived from a diatonic $\hat{1}$–$\hat{7}$–$\hat{1}$ melodic pattern, and realize the A section of "Gone With the Wind" using jazz chorale texture in four voices.[9]

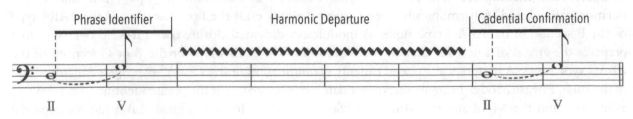

FIGURE 21.7a Phrase Model 2

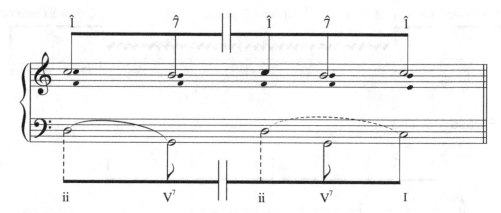

FIGURE 21.7b Phrase Model 2: Contrapuntal Framework

FIGURE 21.7c Phrase Model 2: "Gone With the Wind"

Standard tunes that feature a ii$^{\emptyset}$–V^7 progression at the outset are harmonically more advanced. The consequences of this modal borrowing are felt throughout the phrase such as in "I Love You," where the harmonic departure ventures into the distant major mediant key area.

STANDARD TUNES—PHRASE MODEL 2 _____

Beautiful Love	Poor Butterfly
I Fall in Love Too Easily	Tangerine
If I Were a Bell	That Certain Feeling
Love Is Here to Stay	

Phrase Model 3

Phrase Model 3 also features an off-tonic beginning and it vacillates around the predominant family of chords. Figures 21.8a–21.8c illustrate a basic harmonic layout of the model, show a contrapuntal framework derived from a diatonic $\hat{1}$–$\hat{7}$–$\hat{1}$ melodic pattern, and realize the A section of "Almost Like Being in Love" using jazz chorale texture in five voices.[10]

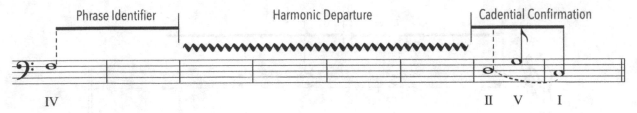

FIGURE 21.8a Phrase Model 3

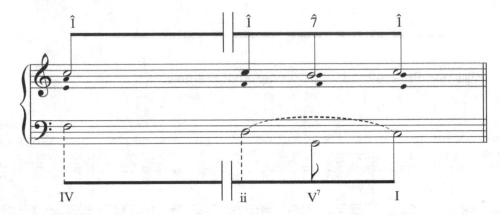

FIGURE 21.8b Phrase Model 3: Contrapuntal Framework

FIGURE 21.8c Phrase Model 3: "Almost Like Being in Love"

Phrase Model 3 accommodates different phrase identifiers, which, in turn, influence the overall content of the phrase. Despite their different surface manifestations, however, they can be derived from the fundamental IV–I motion. As you analyze the phrase structure of the following tunes, pay attention to the relationship between the melody and harmony, and how this interaction produces different harmonic outcomes.

STANDARD TUNES—PHRASE MODEL 3 _____

After You've Gone	Love For Sale
Almost Like Being in Love	Remember
Just Friends	September Song
I'll See You in My Dreams	

Phrase Model 4

In a certain sense, the phrase identifier of **Phrase Model 4**, I–VI–II–V, constitutes a basic expansion of the phrase identifier of **Phrase Model 1**. One cannot help but notice, however, that the number of standard tunes with a clear manifestation of the I–VI–II–V progression is quite impressive. This progression is an important harmonic statement—fully integrated with the melodic structure—and therefore deserves a separate category. Figures 21.9a–21.9c demonstrate a basic harmonic layout of **Phrase Model 4**, show a contrapuntal framework derived from a diatonic $\hat{1}$–$\hat{7}$–$\hat{1}$ melodic pattern, and realize the A section of "My Ship" using jazz chorale texture in four voices.[11]

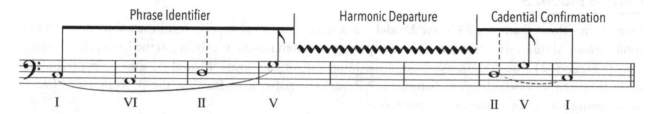

FIGURE 21.9a Phrase Model 4

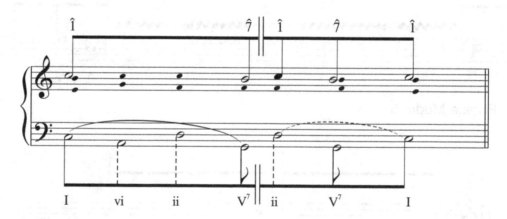

FIGURE 21.9b Phrase Model 4: Contrapuntal Framework

FIGURE 21.9c Phrase Model 4: "My Ship"

One of the characteristics of **Phrase Model 4** is its flexible phrase identifier, which can occur in many different forms, as shown in Figure 21.9c. While some of these harmonic transformations are integrated in the context of standard tunes, such as "Love You Madly" or "Memories of You," others can be freely applied as effective harmonic substitutions.

Phrase Model 5

One of the salient features of **Phrase Model 5** is a large-scale tonal motion from the submediant to the tonic. Standard tunes with this characteristic opening are often mistaken as being in the key of the opening chord. Figures 21.10a–21.10c illustrate a harmonic layout of **Phrase Model 5**, show a contrapuntal derivation of the model from a diatonic $\hat{1}$–$\hat{7}$–$\hat{1}$ melodic pattern, and realize the A section of "Lover Man" using jazz chorale texture in five voices.[12]

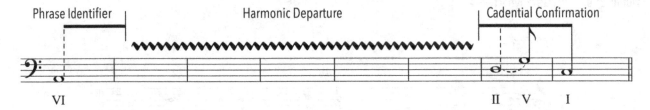

FIGURE 21.10a Phrase Model 5

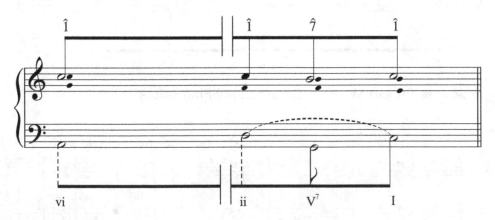

FIGURE 21.10b Phrase Model 5: Contrapuntal Framework

FIGURE 21.10c Phrase Model 5: "Lover Man"

The harmonic variety of **Phrase Model 5** is truly remarkable. The submediant chord can be cadentially confirmed as in "How Deep Is the Ocean," immediately departed from as in "I Hear a Rhapsody," reached by arrival as in "The Shadow of Your Smile," or it can function as the initial chord of a longer sequential progression as in "Fly Me to the Moon."

STANDARD TUNES—PHRASE MODEL 5 _____

Blue Skies   I Hear a Rhapsody

Cry Me a River   If I Should Lose You

Fly Me to the Moon   Lover Man

How Deep Is the Ocean   The Shadow of Your Smile

CHROMATIC PHRASE MODELS

One of the characteristic features of the remaining phrase models is their more intricate harmonic and contrapuntal design. Their phrase identifiers frequently employ tonicizing progressions and, as a consequence, harmonic departures are further removed from the tonic key. With more harmonic activities associated with the forthcoming phrase models, we can ask ourselves whether the different phrase identifiers are further elaborations of the fundamental diatonic frameworks or not. While this is definitely a possibility, the intention here is to show the more harmonic variety and salient characteristics of standard tunes.

Phrase Model 6

Phrase Model 6 has a characteristic phrase identifier that tonicizes the supertonic key area. This phrase identifier has tonicizing qualities and is frequently reinforced by the occurrence of specific notes in the melody. In the tunes "But Beautiful" or "Don't Blame Me," for example, $\flat\hat{7}$ is rendered as a $\flat$5th and $\flat$9th of the corresponding $(ii^{\varnothing}-V^7)/ii$ progression. Figures 21.11a–21.11c provide a harmonic layout of **Phrase Model 6**, show a contrapuntal framework derived from a chromatic $\hat{1}-\hat{2}-\sharp\hat{1}-\hat{1}-\hat{7}-\hat{1}$ melodic pattern, and realize the A section of "East of the Sun" using jazz chorale texture in four voices.[13] The melodic pattern of this model features an extended double neighbor figure with a chromatic pitch, $\sharp\hat{1}$, functioning as the major 3rd of V/ii.

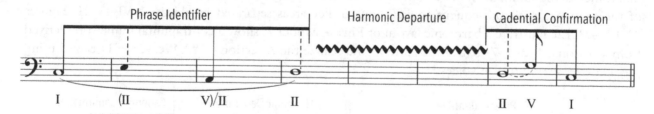

FIGURE 21.11a Phrase Model 6

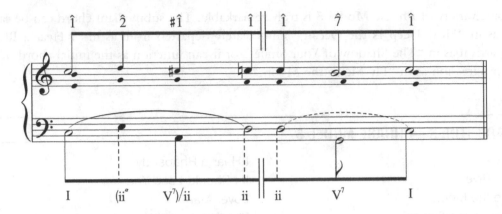

FIGURE 21.11b Phrase Model 6: Contrapuntal Framework

FIGURE 21.11c Phrase Model 6: "East of the Sun"

STANDARD TUNES—PHRASE MODEL 6 _____

But Beautiful   My Foolish Heart

Don't Blame Me   On a Slow Boat to China

East of the Sun   That Old Feeling

It Could Happen to You

Phrase Model 7

The harmonic design of **Phrase Model 7** constitutes an important jazz progression with a phrase identifier that tonicizes the submediant key area. This characteristic progression frequently implies the continuation of the sequence with subsequent tonicizations of key areas separated by thirds: I–VI–IV–II. Figures 21.12a–21.12c illustrate a harmonic layout of **Phrase Model 7**, show a contrapuntal framework derived from a diatonic $\hat{1}$–$\hat{2}$–$\hat{1}$–$\hat{7}$–$\hat{1}$ melodic pattern, and realize the A section of "A Weaver of Dreams" using jazz chorale texture in five voices.[14]

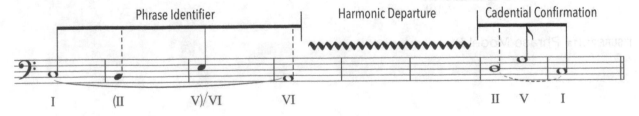

FIGURE 21.12a Phrase Model 7

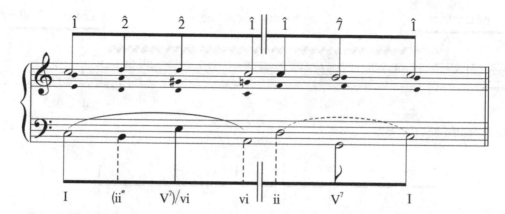

FIGURE 21.12b Phrase Model 7: Contrapuntal Framework

FIGURE 21.12c Phrase Model 7: "A Weaver of Dreams"

Phrase Model 7 is related to the cycle of the dominant 7ths progression: III–VI⁷–II–V⁷. In the context of standard tunes, the submediant chord can function as a tonicized key area as in "Come Rain or Come Shine," or as a passing harmony as in "There Will Never Be Another You."

STANDARD TUNES—PHRASE MODEL 7 _____

A Weaver of Dreams	I'll Close My Eyes
All Through the Night	Just in Time
Bluesette	There Will Never Be Another You
Come Rain or Come Shine	

Phrase Model 8

Phrase Model 8 is a prototype for the important subset of harmonic progressions frequently found in the repertory of standard tunes. The phrase identifier features a motion from I to IV. Since this fundamental harmonic motion has strong blues implications, the subdominant harmony often takes the form of a dominant 7th as in "Willow Weep For Me" or "Tenderly." Figures 21.13a–21.13c illustrate a harmonic layout of **Phrase Model 8**, show a contrapuntal framework derived from a diatonic $\hat{1}$–$\hat{7}$–$\hat{1}$ melodic pattern, and realize the A section of "Willow Weep For Me" using jazz chorale texture in four voices.[15]

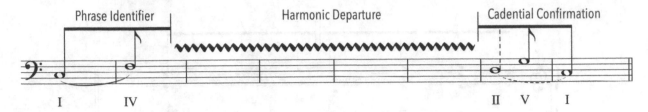

FIGURE 21.13a Phrase Model 8

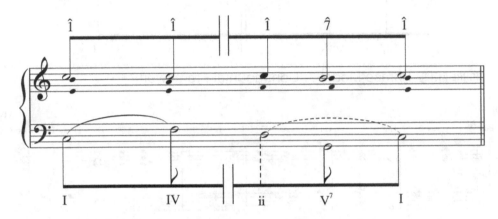

FIGURE 21.13b Phrase Model 8: Contrapuntal Framework

FIGURE 21.13c Phrase Model 8: "Willow Weep For Me"

STANDARD TUNES—PHRASE MODEL 8

A Portrait of Jenny	Tenderly
God Bless the Child	The Nearness of You
On a Clear Day	Willow Weep For Me

Phrase Model 9

Phrase Model 9 features a chromatic phrase identifier that pulls the phrase into the flat submediant key area. Figures 21.14a–21.14c illustrate a harmonic layout of **Phrase Model 9**, show a contrapuntal framework originating from a chromatic $\hat{1}$–$\flat\hat{2}$–$\hat{1}$–$\hat{7}$–$\hat{1}$ melodic pattern, and realize the A section of "What's New?" using jazz chorale texture in five voices.[16] Scale-degree flat two is reinterpreted as the minor 3rd and minor 7th of a (ii–V[7])/$\flat$VI progression. The resolution to $\hat{1}$ over the $\flat$VI harmony fulfills the rules of counterpoint.

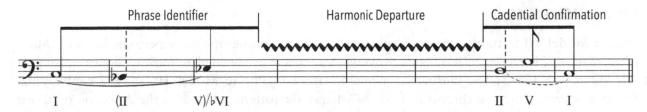

FIGURE 21.14a Phrase Model 9

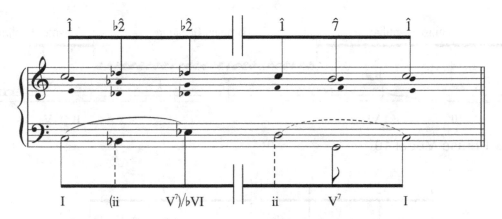

FIGURE 21.14b Phrase Model 9: Contrapuntal Framework

FIGURE 21.14c Phrase Model 9: "What's New?"

The selection of songs featuring this particular phrase identifier is rather small. In the case of "What's New?" and "We'll Be Together Again," the phrase identifier and the ♭VI key area are clearly articulated. "You Stepped Out of a Dream," however, presents a more ambiguous case because the intervening ♭II harmony in the opening phrase expands the tonic before the (ii–V⁷)/♭VI phrase identifier occurs.

STANDARD TUNES—PHRASE MODEL 9 _____

Here's That Rainy Day
What's New?
You Stepped Out of a Dream

Phrase Model 10

Phrase Model 10 features a chromatic phrase identifier tonicizing: the flat supertonic key area. More often than not, however, a [ii–V⁷]/♭II progression occurs in an incomplete form without resolving to ♭II. Figures 21.15a–21.15c illustrate a harmonic layout of **Phrase Model 10**, show a contrapuntal framework derived from a chromatic $\hat{1}$–♭$\hat{2}$–$\hat{1}$–$\hat{7}$–$\hat{1}$ melodic pattern, and realize the A section of "Darn That Dream" using jazz chorale texture in four voices.[17] In **Phrase Model 10**, ♭$\hat{2}$ functions as a minor 7th of the underlying ii/♭II harmony. The resolution to $\hat{1}$ over V/♭II satisfies the rules of voice leading.

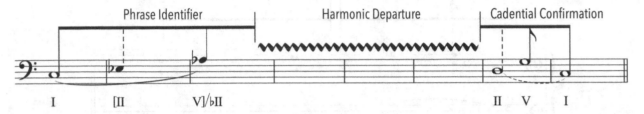

FIGURE 21.15a Phrase Model 10

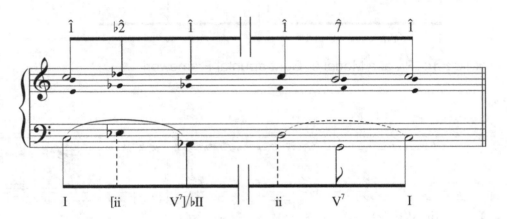

FIGURE 21.15b Phrase Model 10: Contrapuntal Framework

FIGURE 21.15c Phrase Model 10: "Darn That Dream"

What is interesting about the [ii–V⁷]/♭II progression is that it frequently functions as an effective harmonic substitution provided that the melody note establishes a convincing chord/scale relationship with the underlying harmony. After all, it is situated a minor 2nd away from the structural ii–V⁷ progression and, as discussed in Chapter 6, the [ii–V⁷]/♭II often functions as a chromatic sidestepping progression. In the context of "Darn That Dream" or "Out of Nowhere," however, the [ii–V⁷]/♭II is fully integrated within the harmonic structure of these tunes. In "The Lady Is a Tramp" and "I Guess I'll Hang My Tears Out to Dry" only the [ii]/♭II is employed as a chromatic elaboration of the otherwise diatonic opening.

STANDARD TUNES—PHRASE MODEL 10 _____

Darn That Dream	The Lady Is a Tramp
I Guess I'll Hang My Tears Out to Dry	Three Little Words
Out of Nowhere	We'll Be Together Again
San	

Phrase Model 11

Phrase Model 11 features a descending major 2nd cycle beginning on the tonic and—following the subsequent tonicizations of ♭VII and ♭VI—ending on ♭VI. Even though there are only a handful of tunes that use this progression in its entirety, an incomplete **Phrase Model 11** (with a partial descending major 2nd cycle) can occur in the context of different harmonic progressions. Figures 21.16a–21.16c show a chord structure of **Phrase Model 11**, illustrate a contrapuntal derivation from a $\hat{1}$–$\hat{7}$–$\hat{1}$ melodic pattern, and realize the A section of "How High the Moon" using jazz chorale texture in five voices.[18]

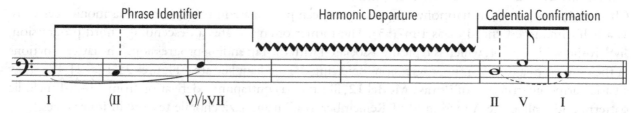

FIGURE 21.16a Phrase Model 11

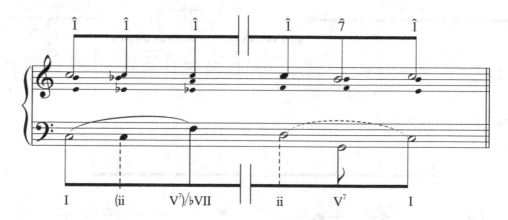

FIGURE 21.16b Phrase Model 11: Contrapuntal Framework

FIGURE 21.16c Phrase Model 11: "How High the Moon"

The most famous occurrence of **Phrase Model 11** is found in "How High the Moon." Apparently, this harmonic sequence was very appealing to a host of musicians from the 1940s and beyond, as they often used this challenging chord progression to test their improvisational prowess. Other tunes from the list, such as "Star Eyes" or "Twilight World" cleverly manipulate the model. Still others, such as "Midnight Sun" or "Early Autumn" use a highly chromatic melody to reinforce the sequential nature of the chord progression.

STANDARD TUNES—PHRASE MODEL 11 _____

How High the Moon   The End of a Love Affair
Midnight Sun   Twilight World
Star Eyes

Phrase Model 12

Phrase Model 12 has a characteristic phrase identifier that features a ♯IV harmony. As explained in Chapter 4, this particular harmony supports $\hat{1}$ and can participate in two common harmonic scenarios: as a half-diminished chord or as a m7(♭5). The former often initiates a descending chord progression, ♯iv⁰–iv–iii–♭iii⁰–ii–V⁷–I, which is typically associated with the tag ending progression. The latter functions in the context of a (ii⁰–V⁷)/iii progression tonicizing the mediant key area. Figures 21.17a–21.17c show a basic harmonic structure of **Phrase Model 12**, illustrate a contrapuntal derivation from a $\hat{1}$–$\hat{7}$–$\hat{1}$ melodic pattern, and realize the A section of "I Remember You" using jazz chorale texture in four voices.[19]

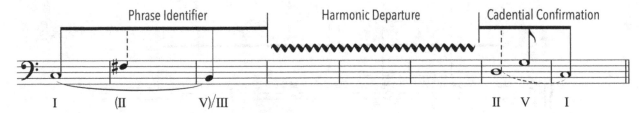

FIGURE 21.17a Phrase Model 12

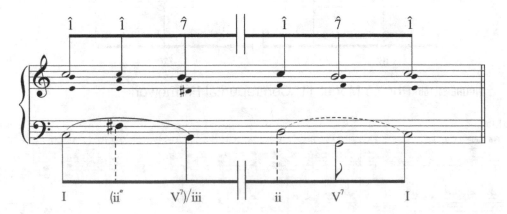

FIGURE 21.17b Phrase Model 12: Contrapuntal Framework

FIGURE 21.17c Phrase Model 12: "I Remember You"

When you examine the list of tunes that share **Phrase Model 12**, you can see how crucial the chord–scale relationships are between the melody and the phrase identifier. In "I Remember You" or "Whispering," the iiᵒ/iii harmony supports $\hat{7}$, which locally functions as an 11th of the underlying chord. "Stella by Starlight" or Miles Davis's version of "I Thought About You" do not begin with the opening tonic; this suggests the possibility of an off-tonic version of the model as well.[20]

One interesting aspect of the progression is its potential for reharmonization. The phrase identifier of this model (either with or without the opening tonic) can be employed as a substitute progression for **Phrase Model 2** provided that the structure of the melody permits for such a substitution. The design of the melody, then, is the ultimate factor allowing the implementation of this substitution. For instance, the A section of "Over the Rainbow" can be reharmonized with the phrase identifier of **Phrase Model 12**. Also, the A sections of "I Should Care" or "Our Love Is Here to Stay," which share **Phrase Model 2**, can also be realized with **Phrase Model 12**.

STANDARD TUNES—PHRASE MODEL 12 _____

I Remember You	Someone to Watch Over Me
I Thought About You	Stella by Starlight
I'm Getting Sentimental Over You	You're My Everything
Lover	

Phrase Model 13

Phrase Model 13 concludes the inventory of phrase models in standard tunes. In contrast to other phrase models, this model constitutes a harmonic sequence of dominant 7th chords and is largely associated with the harmonic structure of the bridge in "I Got Rhythm" and its countless contrafacts. Figures 21.18a–21.18c illustrate a basic harmonic framework of **Phrase Model 13**, show a contrapuntal derivation from a $\hat{3}$–$\hat{2}$ melodic pattern, and realize the A section of "Nice Work If You Can Get It" using jazz chorale texture in five voices.[21]

FIGURE 21.18a Phrase Model 13

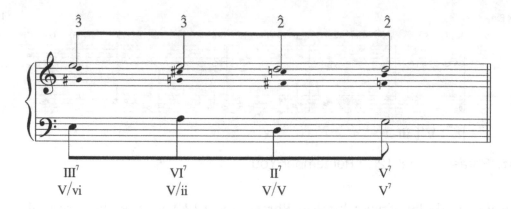

FIGURE 21.18b Phrase Model 13: Contrapuntal Framework

FIGURE 21.18c Phrase Model 13: "Nice Work If You Can Get It"

STANDARD TUNES—PHRASE MODEL 13 _____

A Good Man Is Hard to Find   Nice Work If You Can Get It
Alabama Jubilee   Sweet Georgia Brown
I Hear Music   (Up a) Lazy River
Miss Brown to You

Phrase Models 13 often occurs in an incomplete form (i.e. without the opening III⁷). Tunes, such as "Lazy River," "Alabama Jubilee," "Miss Brown to You," "Old Man Moon," or "Sweet Georgia Brown" begin with an incomplete **Phrase Model 13**.

NOTES

1 The term *standard* refers primarily to American *popular* tunes performed frequently by countless musicians working from ca. 1920 to ca. 1960.
2 Even though this discussion is focused on eight-bar phrase models, the same properties can be used to explain the structure of 16-bar phrases that occur in extended forms and/or more complicated tunes.
3 Melodic patterns are reductions of actual melodies to their structural pitch content.
4 One of the explanations for the primacy of fifth-root movement is related to the occurrence of the perfect 5th in the overtone series between the low-integer ratio (3:2).
5 François Campion's *Traité d'accompagnement et de composition, selon la règle des octaves* offers harmonization of both major and minor scales. See L. Dragnone, "François Campion's Treatise on Accompaniment: A Translation and Commentary."
6 For different harmonic settings of the Rule of the Octave visit the CW.

7 In his description of prolongation in "Jazz Harmony: A Syntactic Background," Henry Martin claims that "many popular jazz songs project a key by *arrival* rather than by simple prolongation of a single tonality designated early on." The terms *on-tonic* and *off-tonic* employed in this book are modeled on Martin's pioneering explanation of the tonality of popular tunes.

8 For more harmonic variations of **Phrase Model 1**, visit the CW.

9 For more harmonic variations of **Phrase Model 2**, visit the CW.

10 For more harmonic variations of **Phrase Model 3**, visit the CW.

11 For more harmonic variations of **Phrase Model 4**, visit the CW.

12 For more harmonic variations of **Phrase Model 5**, visit the CW.

13 For more harmonic variations of **Phrase Model 6**, visit the CW.

14 For more harmonic variations of **Phrase Model 7**, visit the CW.

15 For more harmonic variations of **Phrase Model 8**, visit the CW.

16 For more harmonic variations of **Phrase Model 9**, visit the CW.

17 For more harmonic variations of **Phrase Model 10**, visit the CW.

18 For more harmonic variations of **Phrase Model 11**, visit the CW.

19 For more harmonic variations of **Phrase Model 12**, visit the CW.

20 Miles Davis, *Someday My Prince Will Come*.

21 For more harmonic variations of **Phrase Model 13**, visit the CW.

CHAPTER 22

Song Forms

CHAPTER SUMMARY

Chapter 22 undertakes a study of song forms and its most common types: the 32-bar AABA and the 32-bar ABAC. For each formal paradigm, two tonal variants, on-tonic and off-tonic, are examined. This chapter ends with a discussion of extended and unusual forms.

CONCEPTS AND TERMS

- Analysis:
  - Formal
  - Melodic
  - Tonal
  - Harmonic
- Binary interrupted form
- Bridge (Release)
- Chorus
- Extended structures

- Formal prototypes
- Interruption
- Mixture chord
- Modal mixture
- "Night and Day" duality
- Original sheet music
- Reaching by arrival
- Sentence structure
- Standard tunes

- 32-bar AABA:
  - On-tonic
  - Off-tonic
- 32-bar ABAC:
  - On-tonic
  - Off-tonic
- Verse

FORMAL PROTOTYPES

The term **standard** is often used to denote tunes that make up the core repertory of jazz. The term is an interesting one because it implies that a particular object satisfies certain accepted constraints or that its representation has become, to a certain degree, institutionalized. Tunes that jazz musicians consider standards were largely composed by American songwriters active in the first half of the 20th century, many of whom have become household names in jazz history: Irving Berlin, George Gershwin, Cole Porter, Victor Young, Richard Rodgers, Jerome Kern, Harold Arlen, Jimmy Van Heusen, Frank Loesser, Howard Dietz, Jule Styne, Hoagy Carmichael, and many others. These prolific composers often collaborated with equally remarkable lyricists (Ira Gershwin, Lorenz Hart, Oscar Hammerstein, E.Y. "Yip" Harburg, Dorothy Fields, Johnny Mercer, Sammy Cahn, Ted Koehler) and together they produced hundreds of excellent songs that eventually made their way into the repertory of jazz.

The **32-bar AABA form** is the most common formal prototype underlying the repertory of standard tunes. In the overview of this formal model, we will distinguish between two distinct tonal variants: **on-tonic** and **off-tonic**. These variants are ultimately related to the type of phrase models that occur at the beginning of a tune. In Chapter 21, **Phrase Models 2, 3, 5,** and **13** featured an off-tonic phrase identifier, while the remaining models began on the tonic chord. Whereas phrase models capture the harmonic characteristics of common eight-bar phrases that occur in the A, B, and C sections of the tune, the **formal prototypes** combine phrase models in their most basic harmonic setting and illustrate possible tonal departures in the bridge (or other sections). Depending on the complexity of the tune, the prototype may include anywhere from one to four phrase models. "Can't We Talk It Over," for instance, features only one phrase model; whereas "Stella by Starlight" combines four distinct phrase models, one for each eight-bar phrase in the song. By and large, the formal prototype with two unique phrase models (albeit with some melodic and harmonic variations) is by far the most common.

Broadly speaking, the phrase structure of the tunes in AABA consists of four eight-bar sections and uses a single phrase model for the A sections and a different phrase model for the B section. The phrase model for the B section is usually accompanied by the harmonic motion to a new key area. Each of the eight-bar sections is typically divided into two four-bar phrases. This regular phrase subdivision is emphasized by the fairly regular distribution of chords and harmonic progressions. In certain tunes, such as "I'm Getting Sentimental Over You" or "The Nearness of You," a four-bar phrase extension expands the final A section. The melody of standard tunes is always accompanied by the lyrics. The lyrics frequently reinforce salient features of the melody and highlight important harmonic events. They can even disguise the symmetry of eight-bar phrases by placing textual cadences at locations different from those supplied by the musical meter.

In the process of learning new tunes, it is useful to find the earliest vocal version of the tune that you intend to learn. Even though early vocal performances might not be in keeping with jazz performance practice, they are helpful in authenticating the song's mood, tempo, phrasing, and even some of its harmonic intricacies. It is more valuable to learn a tune from the original recording since later recorded versions might represent transformed versions of the song's harmony, melody, or rhythm. Listen to the words and how the singer phrases the words. Learn the lyrics. Keep them in mind when you decide how you want to phrase the song. Finding the **original sheet music** of the tune that you want to learn may also be beneficial. The harmonic and melodic information included in the original sheet music is often different from fake-book lead sheets. Not only does the original contain the correct melody, harmony (realized as the piano accompaniment), and lyrics as intended by the composer, but it also includes the verse, which is often omitted from the fake-book version. You may be surprised to discover how different composers use the **verse** to foreshadow the overall mood of the song or highlight some salient features that later resurface in the **chorus**. This information can in turn influence your rendition of the song.

THE AABA ON-TONIC DESIGN

The AABA on-tonic design usually features two phrase models: one for the A sections; the other for the B section, also known as the **bridge** or **release**. The tonic chord is clearly announced at the outset of a tune. The first A section is harmonically open and typically ends with a ii–V^7 progression in m. 8. The second A section is tonally closed and, following the cadential confirmation of the main key, ushers in a new phrase model. The bridge introduces contrasting melodic and harmonic material that balances the overall distribution of phrase models. The end of the bridge includes an important formal event, an **interruption**: this event signals the conclusion of the first part of the tune and marks the return of the main key.[1] The harmonic interruption might also overlap with a more substantial harmonic departure occurring in the bridge. For instance, the B section of "I've Never Been in Love Before" begins on IV and features a harmonic departure on III, before the reinstatement of the tonic with a ii–V^7 progression in m. 24.

Figure 22.1 illustrates a generic distribution of phrase models in the AABA on-tonic formal prototype.

PHRASE MODEL **A**	PHRASE MODEL **A**	PHRASE MODEL **B**	PHRASE MODEL **A**
I--------------ii–V^7	I-----------(ii–V^7)/X	X---------(ii–V^7)/I	I-------------------I
A	**A**	**B**	**A**

FIGURE 22.1 The AABA On-Tonic Formal Prototype

The harmonic design of the B section is a defining feature of the song and enables the classification of standard tunes according to their shared tonal and harmonic characteristics. There are a few different scenarios that may happen at the beginning of the bridge. In the most basic scenario, a new chord— still within the orbit of the main tonality—initiates a different (from the A section) chord progression. This new chord can be further reinforced with a local ii–V^7 progression occurring at the end of the second A section. For instance, the bridge sections of "There's a Small Hotel" or "Imagination" begin on IV. However, these subdominant chords do not function as new key areas; in neither case are they confirmed by a cadence or reinforced as a local tonic. In the second, more intricate scenario, the new key area of the bridge is tonicized at the end of the second A or **reached by arrival** at some point during the bridge. For instance, in "Mean to Me" the subdominant key area is clearly tonicized in m. 16 and subsequently prolonged during the first part of the bridge. In "I Can't Get Started With You" the arrival onto the supertonic key area is reached in m. 19 following a tonicized ii–V^7 progression in mm. 17–18. In addition, there are also tunes with tonally ambiguous bridges that cannot be easily classified. Even though the bridge of "Don't Blame Me," for instance, starts on the subdominant, this chord inevitably leads to the hierarchically more important mediant harmony two measures later.

Classification of Standard Tunes[2]

Below is a partial list of standard tunes cast in the AABA on-tonic form that share similar harmonic traits at the outset of the bridge. For a more complete list of tunes and different key areas of the bridge visit the CW. Unlike in Chapter 21, where standard tunes were classified according to the harmonic similarities occurring at the phrase level, this list is organized according to the tonal characteristics at the formal level. Standard tunes with direct or indirect harmonic motion to the subdominant are by far the most common. An "*" indicates tunes where the key area (or hierarchically more important chord) at the beginning of the bridge is reached by arrival.

KEY OF THE BRIDGE—IV	**KEY OF THE BRIDGE—III**	**KEY OF THE BRIDGE—♭VI**
Day Dream	I Never Knew	Darn That Dream
Skylark	I'm Through With Love	Easy Living
Sweet Lorraine	My One and Only Love	I'll Take Romance*
The Surrey With the Fringe on Top*	Polka Dots and Moonbeams	Smoke Gets in Your Eyes

THE AABA OFF-TONIC DESIGN

In addition to the on-tonic model, the **AABA off-tonic design** is an important formal prototype in standard tunes. The main characteristic of the off-tonic design is the absence of the tonic at the beginning of the tune. Since **Phrase Models 2, 3, 5**, and **13** have phrase identifiers that do not start on the tonic chord, tunes sharing this type of design are likely to employ these phrase models for the A sections. Figure 22.2 demonstrates a generic distribution of phrase models in the AABA formal prototype.

PHRASE MODEL **A**	PHRASE MODEL **A**	PHRASE MODEL **B**	PHRASE MODEL **A**
X-------------ii–V^7	X----------(ii–V^7)/X	X----------(ii–V^7)/X	X-----------------I
A	**A**	**B**	**A**

FIGURE 22.2 The AABA Off-Tonic Formal Prototype

Classification of Standard Tunes[3]

The partial list of standard tunes below is organized according to the type of harmonic motion that occurs at the outset of the bridge. For a more complete list of tunes and different key areas of the bridge visit the CW. An "*" indicates tunes where the key (or hierarchically more important chord) at the beginning of the bridge is reached by arrival.

KEY OF THE BRIDGE—IV	**KEY OF THE BRIDGE—I**	**KEY OF THE BRIDGE— VII/♭VII**
Everything Happens to Me*	I Cover the Waterfront*	
How Long Has This Been Going On?	I Didn't Know What Time It Was	All the Things You Are*
I Didn't Know About You*	I Love You*	Sophisticated Lady
Too Marvelous For Words*	My Funny Valentine	What Is This Thing Called Love?*
Why Try to Change Me Now?*	Old Folks	

"HAVE YOU MET MISS JONES?"—AN ANALYSIS

Figure 22.3 gives the original sheet music for the tune "Have You Met Miss Jones?" by Richard Rodgers and Lorenz Hart.[4] This song is an example of the 32-bar AABA on-tonic form. The top stave includes the chord changes from a published lead-sheet version. Since the chord changes differ from the piano accompaniment, both will be used in the following analysis. Figure 22.3 also includes the verse, which in the hands of great songwriters has interesting features that later resurface in the chorus.

FIGURE 22.3 "Have You Met Miss Jones?"—Original Sheet Music

FIGURE 22.3 continued

FIGURE 22.3 continued

The Verse

After a four-measure introduction, the verse of "Have You Met Miss Jones?" is 12 bars long and, like a typical blues, contains three symmetrical four-bar phrases. The first two phrases (mm. 1–8) are variants of one another. The third phrase (mm. 9–12) features a descending octave (overshot by an upper chromatic neighbor, D♭5) from C5 to C4 and uses the basic melodic gestures from the opening phrase. The first phrase is harmonically open and ends with a ii–V^7 progression in the tonic key. The second phrase (mm. 5–8) is tonally closed, but a tonicization of the subdominant in m. 8 with the resolution in m. 9 creates a sense of harmonic momentum. After the subdominant departure, the phrase proceeds to a half cadence in m. 12 using a modified cycle of fifth progression.

The melody of the verse establishes an interesting chord–scale relationship. The sense of eagerness that emanates from the narrator's murky recollections is captured melodically by the blues inflection of $\hat{3}$ and the occurrence of an unprepared major 9th in mm. 1, 5, and 9. The harmonic support for these two pitches is quite adventurous when consulting the piano accompaniment. The A♭4 in m. 1 in the lead-sheet version receives a harmonic support from the A♭dim7 chord. The piano accompaniment uses the same chord but over the C pedal, which offers a much more interesting harmonic realization. In m. 2, the G4 on beat 4 receives the same pedal point support and the underlying A♭dim renders the melodic pitch as the major 7th. With the lyrics: *And now, you see, we mustn't wait* in m. 8, the melody frees itself from a downward slump and ascends to $\hat{5}$, which is harmonically reinforced with a tonicization of the subdominant. A motivic descent to $\hat{5}$ in m. 12 effectively summarizes the overall arch-like architecture unfolding in the verse.

The Chorus

In order to make our musical analysis pertinent to improvisation, it is necessary to know what attributes make "Have You Met Miss Jones?" stand out from other standards built from similar chord progressions. In other words, the analysis should gather the most relevant information about the tune's properties that can later be explored in improvisation. Four broad characteristics—**formal**, **tonal**, **melodic**, and **harmonic**—can be used to describe salient characteristics of the tune. It is not sufficient, however, to consider these categories as separate entities, but to examine them in relation to one another. The analytical method advocated here asks the following question: What is it that makes "Have You Met Miss Jones?" (or any other tune) unique and distinguishes it from other tunes with similar tonal and formal properties? Finding an answer will lead to a more successful improvisation and better understanding of the tune's properties.

Formal Characteristics

The form of "Have You Met Miss Jones?" uses a 32-bar AABA on-tonic design with harmonic motion to the subdominant at the outset of the B section. As is the case with most standard tunes, the A sections are symmetrical with clear four-bar phrase subdivisions. The B section is more sophisticated and features a 2+2+4 phrase division similar to the **sentence structure**.[5]

Tonal Characteristics

The phrase structure of the tune uses **Phrase Model 4** for the A section and **Phrase Model 3** for the B Section. The harmonic rhythm in the A section is relatively slow with one chord per measure. **Phrase Model 4** occurs in the most basic diatonic form without any unusual harmonic activities in the midst of the phrase. The first A section is tonally open and ends with a structural ii–V^7 supporting $\hat{4}$.

The second A section confirms the tonic and subsequently tonicizes the subdominant emerging at the beginning of the bridge. The chord structure of the bridge is classified as **Phrase Model 3** because of its relationship to the main key and large-scale tonal organization of the song as a whole. The bridge begins on IV, which is tonicized in mm. 15–16, but neither cadentially confirmed nor harmonically prolonged. Even though a chromatic sequence in mm. 18–23 touches on distant key areas and ultimately ends on ♭II in m. 23, a ii–V^7 in m. 24 prepares the reinstatement of the tonic key. Thus the chord structure of the bridge begins on IV—which is then followed by a complex harmonic departure—and ends with an incomplete cadential confirmation of I, just as in **Phrase Model 3**. The final A section includes a stepwise ascent to the climactic E5, which gives the word *die* a new meaning and closes with a complete cadential confirmation of the tonic. The intricate harmonic sequence that occurs in the bridge is the most important tonal event of the song. The subdominant in m. 17 initiates a sequential progression that combines two intervallic cycles: major 2nd and major 3rd. At a macro level, each tonicized key area —IV, ♭II, and VI—creates a major 3rd cycle that projects the roots of a B♭ augmented triad. At a micro level, the progression descends by major 2nds and intersects with the major 3rd cycle.

Melodic Characteristics

The melodic structure of the tune uses the composer's signature trademarks: stepwise melodic motion, motivic parallelism, measured use of skips, melodic rests on harmonically active pitches, and a compound melody. In comparison to the verse, the relationship between the melody and harmony in the A sections is not as daring, and largely depends on the use of chord tones on strong beats and passing/neighbor notes on weak beats. The bridge, on the contrary, creates more melodic tension by highlighting accented 9ths in mm. 17, 19, and 21 (in relation to the corresponding local major chords), which initiate sequential melodic repetitions.

Harmonic Characteristics

The longest note of the tune (B♭4 in mm. 7–8) has interesting harmonic implications. Because of the harmonic support it receives from a diatonic ii–V^7 progression and (potentially) from a chromatic [ii–V^7]/♭II, $\hat{4}$ can participate in both environments. In improvisation, we can effectively capitalize on the note's dual harmonic membership. The projection of the augmented triad in the bridge suggests the use of more adventurous melodic and harmonic vocabulary that could infiltrate our improvisation.

Summary of Features

What is it that makes "Have You Met Miss Jones?" unique? We can answer this question as follows:

1. **Formal considerations**—the symmetrical phrase structure of the chorus parallels the symmetrical structure of melodic lines.

2. **Tonal considerations**—since the B section is more adventurous and provides harmonic relief from the diatonic A section, the solo can explore the contrast between diatonic and chromatic elements.

3. **Melodic considerations**—the blues inflections of the verse and the stepwise melodic design of the chorus imply that melodic lines can have similar characteristics.

4. **Harmonic considerations**—since the phrase identifier of **Phrase Model 4** can be transformed harmonically and the longest note of the tune (B♭4 in mm. 7–8) can be harmonized using ii–V^7 or [ii–V^7]/♭II progressions, the solo can capitalize on these harmonic devices.

THE ABAC ON-TONIC DESIGN

The **32-bar ABAC on-tonic design** (similar to the AABA) is an example of the **binary interrupted form**. The harmonic interruption occurs in m. 16 and divides the form into two large tonal motions: I–V in mm. 1–16 and I–I in mm. 17–32. Because of the absence of a clearly articulated bridge, which is the defining feature of the AABA tunes, the ABAC form is more ambiguous and thus less codifiable. Tunes in the ABAC form have a different phrase distribution and are usually characterized by more complicated melodic, harmonic, and rhythmic designs. Even though the designation "B" and "C" implies the use of different phrase models, in practice these sections are frequently related to one another. Figure 22.4 illustrates a generic distribution of phrase models for the ABAC on-tonic design.

PHRASE MODEL **A**	PHRASE MODEL **B**	PHRASE MODEL **A**	PHRASE MODEL **C**
I----------(ii–V⁷)/X	X--------(ii–V⁷)/X	I----------(ii–V⁷)/X	X---------(ii–V⁷)/I
A	**B**	**A**	**C**

PHRASE MODEL **A**	PHRASE MODEL **B**
A	**B**
(16)	(16)

FIGURE 22.4 The ABAC On-Tonic Formal Prototype

This formal structure suggests two different distributions of phrase models. In the first one, each eight-bar section is analyzed with a unique phrase model just as in "Blame It on My Youth" or "The Touch of Your Lips," which feature a faster harmonic rhythm and more intricate melodic design. In tunes such as "Get Out of Town" or "I Could Write a Book," however, with a slower harmonic rhythm and uninterrupted melodic flow spanning mm. 1–16 and mm. 17–32, only a single phrase model suffices to explain the harmonic properties of both sections.[6]

Classification of Standard Tunes[7]

Below is a partial list of standard tunes compartmentalized according to the key of the B and C sections. For a more comprehensive list, visit the CW.

KEY OF THE B AND/OR C SECTIONS—I	KEY OF THE B AND/OR C SECTIONS—VI
But Beautiful*	Embraceable You
Everything I Love	I Could Write a Book
For All We Know	I'll Be Seeing You
On Green Dolphin Street*	It Had to Be You*
Spring Is Here	Time After Time

THE ABAC OFF-TONIC DESIGN

The **ABAC off-tonic design** has a similar phrase distribution as the ABAC on-tonic form. The only difference is the use of **Phrase Models 2**, **3**, **5**, and **13** for the A sections. The distribution of phrase models for the ABAC off-tonic prototype is shown in Figure 22.5.

PHRASE MODEL **A**	PHRASE MODEL **B**	PHRASE MODEL **A**	PHRASE MODEL **C**
X--------(ii–V^7)/X	X---------(ii–V^7)/X	X---------(ii–V^7)/X	X---------(ii–V^7)/I
A	B	A	C

PHRASE MODEL **A**	PHRASE MODEL **B**
A	B
(16)	(16)

FIGURE 22.5 The ABAC Off-Tonic Formal Prototype

Classification of Standard Tunes[8]

Below is a partial list of standard tunes that share the specific key of the B and/or C sections. For a more comprehensive list, visit the CW.

KEY OF THE B AND/OR C SECTIONS—I	KEY OF THE B AND/OR C SECTIONS—VI	KEY OF THE B AND/OR C SECTIONS—♭III
All of You	Day by Day*	Autumn in New York*
Easy to Love*	I've Found a New Baby*	It's You or No One*
I Should Care	Two For the Road	Laura*
I Wish I Knew*	What a Difference a Day	
I'll Never Smile Again*	Made*	
	You'd Be So Nice to Come	
	Home to*	

"ALL OF YOU"—AN ANALYSIS

Figure 22.6 illustrates the original sheet music of Cole Porter's "All of You."[9] This song is an example of the 32-bar ABAC off-tonic form. The top stave includes the chord changes from a published lead-sheet version. Since the chord changes differ from the piano accompaniment, both will be used in the following analysis.

FIGURE 22.6 "All of You"—Original Sheet Music

FIGURE 22.6 continued

FIGURE 22.6 continued

The Verse

The verse sets the overall character of the song and foreshadows certain events that become more apparent in the chorus. For instance, a two-note melodic anacrusis in the verse becomes a three-note gesture in the chorus; an off-tonic beginning on B♭7/F in the verse is mirrored by an off-tonic beginning on A♭, A♭m6, or Fm7(♭5) in the chorus, depending on the version. Each four-bar phrase in the verse has basically the same melodic architecture with a balanced contour and the prevalent use of stepwise motion. The melody establishes a strong chord–scale relationship with the chord tones aligned with beats 1 and 3, and passing notes placed on beats 2 and 4. This lack of melodic/harmonic tensions suddenly becomes disrupted in the chorus where the chromatic chord–scale relationships prevail and larger intervallic leaps dominate the melody. The verse concludes with the words: *And it's not a passing fancy or a fancy pass*, with a perfectly balanced melody supported by an expanded ii–V^7 progression. In the original piano accompaniment, Porter elaborates the dominant 7th in m. 15 with Edim7.

The Chorus

In the forthcoming analysis, we will concentrate on tonal, melodic, harmonic, and metric/rhythmic characteristics of the tune and discuss ways in which they influence the overall approach to improvisation. The chorus has a relatively uniform tonal architecture: the first A section uses **Phrase Model 3** with an open cadence on V^7 in m. 8, while the B section employs **Phrase Model 1** with a modified phrase identifier (notice the interpolation of ♭iii^O in m. 10) and an open cadence on V^7 in m. 16. The second A section differs from the first A, particularly in mm. 21–24. At the end of this section, an elided [ii–V^7]/ii anticipates the arrival of the C section. Rather than resolving the [ii–V^7]/ii to the expected minor supertonic, Porter thwarts our expectations and shifts the music to IV in m. 25. The C section utilizes **Phrase Model 3** with a tonicization of ii in m. 26. Notice that this harmonic departure is initiated by chromatic sidestepping (ii^Ø–V^7)/iii that triggers a sequence of ii–V^{7}s in mm. 27–30 and brings the tune to an end.

The lyrics also contain some important textual associations that enrich our understanding of the song. Each time Porter uses the word *you* in the A section, he accompanies it by a metric, durational, and melodic stress. Its rhymed counterparts—*lure* and *tour*—support ♭$\hat{6}$, giving the melody a characteristic poignancy. This note also triggers the largest and most audacious intervallic leap of a major 7th in m. 7 over the predominant ii^Ø. This chord sounds particularly expressive and its unique quality stimulates the choice of chordal extensions for the V^7 in m. 8.

The tonal architecture of "All of You" features unique harmonic progressions. In mm. 1–2, the succession of iv–I establishes the overall character of the song. This progression, along with its variant ii^Ø–V^7–I, is by far the most common harmonic choice used by jazz musicians. However, it is clear from the original sheet music that Porter had a different harmonic idea for mm. 1–2: his realization features an A♭ major (!) chord over the tonic pedal E♭. Only with the arrival of C♭3 in m. 3 does he change to an A♭ minor chord. The minor subdominant in m. 3 borrows ♭$\hat{6}$ from the parallel minor key, and is known as a **mixture chord.**[10] This and other modal borrowings (e.g. ♭$\hat{7}$ in m. 14) greatly enhance the character of the melody and influence the choice of other harmonies: C7(♭9) in m. 14 and Fm7(♭5) in mm. 3, 7, and 19. With the occurrence of the tonic in m. 2, the A section becomes tonally ambiguous and in search of the tonal stability. Porter makes this search a compelling journey with various harmonic detours (mm. 7–8 and 25–26), deceptive resolutions (mm. 8–9 and 23–25), and modal mixture chords (mm. 3, 7, 14, 17, 19, and 21). When he finally confirms the tonic in mm. 29–32, Porter pulls out all the stops:

he accentuates each word of the final phrase: *For I love all of you*, with half-note values and harmonizes the entire four-bar closing section with a diatonic ii–V^7–I progression. In the piano accompaniment, the bass voice counterpoints the soprano with a $\hat{2}$–$\hat{3}$–$\hat{4}$–$\hat{5}$ ascent with each bass note supporting different chords: Fm–C7/G–A♭6–B♭9, respectively. With such a robust and convincing ending, Porter resolves all previously accumulated melodic and harmonic ambiguities.

The B section of "All of You" uses a harmonically open **Phrase Model 1** that interrupts the form in m. 16. In some versions of the song a different harmony in m. 9 may be encountered. The use of functionally equivalent mediant harmony in place of the tonic, however, is within the limits of acceptable harmonic substitutions. The occurrence of ♭iii^O in m. 10 is a particularly important harmonic event in the B section. This diminished 7th passing chord occupies the whole measure, improves the overall voice leading, and provides a convincing harmonic support for the melody. In addition, it also establishes a chord–scale relationship with a **2/1** octatonic I.

A harmonic shift to the subdominant at the beginning of the C section is in keeping with the tonality of numerous jazz songs where a similar harmonic progression signals the closing section. The harmonic supports for D5 in mm. 25–26 constitute yet another salient feature of "All of You." The D5 is harmonized with A♭M7 in m. 25 and with Am7(♭5)–D7(♭9) in m. 26. These harmonizations suggest specific chord–scale relationships: Lydian in m. 25 and **2/1** octatonic I in m. 26.

Summary of Features

The following points suggest one of many possible directions that can be taken during improvisation on "All of You":

1. **Tonal considerations**—since the tune plays on tonal expectations, the idea of tonal ambiguity can be explored. One that stems from the analysis suggests the use of mixture chords and functionally equivalent harmonic substitutions.

2. **Melodic considerations**—since the melody employs considerable intervallic leaps, melodic lines can have a more angular contour with larger intervallic leaps.

3. **Harmonic considerations**—since the diminished 7th chord in m. 10 and the IV–[ii^O–V^7]/iii progression in mm. 25–26 feature attractive chord–scale relationships, they can be explored during improvisation.

4. **Metric/rhythmic considerations**—the melodic anacrusis in the verse and the chorus suggests a particular design that seems to foreshadow the upcoming harmony rather than retroactively respond to it. This proactive approach to phrasing and harmony creates better melodic flow and can ultimately influence the overall rhythmic architecture of the solo.

EXTENDED AND UNUSUAL SONG FORMS

In addition to the 32-bar AABA and ABAC forms, there are other, less common formal designs with unusual tonal characteristics, different phrase distributions, and **extended structures**. Standard tunes with unusual formal designs might present a challenge to the improviser because they typically unfold in a less regular manner and feature more intricate harmonic progressions. For each song listed in Table 22.1, the length of individual sections is indicated in measures and the length of the form provided. For a more complete list, visit the CW.

TABLE 22.1 Unusual and Extended Standard Forms

Title	Form	Length
A Time For Love	A(8)–A′(8)–B(8)–C(14)	38
Alone Together	A(14)–A(14)–B(8)–A′(8)	44
Dream Dancing	A(16)–A(16)–B(8)–C(12)	52
Falling in Love With Love	A(16)–B(16)–A(16)–C(16)	48
From This Moment On	A(16)–A(16)–B(16)–C(20)	68
I'll Remember April	A(16)–B(16)–A(16)	48
Invitation	A(8)–A′(8)–B(16)–C(16)	48
Moon and Sand	A(24)–B(18)	42
My Favorite Things	A(16)–B(16)–A(16)–C(24)	72
Witchcraft	A(8)–B(8)–C(14)–A(8)	46

"DREAM DANCING"—AN ANALYSIS

Among the numerous songs featuring extended formal designs, "Dream Dancing" by Cole Porter is one of the most interesting.[11] Figure 22.7 illustrates a lead-sheet version of "Dream Dancing" including the verse.

The Verse

The verse is 16 bars long and has recitative-like qualities.[12] For instance, mm. 1–4 introduce a tonic pedal commonly used in recitatives. The melody has a static design, features a syllabic declamation of the words, and receives harmonic support foreshadowing salient characteristics that will become manifested in the chorus. The overall tonal architecture of the verse implies a large motion T–PD–D with the tonic occupying mm. 1–8, the predominant mm. 9–14, and the dominant mm. 15–16. These functional areas feature some interesting harmonic parallelisms. For instance, the progression from mm. 5–7 reappears in a transposed and enlarged version in mm. 9–12. The most striking harmonic event occurs in mm. 13–14 where the lyrics: *to live again* receive a [ii–V^7]/♭II harmonic support.

The Chorus

The phrase structure of "Dream Dancing" does not conform to any traditional formal models: the distribution of phrases, the placement of structural cadences, and the unfolding of lyrics suggest a three-part form. Figure 22.8 illustrates a formal diagram of the tune.

FIGURE 22.7 "Dream Dancing"—Lead Sheet

FIGURE 22.7 continued

A section **a** (8 mm.) + **b** (8 mm.)	A section **a** (8 mm.) + **b** (8 mm.)	B section 8 mm.	C section 12 mm.

FIGURE 22.8 "Dream Dancing"—Formal Diagram

Formal Considerations

The A section is 16 bars long and combines two eight-bar phrases that loosely follow the harmonic structure of an incomplete **Phrase Model 5** for mm. 1–8 and **Phrase Model 3** for mm. 9–16. The B section in mm. 33–40 is eight bars long and resembles **Phrase Model 3** with its characteristic off-tonic phrase identifier on IV. The final C section in mm. 41–52 is 12 bars long and features a 4-bar interpolation of an elided [ii–V^7]/♭II progression from mm. 13–14 of the verse. "Dream Dancing," then, is a composite 52-bar form unlike any existing formal prototype.

Harmonic Considerations

One particularly unusual characteristic of the tune is the harmonic progression in mm. 1–4 and 17–20. The occurrence of the tonally ambivalent major submediant coupled with a chromatic alteration of $\hat{1}$— if heard in the opening progression in the context of C major—are far removed from the main tonic. This opening resembles **Phrase Model 5** with its off-tonic phrase identifier in the submediant. However, unlike other tunes that share this model, "Dream Dancing" begins on V/VI, which tonicizes a local tonic on VI. Given the nature of the opening progression and the subsequent tonicization of IV in m. 8, the tonality of the tune is evasive and neither prolonged nor confirmed.

The tonicization of IV in m. 8 installs an off-tonic **Phrase Model 3** that features an important harmonic event: a [ii–V^7]/♭II progression in m. 13. Porter uses this salient progression to announce the word: *dream*. The other title word: *dancing* receives harmonic support from a ii–V^7 progression. A more forceful confirmation of the tonic occurs in mm. 14–15, but the subsequent tonicization in m. 16, [ii–V^7]/IV, thwarts the tonal expectations and does not resolve to the expected subdominant but to V/VI in m. 17. The chord succession in mm. 16–17 also features two dominant 7th chords a major third apart; in addition to the chromatic progression from m. 13, these sonorities constitute the most important tonal characteristics of the song.

The second part of the tune begins in m. 33 with the lyric: *Dream dancing*. Measures 33–40 resemble **Phrase Model 3** with an off-tonic phrase identifier on IV. The tonality of the song is climactically declared in m. 40 and marks the beginning of the final section of the tune. The arrival of the tonic in m. 41 emphasizes the structural downbeat, features the important word: *love*, and employs **Phrase Model 8**, the only on-tonic phrase model of the entire song. Measures 45–49 interpolate the [ii–V^7]/♭II progression three times in quick succession and, with the lyrics: *Dream dancing, To Paradise prancing, Dream dancing with you*, lead to the final cadence in the tonic, an emphatic end to this fascinating harmonic journey.

Melodic Considerations

The melodic design of "Dream Dancing" is equally interesting. Each time the title words appear in the lyrics they are accompanied by a characteristic melodic gesture. In mm. 13–14, for instance, the motto of the song features a minor third from ♭$\hat{7}$ to $\hat{5}$. In mm. 33–34, the same words project a downward octave leap from $\hat{8}$ to $\hat{1}$. Finally, in mm. 49–50, *dream dancing* highlights a minor third skip from ♭$\hat{3}$ to $\hat{1}$. Notice that in mm. 13 and 45 the minor third skip begins on ♭$\hat{7}$, and in m. 49 on ♭$\hat{3}$: these chromatic pitches allow Porter to inject a subtle blues flavor into the structure of the song.

A chromatic inflection of $\hat{1}$ in mm. 1–4 constitutes an unusual melodic feature of the tune. While in other standard tunes the tonic note is typically left untouched (especially at the outset of a song), in "Dream Dancing" the rhetorical interplay between $\hat{1}$ and $\sharp\hat{1}$ reflects the nature of the lyrics: *When day is gone and night comes on.* The lyrics depict the familiar **"Night and Day" duality**—one of Porter's favorite conceits and something that he highlighted through his choice of melodic notes and harmonic progressions.[13]

Summary of Features

Improvising on a tune like "Dream Dancing" can be an arduous undertaking. Among the numerous challenges, the convincing articulation of the formal structure, correct assessment of the harmonic function of distantly related chords, and the use of chromaticism should be at the center of consideration. The following points offer a summary of features to be explored during improvisation.

1. **Formal considerations**—based on the analysis of the tune, we can see ways in which the composer plays with tonal expectations and postpones the arrival of the tonic until m. 41. This gradual and measured emergence of tonality suggests that the solo can have similar properties especially in the way the local progressions and the climax of the solo are negotiated and articulated.

2. **Melodic considerations**—since the melody features some unusual chromatic inflections, the use of bold chromaticism can be a part of the solo.

3. **Harmonic considerations**—the prominent role of $[\text{ii–V}^7]/\flat\text{II}$ and the dominant 7ths a major third apart suggest the use of these progressions during improvisation with a fitting selection of chord–scale relationships.

4. **Tempo considerations**—with extended formal structures, we can experiment with different tempi and/or time feels. In addition to a swing feel, "Dream Dancing" lends itself to a straight 8th-note feel.

NOTES

1 The concept of interruption is fundamental to the theory of Heinrich Schenker; it is defined as the arresting of the melodic and harmonic motion before the return of the opening material.
2 For the composers and the lyricists, consult Appendix G on the CW.
3 For the composers and the lyricists, consult Appendix G on the CW.
4 For representative recordings, consult Appendix F on the CW.
5 A musical sentence consists of two main components: a basic idea and its repetition organized in 2+2+4 proportions.
6 In the case of "Get Out of Town," a minor version of **Phrase Model 8** with a harmonic departure in $\flat$III for mm. 1–16, and a major version of **Phrase Model 8** with the same harmonic departure for mm. 17–32; in the case of "I Could Write a Book," **Phrase Model 4** with two harmonic departures to vi and iii for mm. 1–16 and **Phrase Model 4** with two harmonic departures to vi and IV for mm. 17–32.
7 For the composers and the lyricists, consult Appendix G on the CW.
8 For the composers and the lyricists, consult Appendix G on the CW.
9 For representative recordings, consult Appendix F on the CW.
10 **Mixture** (also known as **modal mixture**) borrows tonal elements from the parallel mode. In the present instance, notes and chords from E$\flat$ minor that freely interact in the context of E$\flat$ major are regarded as mixture. As a result, the use of mixture greatly enhances melodic, harmonic, and tonal possibilities that can occur in a tune.
11 For representative recordings, consult Appendix F on the CW.
12 Recitative is a type of vocal writing characterized by a speech-like declamation of words. In opera, recitatives precede melodically and formally interesting arias.
13 The most familiar case is his well-known song "Night and Day."

Reharmonization Techniques

CHAPTER SUMMARY

Chapter 23 discusses various approaches to jazz reharmonization. It begins by considering two contrasting approaches to harmony: vertical and horizontal. Basic, intermediate, and advanced techniques of reharmonization are discussed.

CONCEPTS AND TERMS

- Basic techniques:
  - Addition of extensions
  - Diminished 7th chords
  - Harmonic expansion of structural chords
  - Functional exchange
  - Interpolation of auxiliary progressions
  - Melodic recontextualization
- Neighbor formations
- Pedal points
- Tonicizations
- Tritone substitutions
- Block style
- Harmonization
- Harmony:
  - Horizontal
  - Vertical
- Intermediate techniques:
- Cyclic harmony
- Modal harmony
- Signature chords
- Modal pitch centers (MPCs)
- Parallel planing
- Upper-structure triads

INTRODUCTION

The terms *harmonization* and *reharmonization* are somewhat related to one another as they describe the process of *fleshing out* chord progressions with fully or partially realized harmonic structures. **Harmonization** involves supporting a tune with a suitable chord progression. **Reharmonization** then takes that progression and modifies it in a considerable way. While these newly created harmonic modifications might be quite substantial, they are usually traceable to and motivated by the original chord changes. The term *reharmonization* employed in this chapter refers to both processes: realization and harmonic reworking. The process of reharmonization, then, uses both the original and any modified

FIGURE 23.1 "Herzlich tut mich verlangen"—Harmonizations by J.S. Bach

chord progressions to render fully or partially realized harmonic formations. One of the goals of reharmonization is to provide a set of new chord changes that support the melody of a song. The melody, then, is the ultimate source for all harmonic choices.

Historically harmonic explorations of the melody have been tied to the art of composition and improvisation. By studying different genres of composition that primarily focus on harmonic and contrapuntal reworkings of the melody such as passamezzos, folias, passacaglias, toccatas, chaconnes, fantasias, chorale preludes, suites, and the theme and variations, you discover that the practice of reharmonization has indeed been a long and rich tradition.[1] Let's examine how J.S. Bach explored the potential of the chorale melody "Herzlich tut mich verlangen." Figure 23.1 compares three (out of nine) harmonic reworkings of the Passion chorale.[2]

When comparing these versions, you may be surprised at the harmonic flexibility of this relatively simple melody and at Bach's ingenuity in exploring its potential. Each phrase receives harmonic support that clearly delineates the underlying tonality and effectively drives to a cadential repose. How does Bach realize the harmonic potential of the melody? Although there are different answers to this crucial question, it seems that by allowing the melodic phrases to be reinterpreted in the context of closely related key areas and by choosing supporting harmonies that firmly project those key areas, Bach is able to create very different yet compelling harmonic settings. Take, for example, the opening phrase in mm. 1–2. In each case, the pitch E4 that ends the phrase on beat 3 in m. 2 receives distinctive harmonic support. In Figure 23.1a, the E4 is supported by an A major triad, in Figure 23.1b by a C major triad, and in Figure 23.1c, the E4 is harmonized with an E major triad. The choice of these harmonies is predicated on Bach's ability to select chords that inevitably lead to the respective cadential closures. While the cadence in Figure 23.1a functions quite unexpectedly as a sort of Phrygian half cadence in D minor (without an explicit statement to that key), the other cadential gestures are the consequences of prior harmonic progressions. Thus in Figure 23.1b the melody is reinterpreted as $\hat{3}$–$\hat{6}$–$\hat{5}$–$\hat{4}$–$\hat{3}$–$\hat{2}$–$\hat{3}$ in C major and receives a harmonic support from this key area, while in Figure 23.1c, the same phrase functions as $\hat{5}$–$\hat{8}$–$\hat{7}$–$\hat{6}$–$\hat{5}$–$\hat{4}$–$\hat{5}$ in A minor, projects this key with a logical choice of supporting chords, and terminates with a "correct" Phrygian cadence.

Although the independent nature of Bach's inner voices implies a linear approach to reharmonization, each note of the melody is supported by a single harmonic formation, as indicated by the Roman numerals and lead-sheet symbols. The use of melodic diminutions is purely for decorative purposes and confined to local harmonies only. The vertical aspect of these reharmonizations, then, is conveyed by the fast rate of harmonic rhythm and one-to-one ratios between the melody and harmony. Note also that each of these reharmonizations features chord progressions that logically support the underlying key areas, which—as is often the case with the tonal architecture of chorale melodies—change about every two measures. In short, Bach's reharmonizations not only capitalize on the harmonic potential of the melody, but also feature perfectly executed voice leading and unobtrusively support the tonality of individual phrases with a strong cadential confirmation at the end of each phrase.

A very different approach to harmony is shown in Figure 23.2, where the interaction between the three voices creates functional progressions and individual harmonic formations. Figure 23.2 illustrates mm. 1–16 of "Variatio 15. Canone alla Quinta. a 1 Clav." by J.S. Bach from his *Goldberg Variations*.

The rate of harmonic rhythm is considerably slower, with one chord per measure in most cases. The interplay between three independently moving lines creates interesting harmonies that resist a beat-by-beat vertical analysis. Metric displacements, accented passing notes, appoggiaturas, suspensions, and, above all, voice independence (though being a canonic variation certainly helps in this case) are essential features

FIGURE 23.2 "Variatio 15. Canone alla Quinta. a 1 Clav." from *Goldberg Variations* by J.S. Bach

of a linear approach to harmony. The use of these devices creates a sense of harmonic freedom: the many localized harmonies are generated linearly without being confined to individual beats or measures. For instance, mm. 1–4 feature a chromaticized bass span from $\hat{1}$ to $\hat{5}$ which is realized with the traditional chord progression: | i | V⁶–V | iv⁶ | V |. When examining the way Bach handles this standard progression, you can see that voice independence plays an integral role in disguising the structure of individual chords. For instance, the occurrence of V⁶ in m. 2 is postponed by a half beat with a 2–3 bass suspension. In the same measure, the first convergence of three voices at the "and" of beat 2 produces the Daug triad. The chromatic oscillation in the bass voice in m. 3 between E♭3–E♮3 followed by the leap of a diminished 8ve to E♭4, creates a wonderful harmonic ambiguity and further disguises the underlying predominant harmony. Note that each melodic line is melodically and rhythmically independent, with the bass voice providing clear harmonic support for the upper parts. The use of contrary motion between voices (this piece features a canon at the fifth in contrary motion) and stepwise linear spans that create expressive dissonant intervals (mm. 2, 9, and 15), testifies that Bach is probably more interested in cultivating a sense of linear independence and letting the interaction between individual lines dictate the harmonic outcomes than he is in being influenced and confined by the symmetrical unfolding of harmonic progressions.

As mentioned earlier, the study of reharmonization is a vast subject and the forthcoming study does not pretend to be even marginally exhaustive. The primary purpose is to bring an awareness to the huge potential that vertical and linear approaches to reharmonization can offer.

BASIC REHARMONIZATION TECHNIQUES

In this section, several approaches to reharmonization will be discussed and illustrated by using sections from Joseph Kosma's classic tune "Autumn Leaves."[3]

1. Addition of extensions

2. Expansion of structural chords

3. Tonicizations

4. Tritone substitutions

5. Diminished 7th chords

6. Upper-structure triads

7. Neighbor formations

8. Pedal points

9. Functional exchange

10. Melodic recontextualization

11. Interpolation of auxiliary progressions

Addition of Extensions

Chapters 4 and 5 showed how to expand the structure of chords with various extensions and pitch alterations. As a result, 14 four-part chords and 38 five-part chords were introduced. Since the **addition of chordal extensions** will be demonstrated in the context of "Autumn Leaves," the pool of available chords for reharmonization will be considerably smaller and entirely dependent on the structure of the melody. The melody of "Autumn Leaves" (and of any other tune) suggests which chordal extensions will work and which ones will not. Figure 23.3 illustrates mm. 1–8 of "Autumn Leaves" copied from a poorly produced fake book.

FIGURE 23.3 "Autumn Leaves"—mm. 1–8

When trying to realize these chords as faithfully as possible, notice that the realization hardly sounds convincing. If you add appropriate extensions to these chords, however, the progression sounds more idiomatic and in keeping with jazz harmonic practice. To add appropriate extensions, the relationship between the melody and the underlying harmony has to be examined. The notes E♭5 in m. 1, D5 in m. 3, C5 in m. 5, and B♭5 in m. 7, function as minor/major 3rds of the corresponding chords. Notice that each note (with the exception of B♭4 in m. 7) is suspended over the bar line and supported with a different chord. Did you recognize the familiar voice-leading scenario in which the 3rd of one chord becomes a 7th of the next? Each chord tone on the downbeat of mm. 1, 3, 5, and 7 is prepared by a quarter-note melodic ascent. These melodic ascents occur in the harmonic space of particular chords and, as such, suggest the use of specific extensions that can effectively expand the structure of the under-lying chords. Figure 23.4 shows the lead sheet for "Autumn Leaves" analyzed with Roman numerals. The boxed numbers indicate the relationship between melodic notes and supporting harmonies.

FIGURE 23.4 "Autumn Leaves"—Melodic Analysis

Based on this analytical reading, the pool of available extensions becomes more restrictive. For instance, if we were to add a ♭9th to D7 on beat 3 of m. 6, this choice would create a jarring dissonance with the melodic note, E4. Furthermore, the predominant function of Cm7 in m. 1 prevents us from adding a major 7th or a minor 6th to that chord. Also, if we try adding a major 7th to the minor tonic chord in mm. 15 and 31, the presence of G4 in the melody precludes us from using that chromatic alteration, unlike in m. 7 where the melodic B♭4 would have nicely supported that choice. Figure 23.5 demonstrates the addition of available extensions to mm. 1–8 of "Autumn Leaves." The melody with the original chord changes is written on the top stave, while the new harmonic progression is realized using **Model VI** of keyboard playing.

FIGURE 23.5 Addition of Extensions: Variant 1, mm. 1–8

This harmonic expansion is fairly basic and mainly uses a single extension to expand the structure of chords. The only exceptions are F13 in m. 2 and G7(♯9) in m. 8, where the former uses two diatonic extensions: major 9th and major 13th. The latter is more chromatic and employs ♯9th and ♭13th, both of which project the underlying tonality and complement the melody.

What is really fascinating about the addition of available extensions is that one can experiment with different combinations of extensions and voicings to generate different harmonic outcomes. Figure 23.6 illustrates a more challenging selection of extensions for mm. 1–8 of "Autumn Leaves" using the jazz chorale five-part texture.

FIGURE 23.6 Addition of Extensions: Variant 2, mm. 1–8

The rootless Cm11 chord in m. 1 contains two diatonic extensions: major 9th and perfect 11th with an intervallic cluster in the middle of the voicing balanced by perfect 5ths on either side. The accumulation of harmonic tension is highlighted by the diatonic extensions. When examining the harmonic content of mm. 3–5, notice some interesting harmonic choices: | B♭M7(♯5)–B♭M13 | E♭M9(♯11)–E♭M9 | Am7(♭5,♭9) |. This reharmonization is possible because the melodic content allows for the use of these specific chromatic formations. The D5 in m. 3, for instance, functions as a major 3rd of B♭M7 and, as such, effectively supports the inner melodic motion from F♯4 to G4.[4] Since m. 3 initiates the inner line, the content of m. 4 is the consequence of the previous measure as the line continues to ascend to A4 and B♭4. The rather unexpected Am7(♭5,♭9) harmony in m. 5 is the consequence of suspending the B♭4 in m. 4 over the m7(♭5) chord. To put it succinctly, these harmonies are motivated entirely by the melodic content and independent inner lines that cut across the bar lines to supply extensions of the underlying harmonies.

Before leaving this technique, the voice-leading structure of Figure 23.6 must be addressed. Take, for example, the preparation and treatment of extensions in mm. 2–3. The diatonic G4 (major 9th) in m. 2 prepares the F♯4 (♭9th) on beat 4 of the same measure. The F♯4 is suspended over the bar line and becomes a ♯5th of B♭M7(♯5), which in turn initiates the inner line that continues with the suspended preparation of a ♭9th over Am7(♭5,♭9) and a downward resolution to F♯4 in m. 6. The distribution of extensions is hierarchical; more chromatic extensions require more elaborate preparations. For instance, the ♯5th—undoubtedly the most dissonant extension of this reharmonization—requires a two-step preparation: from the diatonic 9th to the chromatic ♭9th and from the chromatic ♭9th to the more chromatic ♯5th.

Harmonic Expansion of Structural Chords

One way in which it is possible to generate harmonic diminutions and increase the sense of harmonic motion is by speeding up the rate of harmonic rhythm. Ballads or tunes with slower harmonic rhythms are better suited for the use of **harmonic expansion of structural chords** rather than tunes with quick moving changes. Broadly speaking, any structural chord with different harmonic diminutions can be expanded. However, your choices must establish a logical relationship with structural chords, anticipate forthcoming harmonies, and occasionally share the same harmonic function. Figure 23.7 illustrates the application of this technique using mm. 1–4 of "Autumn Leaves" realized with the jazz chorale four-part texture.

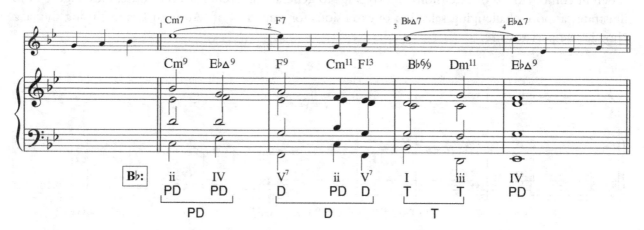

FIGURE 23.7 Expansion of Structural Chords

Even though chords in mm. 1 and 3 share the same harmonic function, they have different qualities. The Cm9 and E♭M9 belong to the predominant category of chords and the B♭M9 and Dm11 belong to the tonic category. In m. 2, the use of a ii–V⁷ progression within the dominant 7th space is one of the most common harmonic expansions. It can be freely implemented with any dominant 7th chord provided that the melody allows for such an expansion. These harmonic diminutions produce forward momentum marked by a faster harmonic rhythm, a stronger cadential drive, and a more convincing voice leading.

Tonicization

Tonicization is a technique that prepares the arrival of minor/major key areas or individual chords (dominant 7th, diminished, and half-diminished chords cannot be tonicized) with appropriate dominant 7ths, ii–V⁷s, ii⁰–V⁷s, or dominant tritone substitutions. As a result of tonicization, harmonic rhythm of the progression speeds up. "Autumn Leaves" features an unusual 32-bar formal design with two eight-bar A sections (mm. 1–16) resembling **Phrase Model 3** and an extended 16-bar B section (mm. 17–32) approximating **Phrase Model 2**. The chord structure in mm. 1–8 forms an uninterrupted sequential

FIGURE 23.8 Tonicization

span that leads to the minor tonic in m. 7. Measure 8, then, is an ideal place to demonstrate the use of tonicization. Figure 23.8 illustrates mm. 7–9 of "Autumn Leaves" realized with **Model IV**.

Even though the tonicization of minor chords requires the iiø–V⁷ progression, the content of the melody in m. 8 prevents the use of this pattern. The melodic span, B♭4–G4–A4–B♭4, suggests a ii–V⁷ progression, which is typically reserved for the tonicization of major chords. In particular, the pitch A4 does not allow the implementation of Dm7(♭5). The pitch B♭4 on beat 4 suggests the use of an altered dominant and, as the potential source of harmonic conflict, suggests the voicing of the supporting harmony. This places the major 3rd in the middle of its structure to avert the overexposed dissonant clash.

Tritone Substitutions

Compare the three different reharmonizations of various sections of "Autumn Leaves" in Figure 23.9 using **tritone substitutions** realized with the jazz chorale five-part texture.

FIGURE 23.9 Tritone Substitutions—Comparison

When listening to the sound of these substitutions, Figure 23.9a may be the least appealing. In this reharmonization, the relationship between the melody and the tritone substitution is not as convincing as it is in the original chord progression. The pitches F4, G4, and A4 in the context of F7 function as root, major 9th, and major 3rd respectively, and as such create a logical melodic succession. When the same pitch segment is examined in the context of the tritone substitution, these notes become ♯11th, ♭13th, and ♭7th of B7 respectively. There are a few problems with this pitch succession. First, it creates an awkward unfolding of chordal extensions. For instance, a ♭13th hardly ever resolves up to a ♭7th. Second, the succession from G4 to A4 demonstrates an incorrect preparation of the chordal 7th in the context of B7. Although the rules of jazz voice leading are not as stringent as they are in common-practice music—at least not on the surface—voice-leading successions like this one should be avoided.

The tritone substitution in Figure 23.9c accommodates the melody notes in a more convincing manner. The pitches Bb4 and D4 function as a b13th and the root of D7, and a major 9th and a #11th of Ab7. The melodic succession 9th–#11th represents a hierarchical unfolding of extensions from diatonic to chromatic and, as such, makes the use of this tritone substitution more effective than the one in Figure 23.9a. When examining the behavior of outer-voice counterpoint, notice that the outer voices move in parallel motion in Figure 23.9b and in contrary motion in Figure 23.9c. In both cases, the melody notes fit nicely in the context of the underlying tritone substitutions, yet the use of contrary motion in Figure 23.9c is probably more effective. The use of tritone substitutions is first and foremost dependent on the melody. If the melody notes function as chord tones and/or diatonic extensions of the intended tritone substitutions, these substitutions are likely to produce satisfactory reharmonizations.

Diminished 7th Chords

Figure 23.10 illustrates the use of two types of **diminished 7th chord**: *passing* and *neighbor*. This realization utilizes the **block style** of harmonization. The main characteristic of this style is the use of close-position voicings with the melody doubled at the octave.

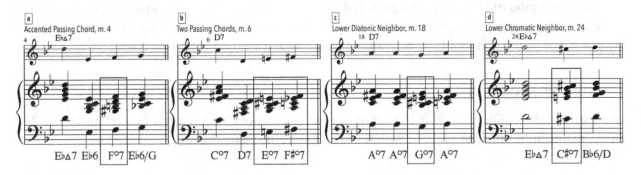

FIGURE 23.10 Diminished 7th Chords

The accented diminished passing chord in Figure 23.10a, Fdim7, connects two chord tones of the underlying harmony: the root and the 3rd. Even though the diminished passing chord typically occupies a metrically weak position, in Figure 23.10a it occurs on beat 3 and adds extra tension to the progression. Figure 23.10b demonstrates the use of two consecutive passing chords, Edim7 and F#dim7. Figure 23.10c shows the use of a lower diatonic diminished neighbor, which is slightly different from the lower chromatic diminished neighbor that occurs in Figure 23.10d. The roots of all diminished 7th chords in Figure 23.10 function as melody notes.

Upper-Structure Triads

The use of **upper-structure triads** is one of the most powerful techniques that can greatly enhance the character of your reharmonizations. Figure 23.11 illustrates the use of upper-structure triads in mm. 22–23 of "Autumn Leaves" realized with six-part harmonic formations. The Roman numerals show the relationship between the upper-structure triad and the underlying chord.

The issues of harmonic hierarchy and voice leading are two of the main themes recurring in our discussion. In Figure 23.11, each consecutive triad is slightly more dissonant than its predecessor. Thus the Bb triad on beat 2 of m. 22 introduces two diatonic extensions, 9th and 11th, and at the same time prepares the chromatic extensions of the following Db by step (albeit, with octave displacements). The choice of

FIGURE 23.11 Upper-Structure Triads

parallel D♭$^6_4$ and B$^6_4$ triads on beats 3 and 4 is very effective, as they gradually accrue harmonic tension over F7 before *resolving* to the chromatic B♭M7(♯5) in m. 23. The choice of upper-structure triads in Figure 23.11 is entirely motivated by the design of the melody.

Neighbor Formations

Broadly speaking, **neighbor formations** come in two types: *upper* and *lower*. The most important considerations controlling the use of neighbor formations is that they adhere to the rules of voice leading and the behavior of outer-voice counterpoint. Figure 23.12 shows the use of different neighbor formations.

FIGURE 23.12 Neighbor Formations

In both cases, the outer voice-counterpoint features contrary motion and stepwise voice leading. The use of neighbor formations is most effective in situations where the melody moves by step in either direction while the lowest voice moves in the opposite direction to the melody.

Pedal Points

The use of dominant **pedal points** is restricted to certain types of harmonic progressions. These progressions typically feature closely related chords, such as ii–V^7–I, ii$^\varnothing$–V^7–i or I–vi–ii–V^7. Dominant pedal points, as the name suggests, utilize the root of V^7 as an anchor that supports moving harmonies in upper parts. In a certain sense, pedal points temporarily suspend the succession of chords and allow for the juxtaposition of different chromatic formations. Figure 23.13 demonstrates the use of two pedal points in mm. 17–24 of "Autumn Leaves."

FIGURE 23.13 Pedal Points

Measures 17–20 feature a dominant pedal point over D while mm. 21–24 suspend the harmonic progression over the F pedal. In both cases, the pedal points are derived from the root of the dominant 7th of the underlying progressions. In addition to being a highly effective reharmonization technique, pedal points are powerful performance-practice devices. Their presence heightens the level of rhythmic activity, invites more interaction between players, renders the underlying progressions as modal (as shown in Figure 23.13) rather than harmonic centers, and allows more chromaticism into the structure of melodic lines. They even justify playing *outside* of the changes.

Functional Exchange

The technique of **functional exchange** is based on a modification of the expected behavior of chords. These modifications typically involve changing a chord's quality or function. A successful implementation of this technique depends on establishing a convincing relationship between the melody and the intended harmonic substitution. In general, melodic pitches that in a new harmonic environment function as chromatic extensions are not ideal choices for the implementation of this technique. Figure 23.14 illustrates a harmonic realization of mm. 1–4 with two functional exchanges.

FIGURE 23.14 Functional Exchange

In m. 1, C7(♯9) substitutes for Cm7. This choice is not particularly effective because the substitute harmony renders the melodic E♭5 as a ♯9th of C7(♯9). This substitution works if it occurs in the 2nd or 3rd chorus and is foreshadowed well in advance. In m. 3, the B♭M7 chord changes its functional status from that of a local tonic to a dominant 7th anticipating the arrival of E♭M7 in m. 4. The technique of functional exchange is melody-sensitive and context-specific. Most common functional exchanges involve changing predominant- to dominant-type chords and tonic- to dominant-type chords. (Others, such as dominant- to tonic-type chords are also plausible, although they might occur in more advanced harmonic settings.)

Melodic Recontextualization

The technique of **melodic recontextualization** provides the most striking and easily recognizable harmonic departure from the original chord changes. A successful application of this technique depends on the recontextualization of the melody notes as diatonic chord tones or diatonic extensions of the intended substitute progression. In addition, the newly formed substitute progression establishes a logical relationship with the underlying harmonic motion. Figure 23.15 demonstrates the use of this technique in mm. 1–4 of "Autumn Leaves" using **Model VI** of keyboard playing.

FIGURE 23.15 Melodic Recontextualization

The Eb5 in m. 1 is recontextualized as a major 9th of Dbm9 and a major 13th of Gb13. This chromatic neighbor progression substitutes the original Cm7 chord and initiates a sequential progression that continues through the phrase. In m. 3, the Bm7–E7 progression substitutes the local tonic BbM7. This substitution is possible because of the diatonic status of D5 in the original and substitute progressions: in the context of BbM7, the D5 functions as a major 3rd; whereas in the context of the substitute progression it functions as a minor 3rd of Bm7 and a minor 7th of E7. The voice leading of the progression uses mostly stepwise motion that prepares and resolves all chromatic extensions.

Interpolation of Auxiliary Progressions

The **interpolation of auxiliary progressions** involves the combination of previously discussed techniques. By now, the idea of melody-specific and context-sensitive harmonic substitutions should be firmly engraved on our musical consciousness. Figure 23.16 interpolates different auxiliary progressions in mm. 1–2 and 7–8 of "Autumn Leaves" using the jazz chorale five-part texture.

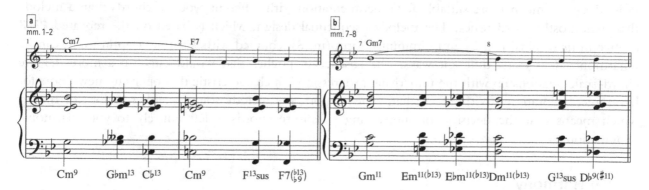

FIGURE 23.16 Interpolation of Auxiliary Progressions

In Figure 23.16a, the melodic E♭5 functions as a minor 3rd of Cm9, a major 13th of G♭m13, and a major 3rd of C♭9. A more advanced interpolation of auxiliary progression occurs in Figure 23.16b. Measures 7–8 combine four reharmonization techniques: the tritone substitution, neighbor formations, tonicization, and melodic recontextualization. The tritone substitution occurs on beat 4 of m. 8 where D♭9(♯11) substitutes a tonicizing G7 formation. The tonicization that foreshadows the arrival of Cm7 in m. 9 should have involved a ii°–V⁷, yet the melody note A4 implies a ii–V⁷ progression. In this case, the tonicizing ii–V⁷ progression is reduced to G13sus and followed by D♭9(♯11) tritone substitution. The arrival of the quartal structure on beat 1 of m. 8 is anticipated by two neighbor formations, which share the same intervallic properties. This technique is also known as **parallel planing**. Not only does the melodic recontextualization of B♭4 in m. 8 as a major 13th of D♭7 allow for the use of tritone substitution, but it also fulfills the tonal conditions and voice-leading requirements that characterize a successful reharmonization. Since the interpolation of auxiliary progression in m. 8 coincides with the cadential preparation of the new formal section, speeding up the rate of harmonic rhythm makes the arrival of the new section in m. 9 more satisfying.

INTERMEDIATE REHARMONIZATION TECHNIQUES

Broadly speaking, **intermediate techniques** of reharmonization can be classified according to the following categories: (1) **modal harmony**, (3) **cyclic harmony**, and (3) **signature chords**. The use of these techniques largely depends on the type of melody you are trying to reharmonize and the overall mood you attempt to convey with your reharmonization. Measures 1–4 of Billy Strayhorn's "Chelsea Bridge," shown in Figure 23.17, could not have been more different from the melody of "Autumn Leaves."

FIGURE 23.17 "Chelsea Bridge"—mm. 1–4

Even in this short excerpt, one can sense a more somber mood created by the pregnant melodic dissonances (major 7ths) metrically outweighing their neighboring chordal roots. Such an accumulation of melodic tension within a relatively short melodic span can influence the kinds of chords and harmonic techniques one can implement. For starters, a melody that highlights dissonances and upper extensions in its design is much more suitable for experimentation with different types of chords than a melody that uses mostly chord tones. The melody's sequential design, which is based on the repeated ♯7–8 motive in its original (m. 2) and diminutive form (m. 3), coupled with a tritone leap in m. 4, can be reharmonized in many different ways. The absence of pitches that would establish a more definite chord–scale relationship with the underlying progression is a characteristic that opens up new doors for harmonic explorations. Without the harmonic support, the melody sounds neither major nor minor, which means that the decision of supplanting substitute chords is left entirely to your harmonic imagination.

Modal Harmony

Since the original changes of "Chelsea Bridge" (mm. 1–4) can be easily substituted using basic techniques of reharmonization, such as: harmonic expansion, melodic recontextualization, functional exchange, and tritone substitutions, so can the underlying scales/modes that support these substitutions and establish chord–scale relationships with them. The use of modal harmonies shifts the focus from functional relationships between chords to more neutral and tonally ambiguous. Rather than using chords that generate grammatically correct units, we can instead implement **modal pitch centers** (MPCs, henceforth), which control fragments of the melody and furnish the harmonic support for it. Since the melody of "Chelsea Bridge" is tonally ambiguous, there are a number of MPCs that can be successfully implemented. The melody in mm. 1–2 establishes a clear chord–scale relationship with the original changes: B♭m(♯7) and A♭m(♯7), respectively. The roots of these chords can function as potential MPCs generating different chord–scale relationships with the melody. Besides occurring in Melodic Minor, the ♯$\hat{7}$–$\hat{8}$ melodic gesture also occurs in Lydian, Lydian Augmented, 2/1 octatonic, Mode IV and VI of limited transposition, and different pentatonic and hexatonic scales. These scales can provide alternate harmonies for the melody. Furthermore, the ♯$\hat{7}$–$\hat{8}$ melodic gesture can be interpreted as an alternate pitch succession over a different MPC which, as a consequence, can further expand the number of harmonic renditions. In a sense, the reinterpretation of melodic gestures is analogous to the technique of melodic recontextualization of individual pitches from Figure 23.15. In this case, however, more than a single pitch is affected. For instance, the ♯$\hat{7}$–$\hat{8}$ pattern can be rendered as: (1) the $\hat{1}$–♭$\hat{2}$ in Phrygian and Locrian, (2) the ♯$\hat{4}$–$\hat{5}$ in Lydian, Mixolydian ♯11, Altered, etc., (3) the $\hat{5}$–♭$\hat{6}$ in Aeolian and Phrygian, (4) the ♯$\hat{5}$–$\hat{6}$ in Lydian Augmented, Mode IV of Limited Transposition, etc., and (6) the $\hat{6}$–♭$\hat{7}$ in Mixolydian, Mixolydian ♯11, etc. These modal reinterpretations utilize melodic pitches whose succession forms a logical pitch succession. For instance, the ♭$\hat{3}$–$\hat{3}$ and ♭$\hat{7}$–♯$\hat{7}$ would not have been viable options (even in this freer, post-tonal harmonic environment) because their inclusion would have violated the rules of proscribing the use of diatonic and chromatic versions of the same pitch within a single chord. The $\hat{3}$–$\hat{4}$, with its Ionian and unambiguous tonal associations, should be treated with caution. Figure 23.18 illustrates some of the more interesting modal reinterpretations of mm. 1–4 of "Chelsea Bridge."

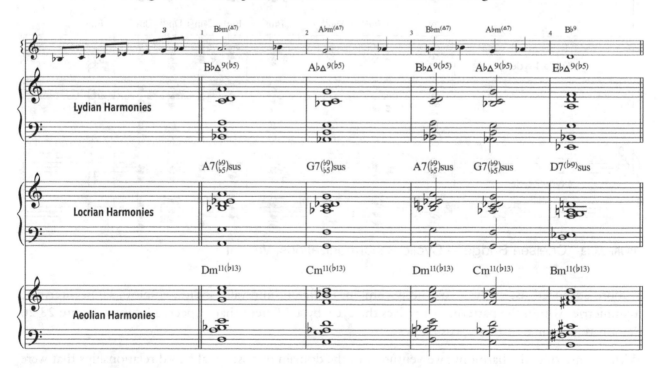

FIGURE 23.18 "Chelsea Bridge"—Modal Reharmonizations

Cyclic Harmony

The main characteristic of cyclic harmony is the use of symmetrical intervallic patterns that controls the unfolding of individual chords within the harmonic progression. For instance, the *Giant Steps* progression is an example of cyclic harmony wherein the structural harmonies establish a major-third cycle: BM7–GM7–E♭M7. That cyclic progression occurs at the macro-level between non-adjacent chords. Cyclic harmony at the micro-level employs adjacent chords, preferably from the same functional family, which establish a recurring intervallic pattern. Cyclic harmony can utilize the following symmetrical root movements: (1) major 2nds (up/down)—whole-tone cycle (2-cycle), (2) minor 3rds (up/down)—minor-third cycle (3-cycle), (3) major 3rds (up/down)—major-third cycle (4-cycle), (4) perfect 4th (up/down)—fourth cycle (5-cycle), and (5) perfect 5th (up/down)—fifth cycle (7-cycle).[5] When experimenting with cyclic harmony, we have to *reinterpret* the melody notes as upper diatonic extensions of the underlying harmonies. The use of cyclic harmony works best for melodies that are already sequential in nature, such as "Chelsea Bridge." The sequential aspect of "Chelsea Bridge" is evident in the opening two measures, which form a descending 2-cycle. Given that the melodic notes can be reinterpreted as 9ths, 11ths, and 13ths, as well as regular chord members, we can find creative ways of experimenting with cyclic harmony. Figure 23.19 illustrates some of the more interesting examples of cyclic harmony.

FIGURE 23.19 "Chelsea Bridge"—Cyclic Reharmonizations, Variant 1

A more advanced use of cyclic harmony combines different intervallic cycles, employs slight intervallic asymmetries within the pattern, or resolves the cycle by a different than expected interval. Figure 23.20 demonstrates some of these possibilities.

With the use of cyclic harmony, we venture into the domain of post-tonal chord relationships that were particularly influential in the late 1950s and 60s, and still continue to inspire many contemporary jazz composers.

FIGURE 23.20 "Chelsea Bridge"—Cyclic Reharmonizations, Variant 2

Signature Chords

By studying the music of different composers (both classical and jazz), one can begin to identify specific trademarks—be they melodic, harmonic, or compositional—that came to define their creative output. In fact, certain harmonic structures became so omnipresent in their works that they even got their own iconic label: *Chopin, Tristan, Salome, Elektra, Mystic, Farben, Marie, Petrushka, Augurs, Psalm, Arc-en-ciel d'innocence, Viennese, Bridge, Dream, So What, Vonetta, Iris, Madness, Purple Haze,* or *Rivello,* etc. Figure 23.21 compiles some of the most famous signature chords by classical, jazz, and pop composers.

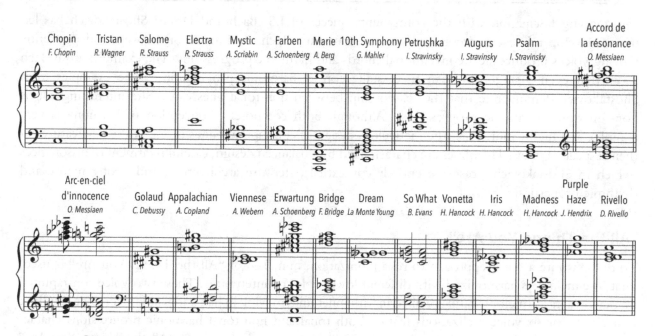

FIGURE 23.21 Signature Chords

Figure 23.22 illustrates ways to implement some of these iconic trademarks in the context of "Chelsea Bridge."

FIGURE 23.22 "Chelsea Bridge"—Signature Chords Harmonizations

ADVANCED REHARMONIZATION TECHNIQUES

My ongoing fascination with the contrapuntal pieces of J.S. Bach and Dmitri Shostakovich has led me to develop a linear conception of jazz harmony in which the interaction between independently moving voices produces less conventional chords and harmonic progressions. The examples from Bach show that even a single line can successfully convey harmonic progressions.[6] The examples from Shostakovich demonstrate that the relationship between non-tonal lines can create interesting, albeit non-functional harmonic progressions.[7] Although both composers' conception of harmony is very complex and highly individual, the meticulous design of contrapuntal lines is one of the key features of their respective styles. Their lines are characterized by a balanced design, careful treatment of dissonances (which in Shostakovich's case are entirely contextual), stepwise architecture, and strong metric and rhythmic properties.

"All the Things You Are"

To demonstrate a linear approach to reharmonization, mm. 1–8 of "All the Things You Are" is used. First, the melody is harmonized with different lower-voice counterpoints. These two-voice contrapuntal frameworks in 1:1 melodic ratio are filled in with inner lines moving in half and whole steps. The resulting four-, five-, or six-voice realizations feature both tonal and non-tonal harmonic progressions characterized by linearly derived chords. Figure 23.23 illustrates the A section of "All the Things You Are" with eight outer-voice counterpoints. Notice that the melody is reduced to its essential structure with whole notes only.

When comparing the structure of the lower counterpoint in Figure 23.23a to other counterpoints, notice that they exhibit more linear characteristics. For instance, the counterpoint in Figure 23.23b moves

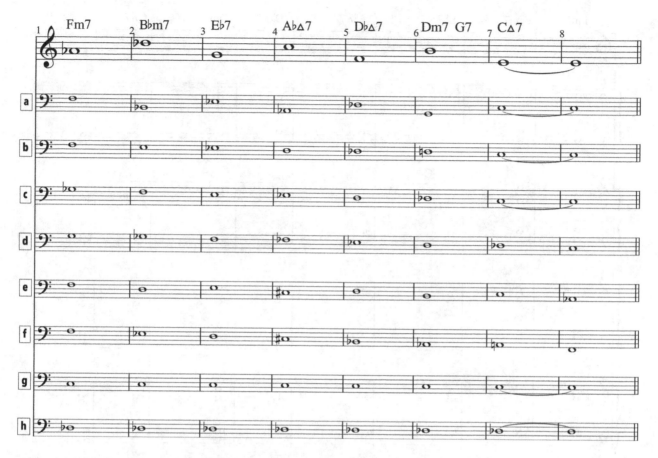

FIGURE 23.23 Linear Approach to Reharmonization: Outer-Voice Frameworks

entirely by half steps starting on the root of the underlying Fm7. The counterpoint in Figure 23.23c moves also by half steps, yet the opening pitch suggests a chord–scale relationship different from the original. A similar scenario occurs in Figure 23.23d, where the opening note of the counterpoint begins on G3 forming the interval of a minor 9th with the melody. Figures 23.23e–f illustrate sequential counterpoints that nicely complement the melody. The former uses a minor 3rd sequence while the latter alternates between major and minor 2nds. Finally, Figures 23.23g–h demonstrate the use of an oblique motion utilizing two pedal points. The choice of tonic pedal point in Figure 23.23g suggests a more conventional reharmonization. The use of Db3 as a pedal point in Figure 23.23h, however, implies a reharmonization outside of the conventional norms.

In *fleshing out* these outer-voice frameworks, the behavior of inner lines is restricted to stepwise motion in either direction or to common tones. For now, leaps are forbidden (except for those occurring in the melody). By adhering to these particular constraints, the voices are prevented from converging onto familiar harmonies. Even though dissonant formations are likely to occur, the larger point is to show how lines produce harmonies and how the flow of harmonic tensions is regulated and resolved.

Figure 23.24 provides eight reharmonizations of the outer-voice counterpoints from Figure 23.23.

These reharmonizations draw on some of the techniques discussed earlier in the chapter. For instance, the realization in Figure 23.24c uses the technique of melodic recontextualization as the opening chord renders the melodic note, Ab4, as a major 9th of Gbm11. In choosing the opening sonorities, familiar structures were avoided in order to experiment with linearly driven harmonic progressions. In a certain sense, the opening sonority sets the character for the entire reharmonization and, at the same time, offers

FIGURE 23.24 Linear Approach to Reharmonization: Realizations

a challenge to find satisfactory harmonic solutions. The difference between Figures 23.24a and 23.24e is very striking. Whereas the former is more conventional because of the tonal framework, the latter is highly dissonant with largely unanalyzable harmonic formations.

"Stella by Starlight"

Written by Victor Young for the movie *The Uninvited*, "Stella by Starlight" has become a favorite standard tune in jazz. Its popularity among jazz musicians is indisputable; almost all of the great jazz artists of the 1950s and beyond recorded it at some point of their career.[8] The lead sheet of the song is provided in Figure 23.25.

The selection includes three sets of changes: *movie soundtrack*, *original*, and *jazz*. By including these changes, we can compare the differences between them and appreciate the composer's original harmonic intentions. Let me first clarify the labeling of the individual progression. The *movie soundtrack* changes refer to the progression that is heard in the movie. The song is played in the keys of D major and B major with lavish orchestration and distinct chord progressions comparatively different from both the *original* and the *jazz* versions. The *original* chord changes—supposedly provided by the composer— were published in a fake book in the 1950s (of an uncertain origin) in the key of G major. The *jazz* changes are readily available in countless fake books and are the ones commonly used by jazz musicians.

What makes "Stella by Starlight" stand out among other standard tunes is its freely unfolding melody, an entity in and of itself that transcends the boundaries of the phrase structure. The melody is characterized by a relatively static rhythmic design and the inclusion of non-harmonic tones as essential melodic components. Suspended notes over the bar lines create tension with the underlying harmonies. Thus the pitch A4 at the beginning constitutes the major 7th of the *original* B♭dim or the 11th of Em7(♭5) of the *jazz* version. In m. 5, the same harmonic change in the *original* and *jazz* versions, F minor, supports the pitch G4, the major 9th. These dissonances usually underscore important words of the lyrics, lending them a particular poignancy. The climax of the tune, occurring in mm. 17–19, corresponds to the lyrics, *That great symphonic theme*; at this point, the melodic E♭5 becomes the ♭13th of G7 and F5 the 11th of Cm11. Measures 20–23 continue to emphasize non-harmonic tones within the melody. Upon reaching $\hat{5}$ in m. 19, the melody features a stepwise descent to $\hat{7}$ in m. 23. This diatonic span, however, receives an unorthodox harmonic treatment: in m. 21, $\hat{3}$ is the major 7th of E♭m7 in the *original* version, or the ♯11th of A♭7 in the *jazz* version; and in m. 23, $\hat{2}$ is supported as the 9th of B♭M7 in both versions.

At first glance, the comparison of the *original* and *jazz* changes seems to reveal significant differences between the two. Upon closer examination, however, the *jazz* changes are seen as a middleground elaboration of the *original* progression. Nowhere is the relationship between the background and middleground more evident than in mm. 1–8. The opening progression of the *original* version, B♭dim–F7, stands out for its stylistic uniqueness and an ominous sound perfectly suitable for a ghost story. Its relationship to the *jazz* changes, Em7(♭5)–A7–Cm7–F7, is classified through common-tone relationships between Em7(♭5)–A7 and B♭dim, as the members of the B♭dim triad are embedded within the structure of A7(♭9). Since it is common in the jazz idiom to precede the dominant 7th with its local predominant ii (provided that melodic notes agree with the harmony), the use of an Em7(♭5)–A7 progression is a well-considered choice for the original B♭dim. Similarly, the space occupied by F7 in the original version is expanded by an embedded ii–V[7] progression. Hierarchically, B♭dim is inferior to F7, since the former, due to its unstable quality, is heard as a contrapuntal elaboration of the more stable F7.

FIGURE 23.25 "Stella by Starlight"—Lead Sheet

FIGURE 23.26 "Stella by Starlight"—A Reharmonization

The evolution of the jazz harmonic syntax from the popular song vocabulary cannot be more evident than in the treatment of IV–V or IV–I harmonic progressions. These are typical of common-practice tonality and the language of popular tunes draws extensively on this practice. There are specific instances pointing to this practice in "Stella by Starlight." For instance, mm. 15–16 tonicize G7 in m. 17. The *original* version employs a local iv–V^7 of G. In the *jazz* version, however, the focus is placed on the cycle of 5ths progression with ii$^\emptyset$ substituting for iv. A similar scenario occurs in mm. 27–30 where local iv–V^7 progressions in the *original* are changed to ii$^\emptyset$–V^7 in the *jazz* version. Measures 21–24 in the original are governed by a iv–I harmonic motion. The relatively weak position of the plagal motion (further emphasized by a minor predominant) is replaced by a more idiomatic ♭VII^7 in m. 21. The use of the back-door ♭VII^7 is consistent with idiomatic jazz practices and anticipates the arrival of the tonic more forcefully. Again, the use of the jazz substitution stems from the original change; E♭m may be interpreted as a "ii" necessarily bringing its "V^7," A♭7.

The *movie soundtrack* and *original* changes are very much related to one another. The former, however, makes great use of chordal inversions and linear bass progressions. For instance, the preparation of the climax in m. 17 begins in m. 9 with the chordal 5th over the B♭ triad. The bass voice subsequently descends to G in m. 17. During this span, it introduces some compelling harmonies, which are quite unexpected, yet masterfully woven into the framework of the progression. In m. 12, D♭7(♭5) nicely anticipates the F/C. The free standing B♭dim in m. 14 offers convincing melodic support and foreshadows the arrival of Am7(♭5).

As a ghost movie theme, the dreamy and mysterious character of "Stella" is expressed in many different ways. The reharmonization of the song attempts to capture its mood through the harmonic vocabulary derived from the hexatonic system discussed in Chapter 18. Remember, the hexatonic system includes major, minor, dominant, suspended, and intermediary categories, each of which features a pitch aggregate that furnishes material for voicings of different sizes and intervallic configurations. In general, the voice leading of the reharmonization shown in Figure 23.26 is mostly stepwise and balances a mixture of contrary, parallel, and oblique motions occurring between the voices.

NOTES

1   A comparison of different harmonic settings of the same chorale melody enables one to appreciate J.S. Bach's conception of harmony. An examination of larger compositions, such as Bach's *Goldberg Variations*, BWV 988; Beethoven's *Diabelli Variations*, Op. 120; Chopin's *Là ci darem la mano*, Op. 2; Brahms's *Variations and Fugue on a Theme by Handel*, Op. 24; or Mompou's *Variations on a Theme by Chopin* reveal how these composers exhausted the harmonic and contrapuntal potential of the melody with which they were working.

2   *178 Chorale Harmonizations of Joh. Seb. Bach: A Comparative Edition for Study*, Volume I by Donald Martino, is an excellent publication that compiles multiple harmonic settings of chorale melodies that allow for easy comparison. This inexpensive publication is strongly recommended.

3   For representative recordings, consult Appendix F on the CW.

4   In common-practice theory this particular melodic motion is known as the retardation or the suspension resolving upwards.

5   The numbers: 2-, 3-, 4-, 5- and 7-cycle refer to the number of semitones within each cycle.

6   J.S. Bach *Das wohltemperierte Klavier I*, BWV 846–869; *Das wohltemperierte Klavier II*, BWV 870–893; 6 *Violin Sonatas and Partitas*, BWV 1001–1006; *Cello Suites*, BWV 1007–1012.

7   D. Shostakovich *Preludes and Fugues*, Op. 87.

8   For representative recordings, consult Appendix F on the CW.

CHAPTER 24

Post-Tonal Jazz—Atonality

CHAPTER SUMMARY

Chapter 24 lays the foundation for cross-disciplinary interactions between post-tonal jazz and atonal music. Basic concepts of atonal music theory are introduced.

CONCEPTS AND TERMS

- Aggregate
- Atonal music
- Cardinality
- Clock face
- Common tones under inversion
- Common tones under transposition
- Enharmonic equivalence
- Index number
- Integer notation
- Interval classes
- Interval-class vector
- Intervals:
  - Ordered
  - Unordered
- Inversion I_n
- Mod 12
- Normal form
- Pitch
- Pitch classes
- Pitch-class (pc) interval
- Pitch-class (pc) set
- Pitch-class space
- Prime form
- Set classes
- Subsets
- Sums
- Supersets
- Transposition T_n
- Trichords

INTRODUCTION

Twentieth-century music offers an amazing variety of styles, harmonic languages, and compositional techniques. As such, it can be used by jazz musicians to broaden their musical horizons, expand their harmonic and melodic vocabularies, experiment with different compositional methods, and engage in exciting stylistic crossovers. Post-tonal theory encompasses numerous theoretical systems, such as atonality or dodecaphony that seek to explain the nature of different kinds of twentieth-century music. Presently, we will concentrate on one particular type of twentieth-century music, so-called **atonal music**, and its corresponding theory.[1] The atonal period is usually identified with the composers of the Second Viennese

School: Arnold Schoenberg, Anton Webern, and Alban Berg. Its golden age lasted for about 17 years, from circa 1905 until 1922. Atonal music is characterized by **unordered** pitch relationships. Any discussion of atonal music along with its theory necessitates the use of a specific jargon that is pertinent to that musical tradition. The familiar topics such as note names, intervals, chord formations, and others, need to be replaced and recontextualized in order to convey the uniqueness of that system. For instance, triads are referred to as **trichords**, notes are labeled with **integers** (not by their traditional letter, scale-degree, or solfège names), and intervals are measured with numbers indicating semitone count. These nomenclatural changes are necessary to reflect the uniqueness of atonal music, in which traditional tonal relationships are generally absent.

BASIC CONCEPTS

Integer Notation

Figure 24.1 shows the notes of the chromatic scale labeled as integers. The pitches A# and B use a "**t**" and an "**e**" to represent integers ten and eleven, respectively.

FIGURE 24.1 Integer Notation

In atonal music, the difference in note spelling is not as crucial as it is in common-practice music. The concept of **enharmonic equivalence** enables us to use the same integer for different spellings of the same pitch. For instance, C# and Db are enharmonically equivalent and are both referred to as pitch class 1 or pc1; A# and Bb are enharmonically equivalent and referred to as pc**t**.

Pitch and Pitch Classes

In our study of post-tonal jazz, the designation **class** is frequently encountered. It signifies an abstract representation that combines shared characteristics of a pitch, an interval, or a chord. A pc3 combines all Ebs, D#s, Fbbs, regardless of their location on the staff, timbre, or other musical characteristics. The differentiation between **pitch** and **pitch class** refers to the distinction between a *literal* sounding pitch and an *abstract* pitch class that combines all like-sounding pitches. Think of all the Gs on the piano, for instance: there are seven distinct pitches that are members of the class pc7. Figure 24.2 illustrates notes between C3 to C6, notated as pitches and pitch classes.

FIGURE 24.2 Pitch and Pitch Classes

Interval and Interval Classes

Intervals in atonal music are labeled and measured differently than they are in tonal music. Pitch intervals measure the distance between two pitches. There are two types of pc intervals: ordered and unordered. An **ordered pc interval** occupies the distance between two pitch classes in ascending order or clockwise direction. For instance, an ordered interval between pc1 and pce is 10, and between pce and pc1 is 2. A formula pcy–pcx, where y stands for the second interval out of the two, helps to make that simple subtraction. There are 12 ordered pc intervals.

An **unordered pc interval** is related to interval classes, which, as the designation *class* implies, represents a further abstraction of intervals. Since each pc interval can be inverted to generate its complement, there are only **six interval classes**, each combining an interval and its inversion. An unordered pc interval constitutes the smallest interval out of the two. The unordered pc interval between pc1 and pce is 2 because interval class 2, written as ic2, combines two intervals—10 and 2—with the smallest one being chosen. Figure 24.3 illustrates traditional interval names, 12 ordered pc intervals, and six unordered interval classes. We will use unordered pc intervals, or interval classes when implementing concepts from the atonal music theory.

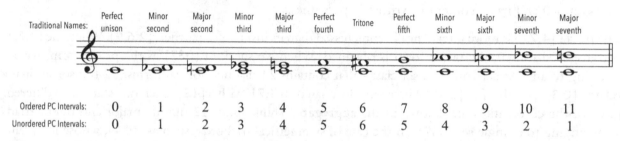

FIGURE 24.3 Ordered and Unordered Intervals

TRICHORDS

In tonal music, root-position triads are considered as being organized in ascending order and in the most intervallically packed manner possible. To figure out the root position of the pitches: F♯, D, and A, for example, put the unordered collection in ascending order: D, F♯, A, or [2,6,9] using integers separated by a comma. For the purpose of representing atonal relationships changing the order in which pitches occur is necessary. In other words, a trichord in root position is analogous to the most packed arrangement of pitches of that trichord in ascending order, or any other trichord or **pitch-class set** (henceforth, **pc-set**) of any cardinality. **Cardinality** refers to the number of pitches, without pitch duplicates, occurring within the set. The trichord [2,6,9] is said to be in the **normal form**, which represents the unordered collection of pitches: F♯, A, and D. The normal form refers to the most intervallically packed arrangement of pitches in ascending order of a pc-set of any cardinality.

When examining the intervallic content of [2,6,9], notice the interval classes 4 and 3 between the adjacent pairs of pitches: pc6–pc2=ic4 and pc9–pc6=ic3. What does the intervallic content of a pc-set tell us? It tells us whether the pc-set is symmetrical or not and whether the trichord [2,6,9] has an inversional partner or not. The intervallic content of [2,6,9] can be written as ic[43]. Note that square brackets are also used to represent the intervallic content of a pc-set; Arabic numbers, however, are listed without a comma. The trichord [2,6,9] comprises two different interval classes: ic4 and ic3, which means that [2,6,9] is asymmetrical and has an inversional counterpart. How do we determine which trichord is inversionally related to [2,6,9]? The easiest and quickest way is to reverse the order of interval classes from ic[43] to ic[34]. When we represent ic[34] as a pc-set starting on pc4, for instance, the result yields the following set: E, G, and B or [4,7,e]. Notice that [4,7,e] is a minor triad and the original set [2,6,9] is a major triad. In atonal music theory, these two normal forms: [2,6,9] and [4,7,e] belong to the same **set class**. This conclusion is based on the fact that the intervallic content of two sets [2,6,9] and [4,7,e] is exactly the same. Remember that in atonal music, the order in which intervals and pitches occur within a set does not affect the interpretation of that set.

In atonal music theory the difference between major and minor qualities is of little significance, simply because major and minor triads, as well as other formations—dominant 7th and half-diminished 7th chords—are inversionally equivalent and belong to the same set class. When the adjacent intervals of [2,6,9], ic[43] and [4,7,e], ic[34] are compared, it is immediately evident that these two trichords are identical in terms of their unordered intervallic content. To figure out the next and final level of abstraction of a pc-set called the **prime form**, (1) put an unordered pitch collection in the normal form, and (2) calculate the intervallic content of that set. Based on this information, examine whether a pc-set has an inversional partner or not. If it does, compare their intervallic content to determine which one is the most packed. Finally, select the most packed set and transpose it to pc0. Prime form or set class always starts on pc0 and its pc content is written in parenthesis.

The pc-set [4,7,e] is more intervallically compressed than its inversional partner, [2,6,9]. When the [4,7,e] is transposed to pc0, the prime form is obtained. When we speak of (037) as the prime form, we are referring to an abstract entity—a set class—that contains 24 distinct normal forms: 12 transpositionally related [0,3,7]s with ic[34] and 12 inversionally related [0,4,7]s with ic[43]. Each one starts on a different pitch of the chromatic scale, known as the **aggregate**. Think about 12 unique major and minor triads as belonging to a single set (037). In the case of symmetrical trichords, such as (024), whose intervallic content yields ic[22], the set class (024) contains only 12 distinct [0,2,4]s built on each note of the aggregate. The (024) is symmetrical and the inversion in **pitch-class space** yields the same pc-set.

Methodology for Figuring Out Normal and Prime Forms

1. Translate any unordered collection of pitches to pitch classes.

2. Put pitch classes in ascending order in the most packed arrangement (i.e. root-position formation).

3. The resulting pc-set is in the normal form, which accounts for the actual sounding, yet unordered pitches of that set.

4. Figure out the unordered intervals (i.e. interval classes) between adjacent pitch classes and determine whether that set has an inversional partner or not.

5. If the answer is yes, select the one that is the most packed in ascending or descending direction.

6. Transpose the most packed set to pc0.

7. The resulting set is in prime form.

8. The prime form is synonymous with set class.

9. Depending on the intervallic content of a pc-set, the prime form might include 24 transpositionally and inversionally pc-sets, or 12 transpositionally related pc-sets only.

"Clock Face" as a Visual Aid to Identify Sets

Figure 24.4 shows a **clock face** that expedites the process of calculating normal and prime forms. Since the clock face has 12 positions corresponding to the 12 pitch classes, it can be quickly drawn and used to locate the pitch classes of a set.

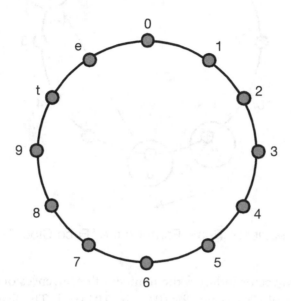

FIGURE 24.4 The "Face Clock"

Given pc7, pc2, and pc6, for instance, it is easy to determine the most packed arrangement of these notes simply by visually examining the set. When examining the collection clockwise (ascending order), notice that by starting at two o'clock, pc2, then moving to six o'clock, pc6, and finally to seven o'clock, pc7, we get the normal form: [2,6,7] with ic[41]. Counterclockwise examination (descending order) starting at seven o'clock, pc7, however, reveals an even more packed intervallic arrangement: the unordered interval between pc7 and pc6 yields ic1, and between pc6 and pc2 is ic4. To calculate the prime form, then, we basically assign pc0 to pc7 and count counterclockwise to determine the integers of the remaining pitch classes: pc6 becomes pc1, and pc2 becomes pc5. Set class (015) is the prime form of [2,6,7]. That method is much faster and, with some practice, it speeds up the translation of any pc-set to normal or prime forms. To generate the prime form, then, assign a movable pc0 to the first note of the most packed arrangement of pitch classes and figure out the position of the remaining pitches. Figure 24.5 demonstrates this process on a clock face.

Interval-Class Vector

In the absence of traditional tonal relationships, the logic of atonal music manifests itself through a network of *intervallic* relationships that can occur at the micro (within a set) or macro (between sets or larger sections) levels of the musical structure. The prominent role of *intervals* in atonal music is also evident in the way the same or similar intervals often undergird the vertical and horizontal dimensions and even control the unfolding of voice leading in an attempt to establish musical coherence in a composition. The sound of a set class of any cardinality can be expressed numerically as a string of six Arabic numbers. Notated in square brackets (with integers without spaces or commas), an **interval-class vector** offers a unique insight into the exact intervallic content of set classes.

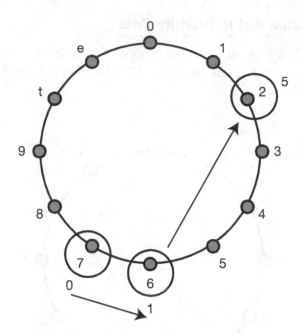

FIGURE 24.5 Prime Form on the "Face Clock"

The value of an interval-class vector indicates the number of occurrences of a particular interval class in a set. For instance, the interval-class vector for (014) is [101100]. The first number [1] of the vector shows the number of ic1=1; the second number [0] shows the number of ic2=0; the third number [1] shows the number of ic3=1; the fourth number [1] shows the number of ic4=1; the fifth number [0] shows the number of ic5=0; and, the six number [0] shows the number of ic6=0.[2] Remember that each interval class (except ic6) includes two inversionally related pitch class intervals: ic1=1/11, ic2=2/10, ic3=3/9, ic4=4/8, ic5=5/7, and ic6=6 because a tritone inverts onto itself.

To calculate the interval-class vector for any sonority (or melodic line) in any pitch order, we have to tally the number of intervals (indicated as interval classes) occurring in that sonority (or melodic line). To keep the score of all interval classes, we first figure out intervals formed with the first member of the sonority, then with the second, third, etc. Given [D♯,G♯,C♯,F♯], we can calculate the interval-class vector of that set as follows:

1. The unordered sonority [D♯,G♯,C♯,F♯] = [3,8,1,6] can be notated in normal form as [1,3,6,8], which is a member of the (0257) set class. To figure out the interval-class vector, both unordered or ordered collections can be used. We will use [3,8,1,6].

2. Figure out the intervals formed between the first member of [3,8,1,6] and the remaining members of the set: 8–3=ic5, 1–3=-2=*mod*12=10=ic2, 6–3=ic3; between the second member of [3,8,1,6] and the remaining ones: 1–8=-7=*mod*12=ic5, 6–8=-2=*mod*12=10=ic2; between the third member of [3,8,1,6] and the remaining one: 6–1=ic5.

3. As we complete the interval-class vector for [3,8,1,6], count the number of occurrences of each interval class within the set. The question—*how many ic1s, ic2s, ic3s, ic4s, ic5s, ic6s are there in [3,8,1,6]?*—is a crucial one. The [3,8,1,6] sonority contains no ic1s, two ic2s, one ic3, no ic4s, three ic5s, and no ic6s. So, the interval-class vector for [3,8,1,6] is [021030]. As with any tetrachord, there are six intervals in all; dyads have one, trichords have four, pentachords have 10, hexachords have 15, septachords have 21, octachords have 28, nonachords have 36, and decachords have 45.

TRANSPOSITION AND INVERSION OF SETS

The [0,2,5] and its inverse [0,3,5] are related by I_5, which means that if you want to **map** the members of the first set onto the members of the second, a compound transformation called an **inversion** (I_n) must be used. The transformation first inverts [0,2,5] around 0 and then transposes each member by +5. When using a mirror inversion around axis 0, you basically flip members of a pc-set to the other side of the clock face. Pitch class 0 inverts onto itself; pc2 inverts onto pct; and pc5 inverts onto pc7. The inverted pitch classes are subsequently transposed clockwise by the **index number**—5, in the present example—to arrive at [0,3,5]. Therefore, pc0 becomes pc5 of [0,3,5]; pct (inverted pc2) becomes pc3 of [0,3,5]; and, pc7 (inverted pc5) becomes pc0 of [0,3,5]. Inversion is a compound operation that involves two steps: (1) the inversion around 0, and (2) clockwise transposition of the inverted set by a specific index number.

When comparing [C,D,F] [0,2,5] and [C,E♭,F] [0,3,5], notice the first member of [0,2,5]: pc0 maps onto the last member of [0,3,5]: pc5; the second member of [0,2,5]: pc2 maps onto the second member of [0,3,5]: pc3; and, the last member of [0,2,5]: pc5 maps onto the first member of [0,3,5]: pc0. These mappings are the consequence of mirror inversion. Given the two sets [0,2,5] and [0,3,5], or any pair of inversionally related sets, it is easy to determine the index number simply by figuring out the **sum** between integers of two sets: 0+5=5, 2+3=5, and 5+0=5. When comparing two inversionally related sets, the first member of the first set is *added* to the last member of the second, the second member to the second, and the third to the first.

Literal relationships between musical events in atonal music are more closely associated with the musical surface and describe ways in which we hear that music. Given the inversionally related sets: [C,D,F] and [C,E♭,F], we can explain their relationships more literally using a slightly different methodology. Since we know that these two sets are related by inversion, the first member of [C, D, F] maps onto the last member of [C, E♭, F]: C→F, D→E♭, and F→C. As a consequence, these inversional pc pairs create an axis of symmetry, which share the same sum 5. Therefore, if we want to express the relationship between these two sets using their actual pitches, the labels: I_F^C, $I_{E♭}^D$, and I_C^F, convey the relationship among pitches more precisely. True, the remaining pairs of pitches which also share sum 5: $E^{C♯}$, $F♯^B$, $G^{B♭}$, $G♯^A$, $A^{A♭}$, $B♭^G$, $B^{F♯}$, and $C♯^E$, use the same inversional pc axis, yet these pitches do not occur in the original sets. By labeling inversions as I_Y^X, we can immediately take notice of certain pitches that might be hierarchically more important than others.

Transposition (T_n) is a single-step transformation that maps the first member of the set onto the first member of the second set, second to second, etc. When you compare two transpositionally related sets to determine the level of transposition or index number between them, *subtract* members of the first set from the members of the second. For instance, [2,4,7] and [t,0,3] are members of (025) and are related by transposition. To calculate the level of transposition or index number, subtract 2 from t=8, 4 from 0=(-4) 8, and 7 from 3=(-4) 8. Notice that in two instances, negative integers are obtained: 0–4=-4 and 3–7=-4. In these cases, apply the *mod 12* operation that brings integers less than 0 and greater than 11 to the pitch-class space between 0 and **e**.

COMMON TONES UNDER TRANSPOSITION AND INVERSION

By examining the interval-class vector of any set, we can predict how many common tones are there between two *transpositionally* related sets. Given [1,2,6,9], which is a member of (0158) with the interval-class vector [101220], a precise number of **common tones under transposition** can be calculated. For instance, the *fifth* number of the vector is [2] and it indicates that under T_5 and/or T_7 there are two notes held in common between sets related by T_5 and/or T_7. Let's verify that [1,2,6,9] at T_5 becomes [6,7,e,2] with the common tones pc2 and pc6, and [1,2,6,9] at T_7 becomes [8,9,1,4] with pc1 and pc9 as common tones. The *first* integer of the interval-class vector, then, reveals the specific number of common tones under T_1 or T_e, which in the case of [1,2,6,9] is one; the *second* integer in the vector shows the number of common tones under T_2 or T_t; the *third* integer shows the number of common tones under T_3 or T_9; the *fourth* integer indicates the number of common tones under T_4 or T_8; the *fifth* integer specifies the number of common tones under T_5 or T_7; and the *sixth* integer tallies the number of common tones under T_6, which in this case is multiplied by 2. Viewed from the perspective of common tones retained between sets, the value of the interval-class vector becomes all the more important particularly as a powerful compositional tool.

Common tones under inversion (I_n) can be determined by examining the **sums** formed by each pair of pitches in a set. Table 24.1, an addition table, calculates the number of notes held in common for [1,3,6,9], which is a member of (0258).

TABLE 24.1 Common Tones Under Inversion: (0258)—Summation Table

+	1	3	6	9
1	2	4	7	t
3	4	6	9	0
6	7	9	0	3
9	t	0	3	6

This table computes all the sums between pairs of pitches in [1,3,6,9]. (The original sets are written in the top row and the left column.) The numbers inside the table, known as index numbers or sums, indicate the occurrence of *one* common tone under a specific inversion represented by that number. For instance, the number 0 occurs three times, which means that there are *three* common tones under I_0; the number 1 does not occur at all, so there are no common tones under I_1; the number 2 occurs only once, so there is one common tone under I_2, etc. Let's verify these findings. There are two 9s inside the table, which means that there should be two common tones under I_9. To invert [1,3,6,9] by I_9, we first invert [1,3,6,9] around 0-axis, which yields [e,9,6,3], then transpose by 9, which yields [8,6,3,0], and finally reverse its order [0,3,6,8]. There are two common tones: pc3 and pc6 between [1,3,6,9] and I_9 [0,3,6,8]. The fact that integer 9 appears at the intersection of 3 and 6 is not inconsequential; it basically confirms that pc3 and pc6 are held in common at I_9 as are the other pitches at different inversions (pc1 and pc3 are held in common under I_4, pc1 and pc9 are held in common under I_t, etc.).

AURAL IDENTIFICATION OF SET CLASSES

Aural identification of pc-sets helps to develop a more abstract way of hearing melodic and harmonic sets. It removes them from the confines of tonality and places them in a tonally neutral environment without any recourse to familiar tonal traits (such as the role of the governing tonic or the referential sound of scale degrees with their functional implications). The prerequisite for pc-set recognition is the ability to identify intervals and interval classes. The correct recognition of interval classes within a pc-set helps to figure out the normal form. This step rearranges unordered pitches and translates them into pitch classes. The next step is more abstract and involves translating normal forms to prime forms. As a practice routine, select a trichord and experiment with different pitch configurations of that trichord, which might include a transposition, reordering, and/or octave displacements, etc. You will be amazed at the number of possibilities and how different all these configurations sound.

In the CW, you are asked to identify melodic and harmonic trichords. Given the pitches C#5, F4, E4, for instance, the following steps are recommended:

1. Identify interval classes between adjacent pitches. The interval class between the first and second pitch is ic4 and between the second and third pitch is ic1. Remember that you might hear the interval between C#5 and F4 as a descending major 6th and between F4 and E4 as a descending minor 2nd. As ordered intervals they yield int4 and int11, but as unordered intervals (i.e. interval classes) they yield ic4 and ic1. We are interested in the latter.

2. Notate pitches: C#5, F4, and E4 as integers: C#5=pc1, F4=pc5, and E4=pc4.

3. With unordered pitch classes: pc1, pc5, and pc4, put them in ascending order: pc1, pc4, and pc5. That is the normal form [1,4,5], written in square brackets with Arabic numbers separated by a comma.

4. Based on the interval content of pc-set [1,4,5], ic[31], you can see that the set can be inverted and that the inversional partner is more intervallically packed, ic[13].

5. Assign pc0 to the first pitch of the most packed arrangement (i.e. start at pc5 and move counterclockwise).

6. The prime form of a [1,4,5] is (014).

To expedite the process of pc-set recognition locate the pitch classes on the clock face. You will immediately see that the counterclockwise arrangement of pitches counting from pc5 produces the prime form (014).

When played simultaneously, the pitches C#5, F4, E4 produce a certain harmonic sound that is unique to (014). Similarly, other set classes exhibit harmonic characteristics that are unique across the multitude of diverse pitch configurations that can occur within the boundaries of a particular set class. The ability to identify that unique sound greatly improves your ears and sharpens your overall harmonic sensitivity.

NOTES

1 Milton Babbitt's "Set Structure as a Compositional Determinant," and Allen Forte's "A Theory of Set-Complexes for Music" and *The Structure of Atonal Music* are considered pioneering works that introduced many of the concepts discussed here.

2 The interval class 6 is counted twice because the interval inverts onto itself.

Set Classes in Jazz

CHAPTER SUMMARY

Chapter 25 examines the harmonic and melodic potential of trichords, tetrachords, pentachords, and hexachords, and demonstrates their usefulness in jazz improvisation and composition.

CONCEPTS AND TERMS

- All-combinatorial
- Categories of trichords:
  - Cyclic
  - Diatonic
  - Semitonal
  - Triadic
- Whole tone
- Combinatoriality
- Hexachords
- I-combinatorial
- PC-Set complex
- Pentachords
- Rotations
- Tetrachords
- Transpositional rotations
- Z-relations

OVERVIEW

One of the most remarkable facts about atonal music theory is its reductive power and the ability to represent a vast array of harmonic and melodic structures using a relatively small number of abstract set classes. The fact that any collection of three pitches without repetition can be represented as one of 12 trichordal set classes, or that any collection of six different pitches can be compartmentalized into one of only 50 possible hexachordal set classes, proves just how powerful the tools of atonal theory really are. With only six dyads, 12 trichords, 29 tetrachords, 38 pentachords, and 50 hexachords, jazz musicians can explore brand new melodic and harmonic plateaus, and begin implementing these structures in improvisation and composition.

In my conversations with Bob Brookmeyer about jazz composition, I remember him posing a lot of intriguing questions, such as: *Can you write a composition using three or more random notes? How can these notes be developed, transformed, modified, and disguised in a composition? How can they influence the form of the piece you are working on? How can you explore the intervallic relationship between these pitches?*

These questions describe ways in which any set class can be used in a composition. Although Bob's questions probed different compositional processes and were meant to reform my views about composition, similar questions can be asked about jazz improvisation: *What kinds of melodic lines can you improvise using (014)? Will your lines work over a tonal or modal progression? Can you improvise a solo that is based entirely on a specific interval-class vector? Can you fit your melodic ideas derived from (013579)—Mystic Chord, into the bridge of a rhythm changes tune?* Still other questions pertaining to harmony and harmonic relationships can be asked: *What kinds of harmonies can be generated using (016) as an upper structure? Can you harmonize a tune using a single set class only? What are the harmonic/tonal implications of 12 trichords, 29 tetrachords, 38 pentachords, and 50 hexachords? How can they expand your understanding of jazz harmony?* With these questions in mind, we can now delve into a fascinating world of atonal music theory and show how the specific concepts can be implemented in jazz improvisation and composition.

TRICHORDS

Any collection of three different pitches can be reduced to *one* out of 12 trichordal set classes with a specific interval-class vector, shown in Table 25.1.

These set classes are compartmentalized into four unique **categories of trichords** that share certain intervallic features and suggest a possible membership in specific harmonic and melodic environments. The **diatonic** category of trichords comprises two pc-sets: (025) and (027). In addition to their independent status, these and other trichords are thought of as **subsets** of larger **supersets**, such as pentatonic, hexatonic, modal, octatonic (MOLT) scales, which in itself is an important characteristic that may be explored in improvisation and composition. Even though they are labeled as *diatonic*, (025) and (027) can intersect with more chromatic supersets as well. The **whole-tone** category includes three set classes: (024), (026), and (048), all of which intersect with the whole-tone scale. The **triadic** category of trichords features two set classes: (036) and (037). The most complex category of trichords is the **semitonal** category. The label *semitonal* indicates that these set classes include ic1 in their pitch structure. The *semitonal* category includes five set classes: (012), (013), (014), (015), and (016).

Figure 25.1 translates the integers from Table 25.1 into pc-sets (written in bold), analyzes the intervallic content of each trichord based on pitch adjacency, and shows inversionally related sets (written in square brackets with integers separated by a comma).

There are 12 transpositionally and inversionally related trichords. When transpositionally related trichords are the only consideration, the number of available sets expands to 19, as shown in Table 25.2. The top row compiles 12 transpositionally and inversionally related trichords; the top and bottom row combines 19 transpositionally related trichords.

Table 25.3 explores the harmonic and melodic potential of transpositionally and inversionally related trichords. The first column: *Allen Forte Name*, provides the names of the set classes in ascending order according to Forte's *The Structure of Atonal Music*. The *Set Class* column lists all the set classes in prime form. The *Inversion* column shows the inversional partners that certain sets have. The *Category* column indicates the potential membership of a trichord in the specific family of chords and describes the trichord's overall characteristics. Unlike in Table 25.2, where each trichord was placed in a single category, Table 25.3 provides multiple categories for some trichords as well as establishing new subcategories. For instance, the **cyclic** category signifies the symmetrical structure of certain trichords. The *Harmonic Interpretation* column analyzes the pitch structure of trichords in the context of traditional tonal formations, incomplete

TABLE 25.1 Interval-Class Vector—Trichords

Set Class	Diatonic		Whole-Tone			Triadic		Semitonal				
	(025)	(027)	(024)	(026)	(048)	(036)	(037)	(012)	(013)	(014)	(015)	(016)
IC Vector	[011010]	[010020]	[020100]	[010101]	[000300]	[002001]	[001110]	[210000]	[111000]	[101100]	[100110]	[100011]

TABLE 25.2 Transpositionally and Inversionally Related Trichords

Category	Diatonic		Whole-Tone			Triadic		Semitonal				
Prime Form	(025)	(027)	(024)	(026)	(048)	(036)	(037)	(012)	(013)	(014)	(015)	(016)
Inversion	[0,3,5]			[0,4,6]			[0,4,7]		[0,2,3]	[0,3,4]	[0,4,5]	[0,5,6]

chords, rootless formations, and upper structures. The *Melodic Interpretation* column provides the occurrence of some trichords as subsets of specific scalar collections. For each trichord, the interval-class vector is provided, whose value offers yet another insight into the structure of trichords. The same generic table will be used later to compile and analyze tetrachords, pentachords, and hexachords.

FIGURE 25.1 Families of Trichords—Pitch Notation

TABLE 25.3 Trichords—Analysis

Allen Forte Name	Set Class	Inversion	Category	Harmonic Interpretation	Melodic Interpretation	Interval-Class Vector
3-1	(012)		Semitonal, Cyclic		Chromatic scale	[210000]
3-2	(013)	[0,2,3]	Semitonal		Octatonic	[111000]
3-3	(014)	[0,3,4]	Semitonal	Incomplete m(#7)	Octatonic	[101100]
3-4	(015)	[0,4,5]	Semitonal	Incomplete M7	Hexatonic	[100110]
3-5	(016)	[0,5,6]	Semitonal	Incomplete 7alt.	Octatonic	[100011]
3-6	(024)		Whole-Tone, Diatonic, Cyclic		Major	[020100]
3-7	(025)	[0,3,5]	Diatonic	Incomplete m7	Pentatonic	[011010]
3-8	(026)	[0,4,6]	Whole-Tone	Incomplete 7/Ø	Octatonic	[010101]
3-9	(027)		Diatonic, Cyclic	Quartal	Pentatonic	[010020]
3-10	(036)		Triadic, Cyclic	Diminished triad	Octatonic	[002001]
3-11	(037)	[0,4,7]	Triadic	Minor/major triad	Major/minor	[001110]
3-12	(048)		Whole-Tone, Cyclic	Augmented triad	Hexatonic	[000300]

HARMONIC POTENTIAL OF TRICHORDS

This section demonstrates the harmonic interpretation of selected pc-set complexes. A **pc-set complex** includes one of 19 transpositionally related trichords and demonstrates how it can function as rootless/incomplete or upper structure within the context of an extended harmonic formation. In other words, a pc-set complex offers a harmonic reinterpretation of set classes and demonstrates how a single set class can participate in a number of different harmonic settings.

Diatonic PC-Set Complexes

The *diatonic* pc-set complexes include three trichords: [0,2,5], [0,3,5], and [0,2,7]. Figure 25.2 illustrates a harmonic interpretation of [0,2,5] and [0,2,7].[1] Since each trichord has two pitch rotations, you can freely experiment with them to produce different chord voicings. In the forthcoming examples, accidentals apply only to the note to which they are attached and do not carry across the measure.

FIGURE 25.2 *Diatonic* PC-Set Complexes

The number of chords that can use *diatonic* sets as upper structures is truly impressive. Because these sets are closely related to one another—[0,2,5] and [0,2,7] share two pitches in common—they often participate in similar harmonic environments. Frequently used as a quartal structure, [0,2,7] constitutes a neutral formation that participates in three pairs of dominant 7th chords, with each pair belonging to a different minor-3rd cycle. As mentioned before, [0,2,5], [0,3,5], and [0,2,7]—and, all the remaining trichords—are very effective as rootless formations. Making them work as such requires an understanding of their functionality. For instance, [0,2,5] in BbM9 exhibits different characteristics than it does in AbM13(#11). In the former, [0,2,5] functions as a major 9th, a major 3rd, and a perfect 5th; in the latter, it functions as a major 3rd, a #11th, and a major 13th.

Whole-Tone PC-Set Complexes

The *whole-tone* pc-set complexes include four trichords: [0,2,4], [0,2,6], [0,4,6], and [0,4,8]. Figure 25.3 provides a harmonic interpretation of [0,2,4] and [0,4,8].[2]

FIGURE 25.3 *Whole-Tone* PC-Set Complexes

The *whole-tone* category of trichords shows an impressive collection of chords, particularly in the dominant 7th category. Since the whole-tone trichords are subsets of the whole-tone scale, the [0,2,4], [0,2,6], and [0,4,8] trichords participate in some form or another in every dominant 7th chords built on each scale degree of the corresponding whole-tone scale. The [0,4,6] trichord can even function as an upper structure in dominant 7th chords, which is derived from two different whole-tone scales, thus showing even greater harmonic flexibility.

Triadic PC-Set Complexes

The *triadic* pc-set complexes include three trichords: [0,3,6], [0,3,7], and [0,4,7]. Figure 25.4 provides a harmonic interpretation of [0,3,7].[3]

FIGURE 25.4 *Triadic* PC-Set Complexes

In the case of [0,3,7]s, you may have recognized the familiar upper-structure triads from Chapter 11. Here, however, the situation is reversed: a single *triadic* trichord functions as an upper structure of different dominant 7ths as opposed to a single dominant 7th supporting different upper-structure triads. The fact that a single trichord can support a plethora of chord types testifies to the remarkable flexibility of trichords and their usefulness in the jazz harmonic syntax.

Semitonal PC-Set Complexes

The *semitonal* pc-set complexes are among the most intricate and include as many as nine trichords: [0,1,2], [0,1,3], [0,2,3], [0,1,4], [0,3,4], [0,1,5], [0,4,5], [0,1,6], and [0,5,6]. Figure 25.5 provides a harmonic interpretation of [0,1,6].[4]

In *semitonal* and other pc-set complexes, what passes for consonance and dissonance is entirely subjective. Even though some of the chords do not sound syntactic, at least not in a traditional sense, a Persichetti-esque caveat that "any note can sound simultaneously with any other note" can be invoked to justify the structure and sound of these formations.

FIGURE 25.5 *Semitonal* PC-Set Complexes

TETRACHORDS

Table 25.4 shows 29 tetrachords, along with their inversional counterparts and interval-class vectors, placed in specific categories, and analyzed based on their harmonic and melodic potentials. There are two set classes with the letter **Z** in their names. Known as **Z-relations**, this label indicates a special relationship that exists between set classes with different pitches, yet with the same interval-class vector. Notice that 4-Z15 and 4-Z29 contain different pitches, (0146) and (0137) respectively, but they share the identical vector [111111].

Some of the categories also include a "+" sign to indicate that there is a single pitch that lies outside of the characteristics of either diatonic, whole-tone, triadic, semitonal, or cyclic categories. For instance, the *cyclic+* label indicates an *almost symmetrical* tetrachord. Sets that are entirely symmetrical, such as 4-1 (0123), 4-21 (0246), or 4-28 (0369), create intervallic patterns and tend to be more predictable and devoid of musical interest. *Almost symmetrical* tetrachords, such as 4-18 (0147), 4-19 (0148), or 4-27 (0258), retain their symmetrical property, but they also contain a single pitch, which does not belong to the underlying intervallic cycle. As a result, that pitch breaks the symmetry, thwarts our musical expectations, and, at the same time, renders the entire tetrachord more interesting. Certain sets, such as 4-18 (0147), are placed in multiple categories and can be implemented according to your musical preferences and compositional needs. The *cyclic+* designation implies that the subset [1,4,7] (036) forms a 3-cycle, with a minor 2nd dyad [0,1] (01) providing a slight asymmetrical imbalance within the collection. The *triadic+* (or *diatonic+*) label indicates that the triadic subset [0,4,7] includes a note, pc1, which lies outside of the triadic and/or diatonic environments. The *gapped x-cycle* label signifies that the non-adjacent pitches of 4-7 (0145) or 4-21 (0246) form the same intervallic 4-cycle. Given 4-21 (0246), the pairs: pc0/pc4 and pc2/pc6 create a 4-cycle, which can be found in Wayne Shorter's "Speak No Evil" mm. 9-10: |Em11–Cm11|Dm11–B♭m11|. Even though multiple categories can be assigned for each tetrachord, Table 25.4 (and forthcoming tables as well) includes only one category.

TABLE 25.4 Tetrachords—Analysis

Allen Forte Name	Set Class	Inversion	Category	Harmonic Interpretation	Melodic Interpretation	Interval-Class Vector
4-1	(0123)		Semitonal		Chromatic	[321000]
4-2	(0124)	[0,2,3,4]	Cyclic+		Chromatic	[221100]
4-3	(0134)		Semitonal		Octatonic	[212100]
4-4	(0125)	[0,3,4,5]	Cyclic+		Mode IV	[211110]
4-5	(0126)	[0,4,5,6]	Whole-Tone+		Mode IV	[210111]
4-6	(0127)		Diatonic+		Mode IV	[210021]
4-7	(0145)		Gapped 4-cycle		Hexatonic	[201210]
4-8	(0156)		Gapped 5-cycle	7alt.	Locrian	[200121]
4-9	(0167)		Gapped 6-cycle	7alt.	Chromatic	[200022]
4-10	(0235)		Gapped 2-cycle	m11	Minor	[122010]
4-11	(0135)	[0,2,4,5]	Cyclic+	M9	Phrygian	[121110]
4-12	(0236)	[0,3,4,6]	Cyclic+	dim(add2)	Octatonic	[112101]
4-13	(0136)	[0,3,5,6]	Cyclic+	m13	Octatonic	[112011]
4-14	(0237)	[0,4,5,7]	Cyclic+	m(add2)	Minor	[111120]
4-Z15	(0146)	[0,2,5,6]		7alt	Altered	[111111]

TABLE 25.4 Continued

Allen Forte Name	Set Class	Inversion	Category	Harmonic Interpretation	Melodic Interpretation	Interval-Class Vector
4-16	(0157)	[0,2,6,7]	Cyclic+	M7(#11); 7alt.; m13	Phrygian	[110121]
4-17	(0347)		Gapped 4-cycle	M/m	Major/minor	[102210]
4-18	(0147)	[0,3,6,7]	Cyclic+	dim(#7)	Octatonic	[102111]
4-19	(0148)	[0,4,7,8]	Cyclic+	m(#7)	Melodic Minor	[101310]
4-20	(0158)		Cyclic+	M7	Locrian	[101220]
4-21	(0246)		Cyclic	9	Whole-tone	[030201]
4-22	(0247)	[0,3,5,7]	Cyclic+	M(add2)	Major/minor	[021120]
4-23	(0257)		5-Cycle	m11	Pentatonic	[021030]
4-24	(0248)		Cyclic+	7(#11,b13)	Whole-tone	[020301]
4-25	(0268)		Whole-tone	7(b5)	Whole-tone	[020202]
4-26	(0358)		Gapped 5-cycle	m7; 6	Minor	[012120]
4-27	(0258)	[0,3,6,8]	Cyclic+	7, ø7	Octatonic	[012111]
4-28	(0369)		3-Cycle	dim7	Octatonic	[004002]
4-Z29	(0137)	[0,4,6,7]	Cyclic+	M9(#11)	Altered	[111111]

IMPROVISATION WITH SET CLASSES

Even though tetrachords in Table 25.4 can be rendered vertically as independent harmonic formations and as members of larger chord structures in the manner shown in Figures 25.2–25.5, the focus now shifts to the melodic potential of set classes; we will use 4-16 (0157) as an example. The forthcoming methodology can be implemented with all remaining tetrachords as well as with trichords, pentachords, and hexachords. With its inversion [0,2,6,7] and interval-class vector [110121], 4-16 is an attractive collection with multiple tonal and modal associations. As a melodic formation, 4-16 is a subset of C Phrygian, B♭ Dorian, D♭ Lydian, A♭ Ionian, G Locrian, A Altered, C Dorian ♭2, C Mode IV, C Mode VI, as well as different pentatonic and hexatonic collections. There are numerous strategies and techniques associated with improvisation/composition with set classes. Here, the emphasis is on the following: (1) **rotations**, (2) **transpositional rotations**, (3) **subsets**, (4) **common tones under transposition**, and (5) **common tones under inversion**. Some of these techniques require preparatory work, such as analyzing sets or creating addition tables. As such, these techniques might be akin to composition rather than to improvisation. Yet with enough practice, they can be mastered and implemented in real time as well.

Since 4-16 has two unique forms: [0,1,5,7] and [0,2,6,7], there are as many as eight different rotations ready for melodic explorations. Figure 25.6 illustrates these rotations.

FIGURE 25.6 4-16 (0157)—Rotations of [0,1,5,7] and [0,2,6,7]

Each rotation has a specific intervallic content written below the staff. Keeping these intervals intact, each rotation is now transposed to the same starting pitch, C4, as demonstrated in Figure 25.7.

FIGURE 25.7 4-16 (0157)—Transposed Rotations

With transposed rotations, 4-16 is explored over a single pitch center, which can also function as the root of a specific modal or tonal environment. Using a single set enables you to focus more keenly on the structural properties of that set.

The idea of using fragments of larger sets is akin to the technique of motivic fragmentation discussed in Chapter 10. The subsets of 4-16, such as (015), (016), (026), and (027), have a potential to function as distinct motives within the improvised line. When concatenated in a line, these subsets are linked by intervals that figure prominently (or not) in the interval vector: [110121]. For instance, ic5 occurs more than any other interval class in the vector; therefore, ic5 can effectively link individual subsets in a line.

With the current discussion, we are gradually steering away from the spontaneous nature of improvisation and begin making overtly calculated decisions, which might seem counterintuitive to improvisation. To develop a sense of improvisatory freedom while improvising with set classes requires a lot of preplanning and practice. The ability to identify set classes aurally and hear intervals in their original and inverted form is central in developing one's atonal improvisatory skills. The good news is that the ideas discussed here are as useful in improvisation as they are in composition. In fact, composing with unordered set classes might be a better starting point to experiment with these concepts; the overall process will force you to calculate your options more methodically and develop them with a well-defined logic. Composing and/or improvising with set classes has enormous potential and offers plenty of opportunities for finding, cultivating, and developing one's creative voice.

Figure 25.8 shows a melodic line composed with four distinct subsets of 4-16: (015), (016), (026), and (027).

4-16 (0157)
Subsets: (015) (016) (026) (027)

FIGURE 25.8 4-16 (0157)—Melodic Phrase—Distinct Subsets

As stated before, the value of an interval-class vector contains a lot of useful information regarding the overall structure of sets. In addition to tallying all available intervals occurring in the set, its value also tells us how many common tones are retained between two sets related by transposition. The interval vector for 4-16 is [110121], which means that by combining T_0 with $T_{1/11}$ there is one common tone (as a reminder, the first integer in the vector corresponds to $T_{1/11}$, the second integer to $T_{2/10}$, etc.); by combining T_0 with $T_{5/7}$ there are two common tones, and by combining T_0 with $T_{3/9}$ there are no common tones, etc. Therefore, if you want to retain more common tones between sets you will likely select $T_{5/7}$. Conversely, if you want to improvise/compose a line with no common tones between transpositionally related sets, you will likely select $T_{3/9}$. Figure 25.9 shows two phrases, which combine T_0 with $T_{5/7}$, and T_0 with $T_{3/9}$. Notice that the pitch content of individual sets is handled with relative freedom with certain notes repeated within the collection. Creative freedom with which you can control

4-16 (0157)
$T_0[0,1,5,7]$; $T_5[\mathbf{5},6,t,\mathbf{0}]$; $T_7[\mathbf{7},8,\mathbf{0},2]$

4-16 (0157)
$T_0[0,1,5,7]$; $T_3[3,4,8,t]$; $T_9[9,t,2,4]$

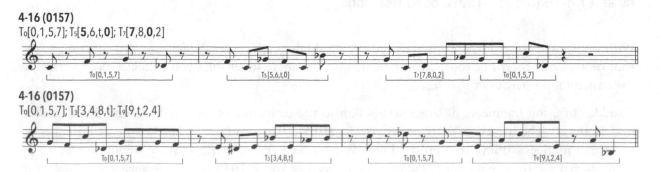

FIGURE 25.9 4-16 (0157)—Melodic Phrase—T_n Forms

the order and/or the recurrence of certain notes in a set is truly liberating and constitutes one of the most attractive aspects of *unordered* music. That freedom enables you to discover creative ways to shape and develop melodic ideas.

To figure out common tones under inversion, an addition table (also known as the summation table or the invariance matrix), similar to that in Table 24.1, is created.[5] Table 25.5 illustrates such a table for 4-16.

TABLE 25.5 4-16 (0157)—Summation Table

+	0	1	5	7
0	0	1	5	7
1	1	2	6	8
5	5	6	t	0
7	7	8	0	2

The integers inside the table indicate the index numbers or sums under which T and I_n forms of 4-16 share common tones. For instance, there are two 1s in the table, which means that $T_0[0,1,5,7]$ and $I_1[6,8,0,1]$ share two common tones: pc0 and pc1. Since unordered pitch relationships are implemented, the order of individual notes within individual sets is subject to creative modifications. The fact that pc0 and pc1 are common for T_0 and I_1 is an important characteristic, which influences the overall design of the melodic line. Figure 25.10 illustrates a line that combines T_0 and I_1.

4-16 (0157)
$T_0[0,1,5,7]$; $I_1[6,8,0,1]$

FIGURE 25.10 4-16 (0157)—Melodic Phrase—T_n and I_n Forms

PENTACHORDS AND HEXACHORDS

It is clearly beyond the scope of this book to explore the melodic and harmonic potential of individual pentachords and hexachords, particularly as they relate to jazz composition and improvisation. Similar techniques of generating harmonies and melodies as discussed before are implemented with larger sets as well. After discussing various atonal techniques, and explaining ways in which they are utilized in practice, the question posed at the beginning of this chapter: *Can you write a composition using three or more random notes?* is seen from a new perspective. One of the characteristics of atonal composition is that the vertical and horizontal forces are often derived from one another and, at the same time, they frequently complement each other. That special relationship manifests itself at various levels of the musical fabric. Since melodic ideas are derived from a particular pitch collection, that collection might also influence

TABLE 25.6 Pentachords—Analysis

Allen Forte Name	Set Class	Inversion	Category	Harmonic Interpretation	Melodic Interpretation	Interval-Class Vector
5-1	(01234)		Cyclic		Chromatic	[432100]
5-2	(01235)	[0,2,3,4,5]	Cyclic+		Chromatic+	[332110]
5-3	(01245)	[0,1,3,4,5]	2-cycle+		Chromatic+	[322210]
5-4	(01236)	[0,3,4,5,6]	3-cycle+		Chromatic+	[322111]
5-5	(01237)	[0,4,5,6,7]	Cyclic+		Chromatic+	[321121]
5-6	(01256)	[0,1,4,5,6]	Chromatic		Chromatic+	[311221]
5-7	(01267)	[0,1,5,6,7]	Chromatic		Chromatic+	[310132]
5-8	(02346)		2-cycle+		Chromatic+	[232201]
5-9	(01246)	[0,2,4,5,6]	2-cycle+			[231211]
5-10	(01346)	[0,2,3,5,6]	3-cycle+			[223111]
5-11	(02347)	[0,3,4,5,7]	Gapped 3-cycle+	dim(#7)		[222220]
5-Z12	(01356)		3-cycle+	M7(add4)		[222121]
5-13	(01248)	[0,4,6,7,8]	2-cycle+			[221311]
5-14	(01257)	[0,2,5,6,7]	Diatonic+		Mode IV	[221131]
5-15	(01268)		2-cycle+	M(#5,#11)	Mode IV	[220222]
5-16	(01347)	[0,3,4,6,7]	3-cycle+	7(#9,#11)	Octatonic	[213211]
5-Z17	(01348)		4-cycle+	m9(#7)	Melodic minor	[212320]
5-Z18	(01457)	[0,2,3,6,7]	4-cycle+	7(#9,b13)	Harmonic minor	[212122]
5-19	(01367)	[0,1,4,6,7]	3-cycle+	dim9(#7)	Octatonic	[212122]

TABLE 25.6 continued

Allen Forte Name	Set Class	Inversion	Category	Harmonic Interpretation	Melodic Interpretation	Interval-Class Vector
5-20	(01568)	[0,2,3,7,8]	Gapped 5-cycle	m9(♭6)	Major	[211231]
5-21	(01458)	[0,3,4,7,8]	Gapped 4-cycle	m(♯7,♭6)	Hexatonic	[202420]
5-22	(01478)		4-cycle+	dim(♯7)		[202321]
5-23	(02357)	[0,2,4,5,7]	Gapped 3-cycle	m11	Minor	[132130]
5-24	(01357)	[0,2,4,6,7]	Diatonic	M9(♯11)	Phrygian	[131221]
5-25	(02358)	[0,3,5,6,8]	Gapped 3-cycle	m13	Dorian	[123121]
5-26	(02458)	[0,3,4,6,8]	2-cycle+	M9; M9(♯5)	Melodic minor	[122311]
5-27	(01358)	[0,3,5,7,8]	Gapped 3(4)-cycle	M9	Locrian	[122230]
5-28	(02368)	[0,2,5,6,8]	Gapped 3-cycle	7(♭5)	Octatonic	[122212]
5-29	(01368)	[0,2,5,7,8]	5-cycle+	m6/9, 7sus(♭9)	Mode II	[122131]
5-30	(01468)	[0,2,4,7,8]	2-cycle+	m(♯7)	Melodic minor	[121321]
5-31	(01369)	[0,3,6,8,9]	3-cycle+	7(♭9)	Octatonic	[114112]
5-32	(01469)	[0,3,5,8,9]	Gapped 3-cycle	dim13(♯7)	Octatonic	[113221]
5-33	(02468)		2-cycle	9(♯11)	Whole-tone	[040402]
5-34	(02469)		2-cycle+	9	Lydian	[032221]
5-35	(02479)		Diatonic	6/9; sus9	Major pentatonic	[032140]
5-Z36	(01247)	[0,3,5,6,7]	3-cycle+	9(♭9)		[222121]
5-Z37	(03458)		Gapped 5-cycle+	m7(♯7)	Minor bebop	[212320]
5-Z38	(01258)	[0,3,6,7,8]	Gapped 5-cycle+	7(♯7)	Mode IV	[212221]

TABLE 25.7 Hexachords—Analysis

Allen Forte Name	Set Class	Inversion	Category	Distinct Subsets	Interval-Class Vector
6-1	(012345)		all-combinatorial	(024)	[543210]
6-2	(012346)	[0,2,3,4,5,6]	I-combinatorial	(014)	[443211]
6-Z3/36	(012356)	[0,1,3,4,5,6]		(016)	[433221]
6-Z4/37	(012456)	[0,1,2,4,5,6]		(0145)	[432321]
6-5	(012367)	[0,1,4,5,6,7]	I-combinatorial	(0236)	[422232]
6-Z6/38	(012567)			(0157)	[421242]
6-7	(012678)		all-combinatorial	(0167)	[420243]
6-8	(023457)		all-combinatorial	(0235)	[343230]
6-9	(012357)	[0,2,4,5,6,7]	I-combinatorial	(0137)	[342231]
6-Z10/39	(013457)	[0,2,3,4,6,7]		(0135)	[333321]
6-Z11/40	(012457)	[0,2,3,5,6,7]		(0247)	[333231]
6-Z12/41	(012467)	[0,1,3,5,6,7]		(0146)	[332232]
6-Z13/42	(013467)			(016)	[324222]
6-14	(013458)	[0,3,4,5,7,8]	P-combinatorial	(015)	[323430]
6-15	(012458)	[0,3,4,6,7,8]	I-combinatorial	(014)	[323421]
6-16	(014568)	[0,2,3,4,7,8]	I-combinatorial	(0145)	[322431]
6-Z17/43	(012478)	[0,1,4,6,7,8]		(0247)	[322332]

TABLE 25.7 continued

Allen Forte Name	Set Class	Inversion	Category	Distinct Subsets	Interval-Class Vector
6-18	(012578)	[0,1,3,6,7,8]	I-combinatorial	(0257)	[322242]
6-Z19/44	(013478)	[0,1,4,5,7,8]		(0134)	[313431]
6-20	(014589)		all-combinatorial	(0158)	[303630]
6-21	(023468)	[0,2,4,5,6,8]	I-combinatorial	(0236)	[242412]
6-22	(012468)	[0,2,4,6,7,8]	I-combinatorial	(0148)	[241422]
6-Z23/45	(023568)			(0258)	[234222]
6-Z24/46	(013468)	[0,2,4,5,7,8]		(013)	[233331]
6-Z25/47	(013568)	[0,2,3,5,7,8]		(015)	[233241]
6-Z26/48	(013578)			(0247)	[232341]
6-27	(013469)	[0,3,5,6,8,9]	I-combinatorial	(0134)	[225222]
6-Z28/49	(013569)			(0136)	[224322]
6-Z29/50	(023679)		RI-combinatorial	(0237)	[224232]
6-30	(013679)	[0,2,3,6,8,9]	I-/R-combinatorial	(0167)	[224223]
6-31	(014579)	[0,2,4,5,8,9]	I-combinatorial	(0145)	[223431]
6-32	(024579)		all-combinatorial	(0247)	[143250]
6-33	(023579)	[0,2,4,6,7,9]	I-combinatorial	(0136)	[143241]
6-34	(013579)	[0,2,4,6,8,9]	I-combinatorial	(025)	[142422]

TABLE 25.7 continued

Allen Forte Name	Set Class	Inversion	Category	Distinct Subsets	Interval-Class Vector
6-35	(02468t)		all-combinatorial	(048)	[060603]
6-Z36/3	(012347)	[0,3,4,5,6,7]		(037)	[433221]
6-Z37/4	(012348)		RI-combinatorial	(0348)	[432321]
6-Z38/6	(012378)		RI-combinatorial	(0137)	[421242]
6-Z39	(023458)	[0,3,4,5,6,8]		(0235)	[333321]
6-Z40/11	(012358)	[0,3,5,6,7,8]		(0125)	[333231]
6-Z41/12	(012368)	[0,2,5,6,7,8]		(016)	[332232]
6-Z42/13	(012369)		RI-combinatorial	(0369)	[324222]
6-Z43/17	(012568)	[0,2,3,6,7,8]		(0146)	[322332]
6-Z44/19	(012569)	[0,3,4,7,8,9]		(0258)	[313431]
6-Z45/23	(023469)		RI-combinatorial	(0369)	[234222]
6-Z46/24	(012469)	[0,3,5,7,8,9]		(0246)	[233331]
6-Z47/25	(012479)	[0,2,5,7,8,9]		(0247)	[233241]
6-Z48/26	(012579)		RI-combinatorial	(0257)	[232341]
6-Z49/28	(013479)		RI-combinatorial	(0347)	[224322]
6-Z50/29	(014679)			(0146)	[224232]

the structure of individual chords as well as the unfolding of chord progressions. For instance, the succession of chordal roots can be derived from the same collection that undergirds the melodic layer and individual chords can be formed from various subsets embedded in the collection and juxtaposed over these roots.[6]

Table 25.6 provides an analysis of 38 pentachords.

Table 25.7 analyzes the structure of 50 hexachords. The *Allen Forte Name* column combines the pairs of Z-related hexachords that share the same interval-class vector. In addition to the familiar characteristics, some hexachords, such as 6-7 (012678) or 6-27 (013469) are labeled as **all-combinatorial** or **I-combinatorial**, respectively. The term **combinatoriality** is reserved for combining a collection of any cardinality with one or more transposed (P-combinatoriality), inverted (I-combinatoriality), retrograded (R-combinatoriality) and retrograde inverted (RI-combinatoriality) versions of itself.[7] For now, it suffices to say, that the six *all-combinatorial* hexachords: 6-1, 6-8, 6-32, 6-7, 6-20, and 6-35 can be combined with either P, I, R, or RI versions of itself to create an aggregate. For instance, to classify as I-combinatorial, a hexachord must form an aggregate by combining the P and I version of itself. The *Distinct Subsets* column provides a partial list of characteristic sets derived from the hexachordal superset.

NOTES

1   For the remaining *diatonic* pc-set complexes, visit the CW.
2   For the remaining *whole-tone* pc-set complexes, visit the CW.
3   For the remaining *triadic* pc-set complexes, visit the CW.
4   For the remaining *semitonal* pc-set complexes, visit the CW.
5   See Bo Alphonse's *The Invariance Matrix*. More on this in the next chapter.
6   For additional possibilities visit the CW.
7   For a thorough discussion of combinatoriality, see Chapter 26.

CHAPTER 26

Twelve-Tone Techniques

CHAPTER SUMMARY

Chapter 26 examines the theory of twelve-tone music. The foundation for its application in jazz composition and improvisation is explored.

CONCEPTS AND TERMS

- All-combinatorial hexachords
- Combinatoriality
- Dodecaphonic
- I-combinatoriality
- Index vector
- Invariance
- Inversion

- Multiplication
- Multiplication inversion
- Order position
- P-combinatoriality
- R-combinatoriality
- Retrograde
- Retrograde inversion
- RI-combinatoriality

- Rotational arrays
- Row
- Series
- Total serialism
- Transposition
- TTO
- Twelve-tone music

OVERVIEW

Arnold Schoenberg declared in June of 1921 that he "discovered something which will assure the supremacy of German music for the next hundred years." And it has taken nearly a hundred years for his groundbreaking ideas to make inroads into the syntax of jazz music. Even though jazz and twelve-tone music seem to be miles apart, there have been successful attempts by jazz musicians to merge both traditions, such as: Gunther Schuller's "Transformation," Hale Smith's "Evocation," Bill Evans's "Twelve Tone Tune," John Carisi's "Moon Taj," and Bill Dobbins's "Concerto For Jazz Orchestra." As atonal music, with its *unordered* pitch relationships, gave way to **twelve-tone** (also known as **dodecaphonic** or **serial**) **music** sometime in the early 1920s, a new compositional system emerged whose influences have been felt in many stylistic trends of the 20th and 21st centuries.[1]

Dodecaphonic music is based on *ordered* pitch relationships, and each note within the **twelve-tone row** or **series** is treated equally, without prioritizing one note over the other. That pitch democracy is manifested in the structure of the twelve-note row, wherein twelve chromatic pitches (without repetition) are employed in an *ordered* succession and function as the principal theme in a twelve-tone composition. Each statement of the row (in any conceivable form or transformation) features a complete aggregate of pitches before the next statement commences. There might be concomitant presentations of different row forms interacting with one another in creative ways, but the underlying premise of twelve-tone music states that these interactions are order and pitch sensitive.[2] Since twelve-tone rows are devoid of any traces of tonality and traditional tonal behaviors (with the noble exceptions of Alban Berg, whose music retains and explores certain *tonal* characteristics), the need of establishing an even stronger connection between horizontal and vertical forces is elevated to a new level.[3] There are as many as 9,985,920 possible twelve-tone rows in the chromatic universe. With that many possible themes at your disposal, to say that there is a budding potential for experimentation with twelve-tone techniques would be a gross understatement.[4]

In keeping with the overall pedagogy of the book, the discussion of serial techniques serves a utilitarian purpose: to suggest practical tools enabling one to excel in jazz composition and twelve-tone improvisation. To better understand how the twelve-tone system works, the following topics will be explored: (1) twelve-tone canonic operations (TTOs), (2) twelve-tone matrices, (3) hexachordal combinatoriality, (4) rotational arrays, (5) twelve-tone harmonization, and (6) twelve-tone improvisation. With the exceptions of the last two original topics, the earlier ones constitute the core of twelve-tone theory.[5] Some of the topics are quite technical and intricate; but it is nonetheless important to master them regardless of their complexities. The ability to invert or retrograde a twelve-tone series, for instance, is required for the development of the principal theme in a composition. Quickly creating a twelve-tone matrix, which offers immediate access to the 48 row forms, is necessary for the selection of specific row forms in a composition. With the matrix on the bandstand, one can even begin improvising with complete twelve-tone rows in a serial manner.

TWELVE-TONE OPERATIONS (TTOs)

Some of the twelve-tone operations (TTOs), such as **transposition** and **inversion**, are familiar transformations and were encountered earlier in the book. Others, such as **retrograde** (R), **retrograde inversion** (RI), **multiplication** (M) and **multiplication inversion** (MI), require further explanation.[6] Since twelve-tone music is based on *ordered* pitch relationships, the interval between adjacent notes reflects their specific order in pitch-class space. Transformations of the twelve-tone series are based entirely on the behavior of intervals between notes in the series. An understanding of that behavior is key to the mechanics of twelve-tone operations. For instance, the succession of pct and pc7 as an *ordered* pitch interval is 9, but as an *unordered* pitch interval it is 3. Table 26.1 summarizes the difference between *ordered* and *unordered* pitch-class intervals.

Transposition

Each TTO is examined according to the behavior of intervals between adjacent pitches in the series. Figure 26.1 illustrates a twelve-tone row from Bill Evans's "Twelve Tone Tune" labeled as P_4 (or P_0). The letter "P" stands for the *prime* form, and the subscript "$_4$" indicates that pc4 is the first note in the series. In addition to the *fixed-pitch* method of labeling rows, the *movable-pitch* method, P_0, is also

TABLE 26.1 Unordered and Ordered Pitch-Class Intervals

Traditional Names	Ordered PC Intervals	Unordered PC Intervals
Perfect Unison	0	0
Minor Second	1	1
Major Second	2	2
Minor Third	3	3
Major Third	4	4
Perfect Fourth	5	5
Augmented Fourth	6	6
Perfect Fifth	7	5
Minor Sixth	8	4
Major Sixth	9	3
Minor Seventh	10	2
Major Seventh	11	1

FIGURE 26.1 "Twelve Tone Tune" by Bill Evans—Row Form

employed. In that method, however, the row is transposed to pc0 (for clarity's sake) and used as a referential collection, which expedites the subsequent transformations of the primary theme. In this chapter, both labels will be used *ad alternatim*.

The status of ordered intervals under transposition remains the same. To transpose a row means to add the level of transposition (counted in semitones) to each note in the series. For instance, to transpose $P_4[4,2,6,7,5,3,8,t,1,0,9,e]$ by a minor 3rd, add 3 (*mod* 12) to each member of the row: $P_7[7,5,9,t,8,6,e,1,4,3,0,2]$.

Inversion

In order to invert a row, each pitch-class interval in the series is inverted. The *ordered* pc interval content for all the P-forms of the row in Figure 26.1 is: <10,4,1,10,10,5,2,3,11,9,2>. The intervallic succession for all inverted forms (I-forms) of the row is: <2,8,11,2,2,7,10,9,1,3,10>. For instance, to create the I_2 form of the row, begin on pc2 and follow the intervallic succession of the inverted version of the row: $I_2[2,4,0,e,1,3,t,8,5,6,9,7]$.

The structure of P_4 and I_4 is explained using dyadic sums between pitches occurring in the same **order position** (OP): OP1/4+4, OP2/2+6, OP3/6+2, OP4/7+1, OP5/5+3, OP6/3+5, OP7/8+0, OP8/t+t, OP9/1+7, OP10/0+8, OP11/9+e, and OP12/e+9. All dyadic pairs share the same *sum* 8, which represents the inversional correspondence between related pitches. Since pc4 is common for both P and I forms, it creates an inversional axis, which maps the corresponding pitches of P and I.

Retrograde

To retrograde a row means to render the pitch content of the P form *backwards* with each interval replaced by its *complement*. The intervallic succession of P <10,4,1,10,10,5,2,3,11,9,2> becomes <10,3,1,9,10,7,2,2,11,8,2> of all retrograde forms (R forms). Since the pitch order in retrograde forms is reversed, to label R forms we use the first note of the corresponding P form. For instance, the last note of P_8 is pc3 and this is the first note of $R_8[3,1,4,5,2,0,7,9,e,t,6,8]$.

Retrograde Inversion

Any twelve-tone series transformed using retrograde inversion *retains* the intervallic content of the P form in *reverse* order. The intervallic succession of the P form, <10,4,1,10,10,5,2,3,11,9,2> becomes <2,9,11,3,2,5,10,10,1,4,10>. For instance, the RI_5 form of the series from Figure 26.1 begins on the last note of I_5: pct. To figure out the last note of the I_5, we basically invert the last note of P_3, pct, around 4-axis, *sum* 8, which gives us pct: pct+pct=sum 8. Since *sum* 8 explains the inversional relationship between notes of all P/R and I/RI forms, RI_5 is inversionally related to R_3, I_5 is related to P_3, P_1 to I_7, etc. The RI_5 form then contains the following pitch classes: [t,0,9,8,e,1,6,4,2,3,7,5].

Multiplication (M) and Multiplication Inversion (MI)

In addition to the basic or canonic TTOs, the M and MI operations complement the TTOs in an interesting way.[7] Unlike TTOs, which retain the fundamental intervallic properties of the series, the M and MI operations do not. The M and MI operations transform the notes of the original series by multiplying its pitches by 5 and 7, respectively. Table 26.2 illustrates the transformation of the aggregate using M and MI operations.

The M operation transforms the chromatic scale into a sequence of descending 5ths with the invariant diminished 7th chord [0,3,6,9]. The MI operation transforms the chromatic scale into a sequence of ascending fifths with the invariant whole-tone subset [0,2,4,6,8,t].

MATRIX

A more convenient way of representing all 48 P, I, R, and RI row forms is to create a two-dimensional 12×12 matrix. Even though there are different ways of generating a matrix, the two methods: *fixed pitch* and *movable pitch* are explained. In the *fixed-pitch* method, the top row includes the P form in its original form as it occurs in the composition. The axis of symmetry between P and I (or R and RI) runs diagonally and features the first number of the P form of the series. In the *movable-pitch* method, the top row includes the P form transposed to pc0. The diagonal axis of symmetry in the *movable-pitch* method is always 0. All row forms read from the left to right side contain 12 P forms, and those that read from right to left include 12 R forms.

To create a matrix using the *fixed-pitch* method, first notate the primary row in the top row. Given the row from Figure 26.1, we know already a couple of things: (1) that the first note of the P-form, pc4, is also the first note of the I-form running from top to bottom, and (2) that the sum of that pitch, pc4+pc4=8, constitutes the index number, which relates all other inversional pairs of P/I and R/RI series. So, if the second pitch of the P_4 is pc2 then the second note of the I_4 is 6, since pc2+pc6=8, etc. The pitches of the completed I form provide the first notes for all P forms, which now need to be completed. For instance, to complete the P_8 form, start on pc8 and add 4 to each member of P_4, since $P_8-P_4=4$, and continue filling each space until the row is complete. Table 26.3 illustrates two *fixed-pitch* and *movable-pitch* matrices.

TABLE 26.2 M and MI Operations

Chromatic Scale	0	1	2	3	4	5	6	7	8	9	t	e
M operation x5 (*mod* 12)	0	5	t	3	8	1	6	e	4	9	2	7
MI operation x7 (*mod* 12)	0	7	2	9	4	e	6	1	8	3	t	5

TABLE 26.3 Twelve-Tone Matrices—Fixed- and Movable-Pitch Methods

Fixed-Pitch Method

	I_4	I_2	I_6	I_7	I_5	I_3	I_8	I_t	I_1	I_0	I_9	I_c	
P_4	4	2	6	7	5	3	8	t	1	0	9	e	R_4
P_6	6	4	8	9	7	5	t	0	3	2	e	1	R_6
P_2	2	0	4	5	3	1	6	8	e	t	7	9	R_2
P_1	1	e	3	4	2	0	5	7	t	9	6	8	R_1
P_3	3	1	5	6	4	2	7	9	0	e	8	t	R_3
P_5	5	3	7	8	6	4	9	e	2	1	t	0	R_5
P_0	0	t	2	3	1	e	4	6	9	8	5	7	R_0
P_t	t	8	0	1	e	9	2	4	7	6	3	5	R_t
P_7	7	5	9	t	8	6	e	1	4	3	0	2	R_7
P_8	8	6	t	e	9	7	0	2	5	4	1	3	R_8
P_c	e	9	1	2	0	t	3	5	8	7	4	6	R_c
P_9	9	7	e	0	t	8	1	3	6	5	2	4	R_9
	RI_4	RI_2	RI_6	RI_7	RI_5	RI_3	RI_8	RI_t	RI_1	RI_0	RI_9	RI_c	

Movable-Pitch Method

	I_7	I_5	I_8	I_9	I_6	I_4	I_c	I_1	I_3	I_2	I_t	I_0	
P_0	7	5	8	9	6	4	e	1	3	2	t	0	R_0
P_2	9	7	t	e	8	6	1	3	5	4	0	2	R_2
P_t	5	3	6	7	4	2	9	e	1	0	8	t	R_t
P_9	4	2	5	6	3	1	8	t	0	e	7	9	R_9
P_c	6	4	7	8	5	3	t	0	2	1	9	e	R_c
P_1	8	6	9	t	7	5	0	2	4	3	e	1	R_1
P_8	3	1	4	5	2	0	7	9	e	t	6	8	R_8
P_6	1	e	2	3	0	t	5	7	9	8	4	6	R_6
P_3	t	8	e	0	9	7	2	4	6	5	1	3	R_3
P_4	e	9	0	1	t	8	3	5	7	6	2	4	R_4
P_7	2	0	3	4	1	e	6	8	t	9	5	7	R_7
P_5	0	t	1	2	e	9	4	6	8	7	3	5	R_5
	RI_7	RI_5	RI_8	RI_9	RI_6	RI_4	RI_c	RI_1	RI_3	RI_2	RI_t	RI_0	

ANALYZING TWELVE-TONE ROWS

The process of selecting or composing a twelve-tone row is the most important step, which determines whether your composition will be successful or not. In order to possess a developmental potential, the row needs to have an attractive pitch content, which manifests itself through: (1) distinct subsets—using trichords, tetrachords, pentachords, and hexachords derived from the same set class, (2) pitch symmetry—selecting dyadic pairs that share the same axis of symmetry, (3) row symmetry—employing the first and last trichord that is a member of the same class, (4) distinct intervals—using a handful of pc intervals or all available pc intervals, as in the all-interval row, (6) intervallic cycles—creating different cycles between adjacent and non-adjacent pitches, (7) tonal/atonal dichotomy, etc.

The structure of twelve-tone rows can be analyzed from many different angles. First, determine the row's intervallic content and look for the recurrence of certain intervals or intervallic patterns. Second, examine and compare the structure of the two hexachords comprising the row, or three adjacent tetrachords or four adjacent trichords. Third, compare the beginning and end of the row and determine whether or not any recognizable and hearable connections can be established between the two. Fourth, analyze the row for the presence of overlapping subsets. Fifth, look for some distinct motives that figure prominently in the row. With these suggestions in mind, let's examine the structure of the row from Figure 26.1: $P_4[4,2,6,7,5,3,8,t,1,0,9,e]$. The succession of ordered pc intervals is as follows: <10,4,1,10,10, 5,2,3,11,9,2>. The row divides into two chromatic hexachords: A[2,3,4,5,6,7] and B[8,9,t,e,0,1]—members of 6-1 (012345). Hexachord A contains two symmetrical trichords [2,4,6] and [3,5,7]—members of 3-6 (024). Hexachord B includes two adjacent trichords [8,t,1]—a member of 3-7 (025), and [9,e,0]—a member of 3-2 (013). The first and last intervals in the row are inversions of one another: pc4/pc2=10 and pc9/pce=2, respectively.

These initial observations tell us a lot about the structure of the row and—what is of particular interest—suggest specific row forms that can be potentially implemented in a composition. For starters, the presence of two chromatic hexachords determines the row's highly chromatic character, which Bill Evans attempts to disguise by reordering the pitches to create two whole-tone subsets in hexachord A. The presence of ic2 continues in hexachord B, but that interval does not manifest itself as pronouncedly as it does in hexachord A. The fact that both hexachords belong to the same set class, 6-1, yet their surface melodic characteristics are quite different is an attractive attribute of the row in itself.

In his composition, Bill Evans chose to repeat P_4 twice, each time with different rhythmic designs and characteristic pitch displacements. So, his composition consists of three statements of P_4 only. There are, however, many different directions in which "Twelve Tone Tune" could have unfolded. Let's ruminate about the possibilities. For instance, different row forms could have been chosen based on their inversional symmetry, *sum* 8, between P/I and R/RI forms. The P form could have been combined in counterpoint with a specific I form. R and RI forms could have also been integrated to provide a contrasting material and to demarcate formal sections within the composition. The last note of a P series could have been chosen as the first note of the next row, etc. Evans's treatment of the row proves that even an exact repetition of the pitch content can be successfully implemented in a composition.

HEXACHORDAL COMBINATORIALITY

Hexachords A and B from Bill Evans's "Twelve Tone Tune" have a special property and are known as **all-combinatorial**. The term **combinatoriality** refers to the process of combining a set with one or more P, I, R, or RI forms of itself. In the case of six **all-combinatorial hexachords**: 6-1, 6-7, 6-8, 6-20, 6-32, and 6-35, each hexachord can be combined with *either* P, I, R, *or* RI forms of itself to create an aggregate. In addition to all-combinatorial hexachords, there are also hexachords that are *only* P-, R, I-, or RI-combinatorial, which means that they can be combined with P, R, I *or* RI forms of itself to create an aggregate.

How do we capitalize on the combinatorial properties of hexachords? Given the all-combinatorial hexachord 6-20 (014589)—which for jazz musicians holds a special place in the pantheon of scales—it can be combined with specific P, R, I, or RI forms of itself to create a twelve-tone row. To figure out exactly at which transposition level [0,1,4,5,8,9] forms an aggregate, the interval-class vector of 6-20 [303630] is examined. Under $T_{1/11}$, $T_{3/9}$, $T_{5/7}$, there are three common tones or **invariants** between A[0,1,4,5,8,9] and any of the complementary hexachords under these six transpositions. For instance, A[**0**,1,4,5,8,9] transposed by 3 becomes B[3,**4**,7,**8**,e,**0**], with three common tones written in bold. For **P-combinatoriality**, then, we need *zero* invariant elements under some transpositions. Based on the interval-class vector [303630], $T_{2/10}$ and T_6 yield zero invariants. For instance, A[0,1,4,5,8,9] transposed by 2 becomes B[2,3,6,7,t,e], and the combination of A and B creates an aggregate in the form of P_0[0,1,4,5,8,9||2,3,6,7,t,e].

For **R-combinatoriality**, the interval-class vector is also examined, but instead of *zero* we need *six* invariants (corresponding to the six pitches that would complete the series). The number 6 in the vector corresponds to $T_{4/8}$. Upon transposition by 4, P_0[0,1,4,5,8,9||2,3,6,7,t,e] becomes P_4[4,5,8,9,0,1||6,7,t,e,2,3]. The first hexachord of R_4[3,2,e,t,7,6||1,0,9,8,5,4] (which renders P_4 backwards) is R-combinatorial with A[0,1,4,5,8,9].

For **I-combinatoriality**, a 12-integer **index vector** provides the number of common tones between two inversionally related sets. To generate the index vector, an addition table analogous to that in Table 25.5 is created. The addition table for A[0,1,4,5,8,9] is shown in Table 26.4.

Each integer in the index vector represents a single T_nI level: [T_0I, T_1I, T_2I, T_3I, T_4I, T_5I, T_6I, T_7I, T_8I, T_9I, T_tI, T_eI]. To create an index vector, the numbers inside the table are tallied. For instance, there are three 0s and six 9s, which means that under T_0I there are three common tones, and that under T_9I there are six common tones. The index vector for A[0,1,4,5,8,9] yields the following value: [363036203630]. For I-combinatoriality, we need *zero* invariants between P and I forms of 6-20. Under T_3I, T_7I and T_eI, A[0,1,4,5,8,9] is I-combinatorial. Let's verify that: A[0,1,4,5,8,9] under T_3I becomes B[3,2,e,t,7,6], which completes the aggregate: P_0[0,1,4,5,8,9||3,2,e,t,7,6].

For **RI-combinatoriality**, the index vector is examined for the maximum number of invariants under T_nI. In the case of hexachords that number is 6, in the case of pentachordal combinatoriality that number is 5, etc. The index vector for A[0,1,4,5,8,9] is: [363036203630], and under T_1I, T_5I or T_9I, A[0,1,4,5,8,9] is RI-combinatorial. Let's verify that: under T_5I, P_0[0,1,4,5,8,9||3,2,e,t,7,6] becomes I_5[5,4,1,0,9,8||2,3,6,7,t,e]. The first hexachord of RI_5[e,t,7,6,3,2] is then RI-combinatorial with A[0,1,4,5,8,9].

TABLE 26.4 6-20 (014589)—Summation Table

+	0	1	4	5	8	9
0	0	1	4	5	8	9
1	1	2	5	6	9	t
4	4	5	8	9	0	1
5	5	6	9	t	1	2
8	8	9	0	1	4	5
9	9	t	1	2	5	6

ROTATIONAL ARRAYS

Extensively practiced by Igor Stravinsky in the 1960s, a twelve-tone technique based on **rotational arrays** offers yet another method for developing the pitch content of *ordered* sets of any cardinality.[8] Table 26.5 shows a rotational array for the blues scale [C, E♭, F, G♭, G, B♭]—a member of 6/Z47 (012479).

TABLE 26.5 Rotational Array for 6/Z47 (012479)

C	E♭	F	G♭	G	B♭
E♭	F	G♭	G	B♭	C
F	G♭	G	B♭	C	E♭
G♭	G	B♭	C	E♭	F
G	B♭	C	E♭	F	G♭
B♭	C	E♭	F	G♭	G

TABLE 26.6 Transposed Rotational Array For 6/Z47 (012479)

Rotational Array					
C	Eb	F	Gb	G	Bb
Eb	F	Gb	G	Bb	C
F	Gb	G	Bb	C	Eb
Gb	G	Bb	C	Eb	F
G	Bb	C	Eb	F	Gb
Bb	C	Eb	F	Gb	G

Transposed Rotational Array						
	C	Eb	F	Gb	G	Bb
T_9	C	D	Eb	E	G	A
T_7	C	Db	D	F	G	Bb
T_6	C	Db	E	Gb	A	B
T_5	C	Eb	F	Ab	Bb	B
T_2	C	D	F	G	Ab	A

Each row of the rotational array represents the subsequent rotations of the original collection. For instance, the rotation in the second row begins on the second note of the first row (Eb) and ends with the first note (C); the third row begins on the third note of the first row (F) and finishes with the first two (C, Eb), etc. The rotational array is complete after all possible rotations are explored.

Table 26.5 is order sensitive, and it preserves the succession of sounding pitches of the original form. One of Stravinsky's favorite techniques was to transpose each rotation to the same pitch in the manner shown in Table 26.6.

The second row of the untransposed array is transposed by 9 to C; the third row of the original is transposed by 7 to C; the fourth row by 6 to C; the fifth row by 5 to C; and the sixth row by 2 to C.

To explore rotational arrays in a compositional manner, concatenate rows one after the other (or in any order) to create melodies, use the rotation in counterpoint with each other, or employ sonorities derived from different columns in support of the melody. The use of canonic TTOs renders the original array in transposition, inversion, retrograde, and retrograde inversion (or inversion retrograde).[9] For each transformation a new array is created. For instance, to create an I_3 rotational array, the original set $[0,3,5,6,7,t]$ becomes $I_3[5,8,9,t,0,3]$, which then undergoes five *untransposed* or *transposed* rotations.

TWELVE-TONE COUNTERPOINT AND JAZZ HARMONY

In order to establish a convincing relationship between harmony and melody in the post-tonal environment, both musical dimensions have to be inextricably entwined with one another. In the absence of traditional tonal relationships, the interdependence of vertical and horizontal forces is the key factor in a composition. In serial music, that relationship takes central stage and manifests itself at different levels of the musical fabric.

The role of outer-voice counterpoint and its influence on harmony was discussed in Chapter 23. A few claims regarding the characteristics of a well-designed outer-voice counterpoint were made and emphasized the use of mostly contrary motion between voices, motivic parallelism, and larger intervals in one voice with smaller ones in the other. These and other characteristics of outer-voice counterpoint are also applicable in twelve-tone music and manifest themselves in equal force through the adoption of serial techniques. For instance, the combination of a melody with one of its TTOs can generate an attractive outer-voice counterpoint, which then is harmonized with chords typical of jazz syntax. Or, the combination of a melody with an *untransposed* or *transposed* rotation might result in an appealing outer-voice counterpoint, which undergoes subsequent harmonization. To demonstrate some of these possibilities, Schoenberg's row from his "Five Piano Pieces," Op. 23 is used. Figure 26.2 provides the P_1, I_1, R_1, RI_1, M_1, and MI_1 forms of the row.

Notice the pitch invariance in the M_1 and MI_1 forms: pcs 9, 6, 3, 0 (diminished 7th chord) and pcs 8, 6, t, 2, 4, 0 (whole tone), respectively. All these row forms (at various levels of transposition) can be combined with P_1 to create an outer-voice counterpoint, which then undergoes a harmonic treatment according to specific guidelines. Since there are 48 unique row forms, there are many available options to combine rows in counterpoint with each other. Table 26.7 illustrates a matrix for $P_1[1,9,e,7,8,6,t,2,4,3,0,5]$.

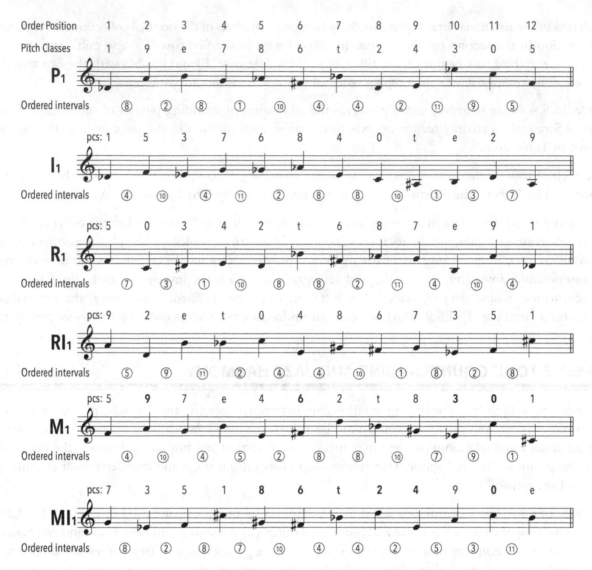

FIGURE 26.2 "Five Piano Pieces," Op. 23 by Arnold Schoenberg—P, I, R, RI, M, MI Row Forms

TABLE 26.7 Twelve-Tone Matrix for P₁[1,9,e,7,8,6,t,2,4,3,0,5]

	I₁	I₉	Iₑ	I₇	I₈	I₆	Iₜ	I₂	I₄	I₃	I₀	I₅	
Fixed-Pitch Method													
P₁	1	9	e	7	8	6	t	2	4	3	0	5	R₁
P₅	5	1	3	e	0	t	2	6	8	7	4	9	R₅
P₃	3	e	1	9	t	8	0	4	6	5	2	7	R₃
P₇	7	3	5	1	2	0	4	8	t	9	6	e	R₇
P₆	6	2	4	0	1	e	3	7	9	8	5	t	R₆
P₈	8	4	6	2	3	1	5	9	e	t	7	0	R₈
P₄	4	0	2	t	e	9	1	5	7	6	3	8	R₄
P₀	0	8	t	6	7	5	9	1	3	2	e	4	R₀
Pₜ	t	6	8	4	5	3	7	e	1	0	9	2	Rₜ
Pₑ	e	7	9	5	6	4	8	0	2	1	t	3	Rₑ
P₂	2	t	0	8	9	7	e	3	5	4	1	6	R₂
P₉	9	5	7	3	4	2	6	t	0	e	8	1	R₉
	RI₁	RI₉	RIₑ	RI₇	RI₈	RI₆	RIₜ	RI₂	RI₄	RI₃	RI₀	RI₅	

Figure 26.3 shows an outer-voice framework using Rₜ in counterpoint with P₁, harmonized with chords typical of the jazz syntax.

This realization demonstrates one of many ways of integrating serial techniques with jazz harmony. Since any melody can be combined in counterpoint with its P, I, R, RI, M, and MI forms, the resulting framework shows a highly coherent structure, which provides a solid foundation for experimentation with different chords and chord progression. The harmonization in Figure 26.3 convincingly supports a non-tonal outer-voice counterpoint, establishes a more modern *harmonic* feel, capitalizes on a

FIGURE 26.3 Twelve-Tone Harmonization

parsimonious voice leading between chords, shows a careful treatment of contextually defined dissonance, balances the use of *stable* and *unstable* sonorities, aims at harmonic parallelism, and finds points of *relative* repose within the harmonization. Harmony in the post-tonal period is defined contextually: what passes for a stable sonority in one harmonic context might be highly unstable in a different context, and vice versa. The context of the harmonization in Figure 26.3 is established with the opening three chords, which feature extended harmonic structures. To create a sense of harmonic continuity and logic, the same quality of chords, 7sus(♭9)/13sus(♭9) or M7(♭5,♯5) for instance, occur four and two times, respectively. The penultimate formation, G♭M7(♭5,♯9), is highly dissonant, yet its occurrence within the progression has been foreshadowed by *less dissonant* chords. The resolution by ic4 to B♭m11(♯7) provides a sense of *non-tonal* closure terminating the progression.

Since there are 48 basic row forms and 24 M-/MI-forms, there are numerous row pairings to be created and then realized. In addition, the row harmonization in Figure 26.3 provides the material for a potential composition *deconstructing* Schoenberg's row from Op. 23. There are 12 unique chords supporting the primary row that can be serialized using TTOs and M/MIs. These chords form chord progressions that provide a harmonic fodder for your composition. Similarly, the serialization of all or selected chords in *untransposed* and/or *transposed* rotational arrays, offers yet another way of generating chord progressions. These and other choices might be quite overwhelming, but they nonetheless provide a number of creative ideas for composition.

TWELVE-TONE IMPROVISATION

The ability to use spontaneously and without visual aid twelve-tone rows in jazz improvisation is next to impossible. Yet, there is a way of improvising with twelve-tone rows by using the matrix as a reference or as a point of departure for your improvisation. An important question might be asked: *What about spontaneity in improvisation?* Since the matrix provides only the pitch classes of 48 row forms, the performance of these rows may unfold in many directions that take into account different factors typically associated with the art of improvisation: communication, interaction, mood, feel, form, and others. With the given pitch-class content of the row, you can improvise on that row while experimenting with different rhythmic ideas, distinct articulation, dynamic and textural contrasts, pitch displacements, and other musical elements. You can even focus on a distinct subset of the row and repeat it for emphasis within a single statement of the row before proceeding to the next row form.[10] Even though twelve-tone improvisation based on the matrix appears to be restricted, there is a lot of creativity involved with the overall presentation of row forms. The ability to *instantaneously* translate integers to actual notes is a prerequisite for successful improvisation. True, while the twelve-tone style of improvisation is still in the infancy stage and is more appropriate for free styles of jazz or streams of musical consciousness, it nonetheless offers a new means of musical expression and provides a unique glimpse into one's musical personality.

NOTES

1 Pierre Boulez (total serialism), Oliver Messiaen (modes of limited transpositions), Milton Babbitt (trichordal arrays), Ruth Crawford Seeger (rotational/transpositional schemes), Ernst Krenek (modal rotations), Józef Koffler (traditional dodecaphony), Elliott Carter (twelve-note chords), George Perle (twelve-tone tonality); Aaron Copland (freely interpreted tonality), George Rochberg (spatialization), Ross Lee Finney (complementarity), Arthur Berger (neoclassic twelve-tone), Louise Talma (tonal serialism), Samuel Barber (twelve-tone neo-romanticism), Gunther Schuller (third stream), Michael Torke (six-tone minimalism), Charles Wuorinen (time-point system), Ursula Mamlok (magic squares), Peter Westergaard (twelve-tone polyphony), Donald Martino (chain forms), Ralph Shapey (twelve-tone arrays), Leonard Rosenman (twelve-tone movie scores), Mel Powell (pitch tableau), Joseph Schwantner (free serialism), Witold Lutosławski (aleatory), Andrew Mead (ordered hexachordspace); see Joseph Straus's *Twelve-Tone Music in America*.

2 As in Webern's *Piano Variations*, Op. 27 and Schoenberg's "String Quartet No. 4," Op. 37/i.

3 Listen to Berg's *Violin Concerto*.

4 In **integral** or **total serialism**, all aspects of the musical composition, such as rhythm, articulation, dynamics, instrumentation, and others are derived from the specific properties of the original row and can be transformed in the same manner as the pitch content.

5 For additional information see: Joseph Straus's *Introduction to Post-Tonal Theory* and Arnold Whittall's *The Cambridge Introduction to Serialism*.

6 Although M and MI are not considered traditional TTOs, their usefulness in jazz renders them equally important.

7 See Robert Morris's *Composition with Pitch-Classes*.

8 Listen to Stravinsky's *Movements, A Sermon, a Narrative, and a Prayer*, and *Requiem Canticles*.

9 Stravinsky preferred the inversion of the retrograde starting on the same first note.

10 Alban Berg in his twelve-tone compositions frequently repeated certain portions of the row within a single statement of that row. Listen to his "Passacaglia" from *Wozzeck*.

Stylistic Crossovers—Developing a New Jazz Repertory

CHAPTER SUMMARY

Chapter 27 crosses the stylistic boundaries of jazz and uses two compositions by Alban Berg to demonstrate how to develop a new jazz repertory.

CONCEPTS AND TERMS

- Musical borrowing
- Hauptstimme
- Nebenstimme

OVERVIEW

The concept of **musical borrowing** has a rich and fascinating tradition. Whether by a conscious decision or an unconscious appropriation of musical ideas from others, composers from different historical periods have enjoyed the challenge of using someone else's material for their own creative purposes. There are many different ways in which the idea of musical borrowing manifests itself in compositional practice. Among the most common types of borrowed material is the theme, such as a waltz by Diabelli or a subject by King Frederick the Great, which then undergoes a masterful treatment in the form of theme and variations by Beethoven in *Diabelli Variations*, Op. 120, and a collection of fugues and canons by J.S. Bach in *The Musical Offering*, BWV 1079, respectively. A famous melody, such as the sequence *Dies Irae*, can be used as the structural foundation for an independent composition, which employs it either overtly as in *Missa pro defunctis* by Palestrina or covertly as in "Intermezzo," Op. 118, No. 6 by Brahms. Borrowed material might also be implemented less conscientiously, when a theme or multiple themes by one composer show similar characteristics to a theme or themes from compositions by other composers. The last movement of Mozart's *Jupiter Symphony* K. 551, for instance, shows curious similarities to the thematic content of Handel's "Father of Heav'n" from Act III of *Judas Maccabeus*, which in turn is loosely based on a Gregorian chant, *Lucis Creator*.[1] Another tradition of musical borrowing involves composers who recycle their own material in different compositions. For instance, the main theme of Beethoven's *Eroica Variations*, Op. 35 (1802) appears in the last movement of his *Eroica Symphony*, Op. 55 (1803); and J.S. Bach's fugal subject from his "Violin Sonata in G minor," No. 1 BWV 1001, serves also as a theme for the fugue in his "Prelude and Fugue in D minor," BWV 539, and "Fugue in G minor," BWV 1000. Lastly, the idea of musical borrowing envelops a very popular tradition of transcribing (intabulating) famous works for different instruments. The most representative examples of such a tradition are countless piano transcriptions by Franz Liszt. Not only did his transcriptions of Beethoven's symphonies, Wagner's operas, Schubert's songs, Bach's organ works, and others, make them readily available to the general public during Liszt's time, they also provide us with a unique insight into the process of making transcriptions.

The idea of musical borrowing has been very popular in jazz, as composers frequently appropriate chord progressions from different standard tunes to write their own compositions.[2] Known as contrafacts, these compositions constitute an important subset of jazz repertory. For instance, Lee Konitz's contrafact "Kary's Trance," based on the tune "Play Fiddle Play," has an interesting genealogy. According to *The Great Song Thesaurus*, "Play Fiddle Play" by Jack Lawrence/Arthur Altman, written in 1932, is based on a popular song from 1898, "Gypsy Love Song" by Harry B. Smith/Victor Herbert, which in turn is based on the first theme of Chopin's *Piano Concerto in E minor No. 1*, Op. 11 (1830).[3] On the one hand, this trajectory establishes a more convoluted pedigree for Konitz's contrafact; on the other, however, it suggests the possibility of exploring classical repertory in the jazz idiom. By and large, the idea of combining both traditions has already been cultivated by different artists as numerous successful projects indicate.[4]

The final chapter of *Jazz Theory* merges jazz and classical traditions into one, in an attempt to develop a new jazz repertory. Since the idea of creating a new jazz repertory is an enormous undertaking and clearly beyond the scope of this book, this chapter presents only two case studies germane to the discussion of atonal and dodecaphonic techniques. Two compositions by Alban Berg, "Schlaffend trägt," No. 2 of his *Vier Lieder aus "Der Glühende,"* Op. 2 and the *Violin Concerto*, serve to demonstrate how these pieces can be transformed, recomposed and/or deconstructed to forge a stylistic merger in the jazz idiom. Berg's compositions are representative of two distinct musical traditions: extended tonality and twelve-tone. The harmonic and melodic structure of "Op. 2, No. 2" verges on a brink of atonality, which makes it very attractive for all kinds of harmonic substitutions and techniques discussed in Chapters 24 and 25. The *Violin Concerto* comes from the dodecaphonic tradition and is particularly relevant to the content of Chapter 26.

The opportunity to adapt classical repertory into the jazz idiom offers a chance to find one's musical voice and to expand one's repertory. There are numerous directions in which transformation, recomposition or deconstruction of the original material can unfold. When listening to different projects listed above, one cannot but notice their stylistic diversities, imaginative reharmonizations, unconventional formal designs, refreshing grooves, conceptual directions, and inventive arrangements. Regardless of the creative route one decides to take, a few preliminary remarks are necessary in order to successfully complete such a project.

First and foremost, a thorough familiarity with the original material is imperative; this is accomplished through a detailed analysis of the form, melody, counterpoint, harmony, rhythm, and the use of compositional techniques. The main purpose of analysis (specifically in this context) is to select a few salient ideas from the original (be they melodic, contrapuntal, harmonic, or rhythmic) that will serve as the main elements of a new composition. Second, a specific style and rhythmic groove for the recomposition need to be determined. This choice is generally influenced by the overall character and feel of the original work. Next, the decision has to be made whether to handle the original material overtly or covertly. For instance, the former might simply involve a reharmonization of the original melody. The latter might control the original material more liberally and disguisedly, and as such might bear little or no resemblance to the original. In both cases, however, the original composition provides the initial stimulus for one's creative impulse that is in keeping with the noble tradition of musical borrowings.

CASE STUDY 1—ALBAN BERG, *VIER LIEDER AUS "DER GLÜHENDE,"* OP. 2, NO. 2: "SCHLAFFEND TRÄGT"

Figure 27.1 shows Berg's "Schlaffend trägt," the second of his *Vier Lieder aus "Der Glühende."*

One of the more attractive features of the song is its extended harmonic vocabulary and the use of cyclic chord progressions supporting a freely unfolding melody. The use of a 7-cycle, realized with dom7(♭5) chords, bears a strong resemblance to the cycle of 5ths found in numerous standard tunes. Since 4-25 (0268), or dom7(♭5), is a symmetrical formation, as well as a subset of the whole-tone collection, 6-35 (02468t), the harmony of the song has a distinct whole-tone feel to it. Even though the piece is in the key of E♭ minor (six flats), the final *tonic* chord—4-25 [1,3,7,9], a member of (0268) or E♭7(♭5)— sounds nothing like what one would expect from a concluding stable sonority. The initial chord of the song—4-25 [2,4,8,t], B♭7(♭5)—functions as the dominant of the home key and that opening is an example of the off-tonic beginning.

"Op. 2, No. 2" has two distinct melodic ideas: *Idea A* in mm. 1–4 and *Idea B* in mm. 9–10. The former utilizes whole-tone subsets [7,e] (04), [6,8,t] (024) and chromatic subset [t,e,0,1] (0123); the latter highlights 3-11 [0,3,7] (037) decorated with the chromatic pc4 and pc6. The closing melodic statement in mm. 14–18 reiterates *Idea A* (mm. 2–4) in augmentation and ends on pc9, which destabilizes the final tonic and emphasizes a highly chromatic nature of the entire composition.

The recomposition of "Op. 2, No. 2" is shown in Figure 27.2.

The treatment of Berg's song retains the original melody but harmonizes it with a vocabulary typical of more contemporary jazz styles. The form features a 27-bar AA'B design with an irregular phrase length in the B section. Its overall mood resembles that of the original, which is somber, dark, and solemn. The chords for the solo section are different from those used to harmonize the melody. The non-tonal chord progression for the solo is derived from the pitches of the original melody occurring in mm. 9–10 [E, E♭, C, G, G♭], as each pitch receives a distinct harmonic support: **EM7(♯11)**, **E♭M7(♯11)**, **Cm11**, **Gm11**, and **G♭M7(♯11)**. The absence of dominant-type chords in favor of extended major and minor harmonic formations is a calculated decision. The use of traditional dominant 7ths would have redirected the progression toward more traditional tonal regions, which the piece deliberately avoids. The 7-cycle controls the unfolding of the progression in the B section.

The choice of harmonic progressions supporting the melody confirms the necessity for the interdependence of horizontal and vertical dimensions. In compositions lacking traditional tonal relationships, that interrelatedness of melodic and harmonic forces is crucial to establish a sense of musical coherence and compositional logic. For instance, the occurrence of a gapped 4-cycle, which is omnipresent in Berg's song, manifests itself in mm. 3–8 of the arrangement as the progression CM/D♭M—Fm11, **BM7(♯11)**–E♭m11 supports the chromatic melody (1-cycle).

The A section of "Op. 2 No. 2" contains two transposed statements of *Idea A*, and the B sections combine *Idea B* (mm. 17–22) with *Idea A* (mm. 23–27). Whereas the A and A' sections highlight 8-bar phrases with subtle inner asymmetries at the sub-phrase level, the B section is 11 bars long with two

FIGURE 27.1 *Vier Lieder aus "Der Glühende,"* Op. 2, No. 2, by Alban Berg

FIGURE 27.2 "Op. 2 No. 2" by Dariusz Terefenko

6- and 5-bar phrases, respectively. The form of the solo section differs from that of the tune and features a 37-bar AA'B design. The fact that the chord progressions for the melody and the solo section are different makes the overall performance more interesting.

CASE STUDY 2—ALBAN BERG, *VIOLIN CONCERTO*

Bearing the famous dedication, *To the memory of an angel*, Berg's *Violin Concerto* is a twelve-tone composition that, in keeping with the composer's overall approach to serialism, cleverly explores the dichotomy between tonal elements and serial compositional procedures. Figure 27.3 illustrates the P_7[7,t,2,6,9,0,4,8,e,1,3,5] form of the row as it first appears in the violin in m. 15.

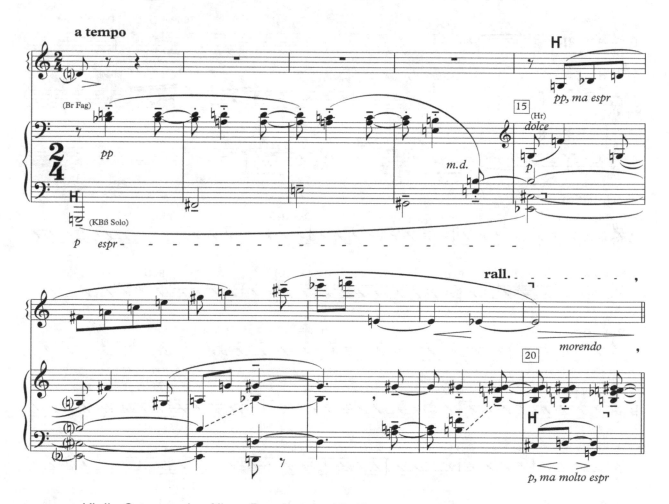

FIGURE 27.3 *Violin Concerto* by Alban Berg—mm. 15–18

Characteristically for Berg, P_7 has strong tonal underpinnings as its overall tertian organization freely alternates between 3- and 4-cycles in order positions 1–8 before shifting to a 2-cycle in order positions 9–12. The first two adjacent tetrachords [7,t,2,6] and [9,0,4,8] are members of 4-19 (0148), and the last tetrachord [e,1,3,5] is a member of 4-21 (0246). From a tonal perspective, the combination of m(#7) chords and a whole-tone segment offers a lot of potential for some creative harmonic and melodic explorations.

FIGURE 27.4 "Angel's Lament" by Dariusz Terefenko

Figure 27.4 shows a lead sheet of "Angel's Lament," which is based on the Berg's row. The piece demonstrates how a single twelve-tone row furnishes the material for the entire jazz composition. Using the preexisting twelve-tone row in jazz composition is comparable, and somewhat related, to the idea of borrowing chord progressions from standard tunes and writing new contrafacts. In both cases, the borrowed material assures that the final products will have integral and coherent structures.

"Angel's Lament" is cast in a 36-bar AB form with a 24-bar A section and a 12-bar B section. The overall mood of the composition is that of grief and conveys the unimaginable feeling of losing a loved one through intense melodic chromaticism and lament-bass harmonic progressions. My composition features five statements of the row: P_7, I_8, and RI_8 in the A section, and R_{11} and P_6 in the B section. The main row of "Angel's Lament," identified with an "H" (**Hauptstimme**), uses the original P_7 with a displaced pitch content and with a different, from the original, rhythmic design. The row is sparsely distributed in mm. 2–11 and clearly conveys its characteristic tertian organization. The I_8 form begins a minor 3rd higher from the last note of P_7, thus connecting both rows using the salient interval of a 3rd. The two pitches in order position 10–11 are repeated for emphasis (which is typical of Berg); the last pitch of I_8, pct, marks the beginning of the next row form, RI_8, as well as the new section. As the piece draws to an end, each occurrence of the row becomes more condensed and rhythmically more intricate.

Since there are 48 row forms that can be freely used in a twelve-tone composition, a couple of important questions need to be raised: (1) What criteria should determine the implementation of specific row forms in the composition? (2) How many row forms in total should there be in the composition? In "Angel's Lament" some series (P_7 and P_6) are carefully selected in an attempt to establish a convincing relationship between the melody and the underlying harmony. All the notes of P_7, for instance, fit into the structure of the supporting chords in fairly traditional ways. This initial melodic/harmonic equilibrium, however, rapidly disintegrates, as the subsequent row statements (I_8, RI_8, and R_{11}) introduce distantly related chromaticism that creates a stark contrast with the supporting harmonies. For instance, the beginning of I_8 [8,5,1]—3-11 (037)—renders the notes as a ♯11, m3, and M7 of Dm(add2); in m. 18, the notes of [6,3,e,7]—4-19 (0148)—function as M13, ♯11, 9, and m7 of Am(add2). The four statements of the row, identified in the score with an "N" (**Nebenstimme**), feature one of each canonic transformations: I_8, RI_8, R_{11}, and P_6, respectively.

In addition to possessing a dirge-like quality, the underlying chord progression of "Angel's Lament" highlights an *almost* symmetrical organization with 1- and 3-cycles alternating in the A section, and with a 1-cycle unfolding in the B section. Historically, the use of a descending 1-cycle has been reserved for the musical narrative typically associated with the topic of lament, which is fitting for this composition. As is the case in "Op. 2 No. 2," the supporting chord progressions deliberately avoid any hints of functional tonality. The use of intervallic cycles is more obvious in the 46-bar solo section as an ascending 2-cycle controls the level of transposition between individual phrases in the A section: m. 1—**D♭m**(add2), m. 9—**E♭m**(add2), and m. 17—**Fm**(add2); and an ascending 4-cycle controls the level of transposition between individual phrases in the B section: m. 23—**E♭m**(add2), m. 31—**Gm**(add2), and m. 39—**Bm**(add2).

Improvising on tunes like "Angel's Lament" presents a challenge, particularly if the focus is exclusively on twelve-tone improvisation, which is pitch and order sensitive. To accomplish this, the matrix, shown in Table 27.1, provides a useful reference.

TABLE 27.1 Twelve-Tone Matrix for P₇[7,t,2,6,9,0,4,8,e,1,3,5]

	I₇	Iₜ	I₂	I₆	I₉	I₀	I₄	I₈	Iₑ	I₁	I₃	I₅	
P₇	G	B♭	D	F♯	A	C	E	G♯	B	C♯	E♭	F	R₇
P₄	E	G	B	E♭	F♯	A	C♯	F	G♯	B♭	C	D	R₄
P₀	C	E♭	G	B	D	F	A	C♭	E	F♯	G♯	B♭	R₀
P₈	G♯	B	E♭	G	B♭	C♯	F	A	C	D	E	F♯	R₈
P₅	F	G♯	C	E	G	B♭	D	F♯	A	B	C♯	E♭	R₅
P₂	D	F	A	C♯	E	G	B	E♭	F♯	G♯	B♭	C	R₂
Pₜ	B♭	C♯	F	A	C	E♭	G	B	D	E	F♯	G♯	Rₜ
P₆	F♯	A	C♯	F	G♯	B	E♭	G	B♭	C	D	E	R₆
P₃	E♭	F♯	B♭	D	F	G♯	C	E	G	A	B	C♯	R₃
P₁	C♯	E	G♯	C	E♭	F♯	B♭	D	F	G	A	B	R₁
Pₑ	B	D	F♯	B♭	C♯	E	G♯	C	E♭	F	G	A	Rₑ
P₉	A	C	E	G♯	B	D	F♯	B♭	C♯	E♭	F	G	R₉
	RI₇	RIₜ	RI₂	RI₆	RI₉	RI₀	RI₄	RI₈	RIₑ	RI₁	RI₃	RI₅	

One of the most attractive attributes of Berg's row is its pitch content, which undeniably has strong tonal characteristics. The row, along with its corresponding P, I, R, and RI forms, then, can be easily internalized, memorized and explored. In order to improvise in twelve-tone style (in a true sense of the word), the specific pitch order occurring in the original series needs to be preserved and followed thoroughly. Given the relative freedom with which Berg handled the pitch content in his twelve-tone compositions, in a successful improvisation the row can occupy larger swaths of music and can be partitioned into motivically charged subsets with certain notes repeated for emphasis. The partition of the row's content into order- and pitch-sensitive subsets allows the improviser to use his/her discretion to perform each segment and the subsequent row forms with a high degree of improvisatory freedom.

NOTES

1   See Ian Woodfield's "Mozart's Jupiter: A Symphony of Light?"

2   Some of the most common chord progressions are borrowed from the following tunes: "What Is This Thing Called Love?," "All the Things You Are," "How High the Moon," "It's You or No One," "I Remember April," "All of Me," "Just Friends," "Exactly Like You," "Honeysuckle Rose," "Out of Nowhere," "Pennies From Heaven," and "Just Friends."

3   In the section of *The Great Song Thesaurus* entitled "Elegant Plagiarisms," Lax and Smith trace the heritage of other standard tunes.

4   Such as Mal Waldron's *Maturity 2—Klassics*, Warne Marsh's *Ne Plus Ultra*, Keith Jarrett's *Expectations*, Joe Zawinul's *Stories from the Danube*, Dominik Wania's *Ravel*, Duke Ellington's *Nutcracker Suite*, Michael Brecker's *Scriabin*, Modern Jazz Quartet's "Blues on Bach," Fred Hersch's "24 Variations on a Bach Chorale," Jacques Loussier's recordings of Bach, Bud Powell's "Bud on Bach," Clare Fischer's "Igor" and "Passacaglia," and Uri Caine's *Ulricht/Primal Light*.

Appendix A
200 Essential Standard Tunes That You Should Know

1. A Foggy Day—George Gershwin/Ira Gershwin

2. After You've Gone—Turner Layton/Henry Creamer

3. Ain't Misbehavin'—Fats Waller/Andy Razaf

4. All of Me—Gerald Marks/Seymour Simons

5. All of You—Cole Porter

6. All the Things You Are—Jerome Kern/Oscar Hammerstein II

7. Almost Like Being in Love—Frederick Loewe/Alan Jay Lerner

8. Alone Together—Arthur Schwartz/Howard Dietz

9. Angel Eyes—Matt Dennis/Earl Brent

10. April in Paris—Vernon Duke/E.Y. Harburg

11. Autumn in New York—Vernon Duke

12. Autumn Leaves—Joseph Kosma/Johnny Mercer

13. Basin Street Blues—Spencer Williams

14. Between the Devil and the Deep Blue Sea—Harold Arlen/Ted Koehler

15. Blame It on My Youth—Oscar Levant/Edward Heyman

16. Blue Moon—Richard Rodgers/Lorenz Hart

17. Body and Soul—Johnny Green/Edward Heyman

18. But Beautiful—Jimmy Van Heusen/Johnny Burke

19. But Not For Me—George Gershwin/Ira Gershwin

20. Bye Bye Blackbird—Ray Henderson/Mort Dixon

21. Caravan—Juan Tizol/Duke Ellington

22. Cherokee—Ray Noble

23. Come Rain or Come Shine—Harold Arlen/Johnny Mercer

24. Dancing in the Dark—Arthur Schwartz/Howard Dietz

25. Dancing on the Ceiling—Richard Rodgers/Lorenz Hart

26. Darn That Dream—Jimmy Van Heusen/Eddie De Lange

27. Day By Day—Paul Weston/Axel Stordahl/Sammy Cahn

28. Days of Wine and Roses—Henry Mancini/Johnny Mercer

29. Do Nothin' Till You Hear From Me—Duke Ellington/Bob Russell

30. Don't Blame Me—Jimmy McHugh/Dorothy Fields

31. Don't Get Around Much Anymore—Duke Ellington/Bob Russell

32. Dream Dancing—Cole Porter

33. East of the Sun and West of the Moon—Brooks Bowman

34. Easy Living—Ralph Rainger/Leo Robin

35. Easy to Love—Cole Porter

36. Embraceable You—George Gershwin/Ira Gershwin

37. Emily—Johnny Mandel/Johnny Mercer

38. Ev'ry Time We Say Goodbye—Cole Porter

39. Everything Happens to Me—Matt Dennis/Thomas A. Adair

40. Everything I Love—Cole Porter

41. Exactly Like You—Jimmy McHugh/Dorothy Fields

42. Falling in Love With Love—Richard Rodgers/Lorenz Hart

43. Fly Me to the Moon—Bart Howard

44. For All We Know—J. Fred Coots/Sam Lewis

45. From This Moment On—Cole Porter

46. Georgia on My Mind—Hoagy Carmichael/Stuart Gorrell

47. Get Out of Town—Cole Porter

48. God Bless the Child—Billie Holiday/Arthur Herzog Jr.

49. Gone With the Wind—Allie Wrubel/Herb Magidson

50. Haunted Heart—John Green/Howard Dietz

51. Have You Met Miss Jones?—Richard Rodgers/Lorenz Hart

52. Heart and Soul—Hoagy Carmichael/Frank Loesser

53. Here's That Rainy Day—Jimmy Van Heusen/Johnny Burke

54. Honeysuckle Rose—Fats Waller/Andy Razaf

55. How About You?—Burton Lane/Ralph Freed

56. How Deep Is the Ocean—Irving Berlin

57. How High the Moon—Morgan Lewis/Nancy Hamilton

58. How Long Has This Been Going On?—George Gershwin/Ira Gershwin

59. I Can't Get Started With You—Vernon Duke/Ira Gershwin

60. I Concentrate on You—Cole Porter

61. I Could Write a Book—Richard Rodgers/Lorenz Hart

62. I Didn't Know What Time It Was—Richard Rodgers/Lorenz Hart

63. I Don't Stand a Ghost of a Chance—Victor Young/Ned Washington

64. I Fall in Love Too Easily—Jule Styne/Sammy Cahn

65. I Get a Kick Out of You—Cole Porter

66. I Got It Bad—Duke Ellington/Paul Webster

67. I Got Rhythm—George Gershwin/Ira Gershwin

68. I Hear a Rhapsody—Dick Gasparre/Jack Baker/George Frajos

69. I Love You—Cole Porter

70. I Loves You Porgy—George Gershwin/DuBose Heyward/Ira Gershwin

71. I Never Knew—Ted Fiorito/Gus Kahn

72. I Remember You—Victor Schertzinger/Johnny Mercer

73. I Should Care—Paul Weston/Axel Stordahl/Sammy Cahn

74. I Thought About You—Jimmy Van Heusen/Johnny Mercer

75. I'll Be Around—Alec Wilder

76. I'll Be Seeing You—Sammy Fain/Irving Kahal

77. I'll Remember April—Don Raye/Gene De Paul/Pat Johnson

78. I'll Take Romance—Ben Oakland/Oscar Hammerstein II

79. I'm Getting Sentimental Over You—George Bassman/Ned Washington

80. I'm Old Fashioned—Jerome Kern/Johnny Mercer

81. I've Got the World on a String—Harold Arlen/Ted Koehler

82. I've Got You Under My Skin—Cole Porter

83. I've Grown Accustomed to Her Face—Frederick Loewe/Alan Jay Lerner

84. I've Never Been in Love Before—Frank Loesser

85. If I Should Lose You—Ralph Rainger/Leo Robin

86. If I Were a Bell—Frank Loesser

87. If You Could See Me Now—Tadd Dameron/Carl Sigman

88. Imagination—Jimmy Van Heusen/Johnny Burke

89. In a Sentimental Mood—Duke Ellington/Manny Kurtz/Irving Mills

90. Indiana—James F. Hanley/Ballard MacDonald

91. Invitation—Bronislaw Kaper/Paul Francis Webster

92. It Could Happen to You—Jimmy Van Heusen/Johnny Burke

93. It Don't Mean a Thing—Duke Ellington/Irving Mills

94. It Might As Well Be Spring—Richard Rodgers/Oscar Hammerstein II

95. It's All Right With Me—Cole Porter

96. It's You or No One—July Styne/Sammy Cahn

97. Just Friends—John Klenner/Sam M. Lewis

98. Just in Time—Jule Styne/Betty Comden/Adolph Green

99. Just One of Those Things—Cole Porter

100. Lady Be Good—George Gershwin/Ira Gershwin

101. Laura—David Raksin/Johnny Mercer

102. Like Someone in Love—Jimmy Van Heusen/Johnny Burke

103. Long Ago and Far Away—Jerome Kern/Ira Gershwin

104. Love For Sale—Cole Porter

105. Love Is Here to Stay—George Gershwin/Ira Gershwin

106. Lover—Richard Rodgers/Lorenz Hart

107. Lover, Come Back to Me—Sigmund Romberg/Oscar Hammerstein II

108. Lover Man—Jimmy Sherman/Roger Ramirez/Jimmy Davis

109. Lush Life—Billy Strayhorn

110. Mean to Me—Roy Turk/Fred E. Ahlert

111. Memories of You—Eubie Blake/Andy Razaf

112. Misty—Error Garner/Johnny Burke

113. Mood Indigo—Duke Ellington/Irving Mills/Albany Bigard

114. Moonlight in Vermont—Karl Suessdorf/John Blackburn

115. My Favorite Things—Richard Rodgers/Oscar Hammerstein II

116. My Foolish Heart—Victor Young/Ned Washington

117. My Funny Valentine—Richard Rodgers/Lorenz Hart

118. My Heart Stood Still—Richard Rodgers/Lorenz Hart

119. My Old Flame—Sam Coslow/Arthur Johnston

120. My One and Only Love—Guy Wood/Robert Mellin

121. My Romance—Richard Rodgers/Lorenz Hart

122. My Shining Hour—Harold Arlen/Johnny Mercer

123. Namely You—G. De Paul/Johnny Mercer

124. Nancy (With the Laughing Face)—James Van Heusen/Phil Silvers

125. Nice Work If You Can Get It—George Gershwin/Ira Gershwin

126. Night and Day—Cole Porter

127. On Green Dolphin Street—Bronisław Kaper/Ned Washington

128. Over the Rainbow—Harold Arlen/E.Y. Harburg

129. Pennies From Heaven—Arthur Johnson/John Burke

130. Perdido—Duke Ellington/Juan Tizol

131. Polka Dots and Moonbeams—Jimmy Van Heusen/Johnny Burke

132. Poor Butterfly—Raymond Hubbell/John L. Golden

133. Prelude to a Kiss—Duke Ellington/Irving Mills/Irving Gordon

134. Remember—Irving Berlin

135. Secret Love—Sammy Fain/Paul Webster

136. September Song—Kurt Weill/Maxwell Anderson

137. Skylark—Hoagy Carmichael/Johnny Mercer

138. So in Love (Am I)—Cole Porter

139. Softly, as in a Morning Sunrise—Sigmund Romberg/Oscar Hammerstein II

140. Solitude—Duke Ellington/Irving Mills/Eddie De Lange

141. Somebody Loves Me—George Gershwin/B.G. DeSylva

142. Someday My Prince Will Come—Frank Churchill/Larry Morey

143. Someone to Watch Over Me—George Gershwin/Ira Gershwin

144. Sophisticated Lady—Duke Ellington/Irving Mills/Mitchell Parish

145. Speak Low—Kurt Weill/Ogden Nash

146. Spring Is Here—Richard Rodgers/Lorenz Hart

147. St. Louis Blues—W.C. Handy

148. Star Dust—Hoagy Carmichael/Mitchell Parish

149. Star Eyes—Don Raye/Gene De Paul

150. Stars Fell on Alabama—Frank Perkins/Mitchell Parish

151. Stella by Starlight—Victor Young/Ned Washington

152. Stompin' At the Savoy—Benny Goodman/Andy Razaf/Chick Webb

153. Summertime—George Gershwin/DuBose Heyward/Ira Gershwin

154. Sweet and Lovely—Harry Tobias/Gus Arnheim

155. Sweet Georgia Brown—Maceo Pinkard/Kenneth Casey

156. Sweet Lorraine—Cliff Burwell/Mitchell Parish

157. Take the "A" Train—Billy Strayhorn

158. Taking a Chance on Love—Vernon Duke/John Latouche

159. Tea For Two—Vincent Youmans/Irving Caesar

160. Teach Me Tonight—Gene De Paul/Sammy Cahn

161. Tenderly—Walter Gross/Jack Lawrence

162. The Man I Love—George Gershwin/Ira Gershwin

163. The Masquerade Is Over—Allie Wrubel/Herb Magidson

164. The More I See You—Harry Warren/Mack Gordon

165. The Nearness of You—Hoagy Carmichael/Ned Washington

166. The Night Has a Thousand Eyes—Jerry Brainin/Buddy Bernier

167. The Shadow of Your Smile—Johnny Mandel/Paul Francis Webster

168. The Song Is You—Jerome Kern/Oscar Hammerstein II

169. The Surrey With the Fringe on Top—Richard Rodgers/Oscar Hammerstein II

170. The Touch of Your Lips—Ray Noble

171. The Very Thought of You—Ray Noble

172. The Way You Look Tonight—Jerome Kern/Dorothy Fields

173. There Is No Greater Love—Isham Jones/Marty Symes

174. There Will Never Be Another You—Harry Warren/Mack Gordon

175. There's a Small Hotel—Richard Rodgers/Lorenz Hart

176. These Foolish Things—Jack Strachey/Harry Link/Holt Marvell

177. They Can't Take Away From Me—George Gershwin/Ira Gershwin

178. Things We Did Last Summer—Jule Styne

179. This Is New—Kurt Weill/Ira Gershwin

180. Time After Time—Jule Styne/Sammy Cahn

181. We'll Be Together Again—Carl Fischer/Frankie Laine

182. What Is This Thing Called Love?—Cole Porter

183. What's New?—Bob Haggart/Johnny Burke

184. When I Fall in Love—Victor Young/Edward Heyman

185. When Your Lover Has Gone—E.A. Swan

186. Where or When—Richard Rodgers/Lorenz Hart

187. Who Can I Turn To?—Leslie Bricusse/Anthony Newley

188. Witchcraft—Cy Coleman/Carolyn Leigh

189. Yesterdays—Jerome Kern/Otto Harbach

190. You and the Night and the Music—Arthur Schwartz/Howard Dietz

191. You Are Beautiful—Richard Rodgers/Oscar Hammerstein II

192. You Are Too Beautiful—Richard Rodgers/Lorenz Hart

193. (You Came Along From) Out of Nowhere—Johnny Green/Edward Heyman

194. You Don't Know What Love Is—Gene De Paul/Don Raye

195. You Go to My Head—J. Fred Coots/Haven Gillespie

196. You Stepped Out of a Dream—Nacio Herb Brown/Gus Kahn

197. You Took Advantage of Me—Richard Rodgers/Lorenz Hart

198. You'd Be So Nice to Come Home to—Cole Porter

199. You're My Everything—Harry Warren/Mort Dixon/Joe Young

200. You've Changed—Carl Fisher/Bill Carey

Bibliography

Alphonce, Bo (1974) "The Invariance Matrix." Ph.D. diss., Yale University.

Babbitt, Milton (1961) "Set Structure as a Compositional Determinant." *Journal of Music Theory* 5: 72–94.

Bach, C.P.E. (1949) *Essay on the True Art of Playing Keyboard Instruments*. trans. and ed. William J. Mitchell. New York: W.W. Norton.

Berliner, Paul (1994) *Thinking in Jazz: The Infinite Art of Improvisation*. Chicago: University of Chicago Press.

Block, Steven (1990) "Pitch–Class Transformation in Free Jazz." *Music Theory Spectrum* 12/2: 181–202.

Brown, Matthew (1997) "'Little Wing': A Study in Music Cognition." *Understanding Rock*, ed. John Covach and Graeme Boone. Oxford: Oxford University Press: 155–69.

Brown, Matthew (2005) *Explaining Tonality: Schenkerian Theory and Beyond*. Rochester: University of Rochester Press.

Brownell, John (1994) "Analytical Models of Jazz Improvisation." *Jazzforschung/Jazz Research* 26: 9–29.

Christensen, Thomas (1992) "The *Règle de l'octave* in Thorough-Bass Theory and Practice." *Acta Musicologica* 64: 91–117.

Cooker, Jerry (1991) *Elements of the Jazz Language for the Developing Improviser*. Miami: CPP Belwin.

DeVeaux, Scott (1999) *The Birth of Bebop: A Social and Musical History*. Berkeley: University of California Press, 1997.

Dickinson, Brian (2007) *The Ears Have Walls*. Rottenburg: Advanced Music.

Dobbins, Bill (1994) *A Creative Approach to Jazz Piano Harmony*. Rottenburg: Advanced Music.

Dragnone, L. (1992) "François Campion's Treatise on Accompaniment: A Translation and Commentary." *Theoria* 6: 135–62.

Folio, Cynthia (1997–98) "'The Great Symphonic Theme': Multiple Takes on 'Stella's' Scheme." *Annual Review of Jazz Studies* 9: 3–24.

Forte, Allen (1964) "A Theory of Set-Complexes for Music." *Journal of Music Theory* 8: 136–83.

Forte, Allen (1973) *The Structure of Atonal Music*. Yale: Yale University Press.

Forte, Allen (1995) *The American Popular Ballad of the Golden Era 1924–1950*. Princeton: Princeton University Press.

Forte, Allen (1997–98) "The Real 'Stella' and the 'Real' 'Stella': A response to 'Alternate Takes', (Society For Music Theory, Annual Meeting, Phoenix 1997)." *Annual Review of Jazz Studies* 9: 93–102.

Goia, Ted (2012) *The Jazz Standards: A Guide to Repertoire*. New York: Oxford University Press.

Goldsen, Michael (1978) *Charlie Parker Omnibook*. New York: Atlantic Music.

Kernfeld, Barry (2006) *The Story of Fake Books: Bootlegging Songs to Musicians*. Lanham, MD: Scarecrow.

Larson, Steven Leroy (1993) "Dave McKenna's Performance of 'Have You Met Miss Jones?'" *American Music* 11: 283–315.

Larson, Steven Leroy (1996) "The Art of Charlie Parker's Rhetoric." *Annual Review of Jazz Studies* 8: 141–56.

Larson, Steven Leroy (1997–98) "Triple Play: Bill Evans' Three-Piano Performance of Victor Young's 'Stella by Starlight'." *Annual Review of Jazz Studies* 9: 45–56.

Larson, Steven Leroy (1998) "Schenkerian Analysis of Modern Jazz: Question About Method." *Music Theory Spectrum* 20/2: 209–41.

Larson, Steven Leroy (1999) "Swing and Motive in Three Performances by Oscar Peterson." *Journal of Music Theory* 43/2: 283–314.

Larson, Steven Leroy (2009) *Analyzing Jazz: A Schenkerian Approach*. Hillsdale, NY: Pendragon Press.

Lax, Roger and Frederick Smith (1989) *The Great Song Thesaurus*. New York: Oxford University Press.

Levine, Mark (1995) *The Jazz Theory Book*. Petaluma, CA: Sher Music.

Lindeman, Steve (1997–98) "Miles's 'Stella': A Comparison in the Light of the Two Quintets." *Annual Review of Jazz Studies* 9: 57–76.

Love, Stefan (2013) "Subliminal Dissonance or 'Consonance'? Two Views of Jazz Meter." *Music Theory Spectrum* 35/1: 48–61

Martin, Henry (1988) "Jazz Harmony: A Syntactic Background." *Annual Review of Jazz Studies* 4: 9–30.

Martin, Henry (1996) *Charlie Parker and Thematic Improvisation*. New Brunswick, NJ: Scarecrow Press.

Martin, Henry (1996) "Jazz Theory: An Overview." *Annual Review of Jazz Studies* 8: 1–17.

Martin, Henry (1997–98) "The Nature of Recomposition: Miles Davis and 'Stella by Starlight'." *Annual Review of Jazz Studies* 9: 77–92.

Martin, Henry and Robert Wason (2005) "Constructing a Post-Modern-Jazz Pedagogy." *Jazzforschung/Jazz Research* 37: 163–77.

Martin, Henry and Keith Waters (2006) *Jazz: The First 100 Years*. 2nd ed. Belmont, CA: Cengage.

Martino, Donald (1984) *178 Chorale Harmonizations of Joh. Seb. Bach: A Comparative Edition for Study*. 2 volumes. Newton, MA: Dantalian.

Messiaen, Oliver (1956) *The Technique of My Musical Language*. trans. John Satterfield Paris: Leduc.

Miller, Ron (1996) *Modal Jazz Composition & Harmony*. Rottenburg: Advanced Music.

Morris, Robert (1988) *Composition with Pitch-Classes*. Yale: Yale University Press.

Owens, Thomas (1974) "Charlie Parker: Techniques of Improvisation." Ph.D. diss., University of California, Los Angeles.

Potter, Gary (1992) "Analyzing Improvised Jazz." *College Music Symposium* 32: 143–60.

Potter, Gary (1994) "Jazz Theory Texts: An Overview." *Journal of Music Theory Pedagogy* 8: 201–08.

Pressing, Jeff (1982) "Pitch Class Set Structures in Contemporary Jazz." *JazzForschung/JazzResearch* 14: 133–72.

Pressing, Jeff (1987) "Improvisation: Methods and Models." In *Generative Processes in Music*, ed. John Sloboda. London: Oxford.

Riemenschneider, Albert (1986) *371 Harmonized Chorales and 69 Chorale Melodies with Figured Bass*. New York: Schirmer, Inc.

Rubin, Dave (1989) "Blues Power: The Eight–Bar Blues." *Guitar School* 1/2: 110–11.

Russell, George Allan (1959) *The Lydian-Chromatic Concept of Tonal Organization for Improvisation, for All Instruments.* 2nd ed. New York: Concept.

Samarotto, Frank (1999) "Strange Dimensions: Regularity and Irregularity of Deep Levels of Rhythmic Reductions." In *Schenker Studies*, ed. Carl Schachter and Hedi Siegel. Cambridge: Cambridge University Press.

Sarath, Edward (1999) "A New Look at Improvisation." *Journal of Music Theory* 40: 1–39.

Sarath, Edward (2010) *Music Theory Through Improvisation: A New Approach to Musicianship Training.* New York: Routledge.

Schenker, Heinrich (1954) *Harmony.* ed. Oswald Jonas, trans. Elizabeth Mann Borgese. Cambridge, MA: MIT Press.

Schenker, Heinrich (1977) *Free Composition.* ed. Oswald Jonas, trans. Ernst Oster. New York: Pendragon.

Schoenberg, Arnold (1969) *Structural Functions of Harmony.* ed. by Leonard Stein. New York: W.W. Norton.

Schuller, Gunther (1979) "Sonny Rollins and Thematic Improvising." In *Jazz Panorama*, ed. Martin Williams, 239–52. New York: Da Capo.

Smith, Gregory Eugene (1983) "Homer, Gregory, and Bill Evans? The Theory of Formulaic Composition in the Context of Jazz Piano Improvisation." Ph.D. diss., Harvard University.

Straus, Joseph (2005) *Introduction to Post-Tonal Theory.* New Jersey: Pearson Prentice Hall.

Straus, Joseph (2009) *Twelve-Tone Music in America.* New York: Cambridge University Press.

Strunk, Steven (1979) "The Harmony of Early Bop: A Layered Approach." *Journal of Jazz Studies* 6: 4–53.

Strunk, Steven (1985) "Bebop Melodic Lines: Tonal Characteristics." *Annual Review of Jazz Studies* 3: 79–120.

Strunk, Steven (1988) "Linear Intervallic Patterns in Jazz Repertory." *Annual Review of Jazz Studies* 4: 63–115.

Vogler, Georg Joseph [Abbé] (1800) *Chorale-System.* Copenhagen: Haly.

Waters, Keith (1996) "Blurring the Barline: Metric Displacement in the Piano Solo of Herbie Hancock." *Annual Review of Jazz Studies* 8: 103–34.

Waters, Keith (2005) "Modes, Scales, Functional Harmony, and Nonfunctional Harmony in the Compositions of Herbie Hancock." *Journal of Music Theory* 49: 333–57.

Waters, Keith (2011) *The Studio Recordings of the Miles Davis Quintet, 1965–68.* New York: Oxford University Press.

Whittall, Arnold (2008) *The Cambridge Introduction to Serialism.* New York: Cambridge University Press.

Wilder, Alec (1990) *American Popular Song: The Great Innovators 1900–1950.* New York: Oxford University Press.

Williams, Kent (1997–98) "Oscar Peterson and the Art of Paraphrase: The 1965 Recording of 'Stella By Starlight'." *Annual Review of Jazz Studies* 9: 25–44.

Woodfield, Ian (2006) "Mozart's Jupiter: A Symphony of Light?" *The Musical Times* 147: 25–46.

Credits

Index